COMMUNIST PARTY-STATES

COMPARATIVE AND INTERNATIONAL STUDIES

COMMUNIST PARTY-STATES

COMPARATIVE AND INTERNATIONAL STUDIES

Edited by

JAN F. TRISKA

Stanford University

THE BOBBS-MERRILL COMPANY, INC.
PUBLISHERS INDIANAPOLIS · NEW YORK

PREFACE

The essays in this volume emanate from the Stanford Studies of the Communist System, a research and training program with which all the present authors are or have been associated. Established at Stanford in March 1963, with the assistance of a grant from the Ford Foundation as a part of the expansion of international studies throughout the University, Studies of the Communist System has centered its attention upon the world communist movement *as a system*—as a delineated and interacting universe whose characteristics and behavior affect, and in turn are affected by, its several parts. We view the communist system as a large transformation process in which demands and supports are processed and outputs produced in ways that are typical of the system. We study the system's origin and development, maintenance and growth, behavior and operations, its various subsystems and boundaries, the differential concepts of identification (and self-identification), and the severally perceived beliefs, preferences, and values of communist elites as they affect the system's cohesion. In our studies we emphasize comparative and interactional models applicable to two or more parts of the system, but we support and complement this emphasis by systematic inquiries into those properties of single units of the system that display propensities toward system harmony or system conflict.

Studies of the Communist System is a part of Stanford University's Institute of Political Studies, a research and training center where the authors of the essays in this volume, along with other scholars, pursue or have pursued their work, some as degree candidates, others as faculty, but all as members of a community of scholars deliberately brought together to foster and advance research in political science.

The studies in this volume were written in the 1963–1967 period. The majority of them were originally mimeographed, bound, and distributed to interested scholars in this country and abroad. But we ran out of available copies, and the cost of second editions (we made no charge for those we sent until 1967), added to the original cost, made the mimeographed series expensive. This is why we gladly accepted the Bobbs-Merrill offer to publish the studies in one volume. The decision to publish, however, presented the problem of updating. Some essays, because of their subject and its treatment, were easily updated by the authors, while others, in spite of updating (summer 1967), remain marked by and mirror the time when they were written. We include them here to show the stages of our own learning; to underline the elusiveness of the subject matter of this volume; and to illustrate the relatively rapid social changes they evidence.

This volume is an intellectual product of many creative minds. In addition to the individual contributors, I would like to single out for particular acknowledgment of their original contributions and skilled assistance the following individuals: Murray Adelman, David Beim, Dennis Doolin, Michel Oksenberg, Julian Phillips, Noralou Roos, John Rue, C. Bradley Scharf, Vivienne Burden, Marie Kinzie, and Laurie Smith. Gabriel Almond kindly read, and critically commented on, the whole manuscript. David Finley ably and patiently did his best to help get the volume to the publisher on time and in good shape; we all owe him a special debt of gratitude. C. Bradley Scharf kindly prepared the index.

J. F. T.

August 1967

CONTENTS

THE CONTRIBUTORS

Richard A. Brody is associate professor of political science, associate director of Studies in International Conflict and Integration, and assistant director of Studies of the Communist System at Stanford University.

Charles D. Cary is a Ph.D. candidate in the department of political science and graduate research assistant of Studies of the Communist System at Stanford University.

David D. Finley is assistant professor of political science at Colorado College. He is also assistant director of Studies of the Communist System and in 1966–1967 was visiting assistant professor of political science at Stanford University.

John S. Gillooly is an instructor in the department of history at the University of Massachusetts. At Stanford he was graduate research assistant of Studies of the Communist System.

Ole R. Holsti is associate professor of political science at the University of British Columbia. He was formerly associate director of Studies in International Conflict and Integration and research associate of Studies of the Communist System at Stanford University.

Edward L. Miles is assistant professor of political science at the University of Denver. At Stanford he was graduate research assistant of Studies of the Communist System.

R. Judson Mitchell is assistant professor of political science at Louisiana State University in New Orleans. He was formerly graduate research assistant of Studies of the Communist System at Stanford University.

Robert C. North is professor of political science, director of Studies in International Conflict and Integration, and associate director of Studies of the Communist System at Stanford University.

Dennis C. Pirages is assistant professor of political science at the University of Connecticut. He was graduate research assistant of Studies of the Communist System at Stanford University.

David Ronfeldt is a Ph.D. candidate in the department of political science and graduate research assistant of Studies of the Communist System at Stanford University.

John S. Shippee is a Ph.D. candidate in the department of political science and graduate research assistant of Studies of the Communist System at Stanford University.

Bruce Sievers is a Ph.D. candidate in the department of political science and graduate research assistant of Studies of the Communist System at Stanford University.

Maurice D. Simon is an instructor in the department of political science at Williams College. At Stanford he was graduate research assistant of Studies of the Communist System.

Daniel Tretiak is with the Political and Economic Studies Section, Advanced Studies Group, Westinghouse Electric Corporation. At Stanford he was graduate research assistant of Studies of the Communist System.

Jan F. Triska is professor of political science, director of Studies of the Communist System, and associate director of Studies in International Conflict and Integration at Stanford University.

John F. Vesecky is a Ph.D. candidate in the department of electrical engineering at Stanford University.

INTRODUCTION

In recent years, increasingly numerous attempts have been made to develop theoretical frameworks, hypotheses, and methods useful at all levels of politics. More and more political scientists concerned with international, national or local politics have gathered and used data to establish models of political behavior which could be tested and applied in real world situations. Their theories and methods may provide not only convenient, ready-made tools for study of decision-making in all kinds of political organizations but may lead to synthesis within and across the separate branches of political science.

Traditionally, students of politics of the communist world or of any of its parts tended to regard these theories and methods as alien to their own research. The chronic lack of data would only be compounded, they felt, by theoretical frameworks and methodologies which put emphasis on the empirical study of political behavior. Given the kinds and types of essentially closed political systems they focus upon, they argued, how could they possibly, in addition to their own basic research, test the usefulness of theories emanating from other branches of political science by field studies, interviews, and other forms of empirical research? Given the substantially unique polities they have been examining, how could they safely depart from their own tried and tested modes of analysis, which have been principally historical, institutional, descriptive, and situation-bound, based on a sustained confrontation of primary and secondary sources and on an interpretative content analysis of the meager evidence available?

Indeed, no new work can be undertaken without the pioneering effort of the advanced and sophisticated area-trained analyst who, with insight and understanding, searches for the precious pieces of evidence, inspects them closely, assembles them into a mosaic and patiently explains the results. The erudition, skill and wisdom on which these analyses rest cannot be minimized. Such analyses cannot be displaced—they are part of valid scholarship on the subject. But the above-mentioned theoretical frameworks, hypotheses and methods emanating from other branches of political science do not purport to replace or substitute for the existing scholarly treatises. In fact, such existing substantive studies of communist affairs, on the one hand, and the attempts for theory-building and companion methodological innovations, on the other hand, are not mutually exclusive. Properly employed, both approaches are complementary: the actual research problem, rather than a vested interest, determines the mix. There can be no question, it seems to me, that such combination is good for scholarship focusing on the communist world, as well as for sound, sustained development of political science as a discipline. If we employ in our labors modern methodological facilities and instruments, of which electronic computers are perhaps the most important, and use such tools to test theories developed by our brethren in more advanced branches of political science, the results may be quite impressive.

In an introductory, still fragmentary and experimental way, this volume records the spill-over of attempts to develop and build theory and methodology in political science into the study of communist affairs.

But there is another reason for this book. The focus here is on societies which are less closed now—and give promise of being still less closed in the future—than they used to be even in the recent past. Access to data appears to be somewhat less difficult, though, of course, by no means easy. But the new propensity toward some openness in these societies and in even officially sanctioned field studies, survey research, and other forms of empirical investigation appears to be founded in large part on the profound difficulty in bringing traditional Marxism to bear effectively on practical problems facing the communist world. Resolution of this difficulty seems to lead almost directly to data collection and analysis based on systematic, empirical research of political behavior, taboo as little as a few years ago. Application of sophisticated quantification and analog modeling using advanced mathematical and statistical techniques is no longer either prohibited or ridiculed. In Poland, Hungary, Czechoslovakia, the USSR, and Yugoslavia, and, to a lesser extent in Romania, Bulgaria, and East Germany, such analyses are now permitted and even sought by the political elites. This thaw seems to allow for relatively rapid development of such studies by young, articulate, impatient, and sometimes aggressive professionals and academics in institutions of higher learning associated with social science organizations, including political science associations, in some of the countries; in others these scholars are grouped around youth newspapers and periodicals and television and radio stations. We are presently attempting to couple our own research interests and activities with those of these enthusiastic and resourceful individuals and organizations in Eastern Europe and the USSR, to cooperate with them, to support them, and to ask that they contribute to our own work the data they are collecting and the subsequent analyses they develop.

In the meantime, we offer the introductory essays in this volume as a modest beginning for such synthesis. Ours is an effort which perhaps should be examined and judged for what it is trying to do, rather than for the results already obtained. Briefly, this is what the individual chapters are about:

In the essay entitled "The World Communist System," Jan F. Triska develops the concepts and delineates the boundaries of the communist system. In the context of world politics, he argues, the communist movement may be viewed as a system of communist parties, both ruling and nonruling, because the patterned interactional activities which the communist parties have displayed, within and also without, tend to distinguish them from other systems in international relations.

In particular, this study is an attempt to construct a descriptive, empirical profile of the communist system. As the set of the system's relevant interactions depends on its transformation processes, the concern here is with the system's composition, structures, properties and propensities that condition these processes. A vantage point of orientation and a macro-view of the territory under exploration, this study provides a framework within which subsequent inquiries into the communist system may be located.

"Integration Among the Communist Party-States: Comparative Case Studies," by David D. Finley, makes an exploratory comparison of the Council for Mutual Economic Assistance, the Warsaw Treaty Organization, and the Joint Institute for Nuclear Research as supranational institutions that affect the integration of the communist party-states. A conceptual discussion leads to the specification of four indexes of integration. The institutions are then examined and compared with respect to these indexes, and conclusions are drawn which point the way for further empirical research.

In his essay, "A Theoretical Approach to the Study of Communist International Organizations," R. Judson Mitchell presents a model based primarily upon coalition theory. His assumption is that the organizer will attempt to maintain its initial influence or power position within the coalition. However, the organizer's side-payment costs appear destructive for such an aim; the organizer must utilize strategies that avoid the cost dilemma. A section of the chapter is devoted to the Soviet search for such a strategy within the Council for Mutual Economic Assistance. The model is completed with use of concepts drawn from organization theory relating to the organization's environment and its internal structure and functions.

In "Processes of Interaction Among the Fourteen Communist Party-States: An Exploratory Essay," Edward L. Miles, with John S. Gillooly, makes extensive use of available empirical party-state interactional data—political-military-diplomatic; economic; social-cultural-technical; and treaties and treaty-making. Their findings suggest that fruitful insights into the workings of the communist system may be gained through the assessment of interactional indexes. All the party-states except Yugoslavia appear to be well integrated within the system. The individual party-state may be rank-ordered according to its involvement in the system, with important qualitative appraisals stemming from such rank-ordering.

"Patterns of Soviet Treaty-Making Behavior with Other Communist Party-States," by Charles D. Cary, is an investigation of interaction between the USSR and the other communist party-states through analysis of Soviet treaties (bilateral and plurilateral) with these states in the 1945–1962 period. The theoretical problem here is the relationship between patterns of interaction in the conclusion of treaties and the degree of integration into the communist system thus accomplished. The author contends that the concepts of complete and congruent treaty-networks which he has developed are useful approaches to the study of integration among the communist party-states.

"The Divided Nations: International Integration and National Identity," by Bruce R. Sievers, suggests that although the four divided nations—Germany, Vietnam, Korea and China—have become the most highly integrated members of their respective international systems, they show no sign of losing their sense of identity with the traditional national units. This condition creates a fundamental "identity crisis" for the members of these nations which appears unresolvable. Since the existence of a stable national identity is one of the most basic prerequisites for the successful integration of political communities, the divided nations would appear to remain the most unsettling factor for communist and western systems alike for a long time to come.

In "Cuba's Integration into the World Communist System, 1962–1966: A Preliminary Assessment," David Ronfeldt and Daniel Tretiak analyze aspects of Cuban relations with the communist system and its two subsystems, those led by the Soviet Union and China. The research focuses on Cuba's participation in the international organizations which order the communist system's political, economic, communications, and military functions. The authors conclude that Cuban alliance with the world communist system, and with the Soviet-led subsystem, in particular, has broadened over time, but that actual integration has proceeded with hesitation and remained at a low level.

Maurice D. Simon, in his survey entitled "Communist System Interaction with Developing Afro-Asian States, 1954–1962: A Preliminary Analysis," uses a quantitative analysis of interstate transactions to examine relationships between 26 developing Afro-Asian states and the communist system. He surveys integration theory and evaluates the usefulness of transactional data for generalized statements about political integration. Then he describes the quantitative densities of transactions between the communist system and the developing states in three broad areas: (1) economic interaction; (2) legal and military interaction; and (3) sociocultural interaction. The rankings for the various indexes are then compared and a composite index of interaction is developed.

In his essay, "Socioeconomic Development and Political Access in the Communist Party-States," Dennis C. Pirages focuses on the communist system as a collection of component party-states at various levels of socioeconomic development. Using much of the survey research and aggregate data made available in comparative studies of political systems, he constructs a brief theoretical framework for analysis of the party-states. His main variables of concern are comparative rates of "liberalization" in the party-states as a function of level of socioeconomic development. Also of concern are the rates of economic growth in the party-states as a function of liberalization. This approach yields some new insights into the nature of the relationship between levels of socioeconomic development and the political elites' ability to successfully employ coercive methods.

John S. Shippee, in his chapter, "Empirical Sociology in the Eastern European Communist Party-States," attempts to ascertain the comparative development of empirical sociology in the communist party-states since the death of Stalin. The results indicate the degree to which flexibility in the area of social sciences (or the lack of it) is linked to Stalinism and the extent to which it may be attributed to other factors. The countries chosen for study comprise the

Soviet Union, Poland, Czechoslovakia, Hungary, East Germany, Bulgaria, Romania, Yugoslavia and Albania. In order to compare the revival, development, application and implications of empirical sociological research in these countries, the author devised indexes which order the nations involved in terms of scope, new developments, and international interaction in the area of political sociology.

Ole R. Holsti, in his essay, "External Conflict and Internal Cohesion: The Sino-Soviet Case," examines the hypothesis that a high level of intercoalition conflict tends to increase intracoalition unity, whereas more relaxed conditions between international systems tend to magnify differences within the alliance, in the context of Sino-Soviet relations. Eighty-two documents written by leading Chinese and Soviet decision-makers during seven periods of high and low East-West conflict between the years 1950 and 1965 were analyzed by a program of computer content analysis on the IBM 7090. The hypothesis received strong support from the data, which revealed that, during the periods of highest East-West conflict, Chinese and Soviet perceptions of American policy were similar on three dimensions. During the three periods of lower tension, differences between Chinese and Soviet perceptions were greater along all three dimensions.

"Soviet Openness to Changing Situations: A Critical Evaluation of Certain Hypotheses About Soviet Foreign Policy Behavior," by Richard A. Brody and John F. Vesecky, inventories the basic themes of several schools of Soviet foreign policy, draws out the propositions predicting Soviet responsiveness (or lack of it) from the work of scholars emphasizing Soviet ideology and Soviet national interest, and devises three situations to test the necessity and sufficiency of these two factors. The three tests derive from: (1) a qualitative content analysis of documents on Soviet military doctrine; (2) an aggregate data analysis of Soviet and United States defense budgets; and (3) a computer content analysis and action data scaling of Soviet perceptions and United States action during the October 1962 missile crisis.

All the authors of this volume thus make use of the several scenarios open and available to them, ask questions for which data exist but have not been used, and experiment with and develop further theoretical frameworks, methodologies and research techniques in order to translate the data. They hope that in this way they may see the issues and problems in the communist world more sharply, and they consequently view the exercise as their opportunity to discover something new in communist affairs. In any case, they appreciate the chance of testing the extant hypotheses and theories in the real world of the communist movement, with the added possibility that what may be epiphenomenal for them may prove to be singularly significant for the behavioral theorist.

Within this context, each contributor was essentially free to choose his own topic and mode of analysis. Still, six of the sixteen authors and coauthors chose to examine and test empirically, within the universe of the communist world, what are principally theories of political integration on the supranational level. The reason for this phenomenon is not hard to understand: The communist leaders have maintained for a long time that they are building a

world communist community based on the class solidarity of the world proletariat and leading to organic unification of workers of all countries under the
aegis of communist proletarian internationalism. They have reached the in-
between developmental stage, the period of transition. The fourteen ruling
communist parties constitute at this stage something more than a movement,
but they are not a community; the nonruling communist parties in the world
may—or may not—follow in their paths. But because of the patterned interactional activity among the communist parties, we—and they—speak of an
international system, distinguished and distinguishable from other international systems. To ask, therefore, how valid this distinction is—how much interaction is there, is this interaction integrative and for whose benefit, and is
there an integrated political community emerging—is an important subject of
inquiry.

    The difficulty here is that we do not have as yet a general theory of
political integration. There are several middle-range theories which, although
they move along in the same direction, tend to take different paths; even the
leading theorists themselves tend to differ when they discuss and use their
models in varying instances. Karl W. Deutsch, Bruce M. Russett, Amitai Etzioni, and Ernst Haas, to name the major integration theory-builders, agree
that integration is a matter of inter-unit *interaction*—its quality and quantity—
and the (resultant) *attitude*—mutual identification and responsiveness. (For
pertinent literature, see footnotes to the several studies mentioned below, in
particular that of Maurice D. Simon.) But they disagree on the precise relationship between these two sets of variables and their proper assessment, both
mutually and by themselves. As a consequence, they differ in their definitions
of political integration: Haas criticizes Deutsch for failing to isolate cause
and effect; Deutsch adds that interactions must be visible, easily identifiable,
and differentiated. Issues such as dependence of high interaction or expectation of rewards; the levels of society involved; the function of consensus, compatibility and support; and other similar complex substantive relational
questions and their conceptualization and operationability are still fuzzy and
unresolved.

    As a consequence, the several contributions here that focus on the
problem of political integration in the world communist system vary somewhat in their conceptual frameworks. They all agree that integration is a matter of interaction and attitude *and* that inter-unit interaction is necessary
(though not sufficient—Maurice D. Simon) for integration, though not all
interaction is integrative. They all focus their respective analyses essentially
on interaction (Bruce R. Sievers investigates attitude, as well) of one, several,
or many key interaction variables. David D. Finley emphasizes also the bureaucratic structure of the inter-unit coordination and the basis of authority
which sanctions it, as well as the degree of consensus supporting the process.
Edward L. Miles and John S. Gillooly analyze patterns of interaction as well
as effects of interaction on the participating units and on the system as a whole.
Charles D. Cary postulates that integration equals the degree to which a key
variable—substantive treaty networks within the system—is complete and
congruent. David Ronfeldt and Daniel Tretiak stress that only interactions

which contribute to value-sharing and mutual responsiveness of the units lead to their integration.

The several authors thus tend to concentrate more on the quantity and quality of interaction and/or interaction-plus within the world communist system than on its integration as a potential community based on "mutual ties" *and* feeling of identity. This is understandable. Assuming that a considerable amount of key inter-unit interaction is a prerequisite of political integration, the contributors select and make use of available data on interactional flows as operational indicators of the degree of the integrational process. The "feeling of identity" concept is still difficult to study empirically in communist party-states, as truly pertinent survey data have not been easy to acquire.

For this reason it is perhaps useful and convenient to include here an essay entitled "On Integration: Some Pre-theoretical Observations" by Robert C. North. In it he defines integration, identifies certain integration processes, and provides a brief account—from history and political anthropology—of the ways in which nation-states and empires seem to have evolved and expanded. He pays particular attention to identifiable stages of Russian integration in the historical past. Against this background the author then suggests some of the difficulties in and possibilities for assessing integration among the communist party-states.

JAN F. TRISKA

ON INTEGRATION:

SOME PRE-THEORETICAL OBSERVATIONS

ROBERT C. NORTH

The word integration derives from the Latin *integrare,* "to renew," and it refers to the act, process or instance of forming a whole by the addition or combination of parts or elements. In human terms, it suggests "the unification and mutual adjustment of diverse groups or elements into a relatively coordinated and harmonious society or culture with a consistent body of normative standards."[1]

The term integration is commonly applied both to organic and to to interpersonal (social, economic, political) unification. In terms of the central nervous system it has been asserted that "If two assemblies A and B are repeatedly active at the same time they will tend to be 'associated,' so that A excites B and vice versa. If they are always active at the same time they will tend to merge in a single system—that is, form a single assembly (integrate)—but if they are also active at different times they will remain separate (but associated) systems. (This means that exciting part of A, for example, has a very high probability of exciting all of A, but a definitely lower probability of exciting a separate assembly, B; A may be able to excite B only when some other assembly, C, also facilitates activity in B.)"[2]

By analogy, human individuals (or groups) who interact, even conflictually and perhaps violently, are functioning associatively, perhaps even somewhat integratively—more so than if they had no contact at all. The association is even more integrative to the degree that rules are agreed upon to regulate or govern the conflict and to limit weapons, place or circumstance of bloodshed, burial of the dead, treatment of prisoners, and the like. Yet it seems probable that, with respect to human beings (and groups), interaction *per se* is not sufficient for eventual merging or unification, but that the nature of the interaction tends to be crucial.

Trade relations are likely to suggest a great deal about patterns of interaction between states, for example, and issues of commerce may contribute to the integrative process along with other functions. It may be a serious error to assume, however, that increasing trade between states—or an increase of various other types of interaction, for that matter—is necessarily an indicator of a tendency of the states to merge under a single government. On the contrary, we might expect successful trade partners to continue their commercial give-and-take over several generations without contributing to their merger as a single political entity.

Whenever two or more individuals or groups integrate, they tend to do so in order to perform a particular function or set of functions. This suggests that the repetitive occurrence of a given interaction is likely to give rise to a particular type of organization—that particular type depending upon the central function that is being performed. Historically, men have organized in order to perform functions of raising children, fellowship, religious worship, warfare, commerce, industry, science, and much more. Many of these organizations tend to develop their own hierarchies and their own decision and control subsystems. Hence, the state apparatus appears to constitute a special case, differing from other integrations with respect to the degree to which it overrides the decision and control operations of a variety of subordinate organizations. The distinctive aspect of a state is the relative sovereignty of its decision and control subsystem.

In the study of international relations, we are concerned primarily with those more or less independent, sovereign decision and control systems that override and to some degree regulate all other organizations, as well as individuals, within a given society. Other subordinate organizations are of interest to us largely insofar as they tell us something about states or the interactions of states.

Elman R. Service, an anthropologist, infers five qualitatively distinct means of integration in human society, each emerging from responses to the environment and giving rise to appropriate economic, political, and social forms, with subvarieties on each level: (1) familistic bonds of kinship and marriage which by their nature can integrate only the relatively small and simple societies we call bands; (2) pan-tribal sodalities which can integrate several band-like societies into one (tribe); (3) specialization, redistribution and the related centralization of authority which can integrate still more complex societies, referred to as chiefdoms; (4) the state, further integrated by a bureaucracy employing "legitimatized," "legal" force; (5) an industrial society—probably only beginning to arise —which is (or will be) integrated not only by a state apparatus but also by a complex network of specialized interdependent occupations.[3] Much of the dynamic for raising human organization to these various levels seems to emerge from population growth and the development of technology in a broad sense (the development, organization and application of knowledge and skills). There are some practical difficulties in the Service formulation, but it seems, nevertheless, to provide a useful frame of reference.

The paleolithic era—the span of time from the origins of culture until the beginning of the domestication of plants and animals—was a time when there existed no forms of economy higher than hunting-gathering bands. A band is only an association, more or less residential, of nuclear families, ordinarily numbering 30 to 100 people. Band society is generally egalitarian and lacking in political hierarchies and dominant groups. Leadership is personal, charismatic, and limited to special purposes. There are headmen who lead in warfare, or in the chase, or on the occasion of other special functions.

The neolithic revolution, based on the domestication of plants and animals, gave rise to tribal societies. A tribe is an association of a much larger number of kinship segments composed of families. They are tied together more firmly than bands. The means of solidarity are clans and other *pan-tribal sodalities,* such as age-grade associations and secret societies which cut across component bands. Tribal society remains egalitarian and lacking in political hierarchies and dominant groups. Leadership is personal and charismatic. There are no governmental forms. The "chief" is merely a man of superior influence. External strife and competition among tribes seem to be the factors accounting for a large part of internal unity.

Chiefdoms emerge from societies which have learned how to coordinate economic, social, religious and political activities. They seem to be associated with greater productivity, greater population density, regional or ecological specialization of different local residential units, and the pooling of individual skills in large-scale cooperative production enter-

prises. Many chiefdoms have arisen in habitats consisting of several ecological zones differentiated by climate, soil, rainfall and natural products.
Some have been pastoral, whether nomadic or sedentary.

As described by Service, the chiefdom level is characterized by
authority and centralized direction, but no government; unequal control
over goods and production, but no private property in resources or entre-
preneurial market commerce; rank differences, but no clear socioeconomic
classes. The chiefship is a recognized "office."

A state, however underdeveloped, is distinguished from earlier
forms of sociopolitical organization by the presence of a clearly defined
and unmistakably institutionalized decision and control apparatus involving the consistent threat or application of force by a body of persons
more or less "legitimately" constituted to monopolize and use it.

Bands, and even tribes, are often so insufficiently integrated and so
poorly defined and bounded that an observer is hard put to determine
whether a particular display of armed force constitutes external warfare,
"civil war," rebellion, family feud, or the effort of leaders to maintain
domestic "law and order." Indeed, lacking sufficient integration, specialization, institutionalization, recognized monopoly of force, and other attributes of statehood, these earlier sociopolitical forms can scarcely be
discussed in some of the above-mentioned terms that we take so much for
granted.

Force, as maintained and applied within a state, is the clear monopoly of certain identifiable and continuing offices. Personal, non-govern-
mental force is outlawed within a state, and the presence of a feud, violent
crime, armed rebellion, or other disturbance involving illegitimate use of
force signifies the inadequacy or absence of state power at that time and
place.

Society on the state level is divided into political classes; the civil
bureaucrats, military leaders, and the upper priesthood tend to become
the aristocracy; there is full-time professionalization in arts and crafts and
sometimes in commerce. The state is integrated by a special mechanism
involving legitimatized force; it constitutes itself "legally"; it makes explicit the manner and circumstances of its use of force by lawfully inter-
fering in disputes between individuals and between corporate parts of the
society. A political system is more or less state-like according to the
presence or absence and the functioning or nonfunctioning of these
phenomena or processes. The emergence of states seems to be associated
with increased production through irrigation or other means, increased
centralized control, increased size of cities, and increases in communicative and notational devices (writing, mathematics).

Historically, states have emerged or expanded in a number of
different ways: by military conquest; by federation through common con-

sent—usually in response to a commonly perceived threat; by the lateral expansion of a smaller unit through the migration of its people; by the aggressive, coercive administration of a prince or other sovereign; by purchase of loyalty or territory; by the division or segmentation of a larger state into two or more smaller states; by attraction in situations where individuals or groups on the periphery are drawn to a ruler or his domain by what appear to be considerations of advantage (protection, for example); and, sometimes, through a marriage joining two dynasties.

Service and others assume that each new level of organization tends to include and subsume at least some of the forms characterizing earlier levels. The family, for example, has inclined to survive from level to level, being encompassed by band, tribe, chiefdom and state systems. In a similar fashion, one may still find band, tribal, chiefdom, and, perhaps, primitive or archaic state forms or residues included in a modern nation-state.

A major objection to the Service approach issues from the number of real world exceptions—composite bands, "anomalous" societies, and the like—which do not fit on any one of these somewhat arbitrary levels.[4] The chiefdom, moreover, remains a somewhat controversial category, Service having provided only a few specific examples.[5] Also, Service's discussion is largely limited to his first three levels of integration. He does not say much about the fourth and fifth levels of integration—the state and the industrial state, respectively. Indeed, he does not discuss the latter at all.[6] It is obvious, too—as Service and others have pointed out—that organizations and institutions do not evolve in a single straight line or simple lineage. There are many variations, permitting of no uniform and predictable sequence.

Clearly, it would be counterproductive at this stage in research to take any conceptual scheme of sociopolitical levels or organization too seriously. The problem is essentially empirical, and only empirical research will solve it. On the other hand, Service's scheme does present a construction against which real world, empirical data can be measured. In these qualified terms it may provide a useful starting point, particularly insofar as it raises the possibility that integration operates essentially as an adaptive function and that it may take place somewhat differently at different levels, with kinship functions tending to be more important for integration on earlier levels and decision and control functions predominating as state forms begin to develop.

Whether or not we are currently moving onto a new level—Service's fifth level—remains a matter of speculation. This study will focus upon problems of integration at the state level—essentially where Service left off—and attempt to relate Russian unification to a number of processes which appear to be ubiquitous through time and across cultures.

In 1957, Karl W. Deutsch and a number of colleagues published a study involving ten cases of unification on the nation-state level, eight of them examined intensively.[7] For integration to take place, according to this analysis, there must be present considerable compatibility in the main values held by relevant strata of all the political units involved, and, in some cases, at least a tacit agreement within these strata to deprive remaining incompatible values of their political significance. Thus, it might be decided or tacitly acknowledged that differences in religion would no longer be a matter of political significance. For achieving a sense of community, however, something more than verbal attachment to similar values was needed. Rather, the people and groups involved had to feel mutual sympathy and loyalties—a "we-feeling"—such that they could predict each other's behavior and act confidently in accordance with such predictions.

Integration was more likely to take place as some distinctive way of life developed. Not only did a network of major and minor values have to be developed, but there was required a set of established or emerging habits of behavior corresponding to these values and institutions. This was true even in cases where amalgamation was brought about by conquest.[8]

Integrative processes tended to accelerate with the decline of those party divisions which had previously reinforced boundaries between political units and with the rise, in their place, of party divisions cutting across such boundaries. In this connection, Deutsch and his associates noted how issues of the Reformation cut across the boundaries of England and Wales in the period of English-Welsh union and how, similarly, the division between Whigs and Tories cut across the boundaries between England and Scotland during the generation preceding 1707.

The development of a core area with certain capabilities seems to have been important. Although the emerging core power or federation might be viewed with considerable misgivings at first, its growth tended to be tolerated or welcomed—provided other favorable conditions were present—and in time other units joined it in some form of unification. Examples include the merging first of England, then of England and Wales, prior to that of England-Wales with Scotland; the case of Switzerland, where the confederation of the original three forest cantons (Uri, Schwyz and Nidwalden) was enlarged two generations later by Zurich and Bern; the integration of the original thirteen American colonies; and the North German Confederation, which afterward grew into the German Empire.

In order to achieve integration, this core area, at least, needed to undergo marked economic growth. Conversely, prolonged economic conditions of decline or stagnation comparing unfavorably with those in neighboring regions tended to facilitate disintegration. Widespread expectations of economic reward characterized the Anglo-Scottish union of 1707, the unification of Italy (where the South found itself to some extent disappointed), and the unification of Germany (where expectations were brilliantly fulfilled).

Other factors contributing to union included wide and multiple ranges of reciprocal communications and transactions among the units involved; a broadening of the political, social, or economic elites both in terms of recruitment from more of the social strata and of maintenance of continuing connections with these strata; mobility of persons among the main units; and development of unbroken links of social communication among the political units involved and between relevant social strata within those units in order to provide effective horizontal and vertical channels among both persons and organizations.

Beyond these factors, Deutsch and his colleagues found four others which seemed helpful, but not essential, to unification: a sharp decline in the expectations of war and an increasing reluctance among the units to wage war against each other; some degree of ethnic and linguistic assimilation (although the Swiss case presents a notable exception); strong economic ties among the units to be conjoined; and a commonly perceived outside military threat.

It is possible, however, that the investigation of additional cases may suggest a slightly different analytic emphasis, without in any way detracting from the importance of those conditions which Deutsch and his associates have identified. Over the face of the earth, for example, and down through the centuries of human history, integration by force, aggressive administrative and legal fiat, and coercion has been the rule rather than the exception on the nation-state level. Populations have accepted such unifications because the costs of resistance have seemed too high, or for other reasons, and, often, with the passage of time, they or their descendants have tended to accept and internalize the very system that initially imposed itself by force.

Indeed, in all of recorded history there seem to have been only a relatively few instances in which states or pre-state forms have combined successfully into a single, essentially permanent, encompassing unit through negotiation and voluntary consent. Four among these successful cases have been particularly notable: the Achaean League (*ca.* 280 B.C.), the Swiss Confederation (A.D. 1291), the seven United Provinces of the Netherlands (1579–1795), and the United States of North America (1778). In each of these instances, a more or less commonly perceived threat from the outside was an important, perhaps determining, factor leading to federative integration. Precise circumstances of the Achaean unification are not known, but the threat of Macedonian garrisons appears to have presented a powerful stimulus. Hapsburg expansionism, the Spanish occupation, and British commercial and imperial attitudes and policies tended to influence the Swiss, the Dutch, and the American colonists, respectively, in the direction of federative integration.

In ancient Greece, the Delian League displayed some of the characteristics of a federative unification, but Athens soon used its superior power to exploit and virtually subjugate the other members. Commercial city-states also characterized Kievan Russia (882–1232), but uncertainties about the princely succession combined with other factors—including, ultimately, the Mongol conquest—to inhibit a lasting integration.

In general, the most effective integrations of tribes, chiefdoms, free cities, and rural principalities into states and empires have been accomplished by able and ambitious kings or military chieftains who have enforced unification either by outright conquest or by what might be designated as aggressive and substantially coercive administration.

This does not mean that an aspiring king under such circumstances is the only integrating agent. Clearly, he cannot succeed unless other able men—each motivated according to his own personality and needs—are willing to support him. People on lower levels also must exhibit a contributing frame of mind, whether through fear, or hope for gain, or other considerations. His task will be facilitated, moreover, as a considerable proportion of the conditions identified by Deutsch are present.

Essentially, integration takes place, however, because (1) two or more units, or at least their leaders, voluntarily perceive some reward in unification, or (2) a leader (or a unit through its leader) perceives a reward in unification and the individuals and/or groups composing the other units do not have the capacity or the will to resist a merger which they may consider of dubious value or even penalizing to them.

France, England, and Spain offer three case histories of great national monarchies that were consolidated by ambitious monarchs —although the governmental forms in the three states developed quite differently. Italy and Germany are examples of great states in which the processes of unification and integration were notably delayed. Russia displays patterns of considerable diversity, interest, and local peculiarity.

For a time during the Middle Ages, France embodied no more than a small territory surrounding Paris. It was not until the thirteenth century that we find French kings conquering, inheriting or otherwise incorporating more and more of the surrounding duchies into their domain.[9] Three strong monarchs may be credited with building the foundations of a truly national state in France: Philip Augustus (r. 1180–1223), Louis IX (r. 1226–1270), and Philip IV, "the Fair" (r. 1285–1314).

Philip Augustus undermined feudal power through a number of aggressive measures: requiring vassals to agree that their own vassals would owe their first allegiance to him; converting many feudal reliefs into money payments; levying general taxes; appointing royal seneschals and bailiffs to supervise justice in the various feudal courts; selling charters to cities; hiring mercenary troops and organizing the foundations for a national army for which the towns were required to furnish recruits; enforcing his own rights as royal overlord; and gathering other administrative, fiscal, and judiciary functions into his own hands. Philip Augustus also seized Normandy, which had been a thorn in the royal flank ever since Duke William, though a feudal vassal of France, had made himself and his heirs kings of an increasingly powerful England.

Louis IX used similar methods to consolidate French power for himself. In the course of his reign, he succeeded in issuing ordinances for the whole country without the consent of his vassals; enforcing acceptance of his own currency; extending the right of appeal from decisions in feudal courts to his own royal court; assigning his lawyers to identify cases throughout the realm, especially breaches of the peace and treason, that would be subject to his own direct jurisdiction; and prohibiting private warfare among his vassals.

Philip the Fair converted remaining feudal dues into direct taxes and established new levies under royal supervision. His attempt to tax the church led to a conflict which contributed to the subjugation of the French Catholic Church to the French king.

The Hundred Years' War (1337–1453) further consolidated and strengthened the royal power in France by driving English sovereignty —dating from William the Conqueror—from French soil.

Parallel developments took place in England. The Angles, Saxons, Jutes, and Danes had established petty kingdoms and bit by bit incorporated them through a gradual merging of various independent, though kindred, principalities. The true development of national monarchy in England dates, however, from the reign of William, who, as Duke of Normandy, conquered the island in 1066. From the start, his dominion was stronger than anything the Saxon or Danish kings had been able to effect. Through the Salisbury oath, William required his vassals to swear allegiance to him rather than to their immediate overlords. He was careful, moreover, in distributing English fiefs, not to grant compact estates to his followers, but to disperse their holdings.

Feudalism had already begun to supersede the older liberties of political, economic, and social life in England prior to the Conquest, but William hastened its development. The desperate and almost universal resistance of the English forced him to take strong measures to protect his throne. These were designed to curtail the disintegration that frequently beset feudalism on the continent. Each estate awarded to one of William's followers was granted solely on condition of military service at the king's call. "A whole army was by this means encamped upon the soil, and William's summons could at any moment gather an overwhelming force around his standard."[10]

The rights and feudal dues owing the king from each estate were strictly exacted. Each tenant-vassal was bound to contribute a money "aid" in case of the marriage of his oldest daughter, the knighthood of his oldest son, or the capture in war of the king himself, and, in any case, to appear, if called, three times a year at the royal court. Most manors were further encumbered with special dues or "customs" for the crown, and, in order to fix and record these, William sent his commissioners into each shire to make inquiries, the resulting facts of which were then entered in his Domesday Book.

The second king to consolidate and enhance royal power in England was Henry II (r. 1154–1189). Finding the treasury depleted and his barons powerfully entrenched, he commuted feudal military service obligations to money payments (scutage), levied taxes on personal income and property for the first time in England, demolished many baronial strongholds, and organized a staff of lawyers and itinerant judges whom he dispatched throughout his domain to administer royal justice *in situ*. Decisions of this legal and judiciary staff tended to organize, unify, and supplement local custom and thus led to the growth of English common law.

Space does not permit a detailed consideration of the ways in which Edward I (r. 1272–1307), Henry VII (r. 1485–1509) and other sovereigns furthered the expansion of the country—to include Wales and Scotland—and contributed otherwise to England's unification. In general, however, the integration came about through conquest, centralization of the courts, royal taxation, the building of a national army (together with the elimination of independent military forces controlled by members of the nobility), and other methods of aggressive and often coercive administration, though strong and ambitious parliaments also performed important integrative functions.

During the fourteenth century, the rapid development of commerce and industry in England, the growth of cities, the prevailing scarcity of labor, the increasing use of money, and the continuing extension of the tax system combined to weaken the manorial system and the pattern of feudal power. Moreover, the waging of the Hundred Years' War against France (1337–1453) furthered the centralization of national power under the crown and rendered the king increasingly independent of baronial power.

However, it was the War of the Roses, a civil war between the great noble houses of Lancaster and York (1455–1485) which put an end to feudalism in England. During this struggle, many noblemen were killed, discontent and disgust prevailed among the people, civil disorder was rampant. For the House of York the conflict ended ignominiously at Bosworth Field (1485). It was now possible for the able and ambitious victor and new king, Henry Tudor, or Henry VII (r. 1485–1509) of Lancaster, to rebuild royal power. The two warring lines were united by Henry's marriage to Elizabeth of York. Attempts at revolt occurred, but these served only to demonstrate more clearly the strength that the new monarchy had achieved—partly, at least, as a consequence of the revolution that had taken place in the art of war through the introduction of gunpowder.

The integration of Spain was in many respects unique, being a function of kinship (the marriage of Ferdinand of Aragon and Isabella of Castile), conquest, aggressive and frequently coercive administration, and a program of what amounted to thought control (the Inquisition).

The combined power resulting from the marriage of Ferdinand and Isabella eventually made Spain a great nation and empire under a series of Catholic kings. Yet the newly united rulers themselves faced serious difficulties. The struggles of reconquest from the Muslims had extended over seven hundred years, and continuing local disputes had nurtured a class of fierce and turbulent nobles "as eager to attack a neighbor or their sovereign as the Moor."[11] Many of the populace looked to the crown for strong government and a greater sense of security.

The two monarchs set out to further weaken the nobility by destroying many of their castles, taking over their revenues and limiting their private courts and other jurisdictions. In building a royal bureaucracy, Ferdinand and Isabella more and more enlisted the aid of civil servants or ecclesiastics, rather than nobles of the royal council. Members of the nobility were still attracted to the court, but as obsequious courtiers, rather than as advisers or administrators. Use of these and numerous other procedures for strengthening the Spanish crown was not notably different from the practices of expansionist kings of France and England. The Inquisition, however, though it existed elsewhere, became a royal instrument primarily in Spain. This institution was by no means the only factor in the centralization of imperial authority and the unification and integration of Spain, but it seems to have been an extremely important one.

Among many powers granted to Tomás de Torquemada, first Inquisitor General, was that of modifying earlier rules of the Inquisition, adapting them to the particular requirements of Spain. In his hands, the Spanish Inquisition functioned as "an elaborate institution for the punishment and suppression of unpopular opinions"[12] that in any way might be conceived of as threatening the crown, the church, the Holy Office, the agents of the Inquisition, or even the servants and slaves of the Inquisitors. It compressed "all the fighting force of patriotism in the narrowest and intensest form."[13] Bishops and other clergy were not always exempt from the whims and excessive zeal of the Inquisitors, who enjoyed the right not only to censure books and speeches and to inquire into what people did, but also to examine what people believed and thought. Within the space of a few years, no Spaniard, whether layman or cleric, could escape the Inquisition's sweeping authority. The property of convicted persons was subject to confiscation. Indeed, the greater the number of convictions, the greater the income accruing to the Holy Office. At the peak of its power, the Inquisitors paid no taxes, rendered no accounts of confiscation, and enjoyed the unqualified right to bear arms. In political, strictly functional terms the Inquisition played a role in sixteenth-century Spain not unlike that of Bolshevism in Russia under Lenin and Stalin.

Despite the terror it frequently inspired—and partly because of it —the Inquisition acted as a titanic unifying and integrating force. In terms of Inquisitorial supervision and administration, the political divisions of Aragon, Catalonia, Valencia, Castile and the like no longer existed. In consolidating their strength and that of the crown, moreover, the Inquisitors disregarded the liberties, franchises and privileges which the nobility had previously enjoyed. Power was acutely centralized, and fear of the Holy Office imposed obedience to the point where, over time, more and more Spaniards internalized its symbols and values.

When Russian territory first began to figure in European history it was inhabited by many tribes of Turkish, Mongol, Slavic, and various other stocks. In the seventh century A.D., somewhat disorganized bands of East Slavs, seeking safety from the Avars, established Kiev on the Dnieper. Gradually, the East Slavs spread over a wide, linked system of waterways—the Dnieper, Pripet, Desna, Dvina, Volkhov, Lovat and so forth—and set up trading centers. From 830 on, this region and its Slavic settlements were increasingly penetrated by the Vikings, or Varangians.

Prince Oleg, a Varangian prince, initiated a major consolidation of the early Russian settlements toward the end of the ninth century. Twice during the next generation or two, the Russians undertook military campaigns, accompanied by considerable looting, into the Caucasus, along the southwestern shores of the Caspian, and against Byzantium. The state was further expanded by Sviatoslav, who conquered first the Khazars and then the Bulgars, and who built an empire controlling the lower Danube, the lower Volga, and the forest regions of Kiev and Novgorod. But this unification was short-lived, being challenged by a Turkish tribe, the Pechenegs, and by Byzantium.

Sviatoslav's death in 972, at the hands of the Pechenegs, halted Russian attempts at uniting the steppes with the forest lands and controlling trade on the Black and Caspian seas. By that time, however, Russian peoples occupied almost the whole territory from the Gulf of Finland and Lake Ladoga to the lower Danube, and from the Marosh and Tisza rivers in modern Hungary to the Oka and the Don.

Yaroslav (r. 1019–1054) achieved a decisive victory over the Pechenegs who, defeated and exhausted, in the end became his allies. Their place as an enemy was taken almost immediately, however, by the Polovtsi, who were more numerous and better organized. For generations, Russian energy was largely devoted to keeping them at bay.[14]

From the close of the tenth until the middle of the thirteenth centuries, the territory of the Russians was not substantially altered—although there were gradual losses in the southern steppe where nomadic Turkish peoples blocked access to the Black and Caspian seas.

The Kievan state consisted of several "lands" which at first were united under the authority of the prince of Kiev but were later ruled separately by princes of their own. Each "land" and its lesser towns, or *prigorodi,* tended to center on a *gorod,* or capital city. In these terms, each "land" was essentially a city-state in the classical sense. By the late twelfth century there were twelve "lands": Kiev, Novgorod, Ryazan, Suzdal, Chernigov, Pereyaslav, Smolensk, Galicia, Polotsk, and Valnia.

Since the rules of succession were not clearly established or institutionalized, claims to sovereignty proliferated, and interminable feuds arose among the Kievan princes. Russian energies were increasingly expended upon internecine warfare as well as upon efforts at internal organization, and upon defense against invaders from the steppes. Trade declined as roads were blocked by both domestic and external warfare, and agriculture became more and more important.

Toward the middle of the twelfth century, whatever unity that had existed in the Kievan realm had largely dissipated, and each prince tried to secure leadership for himself, though not with much success, since none was sufficiently stronger than the others. From time to time, certain princes formed temporary alliances which pitted one coalition against another. Occasionally, there were attempts to establish a federation to meet a commonly perceived emergency such as an invasion of peoples from the steppe. Such efforts were of no long-range effect, however, and, in fact, Russia during this period remained divided into separate states.

In 1223, the Mongols appeared from the southeast. Undertaken by Genghis Khan, the Mongolian program of conquest was continued after his death in 1227 by his grandson, Batu, who occupied Kiev in 1240. Thereafter, one Mongolian army advanced against Poland and later against Hungary. A second army under Batu advanced through Hungary to Vienna. Soon the northern Russian forests, the steppes, and the lower Danube had been brought under Mongol control. At approximately the same time, other Mongolian armies completed their subjugation of northern China and Transcaucasia. By the middle of the thirteenth century, Mongol territories extended from the Adriatic Sea to the Pacific Ocean.

Mongol imperialism derived in part from the pastoral background and ideas of the Mongol and Turkish people, in part from traditional

Chinese thought, and in part from two foreign dynasties of China—the Khitans, who appear to have been of Mongol origin, and the Chin, who were Manchus.[15] Originally, Mongol organization had been at the tribal or chiefdom levels. The administrative hierarchy of the empire, however, was relatively complex, having been largely borrowed from early thirteenth-century China.

The Mongol Empire was created almost wholly through military conquest, and the army became the backbone of administration. "It was through the army officers from the myriarch down to the decurion that the great khan's orders reached the population."[16] The great khan was an absolute monarch enjoying authority which, in theory, at least, was unlimited. Russian princes were compelled to submit to him, and the Mongols also appointed their own agents in the major Russian towns with responsibility for collecting revenue and recruiting soldiers. The central concept was personal service to the state on the part of each subject, whether rich or poor.

By the middle of the fourteenth century, the Mongol power in Russia was being seriously disrupted by internal dissension. Indeed, the status of the Mongols increasingly declined. To a greater and greater extent, their territory was broken up into lesser principalities which tended to become vassal to ambitious Russian princes. Employing a combination of peaceful absorption, coercion, purchase, conquest, successful administration, and sometimes "open robbery," the Muscovite princes were especially successful in extending their domain.[17]

Increasingly, the Great Russian stock was integrated into a single society under a single state power ruled by a single political structure. Previously, the Muscovite state had been one of several suzerain principalities in northern Rus. "Now it became the *only* Suzerain Principality in the region, as well as a *national* one, seeing that its boundaries exactly coincided with the distribution of the Great Russian stock."[18]

The decline of the Golden Horde created a kind of vacuum which only the rulers of Russian principalities could easily fill. Moscow seized Yaroslavl in 1463 and purchased half of Rostov. By 1478, Novgorod had been completely subjugated by Moscow. In 1485, Tver was subdued after the reigning prince had tried to ally himself with Lithuania.

During the second half of the fifteenth century, Ivan III (1440–1505), Grand Duke of Moscow, annexed almost all the previously independent cities and principalities of northern Russia. He succeeded also in arousing hostilities among the Tatar kingdoms and in exploiting struggles between Kazan and Kasimov and Crimea against the Golden Horde. However, " . . . the Tatar danger did not disappear after Ivan III's defiance of the Golden Horde. For almost three more centuries Russia had to mobilize a considerable part of her army every year on her southern and southeastern borders; this affected the whole political and social system of Muscovy."[19]

During the Kievan period, the three elements of power in Russia— the monarchic, the aristrocratic and the democratic—had counterbalanced each other, and the people had sustained a considerable voice in government. Even where the monarchial element was strongest, the boyars and the *veche,* or city assembly, had enjoyed a sizable influence over public affairs. By the close of the Mongol period, the situation had been altered. "When the last threads of Tartar control were broken by Moscow, the dukes of Moscow openly regarded themselves as absolute monarchs and considered their people completely subject to their will. All lands within the boundaries of his state were claimed by the duke to be devoted to the interests of the state. The current theory was that the prince was the sole owner of the land, and that all other persons merely had the tenure and use of it temporarily."[20]

The rising Muscovite tsardom emerged from a distinctive concept of society and its relation to the state. Under *krepostnoy ustav,* or statute of bound service, all the classes of the nation except, ironically, the slaves, were compelled to state service. Princes and boyars and courtiers had become servitors of the tsars who, through *pomestia,* or military fiefs, controlled the landed estates of the gentry, as well as the army. In 1494, after a war with Lithuania, Ivan III extorted from that country recognition of his newly-claimed title, Sovereign of All Russia.

With the gradual expansion of their power over the other parts of Russia, the Grand Dukes of Moscow carried Mongolian practices over into wide areas and incorporated them into the new theory of the state that developed over the next two centuries. Inherited from the Mongols, the principle of unquestioning submission of the individual to the larger group became impressed upon the Russian people and institutionalized the concept of universal service to the state.

The success of Muscovite princes depended sometimes upon military capacity, sometimes upon administrative ability, sometimes upon guile, sometimes upon clearer concept of succession. Some of them, including Ivan III, did not hesitate to ally themselves with Tatar leaders against common adversaries. In 1552, Ivan the Terrible (1530–1584), grandson of Ivan III, supported by the Kasimov Tatars, destroyed the kingdom of Kazan, annexing the whole region to Moscow. The Muscovites conquered Astrakhan soon after. Siberia paid homage to Moscow as early as 1555, although annexation took place later, subsequent to the expeditionary campaign of a Cossack force under Yermak in 1584.

Neighboring principalities had been split, meanwhile, into more and more infinitesimal divisions—while Moscow consolidated. "With each successive will of a Moscow prince (and the princes regarded their political power as property to be bequeathed like their territory) the proportion of the eldest son was increased. . . ."[21] To a large extent it was on this foundation that the Russian autocracy initially developed, "not, at the outset, by any theory of government, but by the mere fact that the eldest son could buy up all the rest; that he alone could appease the Golden Horde, or take up arms against it; that the rival princes by their constant subdivisions provided him with a number of separate preys which he could easily absorb piecemeal."[22] By the reign of Ivan III, the Principality of Moscow had been growing at the expense of other principalities for a century and a half. At the same time, moreover, the Muscovite suzerain princes had been enjoying more and more material aggrandizement at the expense of Muscovite *appanage*[23] princes.[24]

For the most part, the territorial acquisitions of the Muscovite princes had come about either through seizure or through private negotiation between neighboring rulers. After the middle of the fifteenth century, however, there arose pro-Muscovite parties in some of the principalities that took an active part in bringing their communities under the control of Moscow.[25] In other instances, neighboring princes submitted to Moscow because of the advantages they saw in serving a wealthy and powerful ruler.[26] Finally, as when Ivan III and his forces were at the gates of Tver, considerable numbers of loyal boyars and *appanage* princes seceded to Moscow, rather than fight, and took an oath of allegiance to the Muscovite prince. Before long, principalities and commonwealths were vying with each other in transferring themselves and their provinces to Muscovite allegiance.

During the eighteenth and nineteenth centuries, Russia reached the "natural geographical limits" of its expansion, that is, it encompassed those territories from the Baltic and Black seas to the Pacific and south to the Pamir Plateau. Space limitations preclude more than passing reference to this general trend. In 1700, the Turkish region of Azov was annexed by Peter the Great (1672–1725), who then moved against Sweden. His forces were defeated at Narva, but, in 1709, he won a decisive victory at Poltava. Subsequently, through the Treaty of Nystad (1721), Sweden ceded Ingria, Estonia, and Latvia to Russia, thus securing St. Petersburg for Peter as "a window to Europe."

During the reign of Elizabeth (r. 1741–1761), Russia advanced its frontier further westward at the expense of Finland. Later, on September 17, 1809, Finland, as an autonomous grand duchy, passed under the sovereignty of Alexander I (r. 1801–1825) and his heirs. By the first partition of Poland (1772), Russia received Vitebsk, Polotsk, and Mogilev, which were populated by Russians. Through the second partition (1793), Russia acquired Minsk, Podolia and part of Volhynia. With the third partition (1795), Russia took Lithuania, Kurland and western Volhynia.

As with the integration of most great monarchies, Russia expanded over these centuries largely as an outcome of conquest and aggressive, essentially coercive, administration, a special characteristic being the ubiquitous concept of service to the state. It seems probable that the dynamics for these processes emerged in Russia and elsewhere from crucial differentials—across territory and people—in population (levels and growth rates) and in levels and growth rates of technology (the organization and application of knowledge and skills). We may postulate that the greater these differentials were, the stronger was the tendency for more effective (stronger and more skilled) leaders and groups to apply their energy surpluses to the imposition of decision and control over the less effective. With the Bolshevik Revolution of 1917, this trend was reinforced by the introduction of Marxism-Leninism, which provided a belief system, as well as police state refinements, analogous, in a secular framework, to the Spanish Inquisition. However, it was still armed force—in this case, the Red Army—which largely accounted for the integration of large peripheral regions during the civil war period and again after World War II.

For a time in the 1940's and early 1950's, Poland, Hungary, Romania, Bulgaria and other Eastern European states were to a considerable degree integrated within the Soviet decision and control system, their governments being held accountable to the Moscow government (or the CPSU), or to its military, police, and diplomatic agents. After Stalin's death, however, and to some extent even before, the governments and parties of these "satellite" states began to gain, relatively, in strength, independence and sovereignty. Thus, national integration seemed to be enhanced in these countries at the expense of an expanded Soviet integration. More or less simultaneously, however, the integration of the bloc of communist party-states *as a coalition or alliance system of more or less independent states* was enhanced, although its cohesion was soon damaged by the Sino-Soviet controversy.

The crucial point to be remembered is this, however: A sharp distinction must be drawn between and among the integrative processes operating to strengthen and expand the decision and control system of the USSR; the integrative processes operating to strengthen Poland, Hungary, Romania, Bulgaria, and so forth, as more or less independent and sovereign states; and the integrative processes operating to strengthen the *coalition* of these more or less independent and sovereign party-states.

NOTES

1. *Webster's Third New International Dictionary* (Springfield, Mass.: G. & C. Merriam, 1961).
2. Donald Olding Hebb, *A Textbook of Psychology* (Philadelphia and London: W. B. Saunders, 1958), p. 105.

3. Elman R. Service, *Primitive Social Organization* (New York: Random House, 1962).

4. The band concept has been derived, in part, at least, from Steward's investigations of the patrilineal band; see Julian H. Steward, *Theory of Culture Change* (Urbana: University of Illinois Press, 1955), pp. 25 and 122ff. Steward was less inclined to view the band as a universal type than as one of a number of types of hunting-gathering societies.

5. Identifiable chiefdoms include the Bontok Igorot, the Kalinga, the Tahitians, the Menangkabau of Indonesia, and certain Asian and Northwest Coast societies.

6. An alternative scheme of sociopolitical levels of organization is presented in George Peter Murdock, "World Ethnographic Sample," *American Anthropologist*, LIX, No. 4 (August 1957), 664–687.

7. Karl W. Deutsch *et al., Political Community and the North Atlantic Area* (Princeton: Princeton University Press, 1957). The cases were: (1) the integration of the thirteen American colonies into the United States in 1789, the breakup of the Union during the Civil War, and the reunion thereafter; (2) the gradual achievement of union between Scotland and England through 1707; (3) the dissolution of the union of Ireland (including Ulster) and the United Kingdom in 1921; (4) the struggle for German unity after the Middle Ages that culminated in unification in 1871; (5) the long delayed achievement of Italian unification in 1859–1861; (6) the long preservation, followed in 1918 by the dissolution, of the Hapsburg Empire; (7) the union of Sweden and Norway in 1814, followed by their separation in 1905; (8) the gradual integration of Switzerland begun in the thirteenth century and not completed until 1848; (9) the union of England and Wales after 1485; and (10) the integration of England itself during the Middle Ages.

8. *Ibid.*, p. 78.

9. Edward A. Freeman, *History of Federal Government in Greece and Italy* (2nd ed.; London: Macmillan, 1893), p. 626.

10. John R. Green, *A Short History of the English People* (New York: American Book, 1916), p. 84.

11. Henry Charles Lea, *A History of the Inquisition of Spain* (New York: The Macmillan Company, 1906), p. 1.

12. George C. Coulton, *The Inquisition* (New York: Jonathan Cape and Harrison Smith, 1929), p. 12.

13. *Ibid.*, p. 66.

14. Bernard Pares, *A History of Russia* (New York: Alfred A. Knopf, 1928), p. 41.

15. George Vernadsky, *The Mongols and Russia* (New Haven: Yale University Press, 1953).

16. *Ibid.*, p. 124.

17. Pares, *History*, p. 74.

18. V. O. Kluchevsky, *A History of Russia* (New York: Russell & Russell, 1960), II, 10.

19. Vernadsky, *Mongols*, p. 335.

20. George Vernadsky, *A History of Russia* (New Haven: Yale University Press, 1930), p. 47.

21. Pares, *History*, p. 82.

22. *Loc. cit.*

23. *Appanage:* grant (as of lands, offices, state revenues, or money) made

by a sovereign or a legislative body for the support of dependent members of the royal family or of the ruler's principal liegemen.

24. Kluchevsky, *History,* II, 4.
25. *Ibid.,* II, 5.
26. This was especially true of West Russian nobles situated in Lithuania who saw many personal advantages in adhering to an ambitious Muscovite state. Oswald Prentiss Backus, *Motives of West Russian Nobles in Deserting Lithuania for Moscow, 1377–1514* (Lawrence: University of Kansas Press, 1957), p. 98.

COMMUNIST PARTY-STATES

ONE

THE WORLD COMMUNIST SYSTEM

JAN F. TRISKA*

Within the universe of global international relations, the communist world may be conveniently analyzed as a system of communist parties. This approach is helpful for several reasons. First, it permits description, ordering, and classification of interacting units, the communist parties, according to their functions. Gradually, generalizations about functions may be reached, and on this basis analytical models may be constructed.[1] Second, political science, and particularly comparative politics, has developed a refined set of functions which offer uniform categories—socialization, recruitment, communication, and so on—for comparisons, as well as ready-made comparative hypotheses which may be tested in the complex, real world of communist parties.[2] Third, the patterned, interactional activities, supportive as well as conflictual, which the communist parties have displayed in the last fifty years have produced important reciprocally influential effects on the parties as well as on the movement; the system approach permits us to relate interaction to effects in a meaningful way.[3] And fourth, while the system approach focuses upon interaction and change, it does not prejudice the content of relations or the direction of change; the terms "communist bloc," "camp," or "movement," on the other hand, tend to emphasize solidarity within and antagonism outside the group of parties. Also, as George Modelski points out, one cannot understand the structure of communist states without understanding the communist parties which rule in these states. Here the communist parties perform basic political functions: "they facilitate communications against the background of common culture, guard solidarity, legitimize the rule, . . . and serve as justification for claims to universality." On the other hand, while communist states could not exist without communist parties, communist parties could and in fact have existed without the states: there were seven national parties with 400,000 members in 1917 and 56 national parties with 4,200,000 members in 1939. This is why communist parties "deserve separate attention as an independent phenomenon of world politics."[4]

Communist parties are either *ruling* parties, that is, parties which have succeeded in capturing control of government within their respective states—we call such states the communist party-states—or *nonruling* parties, which have not succeeded in this objective. The distinction between the two categories is important: The ruling communist parties, with their monopoly of effective governmental control, have displayed interactional activities within the system which have been greatly superior in scope, frequency, and intensity to those of the nonruling communist parties. The nonruling parties either share political power with other parties, compete with them or with other political organizations for rule, or are outlawed and thus outside the legitimate political process in their states. Because of the heterogeneous or even hostile national environment in which they operate, much of the nonruling parties' energy is exhausted locally, in collaboration, competition, and conflict with other national political organizations and groups. For this reason their internal conversion processes have tended toward the unorthodox, and their maintenance and adaptive characteristics toward the flexible. The nonruling parties' contribution to system performance has been secondary to that of the ruling parties. In terms of functional categories, they may be perceived as the secondary system units, whereas the ruling communist parties may be viewed as the primary or key units.

THE COMMUNIST SYSTEM'S GOALS
AND GOAL ACHIEVEMENT

In terms of the system goals, the functional distinction between the ruling and the nonruling parties is even more striking. Like all political systems, the communist system has goals which are encompassing rather then specific. First among its major goals is *system maintenance,* the preservation of the integrity and inviolability of the system so that the respective communist parties can maintain their achievements. The far-reaching changes which have taken place in the communist system since the death of Stalin bear evidence of efforts made to attain this goal. The Sino-Soviet conflict provides eloquent testimony to significant failure in its pursuit.

The second major goal, *system advancement and development,* aims to make the communist party-states as economically advanced and modern as possible, in the shortest possible time, by building into the economy socialist patterns of production, distribution, and consumption, and of ownership and control. The recent spectacular miscarriage of the socialist economy in Czechoslovakia proved again that although the Stalin model of economic development may have been suitable for pastoral, backward societies, it is patently not suited to advanced societies. The Czechoslovak economists finally discovered this hidden, dark side of the Stalin model—as did earlier the Yugoslavs, and the Russians with their Liberman plan of profit and incentive schemes.

The third major goal is *system expansion*—a communist world. Intermediate stages are involved, but ultimately this goal means the conjoining of all national communist parties—as ruling parties—into one world-wide communist system. But on the basis of the overall experience of the nonruling communist parties during the last ten years, this goal today tends to be viewed as illusory.

In addition, the goal of system expansion is related to and dependent upon the other two major goals; failure in either adversely affects and even precludes system expansion. Because all three goals are mutually exclusive in the sense that the system has a finite amount of resources which it must apportion among the three goals by taking from one that which it grants the others, the first goal, system maintenance, is becoming too costly. In fact, the greater the system success in moving toward the third major goal, system expansion, the greater has appeared the deprivation in the pursuit of the first goal, system maintenance. Judging from the mushrooming conflict patterns within the communist party-states, the goal of communist expansion could be achieved, if at all, only by sacrificing the movement as a system. This built-in paradox greatly reduces the system's investment in the goal of expansion, thus further reducing the functions of nonruling communist parties and widening the abyss between them and the ruling parties more than ever. The inverse relationship between the number of successful units—the ruling parties—within the system and the system's solidarity and cohesion would require an allocation of resources to system maintenance that is entirely out of proportion to expenditures on the other two goals. The system advancement and development process tends to deviate from the costly Lenin-Stalin socialist model and goals, and system expansion, via the nonruling parties, has slackened almost to zero. The gradual but increasing abdication of these two major goals, rather than the reinforcing of the third one, has tended to make the goal of system maintenance more precarious than ever before. The system's progress toward all its three major goals has been consistently slowing down. The communist system now shows the limits the movement has reached—and perhaps transgressed—on its way toward self-maintenance, expansion, and socialist development.

THE COMMUNIST SYSTEM'S ORGANIZATIONAL PROBLEMS

To sustain development and growth, large-scale political organizations must continually adapt their organizational structure to the new demands, responsibilities, opportunities and challenges imposed by their very development and growth. In particular, they must constantly relate their *modus operandi* to the increasing ratio of responsibility, influence, and power which their development entails. Failure to do so, whatever the reason, is bound to lead to a series of reversals which, increasing in significance with time, result in a general slowdown, followed by serious breakdowns in the organizational structures which the frantically squeezed controlling valves barely manage to check. By then, not only further development, but the actual existence of the organization, is dangerously threatened. Continuous accommodation and checking of new stresses as they occur within the organization is an enormous but imperative task. The process of disintegration, which reduced and ultimately destroyed all large political organizations in the world in the past, has a tendency to creep in during times of stagnation, and frenzied insistence on preserving the *status quo* becomes incompatible with the very dynamism and vitality on which large-scale political organizations depend for their life.

In 1918, the Russian Soviet Federated Socialist Republic was a highly centralized body politic, the government of which was the pinnacle of a hierarchy of Soviets—central, territorial, regional, area, district—and the Party. In 1923, the RSFSR became the equally centralized Union of Soviet Socialist Republics, then composed of the original RSFSR and the Ukrainian, Byelorussian, and Transcaucasian SSR's. In 1936, the USSR consisted of eleven Union Republics (the RSFSR, the Ukrainian, the Byelorussian, the Uzbek, the Kazakh, the Turkmen, the Tadzhik, the Georgian, the Azerbaidzhanian, the Armenian, and the Kirgiz SSR's). In 1940, the former Baltic states of Estonia, Latvia, and Lithuania became new Soviet Socialist Republics, and, with the acquisition of Bessarabia and Western Bukovina from Romania, the Moldavian Soviet Socialist Republic was created. The Karelo-Finnish SSR "joined" the ranks of the Soviet Union Republics after the Soviet "victory" over Finland in 1940; this increased the number of Union Republics to sixteen. (The last, however, was dissolved in 1955.) Carpatho-Ukraine (formerly part of Czechoslovakia), the Kurils and Southern Sakhalin (formerly part of Japan), Tanna Tuva, and West Prussia and Königsberg became parts of the USSR after World War II.

This Soviet growth by osmosis continued with the appropriation by Stalin of the eight European and three Far Eastern satellites. These were Poland, East Germany, Czechoslovakia, Albania, Bulgaria, Hungary, Romania, and Yugoslavia; and Communist China, North Korea, and North Vietnam (Outer Mongolia was an earlier acquisition).

Soviet effective control thus grew from one political unit in 1918 to four in 1923, eleven in 1936, sixteen in 1940, and became twenty-six "sovereign states" after Stalin's death, comprising fifteen Union Republics and eleven satellite states (minus Yugoslavia).

Such relatively rapid increase was bound to lead to some relaxation of the rigid pattern of centralization insisted upon by Lenin and Stalin. As a matter of fact, denial of any autonomy in time became inconceivable for the new Soviet political organization. The formal but ineffective homage paid by Stalin to decentralization in 1936 and 1944 was far outmatched by the decentralization scheme effected by Khrushchev in 1957 and 1958 in the USSR and by his insistence at the Twenty-First Party Congress in 1959 upon "complete equality"—political, social, economic, and ideological—of all "socialist states." To insist upon centralization today would result in instant and probably final dissolution of the communist alliance. "Autonomy," "equality," "sovereignty," and "commonwealth of socialist nations" are the catchwords employed with great emphasis and frequency from Prague to Pyongyang—in territorial *as well as* in organizational terms.

Stalin's success was also his failure: The Soviet organization was beginning to move beyond its own saturation point; this large-scale political organization ceased to be controllable, with the given safeguard mechanisms, within a framework now inadequate for its operation. While control, enforcement, and conditioning devices to sustain a Stalinist-type regime capable of dominating as much as one-third of humanity living on one-fourth of the world's available space might eventually become available, under the circumstances the Soviet bite was far too big. Modern science and technology are as yet unable to supply adequate controls to permit the sustained continuity, let alone further growth, of the Soviet large-scale political organization without far-reaching, fundamental revision of the assumptions and premises upon which it was built and complete modernization of the machinery.

The problem is how to construct a rational organization which would produce a minimum of undesirable side effects but achieve a maximum of satisfaction compatible with the aims of the organizers.

The successful "socialism in one country" thesis, at a time when great cost to the organization in human terms was thought necessary, brought about the antithesis and polarization of Yugoslavia, Poland, Hungary, China, Albania, Czechoslovakia, and Romania. The synthesis could take the form of a collective break into 14 hostile Yugoslavias, Albanias, Chinas, or worse—undoubtedly worse, once the process of disintegration started in earnest—involving as well the loss of the nonruling communist parties; or, hopefully, by means of skillful surgery, there could be created an organization of "socialist" but autonomous states, supported by and supporting the nonruling communist parties in the world.

Since the demise of the Cominform, however, there has existed no institutionalized association of the communist parties, ruling or nonruling. The parties do have extensive informal relations and communication networks but these are seldom reliable or binding.

The several institutionalized associations of the communist party-states—the Council of Mutual Economic Assistance, the Warsaw Treaty Organization, the Danube Commission, the Joint Institute of Nuclear Research, the Organization for the Collaboration of Railways, the International Broadcasting Organization, and the multilateral functional (and, in most cases, *ad hoc*) conferences on health, fishing industries, plant protection, cultural affairs, and the like—are at best utilitarian agencies which show increasing signs of ossification and retardation. So also are the multitude of other ties among the governmental agencies of communist party-states, between trade unions, youth or women's groups, and other associations.

Historically, the principal instrument which the leaders of the communist system have utilized toward the fulfillment of system goals have been the nonruling communist parties—and these may have gained the assistance in their respective countries of other parties or groups disposed toward their goals, their belief system, or, perhaps, their tactical objectives. The nonruling communist parties may also have developed military forces of their own, either paramilitary or guerilla. Or they may have worked through numerous other methods and organizations, either communist or affinitive, such as trade unions, youth and women's groups, peace movements, street riots and demonstrations. But this instrumentality has proved increasingly defective, unreliable, and imperfect. The conglomeration of pressures and conflicts among the communist ruling parties has made an impressive and sustained impact on the operational codes of the nonruling parties, upon their orientation, and upon their composite relations with their several environments, especially the national. It is only to be expected that, in turn, the nonruling parties were bound to impress deeply the ruling parties with their new demands and expectations, based upon their changed perceptions of mutual relations with the ruling parties.

More recently, the communist party-states have turned their attention to what might be called affinitive regimes. These are ruling elites of countries which seem to exhibit empathy, for one reason or another, for the system. Rather than trying to replace the respective regimes with nonruling communist party elites, the attempt has been gradually to win the ruling regimes to the communist system, or, at least, to bind them so closely to the system that one day they would find extricating themselves difficult. Where they have decided to follow this strategy, the party-states have been willing to abandon the national nonruling communist parties to their own fate: Egypt under Nasser may serve as an example. The overwhelming evidence, however, again shows that the cost of this sustained attempt has exceeded the expectations; the effort has not paid off.

Finally, the communist system has either utilized existing int rnational confederations of national front organizations or created new ones (for example, the World Federation of Trade Unions, the World Peace Movement, the International Association of Democratic Lawyers) in an attempt to influence the national organizations to bolster the nonruling communist parties in their countries or to swing an affinitive regime closer to the communist system. These organizations still meet, attract attention, and pass resolutions. But since they are known for what they are—which had not been often the case in the past—their significance for the communist system goals is limited.

The problem of constructing a rational organization with a minimum of undesirable side effects and maximum satisfaction along the lines posed by the communist system goals has not been solved. The communist parties are becoming more autonomous but less integrated, and they have no new structures to serve their desirable but complex system functions.

THE COMMUNIST SYSTEM IN SEARCH OF A THEORY

If there is no adequate system organization, is there an adequate association theory upon which such an organization could be built? Is there a communist-produced set of ideas linking the several units of the communist system which may be called a theory?

A *theory* may be defined as a generalization asserting that two or more things—activities, situations or events—covary under specified conditions;[5] its acceptance depends on its precision and verifiability. Well-confirmed, a theory is called a *law;* not yet confirmed, a *hypothesis.* The formulation of *concepts* and their linkage into frameworks—just as the construction of *paradigms* or patterns of mutually related questions, propositions and variables—is an analytical exercise which, while useful, may or may not lead to the building of coherent, formal theories.

To start with, the communists have not made claims to possessing a theory linking the several units of the communist movement together. The closest they come to describing the mental underpinning of the world communist system is their talk of *proletarian internationalism,* a set of "principles" which dates back to the Communist Manifesto and the Marxian programmatic postulate, "Workers of the world, unite."[6]

Setting aside for the moment the several definitions—which are more stochastic, normative, and hortatory than definitional (such as that "proletarian internationalism is the ideology and policy of the brotherhood and friendship of the whole working class")—proletarian internationalism, "the antithesis of bourgeois, capitalist nationalism," is a mental construct of considerable historical significance. Nationalism had no place in Marx's scale of values: The emancipation of labor was a social, rather than a local or national, problem which embraced all advanced countries. Nationalism was irrelevant to the common interest and objectives of the proletariat, which were above any limits imposed by nationalism.

Marx's theory, international in origin, character, and purpose, drew upon the elements of national experience which it perceived as universal and historically repetitive. It postulated an international or nationless world, but it was not concerned with the in-between developmental stage —the period of transition from the nation to the no-nation level.

As a consequence, before the Bolshevik Revolution, Lenin's proletarians had no homeland. Their class enemy was international; hence, the conditions for their liberation were international.[7] In this period, only the class solidarity of the proletariat in several countries could express proletarian internationalism, the progress in uniting workers of all countries under the banner of the Communist Manifesto.

After the Bolshevik Revolution, the "toilers" had a homeland. But now, as Lenin put it, "the most important thing, both for us and from the point of view of international socialism, is the *preservation* of Soviet Russia."[8]

Stalin completed the hiatus: "An internationalist is he," he stated, "who unreservedly and without hesitation and without conditions is prepared to defend the USSR because the USSR is the base of the world revolutionary movement, and to defend and to advance this movement without defending the USSR is impossible."[9]

Ending with "the emergence of socialism from the confines of one country," the Soviet stage of development witnessed the testing of proletarian internationalism both horizontally and vertically. *Abroad,* the world movement of workers supported the first communist party-state and in turn, "the toilers of the USSR supported the . . . movement."[10] *In the USSR,* proletarian internationalism was employed as "a national policy" vis-à-vis nationalities and minorities among and within the Union Republics: The Soviet Union was the first political system to demonstrate empirically the possibilities of developing the model and setting the pattern for the future, Soviet theorists maintain.[11] An ideal proving ground, the USSR fulfilled its historical mission by bringing to its nationality and minority groups all the fruits and advantages of unity and solidarity on the basis of equality and self-determination. The Soviet pattern was thus "bound" to become a model of international and intergroup cooperation for the post-World War II community of communist party-states.[12]

The short-lived Hungarian Soviet Republic of 1919 and the aborted Bavarian communist rule provided little opportunity for the Soviet government to indulge in socialist international relations. While a somewhat greater scope for the testing of proletarian internationalism was furnished in relations between Soviet Russia and Mongolia and the Soviet districts in China, it was only after the Second World War that proletarian internationalism could be tested among the several communist party-states, and between them and the nonruling communist parties.

As long as Stalin was alive, the alternatives available to the new ruling parties were limited: either they conformed, or, like Tito, they were expelled. Had Khrushchev not condemned Stalin as clearly as he did in 1956, the Soviet ability to impose its own rule on others would not have been curtailed so rapidly and so dramatically. But the Soviet quarrel with Peking and the ensuing indiscretions of both adversaries became community property. The increasing reluctance of many ruling as well as nonruling parties to take sides and support either of the contestants has been striking evidence of the growing looseness and slackness of relationships among all parties.

In any event, this development could not have been entirely prevented, suppressed, or greatly retarded. But without Khrushchev's speech before the Twentieth Party Congress in Moscow in 1956, it probably could have been better and more discreetly controlled. Khrushchev's subsequent attempts to patch up matters here and there was not the kind of substantive overhaul of the organizational machinery that was needed.

The "new type" of international relations which emerged with Khrushchev's prescription for "the Commonwealth of Socialist Nations" was formulated in 1955, *after* the April Bandung Conference. Like the Bandung Conference, the "Commonwealth" was said to stand for mutual assistance and cooperation, genuine friendly relations, world peace and security for all. In particular, following the Bandung Declaration, the principles of mutual respect for territorial integrity—non-aggression, non-intervention in domestic affairs, sovereign equality, and mutual assistance —were said to link all the communist party-states "headed by the Soviet Union." The domestic construction of socialism in the USSR was essential for the development of the Commonwealth "because such construction involved a continuous search for theoretical principles which would guide development and bind socialist states in true proletarian internationalism."[13] But, in effect, the emphasis has been put on the *communist party-states,* not on the world movement.

The historical term "proletarian internationalism" has denoted relations among all units as well as subunits of the world system; it has extended from relations among *individuals,* such as members of different parties, to relations among the organizations of several *states,* such as the Warsaw Pact or COMECON. The category subordinated to it, both in time and space, has been *"socialist internationalism,"* the "new type" of relationships which pertains exclusively to the communist party-states.[14]

To use taxonomic categories: If general international relations is the class, then proletarian international relations is the order and social international relations the family, the latter two being governed by the principles of proletarian internationalism and socialist internationalism, respectively. As a consequence, proletarian internationalism, while continuing to remain the guiding principle of the world communist movement, has been the principal foundation from which evolve inter-party-state relations: This subsystemic superstructure is called "socialist internationalism."[15]

But socialist internationalism, in contradistinction to, and as a result of, the lesson of the Soviet "socialism in one country" concept, means socialism in each communist party-state as reduced by the existence of several socialist countries. While constructing their own socialisms in their own single countries and thus following the Soviet historical model, the members are also utilizing the advantages of membership in the common economic, ideological, political, cultural, and military system, thus enhancing the socialist community. The communist party-state system is thus not perceived as a mere sum total of a group of states; it is viewed as an economic, ideological, political, cultural, and military community, counterposed to the capitalist system. Each party-state, while an independent sovereign entity, is also a component part of a broader social community.[16]

The *substance* of socialist internationalism is determined by the nature of the social system prevailing in the communist party-states. The liquidation of private property and of capitalists produces conditions which are presumed to be ideal for interstate economic ties and relations. The public ownership of the means of production should preclude exploitation of man by man and create conditions for the close association of different peoples with a common purpose—the victory of socialism and communism in their countries, members of one political, social, and economic system. The resulting "community of equal and sovereign nations marching along the path of socialism and communism" has been proclaimed an achievement, a fulfillment of a promise, and a victory.[17]

Socialist internationalism is said to express the unity of interests, expectations, and hopes of the peoples of the communist party-states. The principal unifiers of the communist party-states are thus assumed to be (1) common aims, (2) common enemy, (3) common interests, and (4) common accomplishments. Respectively, the communist party-states (1) all struggle for socialism and communism; (2) all seek to defend themselves against imperialism; (3) all are closer to each other than to any heterogeneous outsider, because of their similar political, economic, social, and cultural systems; and (4) all participate in building socialism and communism through mutual assistance and cooperation. Hence the party-states are bound together by (a) the socialist international division of labor, (b) the socialist world market, and close (c) political, (d) cultural, and (e) military relations. In other words, the fact that these states are ruled by communist parties establishes basic similarities among them, creating a presumption of common interests and goals and, therefore, military and economic interdependence. It follows that the substantial amounts of sustained transactions rationally conducted among all the party-states should mutually help them all, individually *and* collectively. The 1957 Declaration of Communist Parties, while emphasizing equality, territorial sovereignty, and non-interference in domestic matters of individual party-states, considers the "most striking" expression of socialist internationalism to be "fraternal mutual aid."[18]

Proletarian internationalism, in its socialist internationalism category, has been thus adapted to the realities of "modern" international relations as they are perceived by the communist theoreticians.[19] In the process, socialist internationalism has been deprived of its most forceful ingredient. The language of conventional and traditional international relations, and, in particular, the growing insistence on state sovereignty as the only basis for mutual relations among communist party-states, imply not only formal equality, non-intervention in domestic affairs, independence, and integrity of the party-states in their mutual relations, but also a very important deviation from and contradiction to the commitments of proletarian internationalism. Thus, several problems are created.

First, when, under the impact of 1956 and the Hungarian revolution, Khrushchev implicitly coupled proletarian internationalism with the principles of Bandung, he had to include a strong disclaimer that proletarian internationalism had anything to do with the simple concept of *peaceful coexistence* between socialist states. Had he not done that, the concept of dichotomous world would have been rendered meaningless:

> From the denial of the fact that the world is split into two antagonistic systems and consequently into two camps, the conclusion has been deduced that socialist states allegedly cannot make a distinction in their foreign policy between the socialist and the bourgeois states. This is a point of view alien to proletarian internationalism; it amounts in fact to undermining the unity among the brotherly socialist countries.[20]

Second, after the debacle of the Cominform, with the increasingly unsuccessful and therefore fewer system-wide party meetings and reduced communication, the emphasis on state relations over those of party relations among the communist party-states made, indeed, for less fuss and strain. But the retrogressive deviation from proletarian internationalism that was implied when state sovereignty was proclaimed as the foundation of socialist internationalism marked an un-Marxian return to the Marxian nineteenth-century world in more ways than one.[21]

In fact, some Soviet authors even suggest that differences of views among the ruling parties harmful to socialist internationalism should not be carried over to relations among the party-states:

> For each socialist country, possible differences notwithstanding, can make its contribution to the overall victory of socialism if it strictly observes all its commitments to other socialist countries, extends economic, scientific, technological, and cultural cooperation with them, builds up their joint defense capabilities against imperialism, and joins with them in a united front in the international arena.[22]

Moreover, the Bandung principles, praised on the state level, are beginning to enter the *party* level as well. As the Central Committee of the Romanian Workers' Party put it in April 1964, there were no "parent" and "son" parties—parties that are superior and inferior—but only a family of *completely equal* parties; hence parties must *respect* each other and must not *interfere* in each other's business. No party has a privileged position nor can it impose its line on opinions of other parties.[23]

Third, serious differences exist within the world communist movement and, in particular, among the communist party-states, on several issues, and "it would be unwise to close our eyes to the differences."[24] The communist party-states are still economically unequal; there is a discrepancy between the development of relationships within the various party-states and between different parts of the communist system; there are wide opportunities for multiform ties among the party-states which are not utilized; there are contradictions among them caused by the divergence of specific interests; there is a lack of experience in the imaginative shaping and evolving of multilateral economic and political ties; and the various peoples have been brought up in a nationalistic climate of hatred and mistrust for their neighbors which has not as yet completely disappeared.

For these reasons, search has been under way for more flexible and effective forms of cooperation that would conform to both the "international interests" and "national aspirations" of the nations involved. Programs for such activity have included the Council for Mutual Economic Assistance; the Warsaw Treaty Organization, within which Soviet nuclear and missile capabilities have been of particular significance; meetings of leaders; exchange of information; coordination of foreign policies; and cultural exchange. "But because it is being carried out and tried and tested for the first time in the history of mankind, [socialist internationalism], an exceptionally intricate undertaking," requires new skill, wisdom, and energy to accomplish the task of strengthening the unity of the party-state system.[25]

Fourth, socialist internationalism cannot develop "automatically." Socialism in the several countries may be creating a foundation on which socialist relations among the party-states can develop; but how this opportunity is used depends on the leadership in the several ruling communist parties. The implementation of the principles of proletarian internationalism in the setting of the communist party-states depends especially on the party-states' attitude toward nationalism in their midst. As Palmiro Togliatti, former Secretary-General of the Italian Communist Party, put it:

> A fact worrying us, and one we do not succeed in explaining fully, is the manifestation among the socialist countries of a centrifugal tendency. . . .
>
> Without doubt there is a revival of nationalism. However, we know that the national sentiment remains a permanent factor in the working-class and socialist movement for a long period, also after the conquest of power. Economic progress does not dispel this, it nurtures it. Also, in the socialist camp perhaps (I underline this "perhaps" because many concrete facts are unknown to us), one needs to be on one's guard against the forced exterior uniformity and one must consider that the unity one ought to establish and maintain lies in the diversity and full autonomy of the individual countries.[26]

The nationalist disunities, contradictions, and centrifugal tendencies among the communist party-states that challenge socialist internationalism are assumed, however, to be transient and temporary phenomena. Of the three major dangers to socialist internationalism—the novelty of the transition to socialism of countries with differing social, economic, cultural, and historical backgrounds; the cult of personality of Stalin; and the "erroneous" policy of China based on nationalist distortions and deviations—the third, pseudo-left, nationalist dogmatism, is depicted as the principal one. Chinese leaders are said to counterpose their divisive nationalist line to both socialist and proletarian internationalism. As Lenin is now cited, with tongue in cheek, "One who has adopted nationalistic views naturally desires to erect a Chinese wall around his nationality, his national working-class movement . . . , unembarrassed even by the fact that by his tactics of division and dismemberment *he is reducing to nil* the great call for the rallying and unity of all nations, all races and all languages."[27]

For this reason, the most compelling task for all believing in socialist internationalism is to assist in the healing of the breach and in the establishment of contacts and cooperation with the Chinese communists. Marx and Engels had held regular congresses of the International, and Lenin considered it important systematically to hold congresses of the Comintern. To strengthen both proletarian and socialist internationalism, a new international communist organization would, perhaps, be the best means of overcoming the differences. But under no condition could the present split in the movement serve as a basis for severing relations with or even excommunicating any member.[28]

The Chinese version of the issue of nationalism versus proletarian internationalism and its consequences is somewhat different. True, the Chinese communists support "progressive nationalism," "national independence," and "people's democracy" and oppose "reactionary nationalism" and "domestic reaction."[29] But their view of proletarian internationalism changed with changed conditions. Earlier, it meant support of the USSR; now it means support of all the communist party-states in the camp, their unity, and "the policies which the socialist countries *ought to pursue*":

> It is under new historical conditions that the communist and workers' parties are now carrying on the task of proletarian internationalist unity and struggle. When one socialist country existed and when this country was faced with hostility and jeopardized by all the imperialists and reactionaries because it firmly pursued the correct Marxist-Leninist line and policies, the touchstone of proletarian internationalism for every communist party was whether or not it resolutely defended the only socialist country. Now, there is a socialist camp consisting of 13 countries, Albania, Bulgaria, China, Cuba, Czechoslovakia, the German Democratic Republic, Hungary, the Democratic People's Republic of Korea, Mongolia, Poland, Romania, the Soviet Union, and the Democratic Republic of Vietnam. Under these circumstances, the touchstone of proletarian internationalism for every communist party is whether or not it resolutely defends the whole of the socialist camp, whether or not it defends the unity of all the countries in the camp on the basis of Marxism-Leninism, and whether or not it defends the Marxist-Leninist line and policies which the socialist countries ought to pursue.[30]

Fifth, coercion is not an end but a means to an end. Still, the communists would not use it if the classes departing from history would give up without recourse to violence. But they do not. The reactionaries have tried to cause troubles in several party-states: they tried to unleash civil war in Poland, to engineer putsches in Hungary and Czechoslovakia, and to organize counterrevolutionary armed actions in Romania. They failed only because the means of coercion were now in the hands of the socialist governments in these countries, and, in particular, in the new party-state security bodies, the armies and the people's militias. These enabled the communists to build up the preponderance of strength, limiting the opportunities of the capitalists for counterrevolutions.[31]

Coercion is inexcusable if used against fraternal parties and states. Thus, in the past, it became increasingly obvious that the Comintern as an international organization and center no longer suited the needs of the communist movement. Its interference with the internal matters of communist parties "went as far as the removal and replacement of leading party cadres and even of entire central committees, as far as the imposing from without of leaders, the suppression of distinguished leading cadres of various parties, and as far as the censure and even disowning of communist parties."

These unfortunate coercive practices were again employed in the Cominform. Yugoslavia's party was condemned and excluded from the Cominform, and Yugoslavia, a communist party-state, was expelled from the party-states system. Thus, evil practices were extended from party to state relations, "rendering their consequences the more serious," and there occurred "numerous cases of expulsion from the party, arrests, trials, and suppressions of many leading party and state cadres." Hence, the Central Committee of the Romanian Workers' Party deemed the "sharp divergences now prevailing in the communist movement" of the utmost gravity, as "the danger could arise of a repetition of the methods and practices" of the past.[32]

Lenin's original sentiments are now approvingly cited:

> We want a *voluntary* union of nations—a union which *precludes any coercion* of one nation by another—a union founded on complete confidence, on a clear recognition of brotherly unity, on *absolutely voluntary consent*. Such a union cannot be effected with one stroke; we have to work towards it with the greatest patience and circumspection, so as not to spoil matters and not to arouse distrust and in order that the distrust inherited from centuries of landowner and capitalist oppression, centuries of private property, and the enmity caused by divisions and redivisions may wear off.[33]

Sixth, the new inclusiveness, stratification and particularization of proletarian internationalism, while responding to new needs, creates new difficulties. Proletarian internationalism stands now for the formation of a broad front of political alliance embracing four principal forces: (1) the communist party-states; (2) the nonruling communist parties; (3) the parties and organizations united in the national liberation movement in developing nations; (4) all peoples and organizations everywhere fighting against imperialism and for peace.[34] The line between the world communist system—the communist party-states and nonruling communist parties —and the rest of the world is elusive and even irrelevant: "In the first half of our century, socialism has been a broad stream that attracts ever more countries and social forces."[35] United by the principles of proletarian internationalism, these countries and social forces are interrelated: For example, the *national liberation movement* would not have reached its present level were it not for the advances made by the communist *party-states*. At the same time, however, the struggle of the communists against capitalism would have taken place under much more difficult conditions were it not for the *deprivation of imperialism of its colonial positions*. The *nonruling parties* in the capitalist countries aided by the USSR and the other communist party-states significantly contributed to the progress made by the party-states. And the *nonruling communist parties* benefited greatly in their own development from the assistance rendered to them by the communist party-states.[36]

The significance of proletarian internationalism rests, then, on its quadruple roles. (1) It is a model of unity among the communist party-states. (2) The development of national liberation movements in terms of their most important needs, economic development and defense of national independence, depends on the help of all communists. (3) It unites all, even "the most diverse detachments," engaged in the revolutionary struggle everywhere in the world. (4) It joins all peoples of good will in their struggle against war and reaction and for peace.

Proletarian internationalism is thus expected to strengthen the world socialist system "as the main factor in present-day revolutionary development"; to synchronize the building of socialism and communism by each communist party-state; to defend the unity of the international communist movement against reactionary nationalism, factionalism and schism; to defend and creatively develop Marxism-Leninism as the ideological foundation of the international communist movement; and to unite all progressive forces everywhere.[37]

This set of assumptions, explicitly broadening proletarian internationalism, led to the next apostate round within the communist movement, a profound disagreement concerning not the breadth but the purpose, rank-ordering, and relationships within the concept. The CPSU, supported by its friends, stipulated that all-world (all-state) communism would be achieved *because of the great successes of the communist party-states*. Their economic, social, political, and scientific achievements must and would be so impressive that all mankind will be persuaded that only communism is the way of the future. Thus, the primary purpose of proletarian internationalism must be the victory and consolidation of communism in the several party-states; and, hence, the world proletariat must support all the states which construct socialism (while, in turn, the socialist construction in the communist party-states can proceed only in close association and in cooperation with the world revolutionary movement).[38]

The Chinese Communist Party and its friends, on the other hand, maintain that primacy belongs not to the communist party-states but to the key area in the struggle for ultimate communist victory, namely, the oppressed people of Asia, Africa, and Latin America. All progressive forces everywhere, including the ruling communist parties, have a duty which is primary and non-mutual, to support these peoples in their open, revolutionary struggle for liberation from imperialist oppression:

> The national democratic revolutionary struggles of the people in Asia, Africa, and Latin America are pounding and undermining the foundations of the rule of imperialism and colonialism, old and new, and are now a mighty force in defense of peace. In a sense, therefore, the whole cause of the international proletarian revolution hinges on the outcome of the revolutionary struggles of the peoples of these areas who constitute the overwhelming majority of the world population. Therefore, the anti-imperialist revolutionary struggle of the people in Asia, Africa, and Latin America is definitely not merely a matter of regional significance but one of overall importance for the whole cause of proletarian world revolution.[39]

Those who consider the significance of the national liberation movement secondary to that of the communist party-state system not only "cater to the needs of imperialism," but try to create a new "theory" to justify the continued rule of "superior nations" over "inferior nations." This is not proletarian internationalism, but a serious departure from it, and the theory is "fraudulent."

Not socialist internationalism and the communist party-states, nor even the international communist movement, then, but the national liberation movement is the principal social revolutionary force today. It leads the other forces as "the storm center of world revolution dealing direct blows to imperialism." This is why the future of proletarian internationalism as a world-wide international format and model hinges on the outcome of its struggle.[40]

In addition to these problems—denial of simple, peaceful coexistence among the socialist states; sovereignty of national communist parties; the party-state dichotomy; revival of nationalism; condemnation of coercion; watering down of the proletarian internationalism concept to include "all men of good will"; and the employment of traditional international forms—there are many other issues and ideas on which there is disagreement and which, at least tangentially, affect the general consensus on proletarian internationalism. These include the inevitability of war; resort to armed revolution; the impact of nuclear weapons on communist strategies; the possibility of disarmament; economic relations among party-states; local wars (among and with developing nations); and peaceful world coexistence. The kind of system climate which results is quite adverse to the building of a unified theory of international relations.

The growing national independence of the ruling communist parties, brought about by the reluctant Soviet emphasis on "complete" equality, non-intervention in domestic matters, and respect for the state sovereignty of the communist party-states, largely eliminated the ruling parties' subordination to the "victorious" CPSU. The end of rule by coercion and condemnation, initiated among the communist party-states by Khrushchev with his emphasis on voluntarism principally on the state level, was carried over to the party level and extended to the nonruling parties. True, the Sino-Soviet split was bound to affect all the parties, and pro-Chinese factions were bound to emerge both because of the seriousness of the conflict and the open and sustained challenge to the CPSU by the CCP. But the fact remains that in the process of deciding the issue for themselves, many parties used this opportunity to assert their own growing independence of *any* party. Being able to select from among more than one party gained for them the freedom of formulating their own views and policies and brought home the opportunity of perhaps influencing the movement merely by deviating from the announced policies.

But then, perhaps, the dialectics of the international and national aspects of the communist movement are such that true unity of the movement's units in the long run can be achieved only when this unity is based on the units' independence and equality. This is what some communists claim, urging that the present stage of development, characterized by disagreements, disharmony, and diversity, is, indeed, both unavoidable and necessary and will lead to a new synthesis of more perfect unity.[41]

Others disagree. Adherents of the Soviet wing in the movement complain that to state that discords and splits—both without and within the communist party-states and communist parties—are necessary and unavoidable and that the dialectics of the development of the international working-class movement involves such disunity, as well as unity on a new basis, means to endow the existing Sino-Soviet disharmony with "a theoretical foundation." This is profoundly dangerous—it is, in fact, "a call for a split," they maintain.[42]

But in their replies, the Chinese communists emphasize that, on the contrary:

> The leaders of the CPSU have themselves undermined the basis of the unity of the international communist movement and created the present grave danger of a split by *betraying Marxism-Leninism and proletarian internationalism* and pushing their revisionist and divisive line. . . . They have thus made a mess of the splendid socialist camp . . . [and] pursued a policy of great-power chauvinism and national egoism.[43]

It was the Soviet leaders who "arbitrarily infringed the sovereignty of fraternal countries, interfered in their internal affairs, carried on subversive activities, and tried in every way to control fraternal countries"; it was they who "openly called for the overthrow of the party and government leaders of Albania"; it was they who "violated the Sino-Soviet Treaty of Friendship, Alliance and Mutual Assistance"; and it was they who "provoked incidents on the Sino-Soviet border and carried out large-scale subversive activities in Sinkiang."[44]

Proletarian internationalism may be a true "acid test" or "test supplied by history"; it may be a "slogan" or a "motto" ("unity, unity, and, once again, unity of the world communist movement"); it may be a "reliable tool," an "instrument," a "keystone," a "bond," and a "thesis"; it may be a "set of principles," an "outlook," and even a "policy"; *but it is not a theory.* As a generalization asserting that two or more things covary under specified conditions ("proletarian internationalism is a unity of all progressive forces based on their common struggle against imperialism and for peace"), it is neither precise, systematic, nor verifiable. The premise of the identity of interests on a class basis no longer obtains. In fact, the concept is now so broad that it has little meaning. And the subsequent limitation of the generalization by the particular exceptions designed for "the most advanced detachment" of the movement, namely, the communist party-state, the learning model for the future; the consequent greater concern for relations among states rather than among parties; and the Chinese denial of both these latter propositions and their disagreement on the rank-ordering of the revolutionary forces, make even this limited conceptual framework questionable. The fact that some broad, theoretical presuppositions underlie the crude empirical search for an overall unity and association does not bring the remote ideal any closer. The very hortatory and stochastic nature of the postulate, and the history of the theorizing on the subject, suggest that the concept has emerged not so much to analyze conditions as to make them, and to persuade everyone of their great value. But a wish for unity, without provision of an adequate theoretical base for it, is irrelevant. It is not theory-building—it is at most a mechanistic continuation of a well-established habit.[45]

The conclusion is that there exists no formal theory of association in the world communist system. There is a great deal of theorizing about it, though, which occurs in the form of inductive reviews of *ad hoc* predictions for individual assumptions. This theorizing emanates from normative observations, case studies, and various non-technical sources. Writings on the subject have often raised interesting questions, but have not arrived at a theory of relations. Proletarian internationalism is, *at best,* two rival conceptual frameworks differing both in rank-ordering and in emphasis laid on particular principles; *at worst,* it is several hortatory speculations, unverified, imprecise, and unsystematic.

Or, to borrow their own language, the communist theoreticians have failed to develop creatively Marxist-Leninist teaching on internationalism in keeping with the conditions of the time, with the relations among socialist countries, and with the conditions in the world communist movement.

With obsolete organizational structure and without an association theory upon which a modern, rational organization could be built, the communist system organizers are doomed to patching-up, temporizing, and holding operations, which, in their sum total, are inadequate even for system maintenance, let alone for the socialist development and system development of the communist party-states. Politically stagnating and economically inactive, the system becomes increasingly vulnerable to adversities at home and abroad.

THE COMMUNIST PARTY-STATES' ALLIANCE SYSTEM

To analyze the communist party-states' alliance system, it may be convenient to describe first those major properties and propensities of the party-states which pertain to their alliance.

The 14 states ruled by communist parties (where the CP's "are at the helm") are: the USSR, Chinese People's Republic, People's Republic of Albania, People's Republic of Bulgaria, Hungarian People's Republic, Democratic Republic of Vietnam, German Democratic Republic, Korean People's Democratic Republic, Heroic People of Cuba, Mongolian People's Republic, Czechoslovak Socialist Republic, Polish People's Republic, Romanian People's Republic, and Socialist Federal Republic of Yugoslavia.[46] While both the CPSU and the Chinese CP recognize Cuba as one of the party-states, China excludes Yugoslavia.

A position "at the helm" is most influential for *party membership*. Of the about 44.6 million communists in the world, organized in 87 communist parties, nearly 41 million, or more than 94%, populate the 14 ruling communist parties.[47] Outside the party-states, party membership is on the decline: In the last three years, the nonruling communist parties lost over one-third of their members.

The largest party in the world is the Chinese Communist Party, with more than 17 million members. The Communist Party of the Soviet Union has about 13 million members; the communist parties of Czechoslovakia, East Germany, Poland, North Korea, and Yugoslavia have over one million members each. If we project the CP membership against the total population, then North Korea (12.9%) and Czechoslovakia lead (11.9%), followed by East Germany (11.1%), Romania (9.0%) and Bulgaria (7.2%). The ratios for CP members to adult population are available for all but North Korea and China. The ratio for Czechoslovakia, where 18.3% of all adults are CP members, seems virtually unequalled anywhere.[48] (See Table 1–1.)

The *population* of the communist party-states accounts for "more than one-third [of] the population of the world."[49] China, the most popu-

TABLE 1–1. COMMUNIST PARTY MEMBERSHIP, 1967
(INCLUDES CANDIDATE MEMBERS WHEN APPLICABLE)

Rank	Total	Rank	CP members/ population* (%)	Rank	CP members/ adult population** (%)
1. China	18,500,000†	13	2.6	n.a.	n.a.
2. USSR	12,947,926	7	5.8	6	9.5
3. Poland	1,894,895	6	6.0	5	10.0
4. East Germany	1,769,912	3	11.1	2	16.0
5. Romania	1,730,000	4	9.0	3	13.5
6. Czechoslovakia	1,689,207	2	11.9	1	18.3
7. North Korea	1,600,000††	1	12.9		n.a.
8. Yugoslavia	1,046,018	9	5.3	7	8.8
9. North Vietnam	760,000††	11	4.0	8	8.6
10. Bulgaria	613,393	5	7.2	4	11.1
11. Hungary	584,849	8	5.8	9	8.4
12. Albania	66,327	12	3.5	10	8.1
13. Cuba	60,000	14	.8	11	1.5
14. Mongolia	48,570††	10	4.3	n.a.	n.a.

    * 1966 estimates for population
  ** population distribution from last official census
   † estimate
  †† 1966 claim
  n.a.=not available

lous state in the world, with some 710 million people, is followed by the USSR, the third most populous state in the world, with about 223 million. The other party-states are much smaller.[50] (See Table 1–2.)

The *geographical area* of the party-states accounts for about 26% of the world's territory. The USSR is the largest state in the world (22.4 million square kilometers or almost 8.6 million square miles) and China the third largest (9.56 million square kilometers or 3.76 million square miles). Only one other state unit possesses more than 1 million square kilometers of territory, namely Mongolia (1.53 million square kilometers). All other party-states are small.[51] (See Table 1–2.) (However, when these area figures are translated into *cultivated land* area figures, that is, the proportion of arable land and land under permanent crops to the total area, they present an entirely different rank-ordering of the party-states. Moreover, the economies of the party-states still depend a great deal upon agriculture. In these terms, the Eastern European party-states, with the exception of Albania, rank highest among the party-states.[52] (See Table 1–2.)

The *density of population* of the party-states (with average value

77 per square kilometer, that is, 77 people live on 1 square kilometer) is relatively high (world average value is 25 per square kilometer). East Germany has a considerable lead (with 148 people living on 1 square kilometer) over other party-states; Czechoslovakia (with 107 per square kilometer) is second; and Hungary (with 109 per square kilometer) is third.[53] (See Table 1–2.)

This population is predominantly *rural*—only 23.18% of the communist party-states' population live in cities with 20,000 or more inhabitants (37.85% in Western Europe)[54]—and is still chiefly *engaged in agriculture.* Sixty-three per cent of the Chinese, 53% of the Yugoslavs, 59% of the Romanians, 33% of the Soviet citizens, 59% of the Bulgarians, and 58% of the Albanians are employed in agriculture.[55]

The party-states' *population growth* is somewhat slower (with an average 1.8% annual rate of increase) than the world population growth (average 1.9%). As may be expected, it is more rapid in the Far East and slower in Eastern Europe.[56]

The party-states' *population is relatively young* (especially in the Far East): Children between the ages of five and fourteen account for 21.6% of the total population (while there are only 14.6% children of the same age in Western Europe).[57] The party-states' *infant mortality rate* is still relatively high (particularly in the Far East), however. It almost doubles that of Western Europe.[58]

The *number of physicians and dentists* in proportion to the populations for which they care is quite high and well above the world average in the USSR and Eastern Europe.[59] Communist China has only 21.9 physicians for 100,000 population, and North Vietnam's ratio is 1.8 physicians or dentists for 100,000 people.[60]

In terms of *literacy* and *education* of population, Eastern Europe (again, with the exception of Yugoslavia and Albania) and the USSR stand high above the world average. East Germany and the USSR report only 2% of their population over fifteen years of age who are illiterate, Czechoslovakia and Hungary 3%, Poland 5%, Romania 11%, and Bulgaria 15%. (The Western European average, not including West Germany and great Britain, is 16.3%.)[61] The Far Eastern party-states, on the other hand, are well below the world standard in this respect.[62] This overall pattern will be subject to changes before long, however. The available figures giving percentage of *population enrolled in primary and secondary education* (but especially in primary schools) in the party-states suggest that radical steps are being taken to combat illiteracy in several of the units, especially in China, Yugoslavia, and Albania.[63] With reference to *higher education* (and excluding North Vietnam and Outer Mongolia, for which no data are available), the party-states' average (513.1 students per 100,000 population are enrolled in higher education) is above that of Western Europe (465.7).[64]

In terms of *mass media of communication,* the population of the party-states is relatively well taken care of. In fact, East Germany and Czechoslovakia have more radio receivers per thousand of population than has the average Western European country (256), namely 360 and 316, respectively. East Germany's daily newspaper circulation (400 per 1,000 population) is above, and Czechoslovakia's just below (280) the Western European average (282). The party-states' average[65] is 278 for the radio receivers (as compared with the Western European average of 256) and 184.3 for the newspaper circulation per thousand population (as compared with 282 for Western Europe). The Far Eastern party-states are well below this standard.[66]

In terms of *economic output,* the party-states are said to account for over a third of the world's industrial output. According to official communist data, the communist party-states produced in 1962 about 37% of the world's industrial goods. However, this figure is not supported by the available statistics concerning key commodities and their total party-state production.[67]

For the purpose of overall comparison, the available data are frequently unreliable or obsolete. The most commonly used index, per capita gross national product, cannot be reliably computed from communist account statistics. Therefore, we have elected to use *per capita net material product* (NMP), which is defined as the net value of all goods and "productive" services, including turnover taxes and excluding public administration, defense, personal and professional services, and similar activities which do not directly contribute to material production. The procedure for calculating net material product is essentially similar in all party-states for which data are provided. Thus, the resulting figures in Table 1–3 are comparable within this group, although comparability with most other national economies is lost.[68]

The 1966 *index of national income* illustrates the party-states' economic growth since 1950. The low index of East German economic growth is clearly a reflection of a relatively mature economy, while Bulgaria, on the other hand, despite its rather high growth index, still ranks low in per capita NMP.[69]

The 1965 *crude steel production* data are available for ten communist party-states. The USSR here leads with almost twice as much steel production as the rest of the party-states combined (91 million metric tons). Together, the ten party-states are responsible for about one-third of the world production of steel.[70] (See Table 1–3.) The party-states' *cement output* amounted to about 122 million metric tons in 1965, which was slightly less than a third of the world output.[71] *Petroleum production,* put at 273 million metric tons, amounted to about one-fifth of the world output.[72]

TABLE 1–2

POPULATION (est.) (in thousands)*		AREA				DENSITY OF POPULATION (persons/km²)	
		TOTAL (in million km²)		CULTIVATED (% of total area)			
RANK		RANK		RANK		RANK	
1. China	710,000	1. USSR	22.4	1. Hungary	60.7	1. E. Germany	148
2. USSR	233,180	2. China	9.76	2. Poland	50.6	2. N. Vietnam	123
3. Poland	31,698	3. Mongolia	1.53	3. E. Germany	46.3	3. Czechoslovakia	111
4. Yugoslavia	19,756	4. Poland	.31	4. Romania	43.6	4. Hungary	109
5. N. Vietnam	19,500	5. Yugoslavia	.26	5. Czechoslovakia	42.1	5. N. Korea	103
6. Romania	19,143	6. Romania	.24	6. Bulgaria	41.1	6. Poland	101
7. E. Germany	15,988	7. N. Vietnam	.159	7. Yugoslavia	31.9	7. Romania	81
8. Czechoslovakia	14,420	8. Czechoslovakia	.128	8. Albania	17.4	8. Yugoslavia	77
9. N. Korea	12,400	9. N. Korea	.122	9. Cuba	16.4	9. China	74
10. Hungary	10,179	10. Cuba	.120	10. N. Korea	15.5	10. Bulgaria	74
11. Bulgaria	8,528	11. Bulgaria	.111	11. N. Vietnam	12.7	11. Cuba	68
12. Cuba	7,833	12. E. Germany	.108	12. China	10.3	12. Albania	67
13. Albania	1,914	13. Hungary	.093	13. USSR	10.2	13. USSR	10
14. Mongolia	1,140	14. Albania	.029	14. Mongolia	2.3	14. Mongolia	1

* Estimates to mid-1966 based on annual rates of increase; UN *Demographic Yearbook, 1966*, pp. 120–131.

TABLE 1–3

Per Capita Net Material Product (1965)		Growth of National Income, 1966 Index 1961 = 100		Crude Steel Production (1965) (in thousand metric tons)	
RANK	$*	RANK	INDEX	RANK	TOTAL
1. East Germany	1238	1. Romania	406	1. USSR	91,021
2. Yugoslavia	935	2. Bulgaria	386	2. China	15,000
3. USSR	918**	3. USSR	361	3. Poland	9,088
4. Czechoslovakia	754	4. Albania	299	4. Czechoslovakia	8,598
5. Poland	705	5. East Germany	286	5. E. Germany	3,890
6. Hungary	697	6. Yugoslavia	281	6. Romania	3,426
7. Romania	n.a.	7. Poland	277	7. Hungary	2,520
8. Cuba	516**	8. Hungary	235	8. Yugoslavia	1,769
9. Bulgaria	391	9. Czechoslovakia	227	9. N. Korea	1,230
Albania		North Korea		10. Bulgaria	588
North Vietnam		North Vietnam			
North Korea		China			
China		Albania			
Mongolia		Mongolia			

* Conversion to dollars based on Commercial rate of exchange.
** Conversion to dollars based on Basic (fixed) rate of exchange.

TABLE 1–3 (continued)

Gross Energy Consumption (1965) (metric tons in coal equivalent)		
RANK		KG/CAPITA
1. USSR	832.80	3611
2. China	197.35†	
3. Poland	110.38	3504
4. E. Germany	92.97	5460
5. Czechoslovakia	80.37	5676
6. Romania	38.71	2035
7. Hungary	28.54	2812
8. Yugoslavia	23.26	1192
9. Bulgaria	21.08	2571
10. Cuba	7.25	950
11. Albania	.65	347
N. Korea		
N. Vietnam		
Mongolia		

Installed Capacity of Electrical Energy (1965) (in 1000 kilowatts)	
RANK	TOTAL
1. USSR	114,988
2. China	11,594†
3. E. Germany	10,350
4. Poland	9,672
5. Czechoslovakia	8,186
6. Yugoslavia	3,700
7. Romania	3,258
8. Bulgaria	2,155
9. Hungary	1,998
10. Cuba	976††
11. Albania	61†
N. Korea	
N. Vietnam	
Mongolia	

Wheat Yields‡ (in 100 kg/hectare)	
RANK	YIELD
1. E. Germany	34.8
2. Bulgaria	25.5
3. Czechoslovakia	24.2
4. Hungary	21.7
5. Yugoslavia	20.6
6. Poland	20.6
7. Romania	19.9
8. China	13.0†
9. USSR	8.5
10. Albania	8.0
Cuba	
N. Korea	
N. Vietnam	
Mongolia	

‡ 1965 yield, *FAO Production Yearbook, 1966* (Rome, 1967).
† 1961 figure
†† 1963 figure

Figures pertaining to *consumption of energy* are also available. They relate to the energy equivalents, measured in a common unit, of the consumption of coal and lignite, crude petroleum, natural gas, and hydro-electric power. The communist party-states account for less than one-third (29.48%) of the world energy consumption, while they produce more energy than they consume. The total *energy production* ratio of the party-states to world production is about 1.6 to 5.3 thousand million metric tons of coal equivalent, or 30% of the total world production.[73] (See Table 1–3.)

And, in terms of the 1965 *installed capacity of electric energy* (that is, normal end of year capacity of all generators available for simultaneous operation in both thermo- and hydroelectric plants), eleven of the party-states for which information is available constitute more than one-fifth of the total world production of electricity. Again, the USSR is responsible for almost two-thirds of the total party-states' production of electricity (114.9 million kilowatts annually), while China produces only 11.6 billion kilowatts.[74] (See Table 1–3.)

Thus, the USSR is the largest party-state, possessing about twice as much territory as all the other party-states combined. China has the greatest population, more than double that of the other party-states combined. The Soviet national economy is second largest in the world, after the United States. It is more than four times that estimated for China and almost two-thirds of the total NMP of all party-states.[75] In terms of natural resources, the USSR and China have an overwhelming lead over the other party-states.[76] In terms of military might, the USSR's absolute eminence among the party-states is well established.

Clearly, then, in reference to size or weight, the USSR and China are the giants among the party-states. Together they control over 91% of the total party-states' territory, contain 86% of the party-states' population, and produce over three-fourths of the total GNP. Their share of the party-states' weight approaches monopoly proportions. The other twelve party-states are pygmies in comparison.

Should one member or unit of a coalition of states contain more than 50% of the coalition weight or size, there would be virtually no probability of a rebellious winning coalition of the smaller units without outside assistance, according to William H. Riker in his study of political coalitions.[77] This describes the Stalinist period. With two large units containing an overwhelming proportion of the party-states' weight, however, the temptation for each to increase its payoff by attempting to form a winning coalition is very hard to resist. Their alliance becomes unstable. They are too large, relative to the alliance, to maintain a winning coalition.

When translated into relative or per capita figures, however, neither of the two giants lead the other party-states. In terms of advancement or

modernization, that is, industrialization, urbanization, literacy and en-
lightenment, communication system, affluence and wealth, well-being of
the population, and so forth, the USSR and China are surpassed on the per
capita basis by several small party-states, principally East Germany,
Czechoslovakia, and Poland (and, in several respects, also by Hungary,
Yugoslavia, Romania, Bulgaria, and Cuba). The considerable quantitative
asymmetry between the two principal and the twelve supporting actors
among the party-states is thus greatly aggravated by the qualitative asymmetry between the two large and several of the small party-states.

Since modernization and advancement is professedly a major communist party-state goal, the least advanced party-states might be expected
to stand to profit most from membership in the alliance. The backward
party-states should be enthusiastic members, while the advanced members
should be recalcitrant.[78] The empirical evidence, however, does not support this proposition.

To socialize the new communist party-states at the outset into the
Soviet international system, Stalin, in addition to the transformation of
their respective political organizations, insisted on the complete conversion of their respective economic and social structures as well. He forced
his new allies, as a function of their membership in the alliance, to adopt
indiscriminately the Soviet model. Combined with Soviet demand for heavy
economic dues from the members of the system for the sake of the USSR's
own economic development, this insistence brought about waves of deprivation and poverty in the party-states.

This heavy-handed initial scheme soon became untenable. It
brought about serious complications in Eastern Europe, resulted in the loss
of Yugoslavia, and would have meant the loss of China long before the
Sino-Soviet break. Khrushchev, and Brezhnev and Kosygin after him,
pressed for change far-reaching enough to mollify the party-states' elites
but compatible with the maintenance of the Soviet international system.
The plan as indicated in the later stages of COMECON development, was
to assign the more advanced party-states the prestigious roles of moderniz-
ers of the alliance assisting the more backward members in their economic
advancement. This was meant to give a stake in the alliance to both groups.

Unfortunately, the plan backfired on both counts. The more developed party-states, such as Czechoslovakia, tended to become economically
bankrupt because they were unable to reconcile the stagnating antagonism
between the superimposed centrally planned methods of managing the
economy for the sake of the alliance and the national demands of a complex modern industrialized society. The more backward members of the
communist system, on the other hand, have played hardly any positive role
in the goal of economic system-advancement.

The advanced party-states did not value the backward party-states' condition, and the backward party-states, in turn, valued negatively the advanced party-states. The differences in advancement are so great that "fraternal mutual assistance" could hardly overcome them in the intermediate run. It would impoverish the USSR and Eastern Europe to contribute rapidly and significantly to China's advancement, and China tells the other party-states, rather huffily, that "each socialist country must rely mainly on itself for its own construction."[79]

China, the other major party-state and would-be organizer, is also one of the least advanced members of the alliance. It thus provides a rallying point for the other less advanced members, who, like China, stress system goals *other* than economic development, namely, ideological purity and world revolution.

If we consider additional contributing and analytical factors such as degree of social stability, ethnic differences, degree of internationalization, historical experiences, mode of joining the subsystem, and degree of independence of the communist parties, we obtain multiple stratified and hierarchical rank-orderings of alliance members. The two leading members, the USSR and China, because of their wide differences in achievement and economic progress, prescribe essentially different goal values for the alliance and for the communist system; alliance between the two leading members, too large relative to the coalition, thus becomes unstable. The alliance is in danger of splitting into two separate sub-alliances.[80]

Aside from the Sino-Soviet conflict, but principally as a consequence of the above-mentioned factors, some party-states appear to be more isolated from and less cohesive with the rest of the party-states. Some have stable and others unstable, or even no, alignments with other members. Many disputes and conflicts arise, chiefly over boundaries and minorities, as well as many pre-system suspicions and national jealousies. The European-Asian boundary (the USSR appears to consider itself principally a European, rather than Asian or Eurasian, power)[81] is politically, socially, economically, and ideologically more significant than the respective boundaries among member units (Mongolia in Asia and Albania in Europe being symmetrical exceptions), although the latter boundaries are better guarded against fraternal neighbors than are any boundaries in the West.

The three alliance *organizations*—the Joint Institute of Nuclear Research, the International Broadcasting Organization, and the Organization for the Collaboration of Railways—are useful agencies with little or no political overtones, as are the multilateral functional and *ad hoc* conferences on health, fishing industries, plant protection, and so on. Both the ambitious Council of Mutual Economic Assistance and the military Warsaw Treaty Organization are European organizations (Outer Mongolia in COMECON is a recent exception), while the membership of the Danube Commission, countering the flow of the river, is spilling over from Eastern into Western Europe and includes not only Yugoslavia, but Austria and, tentatively, West Germany as well.

In terms of *internationalization,* that is, the volume and dimension of transactions of the party-states with the outside world, the party-states also differ a great deal. A simple index of internationalization—based on subindexes of (A) participation in the United Nations, (B) participation in other international organizations, (C) per capita imports of foreign goods, and (D) "communications" (the number of foreign tourists and the number of local citizens traveling abroad; the flow of nongovernmental mail in and out of the country; and the percentage of translated books to native language books)[82] where 1.00 is the "average" amount of internationalization[83] and the index is the average of A, B, C, and D—produces the heterogeneous results shown in Table 1–4. (In several cases, information for C and D was not available.)

TABLE 1–4. INDEX OF INTERNATIONALIZATION

	A. UN	B. Int. Orgs.	C. Imports	D. Communications
1. Czechosl.	1.75	1.51	1.63	1.74	2.14
2. Yugosl.	1.45	1.70	1.90	.57	1.63
3. USSR	1.25	3.01	1.42	.31	.26
4. Poland	1.18	1.47	1.83	.67	.77
5. Cuba	1.13	1.24	1.08	1.63	.57
6. Bulgaria	1.07	.83	1.42	1.00	1.06
7. Hungary	1.06	.70	1.63	1.21	.70
8. Romania	.85	.67	1.70	.51	.53
9. E. Germany	.62	.02	.27	1.37	.82
10. Albania	.56	.58	.51	.58	—
11. Mongolia	.54	.15	.13	(1.35)	—
12. N. Vietnam	.09	0	.17	—	—
13. N. Korea	.08	.05	.10	—	—
14. China	.07	0	.13	—	—

NOTE: The A and B figures denote principally governmental activities while the C and D figures refer principally to nongovernmental activities.

Finally, multilateral meetings and communications of communist parties, ruling as well as nonruling, separately or jointly, have been increasingly unsuccessful and therefore fewer. In this matter the communist parties cannot be viewed as possessing either legislative or executive authority, essentially because of the preference—perceived as system necessity—for unanimity and solidarity. A unanimous vote, given the pronounced heterogeneity of the communist parties' national environments as well as their growing propensity for conflict, has produced only watered-down joint proclamations, declarations, and statements of principles. The judicial or arbitration function of the communist parties has never been taken seriously either.

What the communist parties share are, at most, *hybrid and plurilateral coalitions* which fluctuate from issue to issue (Yugoslavia, the 1956 Polish problem, Cuba, the inevitability of war with imperialism) in which the respective exercise of influence by the two major communist party-states, the USSR and China, demands or permits realignment and side-taking by other members. Even the *World Marxist Review: Problems of Peace and Socialism,* a monthly magazine printed in 19 languages (and differing in content from one geographical target area to another), is essentially a Soviet and a European "cultural" tool of communication cohesion (the Chinese withdrew in the spring of 1963).

Stratification, segmentation, and diversity are thus prevalent among the communist party-states on both party and state levels. There is no single state rule-making or policy-articulating organ, although there are contenders for the role. Rule implementation, segmented and compartmentalized in the several party-states' organizations, such as the Council for Mutual Economic Assistance, is carried out principally on state rather than party levels. While there are several state arbitration boards to resolve or contain anticipated functional or economic conflicts, there is no machinery to deal with party or political conflicts. The party-states, the principal and key units of the communist system, possess no institutionalized leadership formula except on *ad hoc,* weight, or size basis. Even a simple conflict-containing mechanism which would routinely deal with outstanding dissension among the party-states is entirely missing. As a consequence, there is no legitimate automatic coercive agency to enforce decisions of party-states either within the alliance or within the system as a whole.

The party-states (as well as the system as a whole) depend for their common endeavor on *agreement and persuasion,* which oscillates from various degrees of assertion to tentative consultative or advisory assistance, depending on the particular actors involved. Increasingly, the two major alliance organizers deny the other members the right to participate and share in community endeavors and benefits, rather than forcing obligations on them as Stalin did.

The principal *unifiers and solidifiers* of the party-states' alliance, on the other hand, are said to be: (1) The *communist parties* ruling the 14 states, creating thereby 14 similar or "socialist" political, economic, social, and legal systems. On the basis of this essential element of similarity, the CPSU includes Yugoslavia, which possesses the other three elements of unity as well, within the system. The Chinese Communist Party—arguing on the basis of solidifier No. (2) that Yugoslavia is not a socialist state— disagrees. (2) The acceptance by the 14 communist party elites of the *"Marxist-Leninist" belief system* as a common source of present and future political, economic, and social means-and-goals orientation. The revisionist-dogmatist disagreement thus adversely affects a principal unifier of the party-states. (3) *The Soviet military might,* especially its thermonuclear weapons and delivery systems, almost symmetrical in weight to the military capability of the principal and most powerful party-states' opponent, the United States, but overwhelmingly asymmetrical in weight within the coalition. In terms of military weight, the USSR is *absolutely* the alliance-dominant party-state. (4) The *geographical contiguity* of the member-units, an ecological prerequisite for recruitment and original membership, and an element which makes the initial Soviet-Chinese sponsorship of Cuban membership in the alliance questionable, while helping to explain both the successful Albanian resistance to de-Stalinization after the Yugoslav defection and the hesitant Soviet recognition of the Ho Chi Minh regime in North Vietnam before contiguity with China was established in 1950.

The last-named is perhaps the weakest of the four elements of cohesion. On balance, it facilitates logistic extension of assertive control better than it fosters consensual entry. Over time, given the conditions prevailing among the party-states and the shrinking of the international system, geographical contiguity may prove to be an element of secondary importance.

With the absence of an organization of the parties, and only partial, functional, and segmented organizations of the states, the chief propensity of the party-states is now toward greater independence, function, utility, and complexity—a disposition leading further away from the initial achievement-oriented paternal hierarchy. The assertion of greater independence by some members has been successfully tested—by Yugoslavia, China, Albania, and Romania. The integrating coercive forces of the USSR which initiated and perpetuated "the Soviet bloc" have much less to do with the present (but, again, Soviet-sponsored) utilitarian phase of communist community building in Eastern Europe. Still, the essential conflict-orientation of the members, coupled with the absolute lack of automatic conflict-containment machinery, does not make coercion as yet entirely obsolete. Czechoslovakia is the case in point.

However, the issue is no longer one of simple possession of means of coercion—superior weapons and delivery systems—but how to utilize the possession most effectively in order to reach the desirable goals *without* applying the means. This, in the last analysis, is the moot problem.

The Chinese challenge, which opened up new alternatives for the communist party-states—a challenge which the Soviet Union has not been able to subdue—raised the cost of coalition-maintenance for the Soviet Union. The coalition members are in a stronger position vis-à-vis the USSR because the implied possibility of their defection to China, the frustrated candidate organizer. Given the present stalemate between the two powers, the more the coalition members ask, the more they get. Their bargaining position is increasing in direct proportion with the increasing bipolarity in the coalition. This new doorway is bound to become irresistible even to the smaller, more docile communist party-states, once they discover the key. Sustained, however, this process has tended to escalate the cost of coalition maintenance for the organizer, the USSR, because the price, the autonomy of members, may become so inflated that the USSR will not be able to afford it unless goals are altered, as in the case of Soviet intervention in Czechoslovakia. Coalition containment is then bound to mean not only containment of anarchy in the coalition, but also the progressive alienation of all parties, ruling and nonruling, in the communist system. The progressive erosion of the communist party-state alliance is bound to spread to the nonruling communist parties and affect adversely their system participation and maintenance.

THE NONRULING COMMUNIST PARTIES' STRATEGIES

The 14 communist party-states have party and state relations with virtually every corner of the globe. The ruling parties relate to nonruling parties and the governments of the party-states relate to governments of non-party states. State relations are easier to define than are party relations, although even here there is ambiguity.

The nonruling communist parties are aspirationally perceived by the communist party-states as *potential ruling parties* within their state units. They are viewed—and rewarded—as outposts, as well as supporters, of the "socialist community." At the same time, they constitute tangible evidence of the present "world" extension of the communist system. The sustained interaction between the party-states and the parties is thus mutually supportive.

The nonruling communist parties' rapport with the ruling parties mirrors the ruling parties' principal problems, stresses, expectations, setbacks, and advances. But local culture and social change requirements, totally different from those of the party-states' microcosms, impose upon local parties demands for varied, imaginative, and seldom pretested operational codes. This flexibility creates misunderstandings with the party-states, misunderstandings which are often compounded by the party-states' overt and sometimes generous material support of the very governments hostile to their local communist parties.

The *nonruling parties* vary in size, local effectiveness, degree to which they are tolerated by their governments, discipline vis-à-vis the ruling parties, "inner democracy," and so forth. Aspirationally, they play the roles of Czechoslovak, Yugoslav, Polish, or Chinese communist parties before the entry of those states into the party-states' subsystem. In fact, they act and have acted as the legitimate native representatives of the party-states. Historically, because they depended for recognition, legitimacy, and support upon the party-states, their interdependence with the party-states was lopsided. Without the existence of the party-states, they would have been simply local parties, equal in status to other parties within their respective states. This lopsidedness has been decreasing in direct proportion to the conflict orientation of the party-states, however. With the party-states' coalition becoming progressively more unstable, the nonruling parties' value as system allies to the ruling parties, and especially to the two coalition organizers, the USSR and China, has been on the upswing.

As the national orientation of the nonruling communist parties tends to increase with their decreasing system orientation, they become subject to growing interaction with their operational environment. This interaction in turn tends to make an impressive and sustained impact on their operational codes and goals. They become subject to the same persistent national pressures which brought about the disunity among the ruling parties in the first place. As a consequence, the less the nonruling parties are willing to sponsor locally the interests of the ruling parties and the more they deviate from their system functions and from their system goals, the more influential they tend to become locally. In fact, this deviation can lead to success: the greater the means-and-ends coincidence between the national environment and the respective nonruling party, the stronger the party. In those countries where the hostility between the party and the national environment persisted—as in Ireland, Canada, or the United States—the nonruling parties declined. They have gained or held their own in those countries—such as France or Italy—where they gave up for all practical purposes their means and goals.

Significant differences must be noted, however; in *developing nations,* the nonruling communist parties tend to be *revolutionary*. Here they follow the traditional Leninist concept of dynamic revolutionary forces in societies which are not yet integrated and often not politicized.

The nonruling parties perform, in addition to their system objectives, the function of socializers toward modernity. They feed the aspirations and ambitions of those frustrated by the inability of the developing society to use their skills. The resulting high want/get ratio brings into the communist party all those wishing to rapidly mobilize and transform their society into modernity.

In *developed nations,* where there is no legitimate function for a revolutionary, deviant system party, the communist parties either persist and go underground, or they give in, conform, and become *electoral parties.* The former alternative tends to mean failure and the latter, success. The electoral parties compete for votes with other national parties, and the competition forces them to reduce greatly their differences from other parties, both structural and functional. They therefore tend to be pragmatic, nonheretic and nonideological, and their ties and interaction with the communist system tend to slacken. The Italian and French communist parties are good examples of this type of nonruling party.

As for *in-between nations,* where segments of the population have not been incorporated and integrated into their social and political systems, the nonruling parties tend to become parties of protest. By defending and articulating the negative interests and dissatisfactions of isolated and alienated sections of society, they tend to integrate more into social than political parties. In postwar France, when the French Communist Party left the protest field and entered the government as an electoral party, the Party members and leaders found the transition difficult. "Denunciation and demagogy were easier and more enjoyable than responsibility."[84] Just as revolutionary communist parties, the parties of protest tend to function principally as *communist system parties,* with all that this function implies.

In addition, the nonruling communist parties are *political parties* because they seek, in competition with other local parties, to control their respective governments. They thus differ from the ruling communist parties which are by definition without competition for rule and hence are not in this sense parties at all. This difference has important consequences in terms of social composition of the nonruling parties, their structures and strategies, and their relations with other communist parties.

The Soviet press spoke of 75 parties (ruling and nonruling) in 1958,[85] 87 in 1960,[86] and 88 in 1962.[87] One could list as many as 94 parties, but several of these receive little acknowledgement from the party-states.

What constitutes a communist party? Some parties identify themselves as communist, whereas others, such as the Irish Workers' League, are communist although their names do not indicate it. Still others, such as the Mexican Workers' and Farmers' Party, have strong communist leanings, although they exist independently of, and sometimes compete with, the local communist party. Some countries have both a communist party-states'-oriented party and a "national" communist party; some countries have these plus a Trotskyite party. Where communism is illegal, numerous left-wing parties may preach Marxist slogans but maintain few connections with the communist party-states.

We count here only those parties which perceive themselves to be a part of the system and are so perceived by the party-states. This automatically excludes all Trotskyite and "national" communist parties, as well as those left-wing parties which do not acknowledge the party-states' leadership. Furthermore, we count only one party per country, selecting that party most closely identified with the communist system.[88]

These criteria yield 90 communist parties. Omitting the 14 ruling parties, Table 1–5 lists the 76 nonruling communist parties of the world, identified by country rather than by official name, as of 1967.[89]

The list of countries is perhaps most interesting in its omissions. Communist parties do not exist in several states of the Middle East (for example, Saudi Arabia, Libya). None of the three Guianas has an organized communist party, although the French overseas departments of Guadeloupe, Martinique, and Réunion all do. There are almost no communist parties in Africa south of the Sahara. Marxist influence certainly exists in African states and their ruling noncommunist parties, but there are only two African communist parties of any standing, those of Sudan and Nigeria. A Malagasy communist party claims fifteen hundred members but probably has less than one hundred.[90] Communist parties were founded in Basutoland and Zanzibar; needless to say, little is known of these parties except that they are small. The Zanzibar (Tanzania) party has probably flourished since the coup in January 1964, but membership statistics for it are not available. The Soviet press has alleged that there are more than forty thousand communists in "Equatorial Africa,"[91] but this claim seems greatly exaggerated.

International meetings of communist parties give one indication of how many countries have communist parties accredited by party-states. Eighty-one parties met in Moscow in November 1960; the Soviet press named 78 of them, and the remaining three were probably those of the USA, Iceland, and Pakistan. Delegations from 79 foreign communist parties were acknowledged at the Twenty-Second CPSU Congress in 1961. Absent or unacknowledged at both meetings were the parties of the Philippines, Cambodia, Laos, South Vietnam, and Egypt, as well as the four marginal African parties of Malagasy, Nigeria, Basutoland, and Zanzibar.

In terms of *membership,* as may be expected, there are many more small parties than large ones. Because many of the small parties are ille-

TABLE 1-5. NONRULING COMMUNIST PARTY MEMBERSHIP

Country	Estimated Membership (1967)	% of Adult Population	Legal Status (1967)	Trend (1953-1967)
1. Italy	1,531,000	4.33	legal	even
2. France	275,000	.84	legal	down
3. Japan	250,000	.39	legal	up
4. South Vietnam	245,000*	n.a.	illegal	up
5. Indonesia	150,000	.31	illegal	down
6. India	125,000	.06	legal	even
7. Argentina	60,000	.44	illegal	up
8. Finland	49,000	1.70	legal	even
9. Great Britain	32,562	.10	legal	even
10. Chile	32,500	.87	legal	even
11. Sweden	29,000	.45	legal	even
12. Austria	27,500	.54	legal	down
13. Greece	27,000	.48	illegal	up
14. Brazil	21,000	.06	illegal	down
15. Uruguay	21,000	1.34	legal	up
16. Cyprus	13,000	4.12	legal	up
17. Belgium	12,500	.19	legal	down
18. Netherlands	11,500	.15	legal	down
19. Colombia	9,000	.12	legal	down
20. Nepal	8,000	n.a.	illegal	up
21. Sudan	7,500	.15	illegal	up
22. West Germany	7,000	.02	illegal	down
23. Denmark	6,000	.19	legal	down
24. Bolivia	6,000	n.a.	illegal	up
25. Lebanon	6,000	n.a.	illegal	even
26. Mexico	5,250	.03	legal	down
27. Paraguay	5,000	.62	illegal	up
28. Peru	5,000	.11	illegal	down
29. Spain	5,000	.02	illegal	even
30. Venezuela	5,000	.12	illegal	down
31. Burma	5,000	.04	illegal	down
32. Australia	5,000	.07	legal	down
33. Switzerland	4,000	.10	legal	even
34. Syria	3,000	.14	illegal	down
35. USA	3,000	.002	semilegal	down
36. Canada	2,500	.02	legal	down
37. Norway	2,500	.17	legal	down

* Includes all communist political and military personnel, except regular North Vietnamese troops.

TABLE 1–5.   NONRULING COMMUNIST PARTY MEMBERSHIP (continued)

Country	Estimated Membership (1967)	% of Adult Population	Legal Status (1967)	Trend (1953–1967)
38. Portugal	2,000	.03	illegal	down
39. Malaysia	2,000	.005	illegal	down
40. Iraq	2,000	.07	illegal	down
41. Ceylon	1,900	.036	legal	down
42. Philippines	1,750	.012	illegal	even
43. Israel	1,600	.11	legal	down
44. Ecuador	1,500	.07	illegal	down
45. Pakistan	1,450	.003	illegal	down
46. Thailand	1,450	.011	illegal	up
47. Dominican Rep.	1,300	.098	illegal	even
48. Turkey	1,250	.006	illegal	even
49. Iceland	1,000	.90	legal	even
50. Iran	1,000	.008	illegal	down
51. Nigeria	1,000	n.a.	illegal	up
52. Guadeloupe	1,000	.68	legal	even
53. Algeria	1,000	.02	illegal	down
54. Guatemala	750	.04	illegal	down
55. Martinique	700	.46	legal	even
56. Honduras	650	.07	illegal	down
57. Costa Rica	550	.096	illegal	even
58. Morocco	500	.008	illegal	even
59. Luxembourg	500	.21	legal	even
60. New Zealand	400	.025	legal	even
61. Jordan	400	.05	illegal	down
62. Panama	250	.04	illegal	even
63. Nicaragua	200	.03	illegal	even
64. El Salvador	200	.02	illegal	down
65. Singapore	200	.03	illegal	down
66. Afghanistan	175	n.a.	illegal	even
67. Ireland	125	.007	legal	even
68. Cambodia	100	.004	legal	down
69. Malagasy Rep.	100	n.a.	legal	down
70. Tunisia	100	.005	illegal	down
71. Mauritius	50	.014	legal	n.a.
72. Laos			legal	n.a.
73. Réunion			legal	n.a.
74. South Africa			illegal	n.a.
75. Haiti			illegal	n.a.
76. Tanzania			legal	n.a.

gal, while many of the large ones are legal, it appears that governmental supervision at least partly causes the skew. But a distribution of legal parties still centers only on the lower ranges, as Table 1–6 indicates.

The two classifications have seven entries each. These would have to be extended to nearly a thousand entries to include all communist parties. If we distribute the parties not by membership but by logarithm of membership, we get something approaching a normal distribution.

Another way of viewing membership distribution is to calculate the ratio of *Communist Party membership to population*. Some small countries, as, for example, Cyprus, have relatively small parties, yet these parties constitute a significant percentage of the population and wield more influence than their size would suggest. Conversely, a large party such as that of Japan comprises only a tiny percentage of the population, and its influence is therefore less than its size indicates.

The ratio of *CP membership to adult population* is even more relevant. Children do not normally join communist parties, so this ratio more accurately reflects the party membership appeal. Furthermore, underdeveloped countries have many more children in the total population. The ratio of adults to total population varies from a low of 43% in Sudan to a high of 75% in Luxembourg.

As Table 1–7 indicates, the distribution of parties according to this ratio is skewed, just as were the previous distributions.

We thus have two measures of a party's strength: membership in absolute terms and membership as a percentage of adult population. It is difficult to balance these two measures in assessing a party's overall influence. Probably, the first figure measures the party's weight in the system as a whole, the second figure its weight in its own country. There is no obvious way of combining the two figures to produce a single meaningful index with which to rank the parties.

The fourth column in Table 1–5 indicates the *legal status* of the communist parties in 1967. Of the 76 parties, only 34 were consistently permitted to operate legally in this period. Forty-two have been outlawed.

Where communist parties are legal, *election results* give the probably best single measure of a communist party's influence in the country. For, despite the size of the party, its composition, organization, or propaganda line, all of which are inputs into the electoral process, the most telling statistic is the single output: How many people, given the choice, select the communist party delegates as their representatives?

Free elections do not prevail in some of the countries in question, but, for 41 of the 76 parties, we have at least some measure of the CP's electoral success. In most cases this is a percentage of seats held in the national legislature. The distribution of these percentages is wide and

TABLE 1-6. NRCPs: MEMBERSHIP DISTRIBUTION

For all communist parties (61 out of 76 CP's, or 80%, have fewer than 14,000 members):

CP Membership:	0–2000	2–4000	4–6000	6–8000	8–10000	10–12000	12–14000
No. of CP's in each range	39	5	10	3	1	1	2

For legal communist parties only (9 of 34 legal CP's had more than 14,000 members in 1967):

| No. of legal CP's in each range | 15 | 3 | 3 | 0 | 1 | 1 | 2 |

TABLE 1–7. NRCPs: RATIO OF MEMBERSHIP TO ADULT POPULATION

For all communist parties, legal and illegal (except where adult population figures were unavailable):

CP Membership as % of Adult Population:	0–.1	.1–.2	.2–.3	.3–.4	.4–.5	.5–.6	.6–.7
	36	11	1	2	3	1	2

No. of CP's in each range	.7–.8	.8–.9	.9–1	1.34	1.70	4.12	4.33
	0	2	1	1	1	1	1

erratic, with no apparent pattern except, again, a general preponderance of parties in the lower ranges.

The most successful parties are (in popular vote): Guadeloupe (37.7%), Italy (25.3%), France (22.4%), Finland (22%), Iceland (16.7%), and Martinique (16.2%). The least successful parties are those of Canada (0.4%), Ireland (0.02%), and, at the very bottom, the USA (where the CP's Earl Browder won only 0.01% of the vote in 1940, the last presidential election in which the communists participated). It must be remembered, however, that variation in electoral systems complicates these comparisons. Comparisons are most meaningful in elections for a single national candidate, usually a presidential candidate, or in a legislative election with a system of proportional representation. Where single-member districts prevail, the communists may only put up candidates in a fraction of the districts and the total vote for communist candidates thus underestimates the appeal of the communist party in the country as a whole.

Eighteen of the 76 parties hold seats in their national legislatures, and five of these hold them through a front organization, rather than in their own name. In only five countries do the local communist parties hold more than 10% of the seats: Italy (27.5%), Finland (20.5%), Iceland (16.7%), France (15%), and Chile (12.5%). Thus, in only five countries has the communist party achieved significant influence in the government through direct popular election. In most democratic countries, the communists have had little success at the polls.

It is interesting to compare a communist party's membership with the number of votes it receives. In the USA, for instance, Browder received 48,579 votes in the 1940 presidential election, but this was approximately the membership of the party. Apparently no one but party members voted for Browder. But in most other relevant countries there exists a broad periphery of voters who do not belong to the party. The Israeli CP gets votes about 20 times in excess of its membership. In Nepal, the communist party got 40 times more votes than it had members. The ratio has risen to 95 in India and 165 in the Malagasy Republic (although the latter was a vote for a front organization, not for the CP).

In some countries, notably the democratic ones, this "local support factor" remains fairly stable. In Denmark, for instance, where party membership has declined from 16,000 in 1953 to 6,000 in 1967, the number of votes for the CP has declined proportionately, so that the ratio has remained about 6:1. But in most countries, this factor jumps about erratically, as governmental suppression causes large changes in party membership or local issues inflate or depress the CP's electoral popularity.

The final column of Table 1–5 is somewhat arbitrary, an estimate of each party's *trend over the fourteen-year period 1953–1967*. It is based both on membership changes and on electoral results. In some cases, the indications are ambiguous. In Uruguay, for example, communist party membership has fallen by a factor of three, but electoral success has doubled. In India, the fortunes of the party rose during the first half of the period and have been falling since. All such dubious cases are labelled "even." These criteria indicate that of the 76 parties, 35 have been falling, 29 have remained even, and only 12 have risen during the twelve years. Of these twelve, two are small, three are medium-sized, and seven are large (over 10,000 members). To these latter seven parties could perhaps be added large parties whose fortunes over the fourteen-year period remained about even, but which enjoyed some electoral gains, namely Italy and Chile. This gives a list of parties both large and rising which might be described as "statistically impressive" during this period. They were as shown in Table 1–8.

But these parties are exceptions. Ninety per cent of all nonruling communist parties have been either declining or holding about even. In particular, all European parties except Cyprus are in this category. The American communist party seems to have been declining faster than any other party in the world.

TABLE 1–8. MEMBERSHIP OF SUCCESSFUL NRCPs

1. Italy	1,531,000
2. Japan	250,000
3. South Vietnam	245,000
4. Argentina	60,000
5. Chile	32,500
6. Greece	27,000
7. Uruguay	21,000

Almost all communist parties reached peaks of membership and popularity during World War II, but the trend since the early 1950's has been toward smaller parties. This can be seen from Table 1–9.

A decline in size alone, however, does not necessarily indicate failure of the party. The Cuban communist party had 30,000 members in 1953, but only 12,000 in 1957; it rose again after the revolution to 27,000 in 1960 and numbered 60,000 by 1967. Similarly, the Laotian CP had 3,500–3,800 members in 1957, but had cut back to 100 members by 1960; its membership has remained at this extremely low level since then, but its paramilitary arm, the Pathet Lao, has expanded from 1,800 in 1960 to 20,000 in 1967.[92]

In 1953, there were 74 nonruling communist parties with about 3 million members; in 1967, there were 76 with about 2 million members (including splinter groups). In 1953, those communist parties commanded some 20 million votes; in 1965, about 27 million. Thus, while CP voters have grown by about 35% over the 12 years, the CP members declined by about one-fifth, and the ratio between them has doubled, from slightly more than six voters per party member to more than 12 voters per party member. World population has grown by 20% over the same period and this accounts for part, if not all, of the electoral gain.

Nearly half the nonruling party members used to be Indonesians. Indeed, until 1965, the entire growth in communist party membership could be credited to the phenomenal expansion of the Indonesian party. But the great majority of the new PKI members were simple peasants who joined because they were promised land. When the party staged an uprising in October 1965, they simply ignored the party's call to rise and the communist coup collapsed. During the eight months of anticommunist terror which followed, some 400,000 communists (including the party leader Aidit) were reported slaughtered; the PKI was apparently virtually wiped out. This drastic development in Indonesia negatively affected the

TABLE 1–9. NUMBER OF NRCPs, 1953–1967

	1953	1963	1967
SMALL PARTIES (0–2,000)	20	36	36
MEDIUM-SIZED PARTIES (2–20,000)	34	27	25
LARGE PARTIES (more than 20,000)	20	15	15
Total	74	78	76

membership figure of the nonruling communist parties: While during the 1953–1967 period the nonruling communist parties minus Indonesia lost membership, the loss now is absolute, in membership as well as in legislative seats.

The trends in communist party membership have fluctuated greatly from one area of the world to another. Summarized, the 1953–1967 trends are shown in Table 1–10.[93]

Beyond Asia, CP membership is on the rise only in Africa, but the meaning of this increase is minimal. And so, in spite of the more than 20% world population growth in the last 14 years, the nonruling communist party membership actually declined somewhat from 3,146,600 to 3,041,-462.

In summary, it may be said that those nonruling communist parties which essentially abdicated their communist system aspirations and functions and became responsible national electoral parties have either slightly gained in membership or held even. But, then, they have tended to be communist parties in name only. Their differences from other national parties have been reduced, by their responsible participation in the national political process, almost to zero. Those nonruling communist parties which have functioned as *protest* or even *revolutionary* parties, on the other hand, have been subject to strong adversities both at home and within the system. The home governments often take hostile attitudes towards them, especially in one-party states, and outlaw them; or they turn into amorphous movements and become victims of the "objective conditions" of the social environment which they were supposed, but failed, to change, as in Ceylon or southern Italy; or new local parties have emerged,

TABLE 1–10.   NRCPs: MEMBERSHIP TRENDS, 1953–1967,
BY AREAS OF THE WORLD

Area	CP Membership, 1953	CP Membership, 1967	Change
Europe	2,582,000	2,023,187	− 22%
Asia	178,000	791,850	+345%
Latin America	247,000	176,900*	− 28%
Middle East	80,000	30,025	− 63%
USA and Canada	50,000	5,500	− 89%
Australia and New Zealand	6,500	5,400	− 16%
Africa (sub-Sahara)	3,100	8,600	+177%

* Does not include Cuba.

left of the communist parties, more modern, responsive, and suitable to the particular unhappy social conditions that prevail, as in some Latin American countries. Within the communist system, the rapidly growing conflict orientation of the ruling communist parties has produced strains and pressures which further weaken the nonruling communist parties, especially the protest and revolutionary types. Deprivation, isolation, and the need to make a choice between the organizers, the USSR and China, have not proved conducive to the maintenance, let alone growth, of the nonruling parties.

CONCLUSION

The world communist movement has been analyzed here as an international system of communist parties. The system approach appeared convenient not only because it afforded a general examination of the movement's means and goals, organization, association theory, alliance system, and strategies, but also because it has served as a basis for subsequent particular studies which center principally on the comparison of and interaction among the communist party-states. Poorly equipped to cope with complexities of the modern world, the communist system has been described, in this study as well as in the subsequent research, as being in a sustained and fairly rapid decline. Drastic alterations of the system priorities, goals, organization, and strategy seem inevitable.

To implement and to add to these findings, further data is needed, and a more extensive, systematic, "second round" research called for. We need to know more about the structures of nonruling communist parties and their changing interaction with their social and political environments, with other parties, and with other systems. We need to know more about the parties' changing ideological orientation and the degree of system cohesion this orientation provides. But most of all, we need an adequate causal explanation of the respective communist parties' emergence and strength: Why have the nonruling parties been vigorous in some national states and not in others?

Bearing these questions in mind, the Studies of the Communist System prepared a comparative paradigm of the nonruling communist parties, the major focus of which is on the *varieties* of communist parties in the world and on the *causes* and the *consequences* of the variations. At the present time, six studies based on the paradigm are being written—on the communist parties of Brazil, Italy, Japan, Argentina, Cyprus, and Austria. The Studies plans to follow with investigations of the communist parties of India, France, Chile, and Laos. Over the next five years, the Studies hopes to provide comparative monographs on as many of the almost eighty communist parties as is reasonably possible, aiming toward a gradual, overall, comparative analysis of all the units of the communist system.

NOTES

*This study is based in part on Jan F. Triska with David Beim and Noralou P. Roos, *The World Communist System,* Research Paper No. 1 (Stanford, Calif.: Stanford Studies of the Communist System, 1963). It is here reprinted, with minor changes, from Jan F. Triska and David D. Finley, *Soviet Foreign Policy* (New York: Macmillan, 1968), pp. 149–202. By permission.

1. See, for example, E. E. Hagen, "Analytical Models in the Study of Social Systems," *American Journal of Sociology,* LXVII (1961), 144–151; Talcott Parsons, *The Social System* (Glencoe, Ill.: Free Press, 1951); Marion J. Levy, Jr., *The Structure of Society* (Princeton, N.J.: Princeton University Press, 1952); Robert K. Merton, *Social Theory and Social Structure* (rev. ed.; Glencoe, Ill.: Free Press, 1954).

2. See Gabriel A. Almond and G. Bingham Powell, Jr., *Comparative Politics: A Developmental Approach* (Boston and Toronto: Little, Brown, 1966); Gabriel A. Almond and James S. Coleman, eds., *The Politics of the Developing Areas* (Princeton, N. J.: Princeton University Press, 1960); see also David Easton, *A Systems Analysis of Political Life* (New York: John Wiley, 1965); Robert A. Dahl, *Modern Political Analysis* (Englewood Cliffs, N. J.: Prentice-Hall, 1963).

3. Morton A. Kaplan, *System and Process in International Relations* (New York: John Wiley, 1957).

4. George Modelski, *The Communist International System* in *International Encyclopedia of the Social Sciences,* III, 126–132. See also his *The Communist International System* (Princeton, N.J.: Center of International Studies, Research Monograph No. 9, 1960).

5. David Easton, *A Systems Analysis of Political Life* (New York: John Wiley, 1965), p. 7.

6. "When a Marxist speaks of proletarian internationalism, the first thing that comes to his mind is the militant revolutionary appeal advanced by Marx and Engels: 'Workers of the world, unite,'" A. K. Azizian, *"Proletarskii internatsionalizm, Znanie,"* Moscow, 1957, p. 98. See also Evgenii L. Korovin, "Proletarskii internatsionalizm i mezhdunarodnoe pravo," *Sovietskii ezhegodnik mezhdunarodnogo prava,* Moscow, 1958, p. 51.

7. Lenin, *Sochineniia,* XXXI, 126, cited by T. Timofeyev, "Certain Aspects of Proletarian Internationalism," *International Affairs,* Moscow, V, May 1957, 46.

8. *Ibid.,* XXVI, 410. Italics added.

9. Stalin, *Collected Works* (Moscow) X, 51.

10. Potelov, "Razvitie sotsializma i proletarskii internatsionalizm," *Kommunist,* No. 1, Moscow, January 1957, p. 18.

11. N. P. Vassil'iev and F. R. Khrustov, *O Sovetskom patriotizme*, Gos. Pol. Literatury, Moscow, 1952, p. 142 cited by Wladyslaw W. Kulski, *Peaceful Coexistence* (Chicago: Henry Regnery Co., 1959), pp. 34–35.

12. G. I. Tunkin, "Socialist Internationalism and International Law," *New Times*, October–December 1957, p. 5; "Novyi tip mezhdunarodnykh otnoshenii i mezhdunarodnoe pravo," *Sovetskoe gosudarstvo i pravo*, No. 1, 1959, pp. 81–94. See also S. Sanakoyev, "The Basis of the Relations between the Socialist Countries," *International Affairs* (Moscow), July 1958, p. 161; Potelov, *op. cit.*, and Liu Shao-Chi, *Internationalism and Nationalism* (Peking: Foreign Language Press, 1949), p. 9.

13. *Kommunist*, No. 14, October 1955, pp. 4–7. See also "On the Principles of Development and Further Strengthening of Friendship and Cooperation between the Soviet Union and Other Socialist States," *Pravda*, October 31, 1956, p. 1.

14. Korovin, *op. cit.*

15. Tunkin, "Socialist Internationalism," p. 10.

16. I. Dudinsky, "A Community of Equal and Sovereign Nations," *International Affairs* (Moscow), No. 11, November 1964, p. 4.

17. Sanakoyev, "Basis," p. 161.

18. Dudinsky, "A Community," pp. 4, 6.

19. Made available by TASS to *The New York Times*, November 7, 1964, p. 8.

20. Potelov, *op. cit.*

21. M. Airepetian and P. Kabanov, "Leninskie printsipy vneshnei politiki Sovetskogo gosudarstva," *Sovetskoe gosudarstvo i pravo*, Moscow, 1957, p. 65, cited by John N. Hazard, "Soviet Socialism as a Public Order System," *Proceedings of the American Society of International Law*, 1959, p. 41; Potelov, *op. cit.*, Timofeyev, "Aspects," p. 46.

22. L. Zieleniec and A. Charakchiev, "Milestone in the March of History," *World Marxist Review*, VIII, No. 5 (May 1965), 22.

23. "Statement on the Stand of the Rumanian Workers' Party Concerning the Problems of the World Communist and Working-Class Movement, Endorsed by the Large Plenum of the Central Committee of the Rumanian Workers' Party Held in April 1964," *Rumania, Documents, Articles and Information, Supplement*, 1964, p. 50. Italics added. See also S. Sanakoyev, "Internationalism and Socialist Diplomacy," *International Affairs* (Moscow), No. 5, 1965, p. 22.

24. Editorial "Unity of Action of the World Communist Movement," *World Marxist Review*, VIII, No. 4 (April 1965), 4, 5.

25. B. N. Ponomaryov (Secretary of the Central Committee of the CPSU), "Proletarian Internationalism Is the Revolutionary Banner of Our Epoch," *Pravda*, September 29, 1964, p. 2; also, *Information Bulletin No. 25, World Marxist Review Publishers*, Prague, Progress Books (Toronto, November 16, 1964), p. 28; Dudinsky, "A Community," p. 6; Zieleniec and Charakchiev, "Milestone," p. 21.

26. Translated from the Italian and with an introduction by Luigi Longo, Togliatti's successor. *New York Times*, September 5, 1964, p. 2; Dudinsky, "A Community," p. 5.

27. Lenin, *Collected Works*, VI, Moscow, 1961, 520–21, cited in Dudinsky, "A Community," p. 5; Z. Zhivkov, "People's Democracy—Tried and Tested Road to Socialism," *World Marxist Review*, VIII, No. 6 (June

1965), 25; Ponomaryov, "Proletarian Internationalism," pp. 34–35.

28. "For Marxist-Leninist Unity of the Communist Movement, For Solidarity of the Countries of Socialism," *Pravda*, February 10, 1963, p. 3.

29. Zieleniec and Charakchiev, "Milestone," p. 16.

30. A letter sent on June 14 by the Central Committee of the Chinese Communist Party to the Central Committee of the Soviet Communist Party, as printed in the Chinese weekly *Peking Review*. *New York Times*, Western Edition, July 5, 1963, p. 4. Italics added.

31. "Statement on the Stand of the Rumanian Workers' Party," pp. 48, 49.

32. *Ibid.*

33. Lenin, *Selected Works*, III, Moscow, 1961, p. 342, cited by Dudinsky, "A Community," p. 6. Italics added.

34. Ponomaryov, "Proletarian Internationalism," p. 30.

35. *Pravda*, August 15, 1965, p. 1.

36. Editorial, "Unity of Action," p. 4.

37. Ponomaryov, "Proletarian Internationalism," pp. 28–29.

38. Azizian, "Proletarskii internatsionalizm," p. 98; Korovin, *op. cit.*, p. 71; S. Sanakoyev, "Basis," p. 161.

39. A letter sent on June 14, p. 4.

40. *Ibid.*

41. Sanakoyev, "Basis," p. 21; Dudinsky, "Milestone," p. 7.

42. "Statement on the Stand of the Rumanian Workers' Party," p. 50.

43. Editorial in *Hung Chi*, as published in *Yenmin Jih Pao*, February 5, 1964. *New York Times*, February 7, 1964, p. 8. Italic added.

44. *Ibid.*

45. See Editorial, *Pravda*, June 20, 1965, pp. 3–5; G. Shanshiev, "Under the Banner of Proletarian Internationalism," *World Marxist Review*, VIII, No. 8 (1965), 60, citing R. Palme Dutt, *The International* (London: Terrence and Wishart, 1964).

46. "Party Central Committee's Slogans for May 1, 1963," *Pravda*, April 8, 1963, pp. 1–2; *Pravda*, April 14, 1964, pp. 1–2; *Izvestiia*, April 15, 1964, pp. 1–2. See "For Marxist-Leninist Unity of the Countries of Socialism," *Pravda*, February 10, 1963, pp. 2–3. In the original 1963 *Pravda* listing of April 8, cited above, the Socialist Federal Republic of Yugoslavia was introduced as the Federal People's Republic of Yugoslavia. Three days later, the mistake was corrected; see "Correction," *Pravda*, April 11, 1963, p. 1.

47. For example, 80% or 13.5 million of the 1963 Communist Chinese Party members had joined the party after 1949 (70% after 1953). *China Quarterly*, No. 7 (April–June 1961), p. 16.

48. U.S. Department of State, Bureau of Intelligence and Research, *World Strength of Communist Party Organizations*, January 1968. See also United Nations *Demographic Yearbook, 1966*, New York, 1967, pp. 120–31. ("Adults" are age twenty and older.)

49. "For Marxist-Leninist Unity," p. 2. In mid-1960, the party-states had an estimated 984.5 million people (almost 1.3 billion in 1963). UN *Demographic Yearbook, 1962*, New York, 1962, Table 1, pp. 106–123.

Unless specific, particular sources are given, the statistical data below are from a supplement to the *Problems of Peace and Socialism*, No. 8, August 1963 (published in Prague in Russian language) entitled "The Economic Development of the Socialist Countries."

50. UN *Demographic Yearbook, 1966.*

51. United Nations *Statistical Yearbook, 1962,* New York, 1963, Table 1, pp. 24–39. Cuba has 0.12 million square kilometers.

52. The party-states' average is 11.4%. FAO, *Production Yearbook, 1966,* Rome, 1967, pp. 3–8.

53. UN *Demographic Yearbook, 1966,* pp. 96–114.

54. *United Nations Compendium of Social Statistics, 1963,* New York, 1963, Table 5, pp. 70–80. Only the USSR, Cuba, East Germany, and Hungary with 35.5%, 34.7%, 34.6%, and 31.5% of their respective populations living in cities of 20,000 or more inhabitants) have more than 30% of urban population. The rest of the party-states rank from high of Bulgaria and Czechoslovakia (24.7% and 21.6%, respectively) to low of Mongolia (13.0%) and China (8.3%).

55. None of these figures are recent, however. No data are available for Mongolia, North Korea and North Vietnam, all predominantly agricultural states. Only East Germany (21.7%), Czechoslovakia (25%), Hungary (36%), Poland (38%), and Cuba (42%) have less than 50% of their populations dependent upon agriculture, FAO, *Production Yearbook, 1961,* Rome, 1961, Table 5A, p. 19.

56. Population growth is most rapid in the Far East: North Vietnam (3.3%), Mongolia (3.0%), North Korea (2.9%), China (1.5%). Eastern Europe is led by Albania (3.0%), followed by the Soviet Union (1.5%), Yugoslavia and Poland (1.2%), Bulgaria (0.8%), Czechoslovakia and Romania (0.7%), and Hungary (0.4%). Cuba has a growth rate of 2.3%. An eight-year average still shows a negative rate for East Germany (−0.2%). UN *Demographic Yearbook, 1966,* pp. 96–114.

57. UN *Demographic Yearbook, 1961,* Table 5, pp. 138–61. As a consequence of the uneven population growth in economically accelerated Eastern Europe, the Far Eastern sector is younger in population composition and has many more children than Eastern Europe. Unfortunately, no data are available for three party-states, Mongolia, North Korea, and Albania, and the only available age breakdown expressed in the percentage of the total population as compared with the young is 5–14 years of age. On this basis, the four states leading the party-states in youthfulness of population are the USSR, North Vietnam, Cuba, and China with 37.4%, 26.6%, 23.7%, and 20.6% of the population in the 5–14 years age bracket respectively. Czechoslovakia (17.9%), Bulgaria, (17.7%), Hungary (17.2%), and East Germany (11.98%) have the fewest children of 5–14 years among the communist party-states. UNESCO, *World Survey of Education, II: Primary Education,* Paris, 1958.

58. No data are available for the Far Eastern party-states. For the others infant mortality varies from Albania (85.3 infant deaths—under one-year-old—per 1000 live births) and Yugoslavia (81.5) to East Germany (33.8), the USSR (32), and Czechoslovakia (22.5). UN *Demographic Yearbook, 1966,* pp. 280–95.

59. In East Germany there is one dentist or physician for every 166.4 persons; in Czechoslovakia the ratio is 1: 250.7; in Poland 1: 241.9; in the USSR 1: 511.9; in Bulgaria, 1: 615.3; in Hungary, 1: 655.6; and Romania, 1: 736.6. However, the ratios of Yugoslavia and Albania are

1: 1365.4 and 1: 3411.0, respectively. UN *Statistical Yearbook, 1962,* Table 175, pp. 603–09.

60. The last two figures are somewhat dated, however. The first comes from the 1958 *Chinese People's Handbook* (Peking), and the second from the UN *Statistical Yearbook,* New York, 1956, both cited in Norton Ginsburg, *Atlas of Economic Development* (Chicago: University of Chicago Press, N.D.), p. 28. The rest of the figures come from the UN *Statistical Yearbook, 1962,* Tables 1 and 175, cited above. No data are available for North Korea and North Vietnam. Cuba has one physician or dentist for every 677.1 persons.

61. UN *Compendium of Social Statistics, 1963,* Table 59, pp. 303–12.

62. 80% of the North Vietnamese, 60% of the North Koreans, 50% of the Chinese, and 40% of the Mongolians are illiterate. However, these are 1957 or older figures. See UNESCO, *World Illiteracy at Mid-Century,* Paris, 1957, Table 7, p. 39, and Table 10, p. 43.

63. No figures are available for North Korea, Outer Mongolia, and North Vietnam. Still, the party-states' average (61.8% of population aged 5–19 enrolled in primary education) appears to compare favorably with the Western European average of 65.39%. Czechoslovakia (71%), Poland (69%), Hungary (66%), and Bulgaria (66%) lead the list. UN *Compendium of Social Statistics, 1963,* Table 61, pp. 323–28.

64. UN *Compendium of Social Statistics, 1963,* Table 62, pp. 329–31.

65. This average excludes the Far Eastern party-states for which no recent figures are available and which would lower the average considerably.

66. UN *Statistical Yearbook, 1966,* pp. 754–57, 762–63.

67. *Problems of Peace and Socialism,* Supplement, p. 4.

68. UN *Yearbook of National Accounts Statistics, 1966,* New York, 1967, pp. 3–600; UN *Statistical Yearbook, 1966,* p. 583.

69. *Mir sotsializma v tsifrakh i faktakh 1965 god* (Moscow: Izdatel'stvo politicheskoi literatury, 1966).

70. UN *Statistical Yearbook, 1966,* p. 301.

71. *Ibid.,* p. 298.

72. *Ibid.,* p. 285.

73. *Ibid.,* pp. 344–47.

74. *Ibid.,* pp. 348–55.

75. UN *Yearbook of National Accounts Statistics, 1966,* pp. 3–600.

76. The USSR is first in the world in iron ore deposits, manganese ore, and timber, and second in bauxite reserves, gold, lead, and zinc, while China has more bauxite reserves than all the other party-states combined, twice the antimony reserves of the rest of the world, 21.3% of the world's coal reserves, and so on. (But the USSR has 26 billion barrels of proved petroleum reserves while China has virtually none.) *Oxford Economics Atlas* (prepared by the Economics Intelligence Unit, Cartographic Department of Clarendon Press, New York, 2nd ed.; Oxford University Press, 1959).

77. *The Theory of Political Coalitions* (New Haven: Yale University Press, 1962).

78. F. Bruce Dodge, "Comparative Enthusiasm at the International Level: A Research Design and an Application to Eastern Europe" (Honors Thesis, Stanford University, 1964).

79. A letter sent on June 14, 1963.

80. See Morton A. Kaplan, *System and Process in International Politics,* pp. 36 ff.

81. See "For Unity in the Struggle for Peace, Freedom, and National Independence," *Pravda,* May 5, 1964, p. 1: "Every educated person knows that the Soviet Union is not only the biggest European power but the biggest Asian power as well. Approximately 40% of the territory of Asia falls within the boundaries of the Soviet Union. The Asian part of the USSR is almost twice as big as the territory of the whole of China. Furthermore, such major Asian countries as China, India, Indonesia, Pakistan, Burma, and Japan taken together could be accommodated in the expanses of the Asian part of the USSR!"

82. (A) *United Nations Participation.* Ten of the 14 party-states are members of the United Nations (the 3 divided states and China are not members), but they participate in varying degree in its activities. Assuming that a nation has 18 major ways of participating in the UN, we have devised the following index of participation (half a point is given for "observer" or "associate" status):

Yugoslavia	14.5	(1.55)
Cuba	12	(1.29)
Poland	11.5	(1.23)
Czechoslovakia	10	(1.07)
USSR	9	(.96)
Bulgaria	9	(.96)
Hungary	9	(.96)
Romania	9	(.96)
Albania	8	(.86)
Mongolia	1	(.10)

The index in parenthesis was calculated by dividing the first figure by the average of all first figures. Amos Peaslee, *International Governmental Organizations* (The Hague: Martinus Nijhoff, 1956).

All countries, whether members of the UN or not, are free to submit documents to it. How many documents each country submits provides some measure of the role it sees for itself in directing international affairs through the UN. In 1961, the party-states submitted the following number of documents:

USSR	166	(5.07)
Czechoslovakia	64	(1.95)
Yugoslavia	61	(1.86)
Poland	56	(1.71)
Cuba	39	(1.19)
Bulgaria	23	(.70)
Hungary	15	(.45)
Romania	13	(.39)
Albania	10	(.30)
Mongolia	7	(.21)
North Korea	3	(.09)
East Germany	1	(.03)
North Vietnam	0	(0)
China	0	(0)

The two indexes are averaged to give the figure under (A). Note that only in the cases of the USSR and Czechoslovakia is there a broad discrepancy between the two measures of UN participation.

(B) *International Organizations.* Listed below are the numbers of international organizations of which the various party-states are members. As under (A), half a point is given for "observer" or "associate" status. All organizations counted have permanent consultative bodies, except the Bandung Conference, which was included because of its unique importance. (The data are, again, from Peaslee's two-volume work, *International Governmental Organizations,* cited above.)

Yugoslavia	28	(1.90)
Poland	27	(1.83)
Romania	25	(1.70)
Czechoslovakia	24	(1.63)
Hungary	24	(1.63)
USSR	21	(1.42)
Bulgaria	21	(1.42)
Cuba	16	(1.08)
Albania	7.5	(.51)
East Germany	4	(.27)
North Vietnam	2.5	(.17)
Mongolia	2	(.13)
China	2	(.13)
North Korea	1.5	(.10)

(C) *Imports.* A country's total imports are less significant, as a measure of internationalization, than is the ratio of these imports to the size of the population; that is, a given quantity of imported goods has a greater internationalizing effect on a small country than on a large one. Ideally, we should take the ratio of imports to gross national product; but since GNP figures are not available for most communist countries, we use the ratio of imports to population, instead.

The first figure in the table below gives the party-states' imports in 1965, in millions of dollars. The second figure is the ratio of the first figure to the populations, in millions—that is, the per capita imports. These ratios are then averaged to form an index:

	i	ii	iii
Czechoslovakia	2,673	188	1.79
East Germany	2,802	175	1.68
Hungary	1,521	149	1.43
Bulgaria	1,176	138	1.32
Cuba	865	110	1.06
Poland	2,340	74	.71
Yugoslavia	1,287	65	.62
Romania	1,077	56	.54
Albania	98	51	.49
USSR	8,053	35	.33

UN *Yearbook of International Trade Statistics, 1965,* New York, 1967. Note that this list, the first of the "society" indexes, presents quite a different typology from the "state" indexes considered thus far.

(D) *Communications.* This is the most difficult factor to quantify. Data are hard to obtain, and it is not clear which of the many possible measurements are the most significant. Our calculations are based on four separate quantities, insofar as they were available:

i. Ratio of the annual number of citizens traveling abroad to total population. Travelers returning from foreign countries, it seems, are one of the most powerful internationalizing forces in a society.

ii. Ratio of annual foreign visitors visiting country to total population. The presence of foreign visitors, while probably less important than local citizens who have been abroad, is still an important factor internationalizing the society.

iii. Ratio of letters sent abroad and received from abroad to domestic letters. The ratios for "sent" and "received" are averaged. Unfortunately, data are available for only three party-states.

iv. Ratio of foreign book translations to domestic book publication. This may be viewed as another important way in which a society is internationalized.

The table below omits the raw data, showing only the index number for each of the four categories and the average index:

	Ave.	i	ii	iii	iv
Czechoslovakia	1.78	1.81	2.22		1.30
Hungary	1.72	2.12	1.89		1.16
East Germany	1.35	1.71		.99	
Bulgaria	1.20	.49	1.87		1.24
Yugoslavia	1.19	.93	1.44	1.01	1.39
Poland	.56	.71	.37		.59
Romania	.41	.20	.16		.86
USSR	.15	.03	.05		.38
Albania	(1.11)				1.11

UN *Statistical Yearbook, 1966*, pp. 470–87, 745–51. Note that Czechoslovakia sends an extraordinary number of citizens abroad each year, more than any other party-state, in both relative and absolute terms. This typology is quite different from (C) but closer to (C) than to either of the state typologies (A) and (B).

83. To compute the "average," take, for instance, the figures of membership in United Nation agencies. Ten of the party-states are shown to belong to between one and 14.5 agencies. Adding the column for all ten party-states yields 93.0, or an *average* (dividing by ten) of 9.3 agencies per party-state. The average party-state, then, belongs to just 9.3 agencies, so that Czechoslovakia is a little above average and the USSR is a little below average in this respect. To get the index, we simply divide each membership figure by the average membership figure, 9.3. For instance, 14.5/9.3 = 1.55 for Yugoslavia. If there were a hypothetical state between Czechoslovakia and the USSR, which belonged to exactly 9.3 agencies, it would have an index of 1.00, showing it was a completely average case.

84. Hugh Seton, *From Lenin to Khrushchev* (New York: Praeger, 1961), p. 320.

85. B. N. Ponomaryov, "Communist Parties—Decisive Weapon of the Working Class," *Pravda*, April 28, 1958, p. 4.

86. Editorial, "Solidarity Under the Banner of Marxism-Leninism," *Pravda,* November 23, 1960, p. 1.

87. V. Tolstikov, "The Great Strength of the Contemporary Situation," *Sovetskaia Rossiia,* October 16, 1962, p. 3.

88. We do, however, count separate parties for Northern Ireland and the French overseas departments of Réunion, Guadeloupe and Martinique, for the communists do not acknowledge these areas to be actually part of the countries concerned and advance separatist claims.

89. These figures are drawn primarily from *World Strength of the Communist Party Organizations,* U.S. Department of State, January 1968, and UN *Demographic Yearbook, 1966,* pp. 120–31.

90. U.S. Department of State, *op. cit.,* p. 138.

91. *Ibid.,* pp. 126–55.

92. Our survey has used Pathet Lao figures to represent Laos, but the distinction between the two organizations and the opposite trends in membership are worth bearing in mind.

93. Figures for Latin America include pre-revolutionary Cuba; Cyprus is counted as part of the Middle East.

TWO

INTEGRATION AMONG THE
COMMUNIST PARTY-STATES:
COMPARATIVE CASE STUDIES

DAVID D. FINLEY

In the following pages, we shall draw an exploratory comparison of three supranational institutions of the communist system. We are concerned with them as agencies for the integration of the party-states, and our effort will be to illuminate the process of international integration as it emerges through various aspects of the party-states' experience. The institutions are COMECON (Council for Mutual Economic Assistance), the WTO (Warsaw Treaty Organization), and the JINR (Joint Institute for Nuclear Research).[1]

The three differ significantly in the substantive activities they purport to integrate, in the scope and extent of their achievement, and in their respective bureaucratic structures and bases for authority. In common, they share the Soviet Union's purpose of welding together into a single cohesive unit the politically essential decision-making apparatus of the European party-states. It is the differences in the company of a common purpose that makes comparison instructive and perhaps throws light upon the general process of international integration.

CONCEPTS

Drawing heavily upon the work of other scholars,[2] we recognize *integration* as both a condition and a process. As a condition, we conceive integration as describing cooperative behavior in an action system, arrived at through practices and institutions which allow coordination of the system members' courses of action. As used here, cooperation specifies joint action toward a common end; and coordination is (1) sharing of information, and (2) adjustment of individual courses of action to facilitate achievement of a common end. Cooperation thus presupposes interaction, which means an action system must be established before an opportunity for integration can arise.

As we have no pre-established scale with which to compare a given system in order to say it shows high or low integration, usually we must be content with comparing one system, or subsystem, with another. A decision-making orientation has proven useful here. If the informational inputs (both cognitive and affective) for a decision which binds the system as a whole are drawn from all units of the system, then the decision represents integrated behavior. This affords us one guide to research. All indicators of the presence or absence of system-binding decisions based upon system-wide information gathering give evidence of the extent of system integration. Similarly, indicators of decisions made outside a unit, yet binding upon that unit, evidence a degree of unit integration with a larger whole.

The process of decision-making is frequently obscured from our direct observation. Some alternative indicators which may be more objectively assessed in given cases have been suggested by North, Koch, and Zinnes. They include the probability of violence given a conflict among the units, the frequency of conflicts among the units, the agreement of the units on policy conditions, the degree of interdependency among units, the presence of interlocking communications systems or structure, and the overlapping of unit membership in common organizations.[3]

But we have pointed out already that integration is a process as well as a condition. It is the process of so changing the conditions of a system that integrated behavior (as defined above) becomes a more frequent function. It may be that some practices and institutions by which integrated behavior is achieved reinforce or augment the future probability of integrated behavior, while others are deleterious and lower that probability. As we proceed, we shall have to bear in mind this duality in our usage of the term integration. We shall see later that it becomes critical in analyzing attempts at international integration among the party-states.

It is apparent that a system may be integrated in a variety of institutional forms; that is, a variety of role structures will allow the coordination necessary for cooperative action. Toward one end of a continuum of structural varieties, which we shall awkwardly designate "top-level institutional integration" for the present, system-binding decisions are made only at the highest institutional echelon of the authority pyramid. An example of such integration was Stalin's domination of economic decision-making for the USSR and most of Eastern Europe from about 1949 to his death in 1953. Coordination took place only at the top command echelon, with subordinate units acting in conformance with higher directives while pursuing a minimum of self-reliant adjustments with other units on their same level.

Toward the other pole of the continuum, which we shall call "institutional integration in depth," system-binding decisions are made by subordinate authority echelons far down into a supranational bureaucratic structure. The vision of the "Europeans" for later stages of the European Economic Community serves as an example, a vision remarkably similar to that propounded for COMECON by Nikita Khrushchev in the early 1960's.[4] This sort of institutional integration implies mutual adjustment of courses of action by a matrix of commissions and subcommissions representing the diverse units of the system, each acting with decisive effect in its own narrow area of jurisdiction.

The continuum of possible institutional forms provides us with one index for comparison of the modes of integration among our selected supranational institutions of the party-states. Given decisions binding the system as a whole or decisions made supranationally and binding a unit, we ask of each how the adjustments of courses of action have been arrived at. Did the Central Committee of the Communist Party of the Soviet Union issue a directive followed independently by the party-states? Or did commissions of experts from several party-states build up a recommendation which was subsequently ratified and implemented in each state represented?

Just as the extent of integration of a unit into the system or the integration of the system as a whole seem to us to be analytically independent of the institutional form of integration, the basis of authority for system integration seems similarly independent. It may be found at some point on another continuum running between the conceptual poles of pure coercion and pure volition. Authoritarian government may theoretically find its support in consensus just as well as in the power to impose unacceptable deprivations.[5] It is this distinction among authority patterns that leads us to discriminate between *integration* and *community* and to treat the two as hypothetically related but analytically distinct phenomena. We define *community* as an integrated system in which authority is preponderantly based upon consensus of values or volition. It appears to us that whereas in the years just prior to Stalin's death the party-states were relatively highly integrated in several respects, there was little community evident. Today, among these same party-states, there may be less extensive system integration, but such as there is may be based more upon consensus and thus provide reason to speak correctly of a growth of *community*.

The continuum of possible authority bases thus provides another index for comparing the modes of integration reflected in our three supranational institutions. Given instances of integrated behavior as the output of one of these, what was the nature of the authority which sanctioned them? What were the proportions of coercion and volition involved, and what were their genesis?

Finally, before turning to the first of our three institutions, let us consider a fourth index by which we should compare them. It is *scope*. In the totality of politically significant decisions affecting the system, what proportion are influenced by integration or disintegration of decision-making in a particular sector of substantive activity? Clearly, breadth of scope is a condition independent of the extent of integration. Less extensive integration over a broader substantive scope may be more politically significant for the system than a very high degree of integration in a very narrow purview. Additionally, the various possible purviews in which decision-making may be integrated differ markedly in their intrinsic political significance for the system. Decisions to employ nuclear weapons and decisions to raise or lower interstate tariffs may each be highly integrated or not. One, however, is more intrinsically significant than the other, and as indicators they should be differentiated clearly. Lastly, some decisions ramify further upon the subsequent integration or disintegration of a system than do others. The nature and breadth of the scope of integration determine whether, in Ernst Haas's formulation, the integration is "inherently expansive."[6]

COUNCIL FOR MUTUAL ECONOMIC ASSISTANCE

Let us turn now from concepts to facts and specifically to the Eastern European supranational institution for economic integration commonly known in the West as COMECON. We shall examine it with respect to the scope and extent of its activity, its bureaucratic structure, and the basis of authority which sanctions its activity. These data should sustain comparison with the WTO and JINR and conclusions about their relative achievements and potential as vehicles for integration of the party-states.

COMECON was created in January 1949 as a servant of Stalin's policy, reflecting his concern over the successful defection of Yugoslavia from his empire and his determination that no further disintegration should occur. The prior economic organization of Eastern Europe in the post-World-War-II years had been characterized by blatant Soviet exploitation of the resources of satellite states. Exploitation was carried on under the aegis of bilateral agreements between the Soviet Union and each satellite. Autarchic economic development and the servo-mechanical operation of Soviet puppet administrations, reinforced by the Soviet secret police, rapidly broke down old bonds among the satellites. What emerged was a grouping of economically irrational appendages to the USSR, moved more and more by coercion to produce those goods, chiefly capital goods, determined by Stalin to be necessary for the economic recovery and expansion of the Soviet Union.

The Yugoslav defection bore evidence of widespread and growing restiveness in the face of such oppression. The European Recovery Program, successfully launched and now advancing war-prostrated Western Europe toward new economic prosperity, augmented the challenge to Stalin to revise his grip upon his new empire. COMECON reflected at its outset no more than a mode for strengthening his economic domination by multilateralizing the web of trade commitments which had heretofore run predominantly to Moscow.

It was not until Stalin's successors perceived the long-term inadequacy of multiple economic autarchy, supported by ideological allegiance or totalitarian terror, for maintaining Soviet hegemony against Eastern European disgruntlement, that the necessity of a new economic model for the whole region was recognized. COMECON was resurrected as the agency for transforming Eastern Europe to fit the new image. The early Soviet profession that COMECON was an association of equal, sovereign states was approached in the establishment of an extensive bureaucratic structure of commissions and subcommissions of technical experts, called upon to formulate economic standards, allocations and perspectives oriented toward economic progress for the region as a whole. Assiduously democratic procedures were codified, under the assumption that the enormous material advantage of Soviet economic resources would prove decisive leverage for determining in what direction the supranational economy should move.

The model of Eastern European economic organization to which Khrushchev aspired can be characterized as a single amalgamated unit disregarding old national boundaries, highly industrialized as a whole but with each geographic portion producing only what its natural resources dictated could be most efficiently produced there. Comparative advantage would not be construed in terms of costs based on preexisting industrialization. The distribution of labor skills would similarly be regarded as secondary. Distribution of basic resources would be the ultimate criterion; all other factors would eventually be rationalized to conform with this one unchangeable fact. National boundaries, and hence the basis for nationalistic conflict, would be eliminated in the socialist commonwealth. Interdependence would create mutual self-interests which would reinforce themselves in their material implementation:

> Lenin foresaw the future collaboration of socialist nations as taking place in a single world-wide cooperative in which the economy would be conducted according to a common plan. . . .

The various economies, supplementing one another, will gradually merge into a single streamlined economic complex. . . .

The socialist world system is not just a socio-political union of
countries, it is a world economic system. It follows then that the
coordination should be pursued not within the restricted limits of
each socialist country but on the scale of the socialist world economy, which means overcoming the national exclusiveness inherited
from the past.[7]

The reorganized COMECON after 1956 included a Council of
Representatives, meeting in semi-annual sessions to consult and make
recommendations to their respective governments on matters involving
mutual economic cooperation. A Conference of Deputies appointed by
each member, but headquartered permanently in Moscow, and a Secretariat, also located in Moscow, gave the organization continuity. Most
importantly, a large group[8] of specialized technical and procedural commissions, each empowered to establish subcommissions as needed, was
gradually created to do the work of formulating the recommendations
which would come before the Council sessions. To an ever increasing degree, it was within these commissions and subcommissions that the substantial and cumulative work of COMECON was accomplished. Each
commission was oriented to a particular sector of the supranational
economy or a particular problem obstructing economic cooperation. Each
included representation of all members interested in that sector or problem.

In accord with the increasing prominence of COMECON and its
frequent public association in the Soviet press with the developing unity of
the "socialist commonwealth," the Twelfth Session of the Council in
December 1959 adopted a formal charter and an accompanying convention to specify its legal status. The charter was ratified by all members
and took effect in April 1960, adding another formal prop to the burgeoning supranational bureaucratic apparatus.

From 1957 to 1960 the coordination of trade between pairs of
member countries was facilitated by recommendations arrived at in the
COMECON commissions. A rapid increase in volume transfer between
nearly every pair testifies to a considerable measure of success. However,
all efforts to escape from the restrictions of bilateral barter relations and
to put COMECON trade on a multilateral payments basis were stymied.
A payments union, created in Moscow in 1957 to assume the function
of prior bilateral arrangements and promote a freer flow of goods failed
for lack of a convertible currency and the difficulty of establishing prices
among economic systems formally divorced from the market. Efforts to
overcome the technical obstacles remained alive, and a General Economics Commission of COMECON undertook a study of the problems of

international accounting procedures in the socialist commonwealth. An international bank, opened in January 1964, is one outgrowth of these efforts.

Perhaps the biggest obstacle faced between 1957 and 1960 was the reluctance of the Eastern European states to accept any specialization of production or division of labor that would reduce what self-sufficiency they had already achieved. While Khrushchev frequently insisted that only the USSR and possibly China among the communist states could validly pursue a policy of fully diversified production, he remained temporarily content with a compromise advertised as the "international socialist division of labor." According to this principle, no member state was expected to give up production in any basic economic branch. However, duplication of production of similar items was prevented by bilateral specialization agreements within each industrial subdivison. Thus, the advantages of mass production through automation might conceivably be achieved, although the principle of comparative advantage would be partially thwarted.⁹ Specialization of this limited degree has apparently been best achieved in the machine equipment sector of industry. Party-state writers frequently point with pride to a series of specialization agreements covering over a thousand specific varieties of machine parts, negotiated bilaterally within COMECON.

Little, if any, objection has been raised to the idea of joint projects among the member countries of COMECON, although a certain amount of rivalry for the allocation of scarce resources has been evident. The most frequently used example of the success of this sort of integrated activity is to be found in the "Friendship Pipeline," claimed to reduce drastically the cost of fuel oil in Eastern Europe by connecting most COMECON countries there with the Soviet oil fields. A single electric power grid (the "Peace Power Grid") now integrates energy systems of Eastern Europe and the Ukraine under the guidance of a multilateral directorate located in Prague. Further examples of joint projects include Czech-Polish cooperation in exploiting lignite and copper resources in Poland, the Danube-Oder Canal, development of a cellulose complex in the Danube delta, Intermetall, and other lesser undertakings.

In general, COMECON integration was successful in the latter 1950's. Until then, there was little real threat to the balanced industrial development of each state, no sacrifice of achieved economic independence, and no perception of severe conflicts of interest. But, after 1960, with steady prodding by the USSR toward radical specialization of production, a hiatus was reached. Party-state resistance was manifested first in apathetic implementation of the measures which had received formal approval and been recommended by COMECON. The legal commitment to observe recommendations reached by COMECON organs was open to some questions. Certainly, a tacit obligation to conform existed, although the charter provides an opportunity for members to ratify or not at their discretion. The ambiguity was consistent with our contention that a form of elaborate protection for member sovereignty was to be maintained while Soviet economic pressure operated *sub rosa*. In theory, conflicts of interest between COMECON as a whole and its member units were not a problem to the Marxist ideologue, who could not rationalize any conflict of national interests within world communism once a situation had been correctly analyzed. But, in practice, these discords became the foremost obstacle to COMECON's progress.

Albania, unhappy at the progress of de-Stalinization, rested its charges against the USSR chiefly upon the alleged injustice of proposed economic plans which would eliminate Albanian heavy industrial development. Since the Twenty-Second Party Congress in 1961, she has failed to participate in COMECON activities. In June 1962, sharp resistance to coordinated national plans was voiced by Hungary and Czechoslovakia during the Sixteenth COMECON Council Session in Moscow. Since 1963, Romania's disaffection with the organization's supranational infringement upon her economic sovereignty has grown steadily more vigorous.

Both the Soviet desire to overcome this antagonism and the Soviet determination to expand COMECON as the basis for party-state unity were confirmed by events surrounding the Sixteenth Council Session. Just prior to it, an important meeting was called of First Secretaries of the COMECON states (excluding Albania). Here a new Executive Committee replacing the old Conference of Deputies was established, to consist of Deputy Premiers from each member country charged with taking "concrete measures" to implement decisions of COMECON directed toward more thorough economic integration.[10] Since its creation, the Executive Committee has met approximately every two months, as scheduled. Its value as a facilitator of integrated behavior is hard to judge. On the one hand, its achievements have been inauspicious; the rapid progress of the late 1950's has slowed to insignificance. On the other hand, one may speculate that it has served to forestall the disintegration which might have occurred but for such an elite group apparently devoted to discovering pragmatically the full extent of cooperation acceptable to the member states. The fact of the Executive Committee's continued activity testifies to both the life and limitations of supranational economic decision-making in COMECON.

It remains to summarize certain salient characteristics of COMECON as the mode of economic integration in Eastern Europe:

1. Trade among the member countries of COMECON is governed by bilateral agreements, negotiated usually for a term of five years in accord with COMECON recommendations for emphasis of economic de-

velopment in each country. The recommendations in turn are guided by a modified principle of comparative advantage. The agreements provide for an increasing amount of intermember trade and the gradual increase of interdependency resulting from it.

2. All economic relations among the member countries and, to a growing degree, the course of domestic economic development are being coordinated in the alleged interest of the region as a whole through the device of 15- to 20-year "perspective agreements" negotiated bilaterally according to recommendations of the permanent commissions of COMECON.

3. Specialization of production according to the "international socialist division of labor" represents a compromise between production according to comparative advantage and a "well-rounded" economy for each member state. Such specialization is making very slow progress against Eastern European resistance to the Soviet vision of an eventually unified supranational economic plan.

4. Strong emphasis is being placed upon cooperative plans for multilateral development of economic resources within Eastern Europe. Projects under way point toward freer international flow of investment capital among the COMECON countries and the creation of more numerous mutual economic interests.

5. Supranational decisions are arrived at by COMECON through assemblage of information by technical experts representing the member states and operating in a highly differentiated bureaucratic structure. These decisions are reviewed and modified by superior international organs (the Council and Executive Committee) according to the perceived limits of political feasibility.

6. Theoretically, the authority base of COMECON is entirely volitional. The output of cooperative behavior is sanctioned by consensus upon goals for the "socialist commonwealth" shared by all the members. In fact, the rather modest limits of consensus are stretched by use of Soviet economic and political leverage.

Drawing together these data regarding COMECON and referring to our earlier conceptual discussion, we may observe that the institution originated as an unsubstantial front for a condition of top-level economic integration directed toward the industrial expansion of the USSR. COMECON was a front inasmuch as it manipulated attractive symbols such as "equality" and "sovereignty." It was unsubstantial inasmuch as these verbal symbols were in no real way reflected in the decision-making process, where Soviet will brooked no opposition and was sanctioned by military power, and where directions of economic effort for satellite states were determined in Moscow in response to Moscow's perceived needs. At COMECON's outset, economic integration was as broad in scope as the ramifications of economic decisions; that is, it affected every inhabitant of Eastern Europe in the homely details of his economic existence. It was extensive; it was sanctioned by coercion; and it was effectively imposed from the very pinnacle of the authority pyramid.

The scope of COMECON remained as broad as ever. But following the Hungarian revolution it became clear to the new Soviet leadership that the Stalinist pattern of economic integration was unstable. As a process, it did not reinforce itself. Coerced cooperative behavior accumulated resentment and international tensions seeking an opportunity for destructive release. Thus, a new life was given COMECON: Some meaning was pumped into the symbols "equality" and "sovereignty"; coercive authority was supplemented by raising new goals of mutual economic development and interdependent economic prosperity; widely drawn technical expertise was incorporated into the decision process through creation of a differentiated international bureaucracy.

The changes which brought COMECON success in the late 1950's, however, brought on the hiatus of the 1960's. Because of concomitant tolerance of national diversity, new limits began to appear to the members' voluntary cooperation. These obstacles, today still growing, have so slowed the process of integration that it is unclear whether an irrevocable threshold of supranational economic community has been reached in Eastern Europe or whether the virulent divisive forces will produce on balance a regressive disintegration.

Let us turn at this point to our second supranational institution among the party-states and examine in parallel to COMECON the scope, structure, authority, and extent of military integration through the Warsaw Treaty Organization.

WARSAW TREATY ORGANIZATION

Shortly after the termination of World War II, the United States advanced to its erstwhile allies a four-power mutual assistance proposal to guarantee the disarmament of Germany and the collective security of Europe. The Soviet Union demurred. Philosophically ill at ease with the principle of general and indefinite collective agreements reaching across ideological frontiers, and with eyes open to his tactical opportunities in war-prostrated Western Europe, Stalin preferred bilateral alliances with the Eastern European states for military as well as economic purposes. Precedent for bilateral treaties of "friendship, cooperation, and mutual assistance" had been set by a pact concluded during the war (1943) with Czechoslovakia. In the postwar period, similar treaties followed with all the new "satellites" except Albania. China was included in 1950, and the German Democratic Republic (over Western objections) in 1964. Pursuant to the Soviet model of an interrelated matrix of autarchic states in the latter forties and early fifties, similar, supplementary treaties of alliance were concluded between satellite pairs in Eastern Europe.

The military purpose of the Soviet Union was probably as well provided for by this matrix of bilateral agreements as by the alternative of a unified collective security organization. Extensive system integration was achieved, a coercive, top-level institutional integration, through the clear predominance of Soviet military power and the presence of Soviet troops. No institutional integration in depth, for instance, through multilateral coordination among satellite armed forces, was attempted by Stalin. Until his death, the structure, extent, and authority of military integration closely resembled that of economic integration.

When collective security arrangements came to Eastern Europe, they came in response to the Western incorporation of the Federal German Republic into the North Atlantic Treaty Organization. Soviet protests against this course of events culminated in the conclusion in Warsaw, on May 14, 1955, of a multilateral "Treaty of Friendship, Cooperation, and Mutual Assistance," which mirrored in its provisions many of the articles of its Western counterpart. The European party-states (with the exception of Yugoslavia) acted, according to the preamble:

> Taking into consideration the situation obtaining in Europe as a result of ratification of the Paris agreements, which provide for the formation of a new military grouping in the shape of the "Western European Union" together with a remilitarized Western Germany in the North Atlantic bloc, which increases the threat of another war and creates a menace to the national security of the peaceloving states. . . .[11]

The treaty, which was promptly ratified by the eight participants, pledged the signatories to render immediate assistance, including armed force as considered necessary, in the event of an armed attack in Europe upon any signatory. In such an event, immediate consultations would be undertaken to determine appropriate joint measures for restoring and upholding international peace and security. Additionally, the signatories agreed to refrain in their international relations from the threat or use of force and to work for the adoption of effective measures toward arms reduction and the prohibition of weapons of mass destruction. Assistance to members who might be the victims of aggression would be provided within the purview of Article 51 of the United Nations Charter and would cease as soon as the UN Security Council had taken measures to ensure peace.

The signatories agreed to consult among themselves on all important international questions relating to their common interests and to cooperate in strengthening their economic and cultural relations, meanwhile observing principles of mutual respect for independence and sovereignty and noninterference in internal affairs. Declared binding on all members for a period of twenty years, the treaty would run an additional ten years for members who did not denounce it within a year of expiration. Additional members might accede to the treaty and participate in its implementation with the consent of the original parties. A final provision declared that the treaty would automatically cease to be effective on the date a general European treaty of collective security might come into force.[12]

The organizational structure arising from the Warsaw Treaty was a simple one. For holding the required consultations and for considering problems arising in connection with their implementation, a Political Consultative Committee was vested with paramount authority. Composed of government ministers or other, specially appointed representatives, the committee might establish auxiliary organs as it determined necessary. Secondly, a Joint Command was created for the members' armed forces, the forces to be assigned by agreement among the states and to function on the basis of jointly defined principles to guarantee frontiers and territories and defend against possible aggression. Marshal I. S. Konev of the USSR was immediately named commander-in-chief of the joint armed forces. Ministers of Defense of the other member countries were designated assistants to the commander-in-chief, and a joint staff composed of permanent representatives of the members' own general staffs was to be established at the organization's headquarters in Moscow. Deployment of joint forces on the territory of member states was to be governed by "the requirements of mutual defense, in agreement among these states."[13]

When the Political Consultative Committee first formally met, during the following January in Prague, it established two subordinate organs: a permanent commission to handle recommendations in the field of foreign policy for the bloc of states, and a secretariat, to be headquartered in Moscow and include representatives of all members. The committee decided to meet whenever necessary but, in any event, not less than twice a year. A statute providing for the organization of the Joint Command was approved, and the inclusion of East German armed forces, a proposal deferred the previous spring in Warsaw, was agreed upon.[14]

The Prague meeting issued a declaration concerning international security. This called for (1) an East-West major-power agreement to exclude nuclear weapons among forces stationed in Germany; (2) continuation of efforts toward general disarmament; (3) a European collective security system and conclusion of bilateral nonaggression pacts; and (4) limitation and control of arms and troops in a zone to include all of Germany.[15]

During the first decade of the WTO's existence the Political Consultative Committee continued to be a sounding board for enunciation of Soviet "cold-war" policies and helped give an aura of collective unanimity to Soviet foreign propaganda. The semi-annual schedule of meetings was not adhered to; sessions occurred irregularly about once a year. As *New York Times* correspondent A. M. Rosenthal has decribed it, they proved a rather ceremonial shadow of their NATO counterparts:

> When the Western military alliance meets it hands out military information and the inside story on political squabbles. When the Communist military alliance meets it hands out smoked salmon. . . .
>
> Three and a half hours were enough for a review of the world situation, the exchange of pleasantries and the approval of a communiqué. Then everybody was ready for the toasts and the buffet table.[16]

The Hungarian revolution of October–November 1956, by all odds the most severe crisis to face the WTO, did not occasion even a meeting of the Political Consultative Committee. The Nagy government's repudiation of the Warsaw Treaty was met first by a Soviet offer to review the status of Soviet troops on other members' territory and then by Soviet armed intervention which violated explicit Soviet legal interpretation of the Treaty clauses,[17] but no formal meeting of the Political Consultative Committee took place until May 1958.

On the Warsaw Treaty Organization's tenth anniversary, in May 1965, its commander-in-chief, Marshal of the Soviet Union Andrei A. Grechko, wrote a long article for *Pravda* in which he celebrated the body's accomplishments (toward preservation of the peace), described its continuing indispensability (against the imperalist threat), and propounded once again the Soviet foreign policy themes which allegedly have persisted over the decade: the need for a German peace treaty, for "normalization" of the status of West Berlin, for renunciation by both German states of nuclear armaments, for a central European atom-free zone and a NATO-WTO nonagression pact, and for a general conference on collective security for all European states. The essay was reminiscent of the declaration issued by the Political Consultative Committee in Prague in January 1956.[18]

What beyond a Soviet propaganda forum has the Warsaw Treaty Organization been since 1955? As a symbolic response to the perceived challenge of the West in drawing West Germany into NATO, the WTO has clearly served usefully as a political playing card for the Soviet Union. Regardless of what its substantive addition to the military capability of

Eastern Europe and the Soviet Union may be, it represents negotiating capital that the series of bilateral agreements did not. But what of its integrative achievement? According to Marshal Grechko, it has achieved standardization of military equipment and training in Eastern Europe, and it has established a unified military doctrine and view of the nature of a future war which are reflected in the common statutes and directives for training. There is little reason to doubt these claims. Since 1961, it has sponsored joint maneuvers and other military exercises of increasing size and multilateral scope. In September 1964, for example, amphibious landings, airborne drops, and artillery defensive operations were carried out in Bulgaria; these included Bulgarian, Romanian, and Soviet troop elements. In the summer of 1963 and twice in 1965, some forty thousand Soviet, Polish, Czech, and East German troops participated in combined air and land exercises in the German Democratic Republic.[19]

The communiqués describing such joint exercises usually note that they have been undertaken as "a component of a general plan for the combat preparation of the armies of the socialist commonwealth" or "in accordance with the plan of combat readiness of the Combined Armed Forces of the member countries of the Warsaw Treaty." The Cuban missile crisis in October–November 1962 produced a report that the deputy commanders-in-chief of the Warsaw Treaty countries had been summoned to Moscow to consider mobilization plans for their respective forces. It seems reasonable to conclude, then, that the WTO has also led to the existence of formal military contingency plans which integrate the capabilities of the member defense organizations.

In the Stalinist years immediately following World War II, Soviet military policy in Eastern Europe, like Soviet economic policy, had as its chief aim the domination of occupied satellites and their exploitation for the unilateral purposes of the USSR. The aim was facilitated by a process of "sovietization" of the armed forces of the countries of Eastern Europe. All Western-oriented and anticommunist personnel were eliminated from offices of responsibility, Soviet officer cadres were introduced into critical positions far down into the chain of command, and local secret police elements were virtually fused with their Soviet counterpart to augment Stalin's control of puppet party elites.

When the Warsaw Treaty was concluded in 1955, there was no immediate change in the condition of the "sovietized" Eastern European armed forces. In fact, one author reports a number of demanding secret stipulations as part of the original treaty: Soviet troops to be assigned in Eastern European countries with the mission of preserving internal order; "host" governments to pay the expenses of maintenance for Soviet elements but to relinquish legal jurisdiction over them; and Soviet troops to remain by right in Eastern European countries other than Czechoslovakia and Bulgaria for a period of twenty years.[20] If, as we have argued, the WTO was established as a conscious political response to incorporation of West Germany into NATO, there is no reason to suppose any envisaged alteration in the master-satellite conception of the relationship between the USSR and the other members.

However, the national resentment of Soviet control which developed in Eastern Europe as a product of economic irrationality, popular disillusionment over Soviet professions, and Soviet vacillation in economic policy following Stalin's death apparently spilled over into new antagonism toward Soviet military dominance in the satellites.

When this hostility was catalyzed by de-Stalinization in the Soviet Union and burst into open revolt in both Poland and Hungary, Khrushchev found it expedient to change to more subtle means of military integration in Eastern Europe than that afforded by "sovietization." The WTO provided the alternative mode.

Between December 1956 and June 1957, new "status of forces" agreements were negotiated by the Soviet Union with Poland, East Germany, Romania, and Hungary which increased the authority of the satellites with respect to Soviet troops on their territories. Since this time, Soviet control has been steadily, if less obtrusively, maintained through the WTO command structure. The Political Consultative Committee reduced to a propaganda forum, command authority runs directly from the Soviet commander-in-chief down through the Eastern European ministers of defense to all of their respective military echelons. WTO missions are accredited to each member state except Poland, and these missions, reporting back to headquarters in Moscow, are, in effect, instruments of Soviet control to replace the old Soviet officer cadres in the respective armed forces.[21] In the event of war, current Soviet strategic thinking makes evident, this chain of command would be even less equivocal. All Warsaw Treaty forces would be under the direct command of the Supreme Headquarters of the Soviet Armed Forces.[22]

Let us now draw back in perspective and look at similarities and differences between COMECON and the WTO as integrating instruments for Soviet foreign policy among the party-states. It is clear, first of all, that neither organization was created consciously for the purpose it later came to serve. COMECON, as conceived in 1949, had the limited purpose of isolating Yugoslavia and establishing a matrix of bilateral satellite dependencies. The WTO was created in 1955 as a political response to the Western incorporation of the Federal German Republic into NATO. But, in subsequent years, as the old integrating mechanisms failed, both COMECON and the WTO provided alternatives for maintenance of Soviet control. COMECON offered in-depth institutional integration of economic decision-making and an authority pattern based upon consensus rather than coercion, thus appealing to economic rationality and, also, at least in the short run, to sentiments of national heterogeneity in Eastern Europe. Yet it permitted the Soviet Union recourse to economic coercion in the event consensus opposed her national aims. The WTO, on the other hand, after the crisis of the Hungarian revolution offered an alternative to "sovietization" of Eastern European armed forces that was less offensive to national sensibilities but retained a structural configuration of top-level institutional integration. Military coordination of the members of the WTO was still achieved by dictate of the Soviet commander-in-chief.

For two reasons, the top-level configuration of the WTO integrated structure was acceptable in Eastern Europe, whereas such a configuration for economic integration was unacceptable. First, military capabilities were more easily discerned from Moscow without low-level bureaucratic integration. Questions were less complex. Achievement of coordinated action in military matters was also less complicated because of the relatively fewer occasions demanding international military rather than economic coordination. Thus, an attempt to impose a joint economic five-year plan from Moscow (as was made in 1954) failed, but the imposition of a joint military readiness plan could succeed.[23]

Secondly, the comparative economic capacities of the Eastern European members of COMECON are such that they need not feel wholly dependent upon the USSR. While the USSR has an economic advantage which can be used coercively or as a lure, most of the other member-states are sufficiently developed economically and in possession of adequate resources so that they are not totally dependent. Thus, they can and do demand a share in the supranational decision-making which only institutional integration in depth can offer. The relative military capacities of Eastern Europe, given conditions of a nuclear age, have appeared so unbalanced in favor of the USSR that through the first decade of the WTO the Eastern European countries have been resigned to total dependence upon the USSR. The Soviet "nuclear umbrella" appeared desirable in the face of perceived "imperialist threat," and even when there may have developed some doubt about the virulence of the "imperialist threat" that Soviet "nuclear umbrella" has seemed inevitable. Hence, there was consent for the top-level institutional configuration of WTO integration during a decade in which consent for that kind of economic integration broke down.

COMECON, representing the goal of consensual, in-depth institutional integration, has, however, run into the obstacles of national reluctance to forego the old aspirations to autarchy. In the case of Albania, and, more clearly, in the present case of Romania, the carrot of economic prosperity has become insufficient lure for acceptance of the Soviet model of the future. We have already analyzed the origins of this stalemate.

As this comparison is drawn, reports from Eastern Europe show unmistakable evidence that nationalistic sentiments are threatening in a like fashion the authority base for the WTO. It is apparent that a conflict exists between Eastern European nationalism and top-level institutional integration through the Warsaw Treaty Organization. Consent has heretofore been maintained by perception of an outside threat ("imperialism"), combined with resignation to the fact of overwhelming Soviet military superiority. But, in 1965 and 1966, doubts crept into this rationale. The socialist-imperialist dichotomy no longer appears as simple. The "nuclear umbrella" seems to pose as much danger as security. Uncertainties in WTO military policy toward the West have been exposed by the Sino-Soviet conflict and the American war in Vietnam. Most of the same disintegrating forces that have beset NATO may, in fact, be observed at work among the members of the WTO.

Replacement of Joint Armed Forces Chief of Staff N. I. Batov by another Soviet general, M. I. Kazakov, in November 1965[24] may or may not reflect cross-pressures within the organization. Certainly, the outspoken challenges of Romanian Communist Party General Secretary Ceausescu to Soviet leadership in the WTO do. As early as the spring of 1964, Romanian objections to economic specialization in COMECON publicly spilled over to dissatisfaction with Soviet hegemony through the WTO. In disregard of her WTO obligations, Romania unilaterally reduced her armed forces from 240,000 to 200,000 and cut down the term of service for conscripts by one-third. Since his succession to the late Gheorghiu-Dej in March 1965, Ceausescu has repeatedly asserted Romanian opposition to all military blocs and to the stationing of troops at bases abroad. The report circulated in the spring of 1966 that Ceausescu had sent confidential notes to fellow Eastern European members of the WTO asking that consideration be given to changing the WTO statutes. Finally, in May 1966, Ceausescu challenged Soviet Party Secretary Brezhnev's call for a strengthened Warsaw Pact by delivering a strong speech to Romanian party elite calling military blocs and bases abroad "an anachronism incompatible with the independence and national sovereignty of the peoples and normal relations between states."[25] The speech immediately preceded a visit by Soviet General Party Secretary Brezhnev to Bucharest and probably occasioned his sharp criticism of Romania. Notably, no one else in Eastern Europe objected to Ceausescu's stand.

JOINT INSTITUTE FOR NUCLEAR RESEARCH

In the immediate postwar years, when the Soviet Union was hastening to match the challenge of Western possession of atomic weapons, the resources of nuclear material available in Eastern Europe were unsurprisingly commandeered to support that effort. "Joint-stock" companies, devices widely used at this time to implement Soviet economic control in Eastern Europe, were established to harness Eastern European capital and labor, under Soviet direction, to produce fissionable uranium for export to the USSR.

The uranium itself, even that emanating from the richer reserves in Czechoslovakia and East Germany, probably was secondary to the Soviet nuclear effort. For our purposes here, it is important to note that the effective Soviet monopoly on prospecting, extracting, and processing nuclear raw material gave the Soviet Union a total monopoly upon developmental applications of nuclear energy (in defense, industry, medicine) and gave her unchallenged leadership in all aspects of nuclear research as well. There were no obstacles to the total integration of all aspects of atomic energy. Of all the party-states, only the Soviet Union was significantly involved, and, because of its unmistakable military and political importance, the entire Soviet effort was tightly integrated at the highest echelon of authority.

Following Stalin's death and the establishment of some balance to the East-West nuclear weapons race, Soviet leadership sought to draw upon the scientific talent of Eastern Europe and to explore the peaceful potential of nuclear energy without losing the total integration which had heretofore existed through the policy of exclusiveness. In January 1955, the Soviet government announced that it would assist in organizing experimental centers outside the USSR for research into the peaceful uses of nuclear energy. The statement was addressed to China, East Germany, Poland, Romania, and Czechoslovakia; but the door was explicitly left open to inclusion of other interested states.[26] Over the subsequent five months, bilateral agreements to implement the January declaration were concluded with Romania, Czechoslovakia, Poland, China, Hungary, and East Germany, in that order. Yugoslavia followed in January 1956. In these agreements, the Soviet Union undertook to furnish each partner with an experimental atomic pile and cyclotron, necessary equipment and fissionable material, technical assistance, and technical and scientific documentation. Finally, the Soviet Union contracted to provide facilities for training scientific personnel from the partner states in Soviet scientific institutions.[27]

The cooperative behavior solicited through these Soviet-initiated bilateral agreements with other party-states was broadened in scope later in 1956 and 1957 to include industrial applications. Agreements with East Germany, Czechoslovakia, and Hungary provided for assistance to these states in construction of atomic power plants. Poland, in addition to a power plant, was promised a second atomic pile.[28]

By opening up an opportunity for other party-states to participate in development of the uses of atomic energy, the Soviet Union stood to benefit materially from employment of an enlarged pool of scientific talent. It might also benefit politically from the propaganda impact of shared nuclear technology. But, at the same time, the Soviet Union risked planting the seeds of eventual challenge to its nuclear leadership and control among the party-states. The Joint Institute for Nuclear Research was the Soviet response to the latter problem. The JINR reflected the Soviet effort to integrate the new field of atomic energy for the party-states and to assimilate it into the service of Soviet policy.

The JINR was created by a multilateral agreement (paralleling COMECON and the WTO) signed in Moscow on March 26, 1956 by all the party-states except North Vietnam.[29] Pursuant to this agreement, a first session of representatives from each signatory met in Dubna, near Moscow, the following September for a week-long initial convocation. Statutes were adopted to endow the Institute as a legal entity and establish its purpose to organize international research in the field of nuclear physics and the peaceful uses of atomic energy.[30]

The statutes provided that the Conference of Representatives Plenipotentiary should be the supreme organ of the Institute. The Conference would elect a director (three-year term) and two deputy directors (two-year terms), adopt amendments to the statutes as recommended by the director, approve the budget, admit new members, and hear reports by the director. Action was to be by a two-thirds vote, with each member represented equally. The director would preside over a Scientific Council, composed of three scholars designated by each member state charged with formulating work proposals for approval by the Conference. A Finance Commission, with membership designated by participating states, would apportion the assessments of members that would underwrite the Institute's activity.[31]

The first session of the Conference admitted the remaining party-state, North Vietnam, to the JINR, distinguishing the Institute from COMECON (in which Mongolia is the only non-European member) and the WTO (entirely European). Members are statutorily authorized to resign from the JINR by giving notice of intent three months before the end of a fiscal year. Thus far, none has done so publicly, but neither the Albanians nor Chinese were participating in 1966. Empowered to associate with other institutes and research organizations on the territory of member states, the center of JINR activity remains its laboratory complex (formerly operated by the Soviet Academy of Sciences) at Dubna.

Thus, in brief, we have the structure of the JINR. It is worth noting, with respect to authority, that Article 22 of the statutes explicitly states that "The Institute's directorate is guided in its activities only by the decisions of the Conference of Representatives Plenipotentiary and the

Scientific Council, and accepts no instructions whatsoever from single member states."[32] As Conference decisions are by a two-thirds vote, there is greater supranational authority and less Soviet control provided by the formal structure of the JINR than is the case in COMECON, and the contrast with the WTO is even greater.

How does the JINR compare with our other two institutions when the four indexes previously utilized are applied? In scope, it is narrowest of all in the mid-1960's. Proportionately far fewer decisions in the party-state system deal with peaceful uses of atomic energy than deal with military problems. An even smaller fraction must be envisaged when atomic energy decisions are compared with the totality of economic decisions within the purview of COMECON. But this assessment of the present should be qualified by noting that no field of human effort promises to ramify more rapidly than that of atomic energy. As a contributor to the *process,* as distinguished from the *condition,* of integration among the party-states, the JINR thus appears to possess importance disproportionate to its present role.

In formal depth and differentiation of decision-making role structure, the JINR more closely resembles COMECON than the WTO. It is technologically oriented, differentiated by scientific subdisciplines, and draws its information from the breadth of its membership rather than from a single political source as does the WTO. But today, in fact, residual Soviet leadership in all phases of nuclear research and continued Soviet control of available fissionable material (outside China) mean that most premises for decision are furnished by the USSR. The monopoly of fissionable material also means that, despite procedures which underline majority rule, the Soviet Union may exert a coercive leverage considerably more effective than it can in COMECON. Centralized training and research planning for the party-states, however, probably foster the creation of a highly integrated community of values.

Finally, the extent of integration within its narrow purview must be assessed as greater for the JINR than that of either the WTO or COMECON. Today it appears that this integration approaches 100 per cent.

CONCLUSIONS

Within each of the preceding two sections of this chapter we have drawn comparisons among our selected supranational institutions. In summary at this point, Figure 2–I relates the three to one another along continua for each of the four indexes of integration utilized:

What may we say on the basis of the exploratory comparisons we have made here about the achievement and potential of these three insti-

FIGURE 2–I. *Comparisons of COMECON, the WTO, and the JINR as Integrating Institutions (Spring, 1966)*

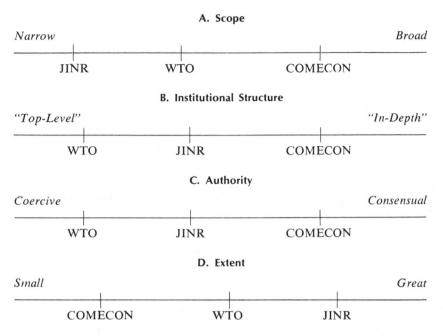

tutions as vehicles for integration of the party-states? Regarding achievement, we may observe that the WTO and JINR have been more effective within their purviews than has COMECON as presently organized. Drawing upon present knowledge, we may tentatively attribute this greater effectiveness to narrower scope or more coercive authority or both together. The authority base appears the more decisive of the two explanatory factors in these cases if we consider the relatively extensive economic integration achieved in Eastern Europe by Stalin through coercion.

When we consider the *condition* of integration as well as the *process,* however, we have grounds for suggesting that, while a coercive authority base has shown itself feasible for developing extensive integrated behavior (COMECON before 1956, and the WTO), it has shown itself weak for maintaining the integrated condition. The experience of COMECON shows that until a conscious effort was made to effect a consensual authority base, the integrated behavior achieved in the system came at the cost of steadily rising, explosive interstate tensions. The recent dissension in the WTO appears to confirm this experience of the economic sector.

Likewise, we can predict that an institutional structure unified only at the top level will, over time, be a liability to an integrated system. The recent difficulties COMECON has faced in moving toward greater integration leave open the question whether an institution delegating significant decision-making authority far down into a well-differentiated bureaucratic structure can be expected to enhance integration when confronted with the need to cope with conflicting values. But it is clear that both in COMECON before 1956 and in the WTO more recently, top-level structural unity has only exacerbated dissatisfactions among those members excluded from participation.

Finally, we put forward the following hypotheses suggested by these comparisons, which appear to warrant further empirical research as potential contributions to a theory of the process of international integration:

1. Coercively obtained supranational integration is self-defeating unless accompanied by a transformation of value conflict into consensus among the integrated units. Put more concisely, durable integration is consensual integration.

2. The narrower the substantive scope of activities to be integrated, the greater the prospect of successful integration of those activities.

3. Structural integration in depth is more compatible with the achievement of consensual integration than is structural integration only at the top level.

4. Integration of activities which must stand a test of rationality necessitates institutional integration in depth.

5. In the presence of expansible value conflicts among system units, coercive authority must supplement consensual to carry integration across a threshold of irreversibility.

NOTES

1. Other studies amply provide the details of structure and development of these institutions. I acknowledge my indebtedness and commend the reader seeking historical and legal description to Michael Kaser, *COMECON* (London: Oxford University Press, 1965); Andrzej Korbonski, "The Evolution of COMECON," *International Conciliation,* No. 549 (September 1964); Kazimierz Grzybowski, *The Socialist Commonwealth of Nations* (New Haven: Yale University Press, 1964); George Modelski, *Atomic Energy in the Communist Bloc* (Melbourne: Melbourne University Press, 1959); and Richard F. Staar, "The East European Alliance System," *United States Naval Institute Proceedings,* XC, No. 9 (September 1964), 26–39. For COMECON, I have also drawn freely on my "A Political Perspective of Economic Relations in the Communist Camp," *Western Political Quarterly,* XVII, No. 2 (June 1964), 294–316.

2. Particularly useful have been Karl Deutsch *et al., Political Community in the North Atlantic Area* (Princeton: Princeton University Press, 1957); Ernst B. Haas, "International Integration," *International Organization,* XV, No. 3 (Summer 1961), pp. 366–92; Leon N. Lindberg, *The Political Dynamics of European Integration* (Stanford: Stanford University Press, 1963); George Modelski, *The Communist International System* (Princeton: Woodrow Wilson School of Public and International Affairs, 1960); and Robert C. North, Howard E. Koch, Jr., and Dina A. Zinnes, "The Integrative Functions of Conflict," *Conflict Resolution,* IV, No. 3 (September 1960), 355–74.

3. North, Koch, and Zinnes, "Integrative Functions," p. 358.

4. See N. S. Khrushchev, "Vital Questions of the Development of the World Socialist System," *Problems of Peace and Socialism,* No. 9 (September 1962), pp. 2–18.

5. The whole body of literature on the phenomenon of "totalitarian democracy" might be cited here.

6. Haas, "International Integration," pp. 366–92. See Leon N. Lindberg. *The Political Dynamics of European Integration* (Stanford: Stanford University Press, 1963), pp. 10–11.

7. Khrushchev, "Vital Questions," pp. 2–11.

8. Reportedly, as many as 25 may have existed in the spring of 1964, according to Korbonski, "Evolution," pp. 22–23.

9. *Pravda,* June 17, 1962, pp. 3–4; V. I. Morosov, "Pravovye aspekty deiatel'nosti organov soveta ekonomicheskoi vzaimopomoshchi," *Sovetskoe gosudarstvo i pravo,* No. 10 (October 1961), pp. 146–55.

10. *Pravda,* June 17, 1962, pp. 3–4.

11. *Soviet News,* May 16, 1955, p. 1.

12. *Ibid.,* pp. 1–2.

13. *Ibid.,* p. 3.

14. Robert M. Slusser and Jan F. Triska, *A Calendar of Soviet Treaties, 1917–1957* (Stanford: Stanford University Press, 1959), p. 348; *Izvestiia,* January 29, 1956, p. 1.

15. *New Times* (Moscow), 1956, No. 6, pp. 33–36; see also *International Organization,* X, No. 2 (Spring 1956), p. 337.

16. "Contrasts Noted Between Two Pacts (NATO and Warsaw Pact)," *New York Times,* December 17, 1959, p. 3.

17. See Grzybowski, *Socialist Commonwealth,* pp. 199–203; Slusser and Triska, *Calendar,* p. 371.

18. *Pravda,* May 13, 1965, p. 3.

19. *Izvestiia,* September 22, 1964, p. 2, and October 22, 1965, p. 1.

20. Staar, "East European Alliance System," p. 30.

21. See Staar, "East European Alliance System," pp. 35–36.

22. V. D. Sokolovskii (ed.), *Soviet Military Strategy* (New York: Praeger, 1963), pp. 367–68.

23. The fact that the economic plan was put to test immediately and the military plan has been tested only by partial simulation may account for some of the contrast here. It is not really established whether or not such top-level military integration could succeed or not. It has been rather conclusively shown in Eastern Europe that such economic integration can not.

24. *Pravda,* November 24, 1965, p. 6.

25. Quoted by David Binder, "Ceausescu of Rumania, Man Battering at the Kremlin Wall," *New York Times Magazine,* May 29, 1966, p. 45.
26. *Pravda,* January 18, 1955, p. 1.
27. Slusser and Triska, *Calendar, passim.;* Grzybowski, *Socialist Commonwealth,* pp. 145–46.
28. Grzybowski, *Socialist Commonwealth,* p. 146.
29. *United Nations Treaty Series* (N. Y.: United Nations Secretariat, 1957), Vol. 259, pp. 125–43; Vol. 274, p. 377.
30. M. M. Lebedenko, "Ustav ob'edinennogo instituta iadernykh issledovanii," *Sovetskoe gosudarstvo i pravo,* No. 2 (February 1957), pp. 116–18.
31. The original agreement to set up the JINR contained a schedule of contributions which obligated the Soviet Union to pay 47.25 per cent of the total, China 20 per cent, and the other party-states radically lower amounts; Grzybowski, *Socialist Commonwealth,* p. 148. See also Modelski, *Atomic Energy,* pp. 134–38.
32. Quoted in Grzybowski, *Socialist Commonwealth,* p. 149. See Lebedenko, "Ustav . . .," p. 118.

THREE

A THEORETICAL APPROACH TO THE STUDY OF COMMUNIST INTERNATIONAL ORGANIZATIONS

R. J U D S O N M I T C H E L L

I. COMMUNIST INTERNATIONAL ORGANIZATIONS

The term "communist international organizations" is an anomaly. In Marxist theory, there is clearly no place for such a linkage of states in formal organizations; the "withering away of the state" makes antithetical the words "communist" and "international." If we use the word "communist" as merely the most convenient designation for the world Marxist-Leninist movement, rather than as a term including all the implications given to it in Marxist theory, we are still confronted with the basic question: Why should Marxist-Leninists unite for specific purposes on the basis of a combination of nation-states, the traditional form of coalition-building? "Communist international organizations" are organizations of states, not of parties.

Existence of communist international organizations surely can be attributed to political and economic exigencies and to the given presence of the nation-state form of political organization. However, it is perhaps significant that an attempt has been made by Marxist theorists to justify organization on a state basis, in terms of the prevailing stage of historical development. In *Foundations of Marxism-Leninism* (1959), edited by O. V. Kuusinen, cooperation by "communist" countries in international organizations is seen as preliminary to the eventual emergence of a single global commonwealth.[1] Furthermore, Khrushchev called for "perfecting the political and economic interrelations among the socialist countries" in order to move toward a "commonwealth of socialist states."[2] Given an ideological position in regard to these international organizations, the possible future evolution of new forms of communist organization cannot be discounted. However, the general tendency of the Soviet Union appears to be toward increasing coordination of the bloc on a national, rather than party, basis.

There are now seven "communist international organizations": the Council for Mutual Economic Assistance (COMECON), the Warsaw Treaty Organization (WTO), the Organization of Cooperation of the Socialist Countries (communications), the Joint Institute for Nuclear Research, the International Broadcasting Organization, the Organization for Collaboration of Railways, and the Danube Commission.[3] The Danube Commission appears to be an international organization set up along traditional lines, not devoted to specifically communist purposes.

These communist international bodies apparently have not yet realized the expectations aroused by their formation. Only COMECON appears to have become a major factor in bloc operations. However, it might be anticipated that the dynamics of the world communist system will require increasing organization across state boundaries. Stability and expansion of such a system demand not merely ideological and political cooperation, but also coordination of the component units on a functional basis to achieve specific objectives. If this be true, then the development of international organizations within the system is one of the more pressing objectives of the communist leadership and examination of their problems and prospects is essential for any appraisal of the system.

This paper is an attempt to develop a theoretical framework for study of these organizations. Since their formation involves the adherence of theoretically independent political units, they may be treated as political coalitions. While coalition theory may not be developed adequately enough to provide a completely acceptable model for the organizations of which we speak, at least it provides certain interesting suggestions which may be utilized for working hypotheses relating to the conditions of formation, growth, and equilibrium of communist international organizations. In section II, some basic postulates of coalition theory will be used to construct a model of organizational behavior. In section III, this model will be applied to COMECON.

Section IV deals with the possible applicability of Riker's two major concepts, the size and disequilibrium principles,[4] to study of the communist international organizations. Certain concepts of organization theory are utilized in sections V and VI for consideration of the organizational environment and internal structure and functions. Sections III and IV concern basic decision-making by the organizer in terms of rational maximization of gains. Sections V and VI treat the circumstances and processes of organizational maintenance and development and the focus of attention is placed upon the organization as a whole, rather than upon the organizer.

II. COALITIONS AND SIDE-PAYMENTS

The purposes sought by organizers in establishing coalitions are varied. Whatever these purposes, the major consideration for the organizer must be the maintenance within the coalition of his position of power, provisionally defined here as the ability to influence coalition decisions. Without the ability to influence decisions, the organizer can have no assurance that his posited coalition goals will be accepted. This power position requires adequate resources to meet the costs involved in goal-setting and goal-seeking. In this section, an attempt will be made to establish the limitations set by resource availability and utilization upon the strategy of the organizer.

Side-payments

Part of the costs for the organizer of a coalition involves his own direct expenditure of resources; part of the costs involves payments to others, payments made to induce them to join, or to remain in, the coalition. In the literature of coalition theory, the latter are referred to as "side-payments."[5] The organizer's willingness to make excessive side-payments in order to maintain his leadership appears in Riker's *The Theory of Political Coalitions* to be a crucial factor in disequilibrium tendencies inherent in coalitions.[6] Moreover, in the demonstration below, it will be seen that, entirely aside from the organizer's willingness to pay, a tendency toward disequilibrium is intrinsic to a situation requiring side-payments due to the quantitative relationship between the organizer's resources and costs and the other members' resources and costs.

Cost Limitations

Available resources and the goal desired set certain theoretical limits upon costs. The costs must exceed the available resources of the organizer, otherwise he will not organize a coalition. If the costs exceed the revenue anticipated from achievement of the goal, it will not be rational for any member of a potential coalition to organize. These limitations upon costs are shown in Table 3–1.

Resources available here are assumed to be the "working capital" of Riker's model. In an extremity, according to Riker, the organizer will even pay out his "fixed assets" in order to continue winning. It is unnecessary to take this possibility into consideration here, since the basic disadvantage of the organizer's position appears already at the stage where he pays out only working capital. Further, while profits are treated in the analysis below, the basic model of Table 3–1 does not include profit because there is no necessary connection between profits and the organizer's power position within the coalition, that is, profits might be divided in proportion to resources expended. However, it should be noted that if shares of profit are promised in advance and yields are not consistently high, the resulting pressures upon the organizer may be even greater than is the case with working capital.

A further basic assumption is that costs are measured in a common currency. "Side-payments" might include such items as military hardware, economic aid payments, tariff concessions, and technical assistance. Obviously, in a real situation, there would be problems of quantification and divisibility, particularly where some side-payments are intangible in nature.[7] However, in a theoretical demonstration, it seems necessary to presuppose a common currency in order to present the problem.[8]

Finally, the other members of the coalition are treated as a unit; it is assumed that the organizer bargains with them as a unit and that they have freedom of action. In Table 3–1, R represents the resources (working capital only) available to the organizer A for achievement of a particular goal. R_1 represents the resources available to other members N. The figures are selected randomly. It is submitted that forty units of resources are available to A, ten units are available to N. Column 1 shows all possible prices for goals between A's resources and total resources.

TABLE 3–1.   COALITION COST LIMITATIONS

Prices for V	Maximum side-payments by A* out of R, or maximum R_1 retained by N
41	9
42	8
43	7
44	6
45	5
46	4
47	3
48	2
49	1

* A=organizer. N=other members. V=resources required for a particular objective. R=resources available to A (working capital)=40. R_1=resources available to N (working capital)=10.

Column 2 shows maximum side-payments that can be made by A out of working capital if all resources of A and N are used.

If the goal costs 49 units, A can pay only one unit out of working capital in side-payments. Or, stating the case differently, N will be required to use nine units of its working capital for achievement of the goal. Its reward must come from profits. However, its percentage of profit is not unlimited, for A must secure at least some profit on his original investment of 40. If the goal costs 41 units, then A can pay up to nine units out of working capital; or, in other words, the minimum payment by N out of working capital is one. N may actually spend more than one; this is subject to bargaining between A and N. But N is definitely in a better bargaining position at 41 than at 49. Obviously, N's risk will be less for the less costly goal. A's risk may be less for the less costly goal, but his risks for the two goals are likely to approach equality, as N's favorable bargaining position at 41 makes it likely that it can force A to commit all or nearly all his available resources. Without N, there can be no achievement of goal, but, at 49, N faces limits upon its exactions from A not faced at the lower figure.

The result of a low-cost victory for N is that it is in a better position than before relative to A, since it has retained most of its working capital. Only a high-yield victory giving disproportionate profits to A could negate this and such a result is unlikely, since N's favorable bargaining position virtually assures it that A will not receive even a proportionate share of the profits. But if victory is achieved at high cost, then N is in a worse position than before, since it has sacrificed virtually all of its working capital. A victory with sufficient yield for N to better its position out of profits is unlikely, since A's revenue must be greater than forty. The lower the yield, the worse is N's position.

If these assumptions are correct, then, over time, a series of such low-cost victories could destroy A's position of power within the coalition. N's power would increase and, if domination of the coalition is a prime consideration for A, then it might be expected that the coalition would disintegrate. The maintenance of A's position of power would appear to depend upon a continuous series of high-cost and/or high-yield victories. However, in regard to high-cost victories, A is caught between Scylla and Charybdis, for it is in the area of higher cost that calculations must be most precise. Low-cost victories may erode A's position vis-à-vis N, but failure to achieve the costly victories may result in disaster—dissolution of the coalition due to non-achievement of goals. If high-cost goals are not achieved, the other coalition members might be expected to be more reluctant to continue than they would be if lower-cost goals were not achieved, due to their greater loss of resources.

Organizer's Strategy

On balance, it thus appears that N's position in the coalition is much more favorable than A's. A's position depends upon the ability to decide goals—and to do so rationally and virtually unerringly—and the ability to fix costs. Since the constant setting of high-cost goals is an extremely hazardous business, A can hardly expect to maintain his position in the long run by this strategy alone. But if the organizer can fix his side-payment costs by means that lie outside the scope of a free bargaining situation, then he might maintain his position indefinitely and even vastly increase his power vis-à-vis the other members. This might be done, for example, by isolating the other members for bargaining purposes. If the organizer is able to bargain with each of the other members individually, then his bargaining strength should be overwhelming. And the greater the organizer's strength vis-à-vis a particular member, the more can he utilize sanctions as negative side-payments, as, for example, a threat to stop delivery of raw materials by A to N. This strategy obviously is not always possible for a coalition organizer. It would appear to be feasible only where the organizer's resources place it in a clearly dominant position vis-à-vis the other members and where alternatives available to the other members are severely limited. Such a situation apparently existed in Eastern Europe for at least a decade after World War II.

Summary

The organizer's power position vis-à-vis other coalition members should be stronger following high-cost victories than low-cost victories, since high-cost victories require a greater contribution of resources, hence lower net gains, by the other members. However, high-cost goals involve greater risks for the system as a whole and thus pose a threat of coalition disintegration. If the organizer wishes to assure maintenance of his position, he must pursue other strategies that avoid the cost dilemma, for instance, isolating other coalition members for bargaining, thus maximizing his own bargaining advantage.

III. THE RECORD OF COMECON

The Council for Mutual Economic Assistance was set up informally in January 1949. Its members included the Soviet Union, East Germany, Poland, Czechoslovakia, Hungary, Romania, and Bulgaria, the same seven nations belonging to the Warsaw Treaty Organization, plus Mongolia.[9] Albania was a full member of the group until it sided with Red China in the Sino-Soviet dispute.[10] Yugoslavia was admitted as an affiliate member in September 1964.[11]

COMECON's history can be divided into four rather distinct periods corresponding to four definite phases of Soviet strategy: the Stalinist period of overt exploitation, 1949–1953; the early Khrushchev years, characterized by a Soviet strategy of bilateralism, 1954–1961; the time of attempted multilateralism and supranational integration, 1962–1963; and the period of strategic readjustment to meet tendencies toward disequilibrium in the coalition, starting in 1963.[12]

First Period

In its early years, COMECON was rather ineffectual and the Soviet Union continued its policy of exploiting the satellites to expedite Soviet economic recovery.[13] Up to 1954, there was no integration of the economies of members. All of the Eastern European countries, beginning in 1949, adopted long-term economic plans which largely duplicated each other. The plans emphasized iron, steel, and heavy machinery, regardless of natural resources.[14] During those years, the main role of COMECON was that of aiding in the preparation of bilateral long-term trade agreements among the members, designed to guarantee minimum supplies of basic materials needed for the separate national economic plans.[15]

Second Period

After his rise to power in the Soviet Union, Khrushchev was quite interested in the problem of economic consolidation of Eastern Europe and COMECON began to assume some organizational substance. However, it was not until April 13, 1960 that a formal charter for the organization (signed December 14, 1959) entered into force.[16]

The flow of economic payments during this second period indicates that the Soviet Union successfully followed the strategy outlined in the model, with reduction of side-payment costs through isolation of the other members for bargaining purposes. Although formal provisions for multilateral clearing had existed for years, the Soviet Union up to 1962 relied almost exclusively upon bilateral trade agreements with member countries.[17]

Measurable payments related to COMECON include trade transactions and economic aid. Payment in the form of economic aid is an obvious example of side-payments as defined in coalition theory. Trade transactions may also contain side-payments: Overpayments by the organizer to the other members would be a form of side-payment; overpayments by the other members to the organizer would constitute a "reverse side-payment," reducing the organizer's net outflow of payment.

Trade. Dr. Horst Mendershausen, an economist of the RAND Corporation has compared prices of commodities sold to, and purchased from, other COMECON countries by the Soviet Union with prices for such commodities prevailing in Soviet trade with Western Europe. He calculated that prima facie losses by other COMECON members between 1955 and 1958 amounted to the equivalent of $645 million.[18] Jan Wszelaki used the same basic data and concluded that net overpayment by the other seven COMECON members to the Soviet Union amounted to $104 million in 1957, $162 million in 1958, and $350 million in 1959.[19] Complaints by economists in the other COMECON countries indicate that this pattern of exploitation continued after 1959.

During the years 1949–1962, the Soviet Union was able to take advantage of the "cost-price" problem within COMECON. Considerable attention has been devoted recently to the subject of a common measure of production costs within COMECON; during the period in question such a measure was entirely lacking. Since prices were established on the basis of the bilateral agreements, the Soviet Union's superior bargaining power made possible pricing policies unfavorable to the other members.[20]

The Soviet Union's political and military power may have an important effect upon its bargaining position vis-à-vis the other COMECON members, but it is not necessary to attribute its favorable position during the second period to these considerations; its purely economic power alone could account for the leverage. The other COMECON members have been heavily dependent upon the Soviet Union for raw materials. While the Soviet Union would suffer greatly without Eastern Europe's machinery and manufactured goods, it is more self-sufficient than any of the other members; the cutting off of Soviet shipments of raw materials could destroy basic industries in Eastern Europe. The Soviet Union apparently took full advantage of its favorable bargaining position up to 1962. There were reported instances of open rejection by other members of Soviet proposals for COMECON production assignments.[21] But when countries demurred on their assigned roles, the Soviet Union threatened to stop deliveries of vital raw materials. Soviet use of this threat to check development of the Polish automobile industry is a case in point.[22]

Economic aid. Data on Soviet credits, loans, and grants indicate a substantial adjustment in the years 1956–1958. It appears that the increase in Soviet payments during these years was due primarily to political developments rather than specific economic problems. Between March 1956 and the end of 1958, Soviet credits to the other COMECON countries amounted to $1,440 million. In 1959–1960, new credits reached only $170 million,[23] indicating that the political crisis which presumably inspired the earlier credits had passed, and, with it, the leverage the other members could exert upon the organizer.

Comparison of payments during 1956–1958 with payments in earlier years yields further evidence to support the thesis that the unusual political developments in Eastern Europe in 1956 gave special bargaining advantages to certain members of the COMECON coalition. Between June 1949 and September 1956, Poland was granted $100 million in credit. Between September 1, 1956 and December 1, 1956, Poland was granted $300 million in credit and a debt amounting to $525 million was cancelled. Hungary was granted no Soviet credits, 1946–1956. Between October 1, 1956 and April 1, 1957, Hungary was granted $243.75 million in credit and a debt of $90 million was cancelled.[24]

Other COMECON countries shared in the large flow of credit, but none came close to the benefits received by the two countries most affected by the political disturbances of 1956. Furthermore, the only credits to East Germany prior to 1956 were granted in July 1953, at a time of serious political troubles in the German Democratic Republic.[25] Also in 1956, the Soviet Union, in accordance with COMECON plans for increasing ferrous metals production in Eastern Europe, agreed to supply the area in 1960 with twice the volume of its 1956 deliveries of high-grade iron ore, despite the likelihood that this would interfere with attainment of Soviet domestic targets.[26] This contrasts starkly with earlier Soviet practices; according to Imre Nagy, the Soviet leaders in 1954 agreed to supply only 36 per cent of the goods Hungary wanted to import from the Soviet Union.[27]

Since the only exceptional Soviet payments to the other COMECON countries followed immediately upon political crises, certain implications for the model are apparent. It appears that the other coalition members, bargaining bilaterally, could not overcome the organizer's favorable position with purely economic leverage. However, the presence of political crisis in a member country offering a potential threat to the organizer's political hegemony could be translated into pressures upon the organizer yielding economic returns. Such pressures, however, can reflect only a short-run strategy. The member's regime can hardly survive a sustained political crisis and, if the crisis is passed, the dominant organizer should be able to reassert its bargaining advantage. The Soviet Union was able to reassert its advantage and reduce its credit expenditures after 1957. Furthermore, if the calculations of Mendershausen and Wszelaki are correct, the Soviet Union recouped a substantial portion of its unusually large side-payments of 1956–1957 through overcharging and underpayment in trade.

Third Period

The major Soviet objective in COMECON during the Khrushchev era was to promote specialization and division of labor. Division of industrial labor among the members was expected to result in reduction of industrial costs and lower prices for industrial products. The Soviet Union would be the principal beneficiary of such reform. Without reducing prices of the basic goods it exported to Eastern Europe, the Soviet Union would be able to purchase industrial goods from the area at lower prices than previously.[28]

Beginning in 1962, the Soviet Union attempted to accomplish this objective through a reorganization of COMECON. The Soviet aim was that the executive committee become a supranational authority, capable of enforcing integration and specialization.[29] The Soviet Union was not able to secure full agreement on either the supranational authority or the broad aim of specialization. Romania refused outright to accept Soviet proposals on these matters and pursued its own plan for all-round economic development; among the other members (with the possible exception of East Germany) there appeared to be a general desire for greater freedom of choice than was offered in the Soviet scheme.[30]

The Soviet Union had changed its strategy in response to a new bargaining situation. Bilateral bargaining was no longer uniformly favorable to the organizer under conditions in which economic alternatives for some of the members, notably Romania, had increased markedly. Available alternatives were unevenly distributed among the other members; decisions of a supranational authority would be equally binding upon those members with many alternatives and those with few, and the Soviet Union would have the strongest voice in such decisions. Moreover, conflicts of interest between the more industrialized countries and the relatively undeveloped countries in COMECON[31] meant that the unity of action necessary to put upon the organizer the kind of stringent side-payment pressure indicated in the model of Section II would probably be lacking.

Fourth Period

The fourth period of COMECON history began in 1963, when the rule of unanimity was dropped and participation in COMECON projects was put on a voluntary basis. This marked the initial step in a Soviet retreat from Khrushchev's multilateral strategy. By the end of 1964, the new Soviet leadership apparently perceived a radical alteration in the relationship between the Soviet Union and other coalition members that called for major tactical readjustments.

This shift was due in part to political pressures generated by the Sino-Soviet split. Romania, in particular, was able to use the splintering of the communist bloc to assure greater freedom of action. At the same time, economic alternatives were opening for COMECON members in noncommunist areas. While Romania was the chief beneficiary of such alternatives, the new advantage was not confined exclusively to the Romanians; in the early 1960's, trade by COMECON members in general with noncommunist countries increased faster than did trade within COMECON.[32] Resistance to Soviet planning has been aggravated by the growing influence of Western technology upon Eastern economic, scientific, and technical cadres.[33] The fall of Khrushchev further weakened the Soviet position vis-à-vis the other COMECON members by indicating a measure of instability in Kremlin leadership. The new leadership would presumably be in no position to exert strong pressure upon other members of the coalition until it had consolidated its position at home.

Romania had consistently opposed proposals to convert COMECON into a supranational organization. It had refused to accept supranational control of joint enterprises and had insisted upon self-determination in its economic planning. Since 1964, it has pursued this independent course even more openly and strongly than before, refusing to participate in such COMECON projects as the Committee on Ball Bearings and Intermetall.[34] New Romanian party leader Nicolae Ceausescu, at the Romanian Party Congress in July 1965, declared that industrialization, especially in heavy industry, was indispensable to national independence and sovereignty.[35] This was in opposition to earlier Soviet propositions that would have sacrificed Romanian industrial development. Moreover, Romania has proposed an expansion of COMECON that would further weaken the position of the Soviet organizer. Under the Romanian plan, non-European communist party-states and even noncommunist countries would be admitted to COMECON.[36]

In the model of Section II, a free bargaining situation appeared as ultimately destructive for the organizer's dominant position, except in circumstances of consistently achieved high-cost and/or high-yield victories. Recent bilateral agreements and COMECON projects indicate that the Soviet Union is pursuing a high-cost goal strategy, that is, attempting to utilize the maximum of resources of other coalition members in trade and economic integration projects within COMECON, leaving minimal resources available for other economic alternatives.[37] However, the other members now possess alternatives not available during the first and second periods of COMECON history. Supranational integration has been favored unequivocally only by the Soviet Union; and, indeed, it appears that only the organizer would gain unmixed advantage from such integration. Since supranational integration has been ruled out, the only alternative available for the organizer has been a return to the earlier bilateral strategy, under much less favorable bargaining conditions. This has been the policy of the Brezhnev-Kosygin leadership—to secure the continuation and expansion of COMECON through such agreements, utilizing whatever advantages remain to the Soviet Union as the major political and economic power of the area. Essentially, it is a second-best approach, but the only feasible one under current conditions.[38]

The Soviet Union, in this new strategic phase, appears to be acting to some degree in the manner indicated for the organizer by Riker in *The Theory of Political Coalitions.* In Riker's model, winning is the only value and the organizer, under conditions of declining profits, will pay excessively in order to maintain the psychological and material advantages of maintaining his status as organizer of a winning coalition.[39] The ultimate result is disintegration of the coalition; the organizer pays himself into bankruptcy. No such outcome can be forecast at this point for the COMECON coalition.

Both Riker's theoretical formulation and the cost-price analysis presented in Section II of this paper are zero-sum, disequilibrium models; that is, winning or goal achievement means that the victorious coalition receives all gains, rather than mixed gains and losses, and operation of a coalition according to the model results ultimately in the coalition's disintegration. It appears that in the case of neither model are all the hypothesized conditions now fulfilled in COMECON. There is, however, a clear tendency toward realization of the conditions of both models. For example, the Soviet Union has consistently granted concessions to maintain the coalition. Some of these, at least, appear to correspond to the overpayments of Riker's model. The bilateral agreements covering the period up to 1970 reportedly have been based largely upon the internal economic requirements of other coalition members,[40] rather than upon Soviet requirements, as was generally the case in earlier years. Notably, the USSR has shown a willingness to increase iron ore exports at a probable sacrifice to its own domestic planning.[41] The Soviet Union has acquiesced com-

TABLE 3–2. SOVIET AID TO EASTERN EUROPE, 1945–1960

| | (in millions of dollars) | | |
	Total	1945–55	1956–60
Albania	162.0	105.5	56.5
Bulgaria	507.1	168.4	338.7
Czechoslovakia	46.5	33.0	13.5
East Germany	663.7	121.2	542.5
Hungary	375.7	37.5	338.2
Poland	887.8	577.8	300.0
Romania	172.5	80.0	92.5
	2,805.3	1,123.4	1,681.9

TABLE 3–3. SOVIET AID AND NATIONAL INVESTMENT, 1956–1960*

(in millions of rubles)

	Soviet loans and credits	Total state investment (gross)	Soviet loans and credits as % of state investment
Albania	226	2875	7.9
Bulgaria	1355	14842	9.1
Czechoslovakia	54	105510	.05
East Germany	2170	98930	2.2
Poland	1200	255967	0.5
Romania	370	59086	0.6
Hungary	1353	23655	5.7

* Computed by Stanislaw Skrzypek, "Soviet Aid: A Balance Sheet," *East Europe*, XI, No. 8 (August 1962), 4.

pletely in regard to Romania's plans for national economic development. In September 1965, Brezhnev conceded in a speech that establishment of a "perfect system of economic cooperation is a complicated matter which requires both time and care" and that it could not be "forced artificially." Further, he declared that the joint use of resources is a "strictly voluntary matter, decided entirely at the discretion of the countries concerned."[42]

Summary

Where possible, the Soviet Union has sought to pursue the rational strategy for the organizer as defined in the model—artificial lowering of costs through isolation of other coalition members in bargaining. When this policy was not feasible, the Soviet Union appears to have attempted maximization of goals, also in accordance with the model. However, Soviet behavior has also indicated a degree of hesitancy in formation of strategy that could be expected from an organizer facing the cost dilemma. The one constant appears to be the Soviet desire for continued leadership of the coalition and a willingness to pay whatever necessary to secure it, the motivation projected by Riker for the organizer in his basic model.

IV. THE SIZE AND DISEQUILIBRIUM PRINCIPLES AND THE DYNAMICS OF COALITIONS

Two principles developed by Riker deserve consideration here for their possible relevance to communist international organizations: the size principle and the disequilibrium principle. According to Riker, winning coalitions tend to be minimal winning coalitions; that is, they contain the smallest number of units that can achieve the coalition goal.[43] Additional members beyond minimal winning size are avoided, since their inclusion involves unnecessary payments. Such minimal winning coalitions tend toward disequilibrium due to the "bias toward decision-making" and the likelihood that the organizer will pay more than winning is objectively worth.[44] This means that: The coalition must act, that is, make decisions, or it ceases to have a *raison d'être* and disintegrates; the organizer must make some form of payment to the other members to induce them to act with him; these payments tend to be too large, since the organizer's desire for victory leads him to overpay rather than risk defections and losses; ultimately, the organizer spends himself into bankruptcy, that is, the strain upon his resources becomes so great that he can no longer organize a winning coalition.

Three Cases

Restriction of the two major communist international organizations to Eastern Europe until June 1962, and the admission at that time of the Mongolian People's Republic into COMECON, make the question of the possible operation of a "size principle" an intriguing one. If the reason for limitation of COMECON to its present membership is that side-payments to less developed bloc countries would exceed any resulting profits to the organizer, then we might be able to predict COMECON's rate of expansion on the basis of economic development statistics for the bloc countries. However, the entrance of Mongolia does not bear out this expectation; its potential economic contribution to COMECON is negligible.

Mongolia's admission appears rather to reflect Soviet use of COMECON as a weapon in its struggle against Red China. Since 1965, when China reportedly incited preparation of a coup in Mongolia, the anti-Chinese orientation of Soviet-Mongolian economic relations has been quite open and obvious, notably in regard to the five-year trade agreement which came into force in January 1966, providing for rapid expansion of Soviet-Mongolian trade.[45]

The cases of Yugoslavia and China also yield evidence that does not readily fit the size principle. Yugoslavia was long excluded from the various communist international organizations on ideological grounds. Its admission as an associate member of COMECON in 1964 was not due to its potential contribution toward specific COMECON goals; rather, the Soviet aim was evidently the prevention of counter-coalition formation. Developing links between Belgrade and Bucharest raised the threat of an economic bloc in the Balkans, led by Romania and Yugoslavia, and posed the ultimate possibility of disintegration of the COMECON coalition.[46]

China's admission to COMECON was considered likely in some quarters as of 1958; the subsequent Sino-Soviet split ended all speculation on this point. However, China's stated position on economic questions actually had precluded its entry into COMECON. As early as September 1956, at the Eighth Party Congress in Peking, Chou En-lai demanded that China set up a "complete industrial system," that is, an autarkic economy, not one designed as a specialized cog in the communist bloc's division of labor. He rejected the view that China could dispense with its own "independent and complete system of industry" and rely exclusively on international support.[47] There has been no reversal of this position since 1956. In the language of coalition theory, no Soviet goal nor any amount of Soviet side-payments was likely to induce China to join the COMECON coalition. In short, China's stand on economic autarky placed it outside the arena of coalition bargaining.

An additional complicating factor in consideration of the size principle is the fact that we are dealing not with one coalition, but with a series of coalitions. It is possible to treat the Soviet Union and the Eastern European countries as one coalition, with organizations such as COMECON and the WTO as mere forms for this coalition. However, since COMECON was organized to achieve certain goals distinct from other coalition goals, I think it must be treated as a separate coalition. Further, if we do treat each communist international organization as a separate coalition, is it logical to assume that each will be a "minimal winning coalition," particularly where membership of two or more coalitions is identical?

This raises the possibility that the organizer pays more in certain coalitions than winning is objectively worth, and less in others. For example, it may be important for country B to join coalition X, in which it would be superfluous for winning. Assume that it is important for the organizer, A, to keep B in coalition Y; A may do this by permitting B to join coalition X, where it would be superfluous. This involves a kind of reverse "side-payment": B's payment for admission to X is the renunciation of its threat to withdraw from Y. These considerations may have relevance for the cases of Mongolia and Yugoslavia. Mongolia may be viewed by the Soviets as part of an anti-Chinese coalition, whose goals are vastly different from those of COMECON; Yugoslavia may be seen as part of an Eastern European coalition opposed to the Western NATO coalition. Mongolia and Yugoslavia would then be necessary members of coalitions that overlap COMECON, in which these states would be superfluous, pushing COMECON above "minimal winning size."

If the organizer operates several coalitions at once, it seems most likely that one or more of them would be above minimal winning size, due to this difficulty of confining calculations to a single coalition. It also appears that the organizer would be more likely to pay too much to members of a minimal winning coalition where members' demands for payment are based partially upon contributions to other coalitions headed by the organizer than he would in a situation where calculations can be confined to a single coalition. If this line of reasoning is correct, then Riker's disequilibrium principle would apply with even greater force to overlapping coalitions than to single ones. However, the second period of COMECON history demonstrates that the disequilibrium principle does not always apply to a single communist international organization. Under certain conditions, a dominant organizer may refrain from paying more than winning is objectively worth and thus maintain his position within the coalition.

Summary

Riker's size principle does not appear to be entirely applicable to communist international organizations. Moreover, where coalitions led by a single organizer overlap, the size principle is unlikely to apply, due to the difficulty of confining calculations to a single coalition. The disequilibrium principle does not necessarily apply to a single communist international organization, since all the conditions of Riker's model are not fulfilled. However, disequilibrium is likely to occur in a system of overlapping coalitions, due to the likelihood of excessive costs in some parts of the system.

V. THE ORGANIZATIONAL MILIEU

Coalition theory has been emphasized in the preceding sections because it presents possibilities for developing concepts with explanatory power not found in more traditional organization theory. But general organization theory also has value for a study of political organizations; insofar as it deals with principles of growth, structure, and maintenance common to all organizations, use of such theory is necessary for an adequate study of formalized political coalitions. Coalition theory offers conceptual tools for explaining the strategy of political organizations, but, for the tactics, techniques, and mechanics of such organizations we must turn elsewhere.

Development of a conceptual scheme for study of organization growth, maintenance, and achievement requires attention to two aspects of the process of organization:

1. The circumstances and environmental conditions attendant upon organization—resources, expectations, perceptions, and alternatives of the units upon organization;

2. The structure and processes of interaction among the organized units—authority, decision-making, integration, specialization, and innovation.

First-order Values

Communist international organizations seem eminently suited to Parsons' categorization of organizations as subsystems within a larger social system.[48] The communist organizations appear in an environment largely determined by the existence of the communist system and it might be expected that perceptions and expectations of the unit decision-makers would be severely limited by this factor. Furthermore, it might be anticipated that these perceptions and expectations would be conditioned not only by the objective circumstances of the environment but also by the superordinate values of the larger system. Commitment by unit decision-makers to the "first-order values"[49] of the larger system would appear superficially to be a feature promoting integration and system maintenance.[50]

Conflict of Value-systems

Important and difficult questions arise, however, when we consider the relationship between "first-order values" and particular goals. To what extent are the superordinate values dysfunctional for subsystem maintenance and growth? It is conceivable that unit decision-makers may be faced with a choice among conflicting goals determined by (a) the superordinate value system; (b) a lower-order value system dictated by specific national interests; (c) a lower-order value system arising from their own unit organizational requirements for maintenance and control. If, in such circumstances, the unit decision-maker must accept unchanged the goals demanded by the superordinate value system, the result is a residue of unresolved conflict in the system.[51]

Resources

Availability of resources is perhaps an even more critical variable in organization maintenance and growth than is value agreement. There exist various possibilities for managing value agreement, but availability of resources sets absolute limitations upon goal realization. Establishment of any goal for an organization requires a degree of "organizational lag," that is, unutilized resources in the system.[52] Herein lie probably the best opportunities for prediction on a quantitative basis about the communist international organizations. While Soviet statistics can hardly be considered absolutely reliable, careful use of such data can yield more productive results than can purely impressionistic guesses about the system. Available resources may be compared with organizational goals to produce predictions about goal realization with an expectation of fair precision in setting outer limits. For example, a goal of increased trade turnover in agricultural products would be largely dependent upon the amount of machinery at hand in farm production; this, in turn, would be dependent upon the availability of iron, steel, rubber, and petroleum. All of these are subject to some degree of measurement.

Important also are the degrees of liquidity, convertibility, and mobility of resources.[53] These factors set limitations upon goal changing, innovation, and adaptation to environment. An important question in approaching communist international organizations is whether a Soviet-type economy, featuring hierarchical controls and the absence of a market mechanism, sets artificial barriers to resource utilization. It might be argued that the ambiguous, fluid quality of the Soviet middle bureaucratic structure would make easier decisions concerning conversion and movement of resources. There is, however, some evidence to the contrary. The bureaucracy's chronic insecurity apparently breeds clique-building among supposedly discrete lower units and this often leads to resource hoarding for lower-unit goal realization that is dysfunctional for the larger system.[54] The issues of liquidity, convertibility, and mobility of resources are, of course, much broader than indicated here, but the most essential point would seem to be the clear relationship between subsystem resource utilization and the management systems of the subunits.

The alternatives available to organization units represents a final principal determinant of the organization's environment. Availability of alternatives to the units is a major factor in bargaining over side-payments. The fewer and less desirable the alternatives available to the other units, the stronger is the organizer's position in the bargaining process. However, closure of alternatives by the organizer may force him to make important strategic adjustments. It appears that the creation of COMECON was made necessary, among other things, by the Soviet refusal to permit the other units to choose the alternative of the European Recovery Program. Given the existence of competing coalition systems, the pressure of competition from the more viable system (unless the competition takes the form of attempts to detach coalition units) should enhance integration and compliance in the less viable system and dominance by the organizer. It appears that the growth of the Common Market has had, at times, such an effect upon COMECON.[55]

Summary

Organization theory provides a conceptual basis for study of communist international organizations that supplements coalition theory. Important environmental aspects include: the relationship between first-order and lower-order value systems; availability, liquidity, convertibility, and mobility of resources; and alternatives available to the organizational units.

VI. THE ORGANIZATIONAL SYSTEM

Decision-making

Decision-making is of central importance in organizational maintenance and growth. The content of decisions, the process of decision-making, and the enforcement of decisions each form a vital link in the chain of organizational continuity. Decisions are basically of three general types: on ultimate goals, on allocation of resources, and on allocation of functions.[56] In our approach to decision-making in communist international organizations, it is essential to account for the close relationships among these different kinds of decisions. Insofar as the ultimate organizational goals are determined by the organizer and serve his interests, decisions on allocation of resources and allocation of functions must be geared to the organizer's interest in those ultimate goals. Therefore, changes in decisions on allocation of resources and allocation of functions should make it possible for us to deduce changes in ultimate goals where such changes are not expressly stated. Stated changes in ultimate goals would make it possible to predict subsequent changes in allocation of resources and allocation of functions.

The effect of decisions upon integration is determined by the three factors mentioned above: content, process, and enforcement. The content and enforcement of decisions may further integration even if the decision-making process leaves unresolved conflict in the system. For example, even if decisions in COMECON on the electric grid system and the Friendship Pipeline had left unresolved conflicts within the system, completion of these projects would lead to greater integration of the system under leadership of the organizer. Therefore, it is necessary to appraise the effect of the content of decisions upon subsequent relationships among the units.

Adaptation

The dynamic quality of an organization is crucially dependent upon its ability to adapt to changes in its environment, through goal changing and innovation.[57] Such changes are, in turn, heavily dependent upon the channels and processes of communication within the system, upon the feedback of accurate information concerning the effects of earlier decisions.[58] It might be expected that bifurcation of interests among the units in these communist organizations would not necessarily lead to formation of subcoalitions,[59] due to the dominant position of the organizer. But such bifurcation of interests might lead to gaps and distortions in the communication process upon which goal changing depends. The subunits may attempt to protect themselves against certain forms of sanction by feeding inaccurate and incomplete information to the decision-makers. The known prevalence of such dysfunctional feedback in the Soviet bureaucracy and diplomatic corps at various times indicates the opportunities for such a phenomenon in a communist subsystem. While it may be out of the question to adequately study the behavior of these communications systems directly, it might be possible to make useful deductions by comparing a series of organizational decisions with the apparent patterns of interest underlying the decisions.

Organization of Authority and Responsibility

The organization of authority and responsibility within the subsystem is an important determinant of the rate of achievement of goals and the degree of integration. In COMECON, there is no clear indication as to the binding character of specific organizational decisions and how such decisions can be enforced. Further, little is known about the structure of authority within the personnel forces. Does organizational authority supersede the authority of their own unit leadership for such personnel, now recognized as having an international character and status?[60]

It might be expected that authority relationships would change over time with increasing complexity of the organizational structure. It might also be anticipated that the increasing complexity of the organizational structure would lead to greater delegation of decision-making. The increasing role of the permanent commissions in COMECON might be studied in terms of two propositions advanced by Selznick: (1) Delegation tends to decrease the differentiation between organization goals and achievement, that is, goals are more often achieved; (2) delegation results in departmentalization and increase in bifurcation of interests among subunits.[61]

The effect of technical skills upon the hierarchical functioning of authority is another important question in the study of authority relationships within the organizations.[62] It is reasonable to assume that the needs for special technical competence in such organizations as COMECON and the Joint Institute for Nuclear Research would pose certain problems of control for the organizer. What is the effect, if any, of the high proportion of Czech personnel in the Institute upon Soviet control of that organization? Further, how does the pooling of technical skills contribute to the broader goal of integration?

Integration

Quantitative measurement of achievement of the broader goals of integration seems quite feasible. The following indicators can be utilized:

1. Statistics on trade turnover
2. Measurement of the degree of specialization

3. Measurement of the flow of bloc resources within and outside the coalition area
4. Measurement of the flow of unit personnel into common organizations
5. Measurement of changes in flow of communications

Insofar as the organizations are dominated by the organizer, such indexes may also be employed as rough gauges of the power of the organizer vis-à-vis the other units. Obviously, all these measurements would not be useful for all the organizations and other measurements might also be available. But at least they provide a starting point for quantitative appraisal of integration, which would seem to be one of the more important objectives in an intensive study of the communist system. Hopefully, use of such measurements will eventually make possible an overall index of integration for each organization.

Summary

A comprehensive model for study of the organizations requires attention also to the structure and functions of the organizational system. Major aspects of the organizational system include: decision-making, communication, the organization of authority, and processes of adaptation to environment and integration.

VII. COALITION THEORY AND ORGANIZATION THEORY: AN INTEGRATED FRAMEWORK

The basic thesis of this paper has been that in order to develop a comprehensive conceptual scheme for the study of communist international organizations it is necessary to integrate coalition theory and more traditional organization theory. An attempt was made to demonstrate the validity of coalition theory for the broad questions of organizational strategy. In our demonstration, it appeared that Riker's size and disequilibrium principles are not readily applicable to communist international organizations for the following reasons: (1) Ideological and other considerations are involved that transcend a particular coalition (we are really dealing with overlapping coalitions, hence the size principle is unlikely to apply to any single coalition); (2) the communist international organizations do not have a completely free bargaining situation, therefore tendencies toward disequilibrium may be checked by the organizer under certain conditions.

Despite these reservations, coalition theory does seem to offer conceptual formulations with explanatory power that cannot be disregarded. In Section II, a model was constructed based upon the concept of side-payments that offered a generally satisfactory explanation of the Soviet behavior outlined in Section III. Moreover, there appears to be a clear relationship between the free bargaining condition and applicability of Riker's model. When COMECON approached a condition of free bargaining (1956 and 1962 to the present), Soviet behavior resembled that of Riker's organizer and tendencies toward disequilibrium became clearly apparent.

While coalition theory appears to offer an incomplete model for communist international organizations, nonetheless all the basic concepts of this paper can be summarized in coalition theory terms. The traditional concerns of organization theory discussed in Sections V and VI relate ultimately to the two major aspects of coalition theory that were not treated fully in Sections II and IV: profits and information. Riker's coalition theory assumes perfect information for the full validity of its basic propositions; it says nothing about the means of achieving profits. The degree and quality of information and the rate of profit depend upon these environmental and systemic factors discussed in Sections V and VI. For these reasons, coalition theory must be supplemented with concepts drawn from organization theory in order to present a comprehensive model for communist international organizations. On the other hand, a model drawn only from organization theory would be equally incomplete, particularly in view of the potentialities of coalition theory in regard to predictability of behavior.

If it is true, as was postulated earlier, that formal organizations will become more important in the future operation of the world communist system, then it is not enough to comprehend the goals, structure, functions, and processes of present organizational mechanisms. We need also some basis for prediction about the future behavior of the communist international organizations. Certain possibilities for such prediction have been pointed out in this paper. I think it not unreasonable to assume that further accumulation of quantitative data, its organization under our basic concepts, and observation of quantitative changes through time will admit of useful predictions concerning the following:

1. Goal realization
2. Behavior of the organizer in making strategic choices
3. Behavior of the other units in making strategic choices
4. Rate of integration
5. Changes in allocation of resources and functions
6. Changes in distribution of economic and political power within the coalitions
7. Response by the organizations to major changes outside the subsystem

It is not claimed that we could make such predictions with even a close approximation to absolute accuracy. However, it seems beyond question that quantification and other behavioral study can yield predictions with far greater accuracy than any guesswork based upon impressionistic conclusions about the communist system.

NOTES

1. O. V. Kuuisinen, *Fundamentals of Marxism-Leninism* (Moscow: Foreign Language Publishing House, 1960), pp. 749–51, quoted in Z. B. Brzezinski, "The Organization of the Communist Camp," *World Politics,* XIII, No. 2 (January 1961), 208.

2. Marshall D. Shulman, "The Communist States and Western Integration," *Problems of Communism,* XII, No. 5 (September–October 1963), 54.

3. Brzezinski, "Organization," pp. 175–82; Jan F. Triska, "The World Communist System," Chap. 1 above.

4. William H. Riker, *The Theory of Political Coalitions* (New Haven: Yale University Press, 1962), pp. 46–47, 191–92, 210–11, 247–48.

5. *Ibid.,* pp. 105–23.

6. *Ibid.,* pp. 188–210.

7. *Ibid.,* pp. 106, 202–10.

8. *Ibid.,* pp. 19–20; see Anthony Downs, *An Economic Theory of Democracy* (New York: Harper and Row, 1957), pp. 36–37.

9. Ruth C. Lawson, *International Regional Organizations: Constitutional Foundations* (New York: Praeger, 1962), p. 210; Klaus Meynert, *Peking and Moscow* (New York: Putnam, 1963), p. 268.

10. See *Pravda,* December 17, 1961, p. 1; *Current Digest of the Soviet Press,* XII, No. 50 (January 19, 1962), 32; William E. Griffith, "Albania: Footnotes on a Conflict," II, *East Europe,* XI, No. 10 (October 1962), 18–24.

11. "Comecon Adopts Flexible Policy," *New York Times,* September 19, 1964, p. 3.

12. See David D. Finley, "A Political Perspective of Economic Relations in the Communist Camp," *Western Political Quarterly,* XVII, No. 2 (June 1964), 294–316; Harry Schwartz, *The Soviet Economy Since Stalin* (New York: J. B. Lippincott, 1965), pp. 218–31.

13. Robert S. Jaster, "CEMA's Influence on Soviet Politics in Eastern Europe," *World Politics,* XIV, No. 3 (April 1962), 508.

14. *East Europe,* VIII, No. 11 (November 1959), 5.

15. Nicholas Spulber, "The Soviet Bloc Foreign Trade System," in Morris Bornstein and Daniel R. Fusfeld (eds.), *The Soviet Economy: A Book of Readings* (Homewood: Richard D. Irwin, 1962), p. 303.

16. Lawson, *International Regional Organizations,* pp. 210–23.

17. Alec Nove, *The Soviet Economy* (New York: Praeger, 1961), p. 191.

18. Jan Wszelaki, "Economic Developments in East-Central Europe," *Orbis,* IV, No. 4 (Winter 1961), 439.
19. *Ibid.,* p. 440.
20. On the problems of cost measurement in a Soviet-type economy, see Robert W. Campbell, *Soviet Economic Power* (Boston: Houghton Mifflin, 1960), pp. 108–10; see also John S. Reshetar, Jr., *Problems of Analyzing and Predicting Soviet Behavior* (New York: Doubleday, 1955), p. 50, and Michael Gamarnikow, "The Future of Comecon," *East Europe,* XI, No. 6 (June 1962), 5.
21. Jaster, "CEMA's Influence," p. 513.
22. *East Europe,* VIII, No. 11 (November 1959), 10.
23. Wszelaki, "Economic Developments," p. 425.
24. Joseph S. Berliner, *Soviet Economic Aid* (New York: Praeger, 1962), pp. 53–55.
25. *Ibid.,* p. 52.
26. Jaster, "CEMA's Influence," p. 515.
27. Imre Nagy, *On Communism* (New York: Frederich A. Praeger, 1957), p. 190, quoted in Jaster, "CEMA's Influence," p. 515.
28. Wszelaki, "Economic Developments," p. 442.
29. Roman Zybenko, "The Economic Problems of COMECON Integration," *Studies on the Soviet Union,* II, No. 4 (November 1963), 60–70.
30. Michael Gamarnikow, "Comecon Today," *East Europe,* XIII, No. 3 (March 1964), 2–9.
31. See George Kemeny, "Economic Integration in the Soviet Bloc," *Problems of Communism,* XIII, No. 5 (September–October 1964), 70–76.
32. Paul Underwood, "Comecon Defers Reform in Prices," *New York Times,* January 21, 1964, p. 8.
33. J. F. Brown, "East Europe: The Soviet Grip Loosens," *Survey,* No. 57 (October 1965), pp. 14–25; see Klaus Meynert, "Westwind über Osteuropa," *Ost Europa,* XVI, No. 1 (1966), 3–17.
34. *New York Times,* January 2, 1965, p. 1.
35. *Washington Post,* July 20, 1965, p. A–18.
36. "Rumania Wants Free Nations in Red Trade Bloc," *Washington Post,* July 8, 1964, p. A–7.
37. See East Berlin *Neues Deutschland,* January 26, 1966, p. 1; V. Isupov, B. Ladygin, and V. Terekhov, "Economic Development of the CEMA Countries at the Present Stage," *World Marxist Review,* IX, No. 1 (January 1966), 40–47; *New Times,* No. 6 (February 9, 1966), pp. 3–5.
38. Lajos Lederer, "Russia and Satellites Make a Deal," *Observer,* December 12, 1965, p. 6; see "Abschluss der Comecon-Tagung in Moskau: Tendenz zum Bilateralismus innerhalb des Ostblocks," *Neue Zürcher Zeitung,* July 20, 1964, p. 2.
39. Riker, *Political Coalitions,* pp. 203–10.
40. Lederer, "Russia and Satellites," p. 6.
41. Kemeny, "Economic Integration," p. 74.
42. Victor Zorza, "Reorganization Plan for Warsaw Pact," *Manchester Guardian,* September 16, 1965, p. 8.
43. Riker, *Political Coalitions,* pp. 47, 247–48.
44. *Ibid.,* pp. 191–92, 211–15.
45. Tass dispatch, Moscow Radio broadcast in English, January 17, 1966.
46. Brown, "East Europe," pp. 22–24.

47. Meynert, *Peking and Moscow,* p. 303.
48. Talcott Parsons, "Suggestions for a Sociological Approach to the Theory of Organizations—I," *Administrative Science Quarterly,* I (June 1956), 66–67.
49. Karl Deutsch, *The Nerves of Government* (Glencoe: The Free Press, 1963), p. 241.
50. See Amitai Etzioni, *A Comparative Analysis of Complex Organizations* (Glencoe: The Free Press, 1961), pp. 129–30.
51. Robert C. North, Howard E. Koch, and Dina Zinnes, "The Integrative Functions of Conflict," *Conflict Resolution,* IV (September 1960), 355–72.
52. R. M. Cyert and J. G. March, "A Behavioral Theory of Organizational Objectives," in Mason Haire (ed.), *Modern Organization Theory* (New York: Wiley, 1959), p. 86.
53. See Parsons, "Suggestions," pp. 69–74.
54. Merle Fainsod, *How Russia is Ruled* (rev. ed.; Cambridge, Mass.: Harvard University Press, 1963), pp. 419–21; Howard R. Swearer, "Khrushchev's Revolution in Industrial Management," *World Politics,* XII, No. 1 (October 1959), 51.
55. Shulman, "The Communist States," p. 53.
56. Cyert and March, "A Behavioral Theory," p. 82; James G. March and Herbert A. Simon, *Organizations* (New York: Wiley, 1958), pp. 122–24.
57. March and Simon, *Organizations,* pp. 129, 182–85.
58. See Deutsch, *Nerves,* pp. 129, 182–85.
59. See March and Simon, *Organizations,* p. 42.
60. Wszelaki, "Economic Developments," p. 450.
61. Quoted by March and Simon, *Organizations,* p. 41.
62. Robert Presthus, "Toward a Theory of Organizational Behavior," *Administrative Science Quarterly,* III (June 1958), 58.

FOUR

PROCESSES OF INTERACTION AMONG THE FOURTEEN COMMUNIST PARTY-STATES: AN EXPLORATORY ESSAY

EDWARD L. MILES
JOHN S. GILLOOLY

INTRODUCTION

In this chapter, we proceed on the assumption, agreed to and supported by several scholars,[1] that the fourteen nation-states in the world today in which communist parties are the ruling entities constitute a system. By "system," we mean that there are particular modes of patterned activity or interaction occurring within and among these communist party-states which tend to distinguish them from other systems in the international arena as a whole.

We assume, also, that not all types of interaction result in continued coordination and cohesion within the system; not all interaction is integrative. Our purpose, then, is to collect and analyze the empirical data relevant to patterns of interaction in all areas of activity within the system and to attempt to determine the effects of differing types and frequencies of interaction on the integration of the system itself. In following this approach, we postulate that integration as a process can fruitfully be studied both interactionally and comparatively; in other words, in terms of the effects of interaction on the participating units and on the system as a whole.[2] It would seem ideal, therefore, to conduct such an investigation on these two levels of analysis simultaneously.

Unfortunately, limitations of time and space do not allow us to proceed with a comparative analysis, but we have categorized four broad types of indexes of interaction which we think are particularly pertinent to such a study and which are likely to provide reliable guidelines for further research. These broad categories we call economic indexes of interaction, social-cultural-technical indexes of interaction, treaties and treaty-making as indexes of interaction, and political-military-diplomatic indexes of interaction. There has been no attempt to rank these indexes in order of importance; such an ordering will have to await the comparative analysis.

ECONOMIC INDEXES OF INTERACTION[3]

In approaching the investigation of this category, we thought we would, first, examine the pattern of trade and aid within the system between 1953 and 1962; and then attempt to determine whether there was a theory of economic development for the entire system which provided, or now provides, guidelines for economic interaction. If there were such a theory, we would next try to determine what conflicts emerge from the incompatibility between setting and adhering to national goals while at the same time achieving system goals. As we expected, the data available pertained more to the Eastern European than to the Asian members of the system.

If we begin with the Eastern European subsystem,[4] we find that for the six years from 1957 to 1962, the percentage of Albania's trade with the system as a whole was always more than 94% of her total trade, except for 1962, when it dropped sharply to 58.98%.[5] The Eastern European area, however, accounted for 93% of Albania's trade until 1960, when it declined to 89.2% and from that to 6.99% in 1962. Significantly, Albanian trade with the Asian area, particularly with China, rose from 2.7% in 1957 to 51.99% in 1962. In 1963, China accounted for 60% of Albanian trade,[6] while trade with the Soviet Union declined from 54.9% in 1957 to .03% in 1962. If we take into account compacts signed by the Albanians in 1963, we find that they have entered into long-term trade agreements (for five years) with all system members except the Soviet Union and that there will be a substantial increase in trade with East Germany.[7]

The Bulgarian case presents no such variations. During the years 1952–1962, Bulgaria's trade with the system as a whole never dropped below 82%, while Eastern Europe accounted for never less than 80% of the total. The Asian area, in its best year of trade with Bulgaria (1958), claimed only 2.6%. The Soviet Union, on the other hand, never accounted for less than 46.2% of Bulgaria's total trade.

Between 1956 and 1959, Czechoslovakia, after Yugoslavia and Poland, did more trade with non-system countries than did any of the other party-states, but the system still claimed between 64.4% and 72% of her total trade.[8] Dealings with Eastern Europe represented between 58.9% and 64.59% of her total trade; and, in commerce with Asia, she ranked third, after the Soviet Union and East Germany (5.0% to 8.12%). Significantly, as in the case of Poland, transactions with the Soviet Union varied between 31.8% and 36.01% The pattern exhibited between the years 1960 and 1963 tells a different story. During this time, not only did Czechoslovakia's trade with Asia drop drastically (from 6.40% in 1960 to .68% in 1963), presumably as a result of the Sino-Soviet rift, but also her total trade with the system rose to 69.73% in 1961 and 74.19% in 1962. The Eastern European subsystem, of course, claimed the largest share of this, but even the percentage of trade with the USSR continued to increase, from 34.42% in 1960 to 38.92% in 1962.

Hungary maintained a 68–75% pattern with Eastern Europe in its total trade between 1953 and 1963; the only exceptions occured in 1955 and 1956, when figures dropped to 60.2% and 61.4% respectively. In 1957, dealings were on the rise once more, with 69.3% of Hungary's trade going to Eastern Europe. Hungary's commerce with Asia never rose above 7.2% (1958), while the Soviet share varied between 22.0% in 1955 (and 23.4% in 1956) and 35.9% in 1962. Hungary's other major trading partners within the system seemed to be Czechoslovakia and East Germany. Trade with non-system countries, on the other hand, appears to have been rising since 1960.[9]

East Germany itself, however, displays some interesting characteristics. Its trade with Eastern Europe varied between 79.7% (1954) and 64.2% (1955) of its total, while the Soviet Union accounted for 50.5% (1954) to 38.2% (1955). In its trade with the Asian subsystem, East Germany maintained the highest percentage after the Soviet Union; in 1954, it was 8.5% and, in 1955, it was 7.8%. In 1961, however, it dropped to 2.5%, and to .95% in 1963.[10]

Poland, like Yugoslavia, exhibits a pattern of trading as much or more with Western Europe and the United States (37.6% in 1954 and 26.2% in 1958) as with the Soviet Union. Unlike Yugoslavia, however, the greater part of Poland's trade is still with the system: from 57.2% in 1954 to 65.08% in 1963. Of course, the Eastern European area accounts for most of her total commerce (from 53.4% in 1954 to 63.79% in 1963), while the Asian portion is extremely small and has even declined (from 3.8% in 1954, to 5.1% in 1958, to 1.29% in 1963). Poland's major trading partners within the system, not including the Soviet Union, are, like Hungary, Czechoslovakia, and East Germany.

Romania, at the moment, seems to be undergoing some transformation in its trade patterns, such that the share of the Asian members, Western Europe (particularly France), and the United States (maybe least of all) in Romania's total is likely to increase.[11] But between 1958 and 1963, the pattern exhibited was a stable one. Trade with the system as a whole varied from 73.2% in 1958 to 67.0% in 1962; of the total, Eastern

Europe accounted for 72.7% to 65.7%, and the Soviet Union, 51.4% to 40.5%. Transactions with Asia were insignificant, varying from .5% in 1958 to 2.55% in 1963.

The USSR from 1955 to 1963 varied, in its total trade from 79.2% with the system in 1955 to 75.8% in 1962, to 70.38% in 1963. Eastern Europe accounted for 53.9% in 1955 and 66.9% in 1962. Asia's share, however, declined from 25.3% of the total in 1955 to 7.18% in 1963. East Germany, Czechoslovakia, and Poland, in that order, seem to be the Soviet Union's major trading partners within the system.

In economic terms, generally, Yugoslavia cannot be considered a strong member of the system. Most of her trade is carried on with the United States and Western Europe. Of her total trade from 1954 to 1963, the system accounted for 11.4% in 1954, 28.7% in 1958, and 22.8% in 1962; and almost all of this trade was with the East European area. There is now (May 1966) almost no trade with Asian members (.01%), while trade with the Soviet Union varied from .4% in 1954, to 9.0% in 1959, to 8.57% in 1963. It must be remembered, too, that Yugoslavia is not a member of the Council for Mutual Economic Assistance (COMECON), although she has recently been granted observer status.

Cuba certainly represents a rather interesting case study within the communist system. Like Mongolia, she clusters with the Eastern European subsystem on all indexes, and this is most pronounced in the case of trade. For instance, Cuban trade with the system went up from 1.66% in 1959 to 83.24% in 1962. Currently (1963), it stands at 75.56%. From 1.59% in 1959, the Eastern European share in Cuba's total commerce increased to 72.10% in 1961 and, in 1963, stood at 63.60%. Oddly enough, her trade with Asia (that is, China and North Korea) rose from .06% in 1959 to 15.37% in 1962; this means that Cuba did more relative trade with the Asian subsystem than any other member (Albania being classified here as a member of the Asian subsystem). In 1963, however, Cuban trade with Asian members dropped to 11.96% and, as a result of Cuba's break with China in 1966, one would expect to see a further drastic fall in the percentage of trade interaction. Not surprisingly, Cuban trade with the Soviet Union has increased from .96% in 1959 to 49.30% in 1962. In 1963, though, it dropped to 44.28%.

It is almost impossible to present any coherent data on Asian trade with Eastern Europe because no complete sources are available. Professor A. Doak Barnett, however, estimates that, in 1950, China's trade with the system amounted to 33.48% of her total trade, and that this progressed to 78.8% in 1952, to 82% in 1955, and to 75.3% in 1956.[12] Barnett also cites Soviet figures which show that, in 1956, China ranked first among Soviet trading partners, coming ahead of East Germany and Czechoslovakia.[13] This is in accord with the statistics provided by the United Nations

Secretariat. Since 1956, however, Chinese trade with the Soviet Union has steadily declined. Finally, Barnett quotes the Chinese assertion in 1959 that 1958 trade with the Soviet Union constituted a little over 40% of China's total, as compared with the previous 50%.[14] It is said that East Germany and Poland rank second and third respectively among China's trading partners.

We might, at this point, attempt to compare these estimates with data provided by the *United Nations Statistical Yearbook* for 1959, 1960, and 1963.[15] These statistics, however, relate only to world exports by provenance and destination. They are given for China from 1956 to 1958 and for the Asian subsystem from 1959 to 1962. In terms of Chinese exports, 62.1% in 1956 went to the USSR (47.8%) and Eastern Europe (14.3%), exclusive of Yugoslavia; in 1957, the distribution was 62.5% (47.4 plus 15.1); and, in 1958, 64.3% (50.5 plus 13.8). Here we have, in fact, the Eastern European share declining while that of the Soviet Union increases. If we take the Asian subsystem as a whole, the breakdown is as follows:

Year	System	USSR	Eastern Europe (excluding Yugoslavia)
1959	70.6%	54.7%	15.9%
1960	66.6%	49.0%	17.6%
1961	60.8%	47.0%	13.8%
1962	56.2%	46.0%	10.2%

Again, there is a rather large gap between the Soviet and Eastern European shares; and, even though both declined, the latter share has declined more rapidly than the former.

These figures, of course, are insufficient to support any conclusions; it seems that much more systematic research needs to be done before any definite statements can be made regarding Chinese and Asian trade patterns. We do think, however, that, in terms of trade, there seem to be two subsystems within the communist system.[16] Furthermore, within the Eastern European subsystem, there appears to be an inner clique of the industrially more advanced members: the Soviet Union, East Germany, Czechoslovakia, and Poland. On the criterion of trade relations, at least, it is doubtful whether Yugoslavia is in the system, particularly as far as the East Germans and the Asians (especially the Chinese) are concerned.

Aid-giving, as well as trade, is an important indicator of economic interaction within the system. The evidence suggests that aid in the form of outright grants is not very popular in Soviet policy.[17] The emphasis, instead, is on an extensive program of technical assistance, supplemented by the granting of loans (usually for ten years at the rate of two per cent interest per annum) and credits. It is, therefore, rather difficult to estimate in absolute figures what the Soviet aid program amounts to. The Chinese, however, appear to use outright grants to the other Asian party-states as political levers in their confrontation with the Soviet Union.

In Eastern Europe, the Soviet Union in her aid practices seems to rely heavily on technical collaboration with the more industrially advanced members though, since 1958 especially, she has paid much more attention, in terms of technical assistance agreements, to the less developed members. This also includes Cuba, which since 1961–1962 has been the recipient of ten technical assistance agreements and at least one equivalent of a grant in the form of the free transfer of Soviet fishing equipment. Surprisingly, however, Poland has also done extremely well in receiving technical assistance from the USSR. As far as industrial import-export patterns are concerned, it has been reported that Eastern Europe is heavily engaged in exchanging fuel and raw materials for manufactured products with the Soviet Union.[18] Soviet imports of machinery and equipment are also significant for the East Europeans; these increased from 660 million rubles in 1955 to 1,459 million in 1962.[19]

Concerning Soviet aid to China, Professor Barnett has said that, on the basis of the public record, the Chinese have never received a single outright grant from the Soviets.[20] The Chinese, however, have remained heavily dependent on the system (that is, the Soviet Union, East Germany, Czechoslovakia, and Poland) for equipment and supplies for industrial development and for technical assistance. Barnett also states that China has given substantial aid to the Asian members and some aid even to Albania and Hungary. China is reported to have given grants of about $388 million to North Korea and North Vietnam and $40 million to Outer Mongolia; these were in addition to an important program of technical assistance, two long-term credits to North Korea, and a long-term loan of $25 million to Outer Mongolia.[21] In fact, in terms of loans and grants, another author estimates that between 1947 and 1961 Mongolia has received a hundred-million-ruble ($25 million) grant and 1,715 million rubles (about $429 million) in loans from the Soviet Union and a 160-million-ruble ($40 million) grant and 300 million rubles ($75 million) in loans from China.[22] Since 1962, also, Mongolia is the only Asian party-state holding membership in COMECON.

As far as aid to North Vietnam is concerned, it seems that China is predominant in the area. Professor Bernard Fall has cited Lê Thanh Nghi, the Minister for Heavy Industry in North Vietnam, as having said that, between 1955 and 1961, North Vietnam received more than one billion dollars in aid from the communist system.[23] Of this amount, the Soviet Union is said to have supplied $365 million, Eastern Europe $38 million, and China $662 million.[24]

We do not have any comparative figures for North Korea,[25] but

Professor Glenn Paige has estimated that 33.4% of North Korean state revenue in 1954 was provided by foreign aid; this had dropped to 4.5% by 1958.[26] At the same time, North Korean trade with the Soviet Union in 1955 represented 80.8% of all its international transactions, but this declined to 57.0% in 1957. But by 1957, China had garnered 27.3% of North Korea's foreign trade, as compared with 9.0% in 1955.[27]

At the moment, there is no one theory of economic development which is accepted by all members of the system. Indeed, the Chinese berate the Soviets for aiding "nonsocialist" nations so generously while they neglect the more backward members of the "socialist camp"; the Soviet Union, East Germany, and Czechoslovakia espouse an approach which seems to aim at facilitating their own industrial development. This, in turn, is opposed by the Romanians and, to some extent, the Hungarians, on the ground that such an approach is not relevant for their own particular needs.

The Soviets call for the development of supranational planning within COMECON under the slogan of the "international socialist division of labor," through which, it is alleged, they hope to promote economic interdependence and political unity.[28] To this end, the Soviets have recently set up a series of intergovernmental commissions for economic and scientific-technical development.[29] The Romanians, in opposition to the Russians, feel that if they accept this plan, their own industrial development will be limited, and they engage in polemics on the matter in the press and on the radio with the Russians, the East Germans, and the Czechs. Hungary, however, feels that a "swifter solution" can be found through bilateral, rather than multilateral, negotiations, treaties, and planning.[30]

The fact that there is neither general agreement on criteria for economic development nor consensus on the means to be employed suggests to us a lack of economic unity within the system. We would submit further that the absence of substantive supranational planning that would lead to the continuous upgrading of system-interests as a whole is a primary indicator that the system does not now possess substantial economic integration.[31] Moreover, we think that the effect of the present pattern of trade and aid within the system as a whole, if continued without supranational planning and development, will serve to widen the emerging cleavage into two subsystems, led by the Soviet Union and China respectively. This assertion is based on evidence showing that Bulgaria and Outer Mongolia conduct more than 50% of their total trade with the Soviet Union; that Cuba, East Germany, and Romania maintain a 40–50% ratio; and that Czechoslovakia, Hungary, Poland, and Yugoslavia all exhibit a pattern of under 40%. China has succeeded in obtaining more than 50% of the total trade of Albania (since 1962) and North Vietnam. North Korea seems to maintain a 40–50% balance between China and the Soviet Union.

In the area of aid-giving, also, the emerging boundaries are comparable. The Soviet Union is engaged to a greater degree with the members of the Eastern European subsystem, which now includes Cuba and Outer Mongolia. And the Chinese have given substantial amounts of aid mainly to the members of the Asian subsystem. The fact that China has assisted Outer Mongolia is probably a manifestation of her challenge to the predominance of the Soviet Union in the area.

The broad pattern of trade between 1953 and 1962 serves also to delineate the boundaries of the system as a whole vis-à-vis the larger international arena. All system-members, except Yugoslavia, conduct 50% of their trade within the system. The rank order of members in terms of percentage of total trade with the system is as follows:

Rank	System-Members	Percentage
1	Albania, Bulgaria, Mongolia, North Korea, North Vietnam	80–95
6	China, East Germany, Soviet Union	70–80
9	Cuba, Czechoslovakia, Hungary, Romania	60–75
13	Poland	50–65
14	Yugoslavia	11–29

SOCIAL-CULTURAL-TECHNICAL INDEXES OF INTERACTION

It is almost a commonplace in the literature concerning the communist system to find statements referring to the similarity of outlook or the communality of values existing within and between member countries. This, however, does not take into account what now appears to be the dysfunctionality of the ideology itself, at least at the highest levels of policy formulation.[32] But this dysfunctionality constitutes a paradoxical situation, since the whole trend of cultural relations within the system from the early 1950's seems to have been deliberately designed to nurture the development of value-sharing capacities. Thus, the problem posed for a study of interaction on this level seemed to us to involve a systematic investigation of educational programs, student and curricula exchange, artistic and technical exchange, patterns of travel, tourist exchange, and their various effects.

We found that the framework within which interaction takes place on this level is very elaborate. It is broadly defined by a network of bilateral agreements among the member countries and supplemented by cooperation between national academies of science, friendship societies, and special functionally-integrative organizations, such as intrasystem conferences of economists, ministers of communication, and, among other things, cooperative bodies in various specialized fields of industry.[33]

The greatest emphasis in these programs of cultural interaction is placed on education, apparently perceived to be the most important means of inculcating common value-systems. The clearest statements relating to the purpose of cultural exchange may be found in the bilateral treaties (in which the terminology employed is very similar in all cases). For instance, the preamble of the Treaty on Cultural Cooperation between Poland and China, signed April 3, 1951, reads:

> The Government of the Polish Republic and the Central People's Gov-
> ernment of the People's Republic of China,
>   Desiring to develop closer ties of friendship between the peoples of
> the two democratic countries, which have a common political, eco-
> nomic, social, and cultural ideology,
>   *Convinced that one of the most effective means towards the achieve-
> ment of this aim is cultural cooperation between the two countries,*
>   Have decided to conclude this Agreement [our italics] ....[34]

The norms of cooperative behavior as stipulated by the treaties are also very similar. The Treaty on Cultural Cooperation between Albania and Poland, signed December 2, 1950,[35] provides an excellent example of the relations carried on. Both parties agree to promote and encourage co-operation between institutions (Article I); to direct the appropriate faculties of their institutions of higher learning to introduce into their cur-ricula lectures on the history, geography, literature, and economic sciences of the other party and to encourage the study of the Polish language in Albania and of the Albanian language in Poland (Article II);[36] to facili-tate translations and publications of books, newspapers, and periodicals (Article III); and to cooperate in radio broadcasting (Article V).

As far as student exchange programs are concerned, we found that the available data were meaningless and required further analysis to determine the effects of this type of interaction. It would be necessary to ascertain what exchange students do when they return home and where they are placed in their countries, geographically, functionally, and hier-archically. Unfortunately, this latter analysis could not be conducted within the confines of the present study.

It has been established, however, that the practice of cultural co-operation in general and student exchange in particular were not looked upon with favor by Soviet policy-planners until the beginnings of de-Stalin-ization in the years 1954–1956.[37] In fact, it has been reported that it was only in 1955 that the dissertations of some students in the field of political economy, as well as some newspapers and periodicals in the Soviet Union, began to be concerned with the problem of intrasystem multilateral co-operation.[38]

We know also that, up to 1956, the pattern of educational exchange moved from the other communist party-states to the Soviet Union. Since 1956, however, the Soviets have signed a series of agreements with the other thirteen party-states on bilateral exchange, particularly in higher education.[39] Professor Frederick Barghoorn estimates that, as of 1955, about 8,000 to 9,000 Eastern European students had studied in the Soviet Union, and he cites an article in *Pravda* for July 3, 1956, which makes the statement that there were more than 12,000 undergraduates and 1,500 graduate students studying at that time in the USSR.[40] Professor David Cattell, on the other hand, gives even more detailed figures but presents no documentation.[41] He asserts that, in 1954, there were 1,100 Bulgarian students in the Soviet Union as compared to 160 in 1953, and 200 Polish students in 1955 as compared with fewer than 100 before 1950. He estimates, also, that there were about 14,000 students from system-countries studying in the Soviet Union in 1956 (about the same number as that given in the *Pravda* article cited by Professor Barghoorn) and 1,200 in Poland in 1957.

Finally, we know from Aleksandr Kaznacheev that the International Relations Institute in Moscow played a most important part in training elite specialists and party-cadres from the Soviet Union and from system-countries at least up to 1963. Kaznacheev asserts that out of a total student body of 2,000 at any given time, there are always about 200 (10%) foreign students at the Institute.[42] The largest number of students allegedly come from China, but all the other countries are also represented. The majority of these students are said to be in the Eastern Division and to have a good knowledge of Russian before they are admitted to the Institute.

Turning to the data on student exchange programs and policies as they exist in the other system-countries, we find that, between 1949 and 1957, more than 7,000 Chinese university and graduate students went to Communist countries for training and that most of these students went to the Soviet Union.[43] One Soviet source, however, states that from 1951 to 1957, China sent more than 6,500 students and 7,100 "practicals" to the Soviet Union to study.[44] This assertion is closer to Herbert Passin's estimate that at least 2,000 Chinese students were sent abroad for study each year, after careful language preparation, and that about 85% of these went to the Soviet Union.[45]

In addition, Passin states that nearly 700 out of more than 1,040 teachers in the People's University of China were trained directly by Soviet experts and, more importantly, that ". . . about one–third of all teachers of political theory courses in the various institutions of higher learning throughout the country were directly or indirectly trained with the assistance of Soviet experts."[46] Passin also describes a pattern of exchange in which the Eastern European countries send limited numbers of students to China to acquire special knowledge of language and other areas. But the majority of foreign students in China are from North Korea, North Vietnam, and Outer Mongolia, and these come for basic education.[47] It is also reported that of the Chinese students who go to Eastern Europe, the majority attend Polish academies to study medicine or technology.[48]

It is reported that North Koreans teach Russian rather than Chinese as a second language,[49] while the North Vietnamese teach both Russian and Chinese.[50] In building up a technical vocabulary, Russian is usually the source of borrowings. In Outer Mongolia, where the Soviet presence has been felt for more than thirty years, the Russian cultural influence is predominant. This extends even to the reconstruction of the Outer Mongolian alphabet into Cyrillic and the use of textbooks translated from Russian. Also, most Outer Mongolian teachers are trained in the Soviet Union.[51]

Data on patterns of student exchange in Eastern Europe, unfortunately, are even more sketchy than those already discussed. Since 1961, Albania is reported to have suffered in the field of educational aid as well as economic aid, as a result of its defiance of the Soviet Union. The 1,213 Albanian students who were in Soviet schools allegedly have been expelled, and all personnel from the Soviet Union and Eastern Europe teaching in Albanian schools have been withdrawn.[52] According to information contained in the United Nations Educational, Scientific, and Cultural Organization publication *Study Abroad* for the years 1954–1961, Albanian students were attending schools in Romania, Czechoslovakia, Yugoslavia, Bulgaria, Poland, and the Soviet Union. The pattern of student exchange in Albania was duplicated in Bulgaria.

Since January 1961, Cuba has signed cultural agreements involving student exchange with Bulgaria, Czechoslovakia, the Korean People's Democratic Republic, Poland, and Romania.[53] The same pattern obtains for Hungary, Romania, the USSR, and Yugoslavia as obtains for Albania and Bulgaria, but data on the number of students studying particular subjects at certain institutions were not available. Poland, however, appears to be the second major system-center for education after the Soviet Union, especially for Asian members.[54]

Apart from the types of cultural interaction indicated above, the types of treaties concluded show that there also exists bilateral interaction on the coordination of social policy and within various technical fields.[55] We have also collected data on tourist exchange and some patterns of immigration and emigration within the system, but we seriously question the importance of this type of interaction for our study.[56]

In the category of cultural interaction, then, the Soviet Union appears to educate more students from more system-members than any other single party-state. Poland appears to be second to the Soviet Union, at least in terms of educating students from the Asian subsystem in the fields of medicine and technology. China, on the other hand, appears to be the leader, *but presently only in basic education,* for North Korea and North Vietnam. Thus, the boundaries between the two subsystems in the area of cultural exchange are rather blurred, but this may be merely the result of ideological necessity.

We would hypothesize that, as a result of the degree of centralized control over the placement of recent graduates by the political elites in each party-state, processes of cultural cooperation and exchange are less important than economic and political transactions for integration *in the short run,* given the current divergences based on apparent differences in national goals and ideological interpretation. The continued widespread exchange of students, radio programs, periodicals, texts, magazines, newspapers, and movies, however, especially if carried on at increasingly higher intensities on wider levels, may have *the long-run effect* of building a basis for a communality of values. This hypothesis assumes also that similar types of ideological training will be carried on at least at the secondary school level.

It may be, too, that where a degree of political consensus exists, that is, where there is no conflict of interpretation over the security of the system, as in most of the Eastern European subsystem, the integrative effect of cultural interaction will be more immediate. This tendency will be reinforced if there already exists a historical similarity in cultural patterns among the individual party-states.

Unfortunately, at the present time, it is not possible to present substantial empirical data to verify or reject propositions or hypotheses relating to the immediate effects of cultural interaction. Not only would we need to know where the students are placed when they return home and what they do, but it would also be necessary to determine the effect of cultural exchange on their cognitive and affective orientation towards the particular subsystem in which their training was acquired and towards the system as a whole. But even though these data cannot be required at this time, the cultural variable in the process of integration remains a factor that should not be totally ignored.

TREATIES AND TREATY-MAKING
AS INDEXES OF INTERACTION

In choosing these categories as broad indexes of interaction, we thought we would be able to obtain data on the frequency and extent, on at least a formal level, of various types of commitments being developed within the communist system. In Parsonian terms, this should be a useful indicator of the degree of functional diffuseness and/or specificity which the system is progressively exhibiting. We resolved, therefore, to study, first, the quantity and types of bilateral and plurilateral[57] treaties concluded by the Soviet Union with other system-states from 1953 to 1962; and, second, the quantity and types of bilateral and plurilateral agreements concluded among and between the Eastern European members of the system, exclusive of the Soviet Union.[58]

Between the years 1953 and 1962, the Soviet Union concluded 340 "economic" treaties with the other 13 members of the communist system. One hundred and six of these were concluded in the period 1953 to 1957 (from the death of Stalin to the qualitative change in Soviet-system relations after 1956); and 234 were concluded from 1958 to 1962 (from the beginnings of the Sino-Soviet dispute to the flowering of "polycentrism" or substantial decentralization). If the absolute increase in the number of this type of treaty concluded is looked at in terms of increases with individual countries, then certain interesting trends become apparent.

Before presenting the evidence for each country, however, we should point out that the number of treaties concluded for either period is quite high relative to other types of treaties concluded. This seems to be a result of the peculiar Soviet style in conducting economic relations with system-countries, whereby trade protocols are signed with each country for each year, in addition to certain long-term trade agreements of four to five years' duration.

If we rank each country in terms of the number of all "economic" treaties (that is, if we take into account trade agreements, grants, loans, credits, and technical assistance) concluded from 1953 to 1962, the order is as follows:

Rank	Party-State	Number of Treaties
1	Mongolia	40
2	Bulgaria	38
3	Poland	34
4	North Korea	27
5	China, North Vietnam	25
7	Yugoslavia	24
8	Cuba*	23
9	Czechoslovakia, Romania	22
11	East Germany	21
12	Hungary	20
13	Albania	19

* The first Soviet bilateral agreements with Cuba were signed on February 13, 1960, after the visit to Cuba of Deputy Premier Anastas Mikoyan.

But let us compare this overall standing with the rankings of 1953 to 1957 and 1958 to 1962. Here we have the following:

1953–1957		*1958–1962*	
1. China, Yugoslavia	12	1. Mongolia	29
3. Mongolia	11	2. Bulgaria	28
4. Bulgaria	10	3. Poland	26
5. East Germany	9	4. Cuba	23
6. Czechoslovakia,		5. North Vietnam	20
Hungary, North Korea,		6. North Korea	19
Poland, Romania	8	7. Czechoslovakia,	
11. Albania	7	Romania	14
12. North Vietnam	5	9. China	13
		10. Albania, East	
		Germany, Hungary,	
		Yugoslavia	12

The spectacular decline of China and Yugoslavia is matched by the equally spectacular ascent of Cuba, North Vietnam, North Korea, and Poland. Bulgaria and Mongolia both gain in the face of the Sino-Soviet confrontation. Both of them do especially well in the field of technical assistance: Mongolia with 18 and Bulgaria with 13 such agreements signed. North Korea received ten technical assistance agreements and one outright grant, a very rare occurrence in Soviet economic relations. Albania, however, received two grants[59] and Cuba, during the period 1961–1962, received ten Soviet technical assistance agreements and one grant of fishing equipment.

As we expected, the information to be gleaned from scanning the military agreements available was negligible. Apart from the Warsaw Treaty (Article 7 of which prohibits parties to it from becoming members of other alliance systems) and defense agreements with China (1950) and North Korea (1961), the other treaties signed by the USSR with East Germany, Hungary, Poland, and Romania regulate questions of legal aid[60] and other minor problems arising out of the fact that Soviet troops were stationed in these countries. It has often been pointed out that three of these agreements, signed with Poland, East Germany, and Hungary during 1956 and 1957, were the direct consequence of Soviet intervention in Hungary in November 1956.

On the other hand, a perusal of the "political-diplomatic" agreements shows that these are used quite frequently to deal with a very broad spectrum of issues. They range from establishing diplomatic relations; to signing consular conventions; to institutionalizing procedures for settling border conflicts; to stipulating ways and means for giving legal aid in civil, family, and criminal matters. In addition, bilateral agreements were used to regulate the procedure by which the Soviet Union turned over its shares in joint-stock companies with individual countries. This was done only with Bulgaria (2), China (4), East Germany (1), Hungary (1), North Korea (2), and Romania (3).

As we indicated in an earlier section, the range of social-cultural-technical activities obtaining between the Soviet Union and the other system-countries may be seen in detail by using treaties of this type as indicators. These relations range from minor agreements providing for the quarantining of plants; to establishing cooperation in radio broad-casting, air communications, telephone, telegraph, and mail communica-tions; to stipulating conditions of student and artistic exchange. In terms of quantity and rank for the period 1953–1962, they are as follows:

	Technical Collaboration Agreements		Social-Cultural Agreements	
Country	*Quantity*	*Rank*	*Quantity*	*Rank*
Albania	7	9	4	12
Bulgaria	6	10	8	3
China	18	1	7	6
Cuba	2	13	5*	10
Czechoslovakia	13	3	7	6
East Germany	18	1	8	3
Hungary	9	6	8	3
Mongolia	8	7	6	8
North Korea	8	7	6	8
North Vietnam	6	10	5	10
Poland	11	4	12	1
Romania	6	10	8	3
Yugoslavia	11	4	9	2

* For the period 1960–1962 only.

Finally, it seems that plurilateral agreements are used to regulate cooperative activities among a stipulated number of countries in certain specific technical areas. During the period 1953 to 1962, there were 31 such agreements involving various members of the system, most of whom, however, were Eastern European.[61] Of the Asian members, China was involved in seven such agreements, Mongolia in six, North Korea in three, and North Vietnam in one.

If we turn to those agreements not involving the Soviet Union, we find that economic agreements constitute approximately only four per cent of all types of treaties signed. Of these economic agreements, Albania has signed one with Yugoslavia relating to the exchange of goods in 1960 (December 29, 1959)[62] and one trade agreement with Cuba (January 16, 1961).[63] Bulgaria has signed one trade and payments agreement (March 16, 1955)[64] and one agreement relating to the settlement of debts for railway traffic (March 16, 1955)[65] with Yugoslavia, and one trade and navigation agreement with Czechoslovakia (March 8, 1963).[66] Cuba signed a trade agreement with Czechoslovakia (June 10, 1960),[67] in addition to an agreement on air transport (March 4, 1961).[68] Czechoslovakia signed treaties of trade and navigation (November 25, 1959) with East Germany[69] and Bulgaria (March 8, 1963);[70] and one agreement with Hungary concerning rail traffic (October 22, 1963).[71]

In 1963, Romania signed a series of agreements which must be seen as directly related to its drive for greater economic independence from the Soviet Union and Eastern Europe. With Albania, she signed two trade agreements (March 7 and December 28, 1963); with China, a cultural exchange agreement (July 6), an agreement on scientific cooperation (July 8), and a trade agreement (December 28, 1963); and with Yugoslavia, a trade agreement (December 24, 1963).[72]

We were not particularly surprised to find that there were drawn up very few bilateral military agreements after 1953, nor that there were no plurilateral agreements exclusive of the Soviet Union. In fact, it is significant, we think, that the only military agreements which hold between party-states exclusive of the Soviet Union are between China and North Korea,[73] and conceivably China and North Vietnam, that is, those involving only the major Asian member with two lesser Asian party-states. But the agreements coming under the "political-diplomatic" category accounted for a little more than 35 per cent of the total number of treaties concluded and reported to the United Nations.[74] They range from consular conventions; to stipulation of procedures for settling border disputes; to mutual legal aid in family, civil, and criminal cases. The patterns here are as follows:

Albania: with Czechoslovakia and Yugoslavia
Bulgaria: with Hungary, Poland, Yugoslavia, Czechoslovakia, and Romania
China: with Czechoslovakia
Cuba: with North Korea
Czechoslovakia: with East Germany, Hungary, Poland, Bulgaria, Albania, Romania, China, Yugoslavia, Mongolia, and North Vietnam
East Germany: with Czechoslovakia, Hungary, Poland, and Romania
Hungary: with Bulgaria, Czechoslovakia, East Germany, Poland, and Romania

Mongolia: with Czechoslovakia
North Korea: with Cuba
Poland: with Bulgaria, Czechoslovakia, Hungary, Yugoslavia, East Germany,
    and Romania
Romania: with Bulgaria, East Germany, Hungary, Czechoslovakia, Poland,
    and Yugoslavia
Yugoslavia: with Albania, Bulgaria, Czechoslovakia, Poland, and Romania

It is striking that in the political-diplomatic category of agreements, only Czechoslovakia is reported to have relations with China and North Vietnam, and that Cuba is involved with North Korea. Inferring from what appear to be close relations between China and Albania, and, perhaps, China and East Germany, it is probable that such agreements exist but have not been reported. Bulgaria and Yugoslavia, as a result of their rapprochement beginning about 1955–1956, have signed a number of agreements in all categories with each other. In the political-diplomatic category alone, they have signed ten agreements, most of them relating to border problems. Czechoslovakia's contacts seem to be the most extensive in this area: she is contractually bound to ten members of the system besides the Soviet Union. As in the areas of trade and cultural cooperation, the East Germans are not at all involved with Yugoslavia.

If we look now at the "social-cultural-technical" category, we see that such agreements constitute more than sixty per cent of all treaties signed. And, especially in the social-cultural field, the Asian members are much more involved. If we separate the "social-cultural" type from the "technical" for greater specificity, the patterns are as follows:

Albania: with Poland and Romania
Bulgaria: with Czechoslovakia, Poland, Romania, and Yugoslavia
China: with Poland
Cuba: with Czechoslovakia, East Germany, North Korea, Poland, and
    Romania
Czechoslovakia: with Yugoslavia, North Korea, Poland, Romania, Hungary,
    Bulgaria, East Germany, and Cuba
East Germany: with Poland, Cuba, Czechoslovakia, Hungary, Romania (and
    China?)
Hungary: with East Germany, Poland, Yugoslavia, and Czechoslovakia
Mongolia: with Romania and Poland
North Korea: with Cuba, Romania, Czechoslovakia, and Poland
North Vietnam: none reported
Poland: with Cuba, Yugoslavia, Hungary, North Korea, Mongolia, North
    Vietnam, Bulgaria, Albania, China, Czechoslovakia, and East Ger-
    many
Romania: with Cuba, North Vietnam, East Germany, Bulgaria, Czechoslo-
    vakia, Yugoslavia, Albania, Mongolia, and North Korea
Yugoslavia: with Poland, Czechoslovakia, Bulgaria, Hungary, and Romania

According to these data, then, Poland and Romania (since 1963) are the only Eastern European system members who maintain cultural relations with at least two Asian members; Poland is linked with all three. Poland's cultural relations within the system appear to be the most extensive: She is contractually involved with twelve nations, while Czechoslovakia and Romania, since 1963, are involved with nine. But why is it, if the evidence is correct, that Romania is the only system-country with which Poland does not have a cultural agreement? Does this mean that there are no cultural relations between the two countries?

On the other hand, the pattern of technical cooperation is as follows:

Albania: with Poland and Yugoslavia
Bulgaria: with Czechoslovakia, Poland, Romania, and Yugoslavia
China: none reported
Cuba: After mid-1961, with Bulgaria, Czechoslovakia, and Romania
Czechoslovakia: with Poland, East Germany, Bulgaria, Hungary, Romania, and Yugoslavia
East Germany: with Poland, Romania, Czechoslovakia, and Hungary
Hungary: with Poland, Romania, East Germany, Czechoslovakia, and Yugoslavia
Mongolia: none reported
North Korea: with Romania
North Vietnam: with Romania
Poland: with Yugoslavia, Czechoslovakia, Albania, Bulgaria, East Germany, and Hungary
Romania: with Yugoslavia, Bulgaria, Czechoslovakia, North Korea, East Germany, Hungary, North Vietnam (and China, since 1963)
Yugoslavia: with Albania, Bulgaria, Czechoslovakia, and Hungary

This time Romania takes the lead in terms of extent of commitment, being involved with seven countries (eight since 1963), while Czechoslovakia and Poland both follow with six. Romania, it should be noted, is also the only Eastern European system-member to be linked with the three Asian members. In Eastern Europe, though, there seems to be a highly complex "core" consisting of Czechoslovakia, Poland, Romania, East Germany, and Hungary. The bilateral involvement of Yugoslavia and Bulgaria continues to be high.

On the basis of the data presented here, it can be seen that the Soviet Union conducts the highest degree of interaction on the widest range of subjects of any party-state. This is so especially in the field of economic interaction, where the Soviet Union maintains a considerable degree of contractual involvement with all the other members of the system. But to look only at the number of treaties concluded with each member in this category without considering the differences in the substantive nature of interaction by a content-analysis of the treaties themselves would be misleading.

The Soviets do the most *reciprocal* trade with the Eastern European subsystem, while most Soviet aid, in the form of technical assistance, goes to the less industrialized Eastern Europeans and to the Asians. As we have seen, the pattern of trade and aid between 1953 and 1958 was affected by the developing Sino-Soviet confrontation with a subsequent decline, after 1961 particularly, in the degree of interaction between the Soviet Union, on the one hand, and China and Albania on the other.

It is interesting to note, also, that Soviet involvement with Poland is highest in the fields of cultural cooperation and technical assistance. In fact, Poland, at least in terms of agreements signed, has received the most technical *assistance* from the Soviets of all the more developed Eastern European members. In the field of technical collaboration, however, East Germany, China, and Czechoslovakia lead the field, in that order, up to 1962. Presumably, the Chinese position has declined since then.

In the category of bilateral, political interaction among and between the other party-states exclusive of the Soviet Union, we find that Albania is involved with Czechoslovakia and Yugoslavia and, particularly since 1961, with China. Although no treaties regulating such interaction were found, Albania is probably now involved also with North Korea and North Vietnam. Yugoslavia maintains political relations only with Albania, Bulgaria, Czechoslovakia, Romania, and Poland, while all the other members of the Eastern European subsystem appear to be highly interconnected.

In terms of political interaction, also, Czechoslovakia maintains the widest extent of commitment and, in fact, is the only Eastern European member reported to have formal political relations with China (although, as indicated previously, such may be true of East Germany). Poland follows Czechoslovakia in extent of commitment in the political category but leads the field in extension and degree of involvement in the social-cultural and technical categories.

Within the system as a whole, it is obvious that the intensity of interaction in the treaty-making category is very high. Apparently, the treaty in general, and the bilateral treaty in particular, is looked upon as a very useful tool for regulating intrasystem interaction on a wide variety of subjects.[75] But the mere fact that the *bilateral* treaty is used so much for such a wide variety of subjects appears to be a symptom of a lack of integration within the system, if not also a contributing factor. Specifically, those treaties designed to regulate procedures for conflict resolution on political questions are always bilateral and deal with relatively minor and usually parochial problems. The areas where the greatest integration appears to be taking place are in certain functionally specific categories which have involved all the members of the system except North Vietnam, at least up to 1962. But even here the Eastern European involvement is higher than the Asian.

On the other hand, the boundaries between the two subsystems are not as clear-cut in terms of treaty-making as in those of substantive economic interaction. The range of treaties concluded indicates at least some channels of communication between individual members of both subsystems in all categories.

POLITICAL-MILITARY-DIPLOMATIC INDEXES OF INTERACTION

These indexes of interaction, that is, those processes which exist because of or in spite of formal ties and procedures, may prove to be the most important for the integration or disintegration of the system over time. But, as a result of the unavailability of data and the limitations of time, we were unable to do more than ask certain questions which are likely to yield some insight into such intrasystem processes.

It seemed to us relevant to inquire, first, what types of party-to-party, state-to-state, and party-to-state interaction there might be. Professor Brzezinski has done pioneering work in cataloging some of the most important contacts since October–November, 1956, that is, contacts among top leaders of the various ruling parties.[76] The following question, however, still remains to be answered: Following what levels of disagreement and on what types of issues are these *ad hoc* consultations resorted to? Furthermore, what processes of communication are available for purposes of general coordination? How important are ambassadors and other diplomatic personnel in this respect?

Professor Triska has shown that most Soviet ambassadors (eight out of ten, including the ambassador to Cuba) to other party-states hold present or past membership or candidate membership in the Central Committee of the Communist Party of the Soviet Union.[77] Furthermore, we know that if the first assignment of a Soviet ambassador is outside the system, he usually continues to serve outside the system.[78] A similar pattern holds for those ambassadors whose first assignments are within the system. It would be useful, we think, to find out whether the same pattern holds for each of the fourteen party-states.[79]

Triska has also pointed out that, as decentralization has spread within the system, *state* relations appear to have assumed much greater importance and, at times, even rivaled *party* relations or considerations.[80] This observation becomes more significant if one compares the current definitions of "proletarian internationalism" that have arisen in the course of the Sino-Soviet confrontation and the Romanian divergence on questions of economic policy with the *Pancha Shila* or "Five Principles of Peaceful Coexistence," previously said to apply only to relations with capitalist states. "Proletarian internationalism" and the *Pancha Shila* now appear to be synonymous, at least for some members.[81]

Finally, we feel that differing evaluations of immediate threat from the United States play a significant role in determining divergences on some political-military policies between the Eastern European and Asian subsystems.

TENTATIVE CONCLUSIONS

On the basis of the economic indexes of interaction, especially trade, all the party-states except Yugoslavia appear to be well integrated within the system. As shown previously, the range of total trade of individual members (excluding Yugoslavia) with the system as a whole extends from 50% to 95%. Poland exhibits the lowest degree of involvement in this category (50–65%), but is very highly involved in the other categories, especially in the cultural field.

The least developed of the members maintain the highest percentage of their total trade with the system: Albania, Bulgaria, Outer Mongolia, North Korea, and North Vietnam all exhibit a pattern of from 80% to 95%. And these are the same members who appear to carry on the least amount of interaction in any category with any states outside the system. By necessity or by choice, they are the most system-oriented of all the party-states. On the other hand, the most industrialized members also conduct a very high percentage of their total trade with the system. East Germany and the Soviet Union maintain a range of 70–80%, while Czechoslovakia's is 60–75%. In addition, China, who appears to be bent on rapid development, maintained a range of 70–80% up to 1962.

We would assume, then, that the effect of economic interaction, objectively and perceptually, differs between the more developed and the less developed of the party-states. This assumption is reinforced by the fact that trade between the more developed (especially the Soviet Union) and less developed party-states takes the form largely of barter, that is, an exchange of manufactured goods, primarily machines, for agricultural produce. This type of trade, of course, may tend to preserve the less developed members in their current condition.

Furthermore, even the aid given to the less developed by the Soviet Union and China, as we indicated earlier, is based not upon plans for their long-term economic development, but is geared to enhance the political leverage of either the Soviet Union or China in their confrontation with each other, thereby sustaining the developing cleavage within the system.

The effect of economic interaction differs also between the more developed and less developed members *of the Eastern European subsystem.* At present, there is considerable suspicion of the highly integrated core of the industrially more advanced party-states (the Soviet Union, Czechoslovakia, East Germany, and Poland) on the part of Romania and, to a lesser extent, Hungary. The latter fear that the type of planning advocated by the former will limit their own industrial development, and this leads them to upgrade their national goals in opposition to the "system goals" as proclaimed by the more developed party-states. Thus, there are three interrelated factors which will tend to inhibit further integration in the economic sector: (1) differences in emphasis on criteria for economic development; (2) the lack of supranational planning on the basis of system interests as a whole; and (3) the developing cleavage within the system as a result of the Sino-Soviet conflict and the use of aid for political rather than strictly economic purposes by both contestants.

It does not appear that Yugoslavia can be considered a full system-member, especially since the Asians and the East Germans appear to reject her membership and do not conduct any relations with her. In addition, we have seen that Yugoslavia's trade with the system constitutes only 11–29% of her total trade. On the other hand, Yugoslavia is involved culturally and technically with all the other members (except, perhaps, with Mongolia), particularly with the Soviet Union. In fact, she ranked fourth in the number of technical collaboration agreements signed and second in the number of cultural agreements concluded. Politically, however, Yugoslavia's relations with the system are deemed not to prejudice her "neutralism." She is a member of neither the Warsaw Treaty Organization nor of the COMECON, although she is a member of the Joint Institute for Nuclear Research and is pledged to secrecy on information gained from the Soviet Union.

Yugoslavia's low involvement with the system in the economic sector, as well as the restrictions on her political involvement and her ideological rejection by the Asians and East Germans, suggest a lack of full membership within the system. As a result, we need to know what the effect of partial membership is on the system. We should point out, also, that in terms of intensity and extent of involvement, Mongolia and Cuba are to be included as members of the Eastern European subsystem. Not surprisingly, these two members are more involved with the Soviet Union than with any other party-state.

The boundaries between the two subsystems appear to be the most clear-cut in the political-military-diplomatic category of interaction. The evidence collected shows that only the Soviet Union and Czechoslovakia are formally involved with the Asians and that Czechoslovakia is involved only with China. The Soviet Union is the only party-state involved with *all* system-members (except Albania, from 1961) and is the only party-state to maintain defense agreements with all the others (the defense agreement with Albania may still be regarded as important by the Soviets vis-à-vis an external threat). In this area, though, there are, as yet, no institutionalized procedures for conflict resolution on a system-wide basis.

The degree of involvement among and between party-states in the social-cultural-technical category is very high, and the boundaries of the two subsystems are much more blurred than in either the political-military-diplomatic or economic provinces. The Soviet Union, Poland, Czechoslovakia, and Romania (since 1963), particularly, are linked with the members of the Asian subsystem. Trade and cultural interaction seem to proceed, to some extent, independently of political conflict. This may be seen in the recent developments in Albanian-Eastern European trade relations, Chinese-Soviet trade relations, some Albanian-Soviet cultural relations,[82] Chinese-Soviet cultural-technical relations, and Chinese-Eastern European cultural relations.

The present intensity of interaction in all the categories considered appears to have a strong centripetal effect, but this is tempered by the emergence of two competing centers within the system itself. In addition to this confrontation on the basis of ideological interpretation and prescriptions for action between the Soviet Union and China, there are two other factors which will tend at least to stabilize, and perhaps even to erode, the current state of system integration. These are, once again, the emerging bipolarity which, in the event of a formal split between the two main loci of power, will probably become more rigid as a result of the degree of dependence of the subsystem members on either leader; and the absence of effective supranational planning designed to upgrade system interests, thereby generating the "spill-over" effect which would serve to maintain the integration process as a going concern.

NOTES

1. On this point see Jan F. Triska, "The World Communist System" (Chap. 1 of the present volume), and George Modelski, *The Communist International System* (Princeton: Center of International Studies, 1960).

2. We are indebted to Jan F. Triska for his enlightening comments on this and other matters.

3. For the tables which provide the data on which the following analysis is based, the reader may write to the Stanford Studies of the Communist System (SSCS), Stanford University.

4. It will become clearer later in the chapter that membership in either the Eastern European or Asian subsystems of the larger communist system is a function of the degree of involvement among and between party-states on all indexes. Thus, the Eastern European subsystem consists of: Albania (only up to 1961), Bulgaria, Cuba, Czechoslovakia, East Ger-

many, Hungary, Mongolia, Poland, Romania, and the Soviet Union. The Asian system comprises: Albania (since 1961), China, North Korea, and North Vietnam. We will see, also, that Yugoslavia appears to be a member of neither subsystem.

5. We found that the statistics included in our tables, although compiled from the United Nations series, *International Trade Statistical Yearbook, 1953–1963* (New York: United Nations), tally closely with Soviet statistics for the same period published in *Vneshniaia Torgovlia.*

6. Radio Free Europe, *Attempts to Expand Albanian Foreign Trade,* June 11, 1964, p. 3.

7. *Ibid.* See also the section on treaties in this chapter.

8. On Czechoslovakia, the UN received statistics for 1956–1957 and from 1960–1963. In *Vneshniaia Torgovlia,* however, there was given a listing of figures for the years 1953–1959. In comparing the two sets of figures, it was found that those published by the Soviet Union often claim a slightly higher percentage of trade with the system.

9. George Mueller and Herman Singer, "Hungary: Can the New Course Survive?", *Problems of Communism,* XIV, No. 1 (January–February 1965), 34.

10. One wonders what could have happened between 1960 (5.1%) and 1961 to account for this drastic decline. This is especially interesting since, by 1960, a rather close relationship seemed to be developing between East Germany and China; see M. J. Esslin, "East Germany: Peking-Pankow Axis?" *China Quarterly,* XIII (September–October 1960), 85–88.

11. See Richard Burks, "Perspective for Eastern Europe," *Problems of Communism,* XIII, No. 2 (March–April 1964), 74.

12. A. Doak Barnett, *Communist China and Asia* (New York: Harper and Bros., 1960), pp. 220-21. For mention of the Soviet role in the development of Chinese industry, see William Hollister, "Capital Formation in Communist China," *China Quarterly,* XVII (January–March 1964), 43.

13. Barnett, *Communist China,* p. 222.

14. *Ibid.,* p. 223.

15. United Nations, *United Nations Statistical Yearbook, 1959,* p. 388; *1960,* p. 398; *1963,* pp. 464–65.

16. On this same point, see Jan F. Triska, "The World Communist System" (Chap. 1 of the present volume).

17. An investigation of Soviet bilateral agreements with the rest of the system between 1953 and 1962 shows a total of five grants: two to Albania, one to Mongolia, one to North Korea, and one to North Vietnam. See the section on treaties in this chapter for an extended discussion of their use as interactional indexes.

18. F. Stransky, "Some Aspects of the Economic Cooperation between the Socialist Countries," *World Marxist Review,* VII, No. 7 (July 1964), 31.

19. *Loc. cit.*

20. Barnett, *Communist China,* pp. 228–29.

21. *Ibid.,* pp. 245–47.

22. Robert A. Rupen, "The Mongolian People's Republic and Sino-Soviet Competition," A. Doak Barnett (ed.), *Communist Strategies in Asia* (New York: Praeger, 1963), p. 175.

23. Bernard Fall, *The Two Viet-Nams* (New York: Praeger, 1963), p. 175.

24. In a private communication to the author (May 25, 1966), Professor Fall estimated that since 1961 Soviet aid had amounted to something over $500 million (including the cost of military hardware) and Chinese aid to approximately $300 million (including twenty thousand Chinese road construction workers and engineers to assist in rebuilding roads and the like).

25. One Soviet author, however, states that since 1953 the "socialist nations" have given almost three billion rubles (old currency) to North Korea, of which 1.3 billion "were granted" by the Soviet Union: I. Krapranov, "Economic Collaboration Between the USSR and the Socialist Countries," *Vneshniaia Torgovlia,* No. 2 (1963), p. 9.

26. Glenn Paige, "North Korea and the Emulation of Russian and Chinese Behavior," in Barnett (ed.), *Communist Strategies,* p. 243.

27. *Loc. cit.*

28. This allegation is made by Fritz Schenk, a former aide to the East German planning chief Bruno Leuschner, in his book *Der Magie der Planwirtschaft* (Cologne: Kiepenheuer & Witsch, 1960), pp. 106 and 122. It is cited by J. B. Thompson, "Romania's Struggle with Comecon," *East Europe,* XIII, No. 6 (June 1964), 2–3. For other statements on Soviet economic goals for the system as a whole, see *Ekonomicheskoe sotrudnichestvo i vzaimopomoshch mezhdu Sovetskim Soiuzom i Evropeiskimi stranami narodnoi demokratii* [*Economic Collaboration and Reciprocity between the Soviet Union and the European Countries of People's Democracies*] (Moscow: Akademiia Nauk SSSR, Institut ekonomiki, 1958); and David D. Finley, "A Political Perspective of Economic Relations in the Communist Camp," *Western Political Quarterly,* XVII, No. 2 (June 1964), 294–316.

29. *Rabotnichesko Delo* (Sofia), February 27, 1964, as reproduced in *East Europe,* XIII, No. 4 (April 1964), 24.

30. *American Assembly of Captive European Nations (ACEN) Survey,* XIV (January–June 1963), 197.

31. A recent article on this matter by a Soviet economist, however, deserves attention. O. Bogomolov, "Economic Cooperation Among the Comecon Countries," *Eastern European Economics,* II, No. 14 (Summer 1964), 3–10. The article is translated from *Planovoe Khoziaistvo,* 1964, No. 4.

Bogomolov argues here that there are a number of projects sponsored by COMECON which are leading to increasing (economic) integration within the system. These may be summarized as:

1. The construction of a trans-European oil pipeline facilitating the supply of Soviet oil to Poland, the German Democratic Republic, Czechoslovakia, and Hungary.

2. Long-term cooperation in the construction of enterprises for extraction of raw materials in those countries having plentiful supplies. This, however, is on a bilateral basis.

3. The unification of power systems involving so far: the German Democratic Republic, Czechoslovakia, Poland, Hungary, Romania, and the Soviet Union.

4. Cooperative power development on the Danube.

5. The standardization of freight cars.

6. The construction of a united system of telephone and television communications.

7. The creation of a bank for international cooperation.

8. The imminent establishment of an international production combine among Czechoslovakia, Poland, and Hungary for the rolling of ferrous metals.

9. Coordinated scientific and technical cooperation on a multilateral, as opposed to an earlier bilateral, basis. This is said to facilitate the efficient diffusion of scientific innovations.

10. The standardization of economic, statistical, and accounting indexes which are the prerequisites for the successful coordination of economic plans and international specialization of production.

It is noteworthy that only in *one* multilateral venture is the Soviet Union *not* involved. What is even more interesting is the following statement by Bogomolov which may be a direct reply to Romanian criticism of plans suggested by the more highly industrialized members of the system: "The Marxist-Leninist theory teaches us that only *the flowering of national forms of political and economic life* opens the way to a voluntary rapprochement between nations" (*ibid.,* p. 7, our italics).

32. For one of the few discussions of this subject, see Richard Lowenthal, "The Rise and Decline of International Communism," *Problems of Communism,* XII, No. 2 (March–April 1963), 19–31, especially 20.

33. For a detailed list of these conferences, see David Cattell, "Multilateral Cooperation in Eastern Europe," *Western Political Quarterly,* XIII, No. 2 (March 1960), 68, n. 9.

34. United Nations, *United Nations Treaty Series (UNTS),* I. 4396, 304:187.

35. *Ibid.,* I. 3707, 260:131.

36. It is interesting that one of the recent measures reflecting increasing national emphasis among the Romanian political elite is manifested in the limitations placed on the teaching of Russian language in Romanian schools of all levels. Russian is no longer obligatory. For details on this point, see Randolph Braham, "Rumania: Onto the Separate Path," *Problems of Communism,* XIII, No. 3 (May–June 1964), 23.

37. Zbigniew Brzezinski, "The Organization of the Communist Camp," *World Politics,* XIII, No. 2 (January 1961), 188–89; and Cattell, "Multilateral Cooperation," pp. 66–67.

38. Cattell, "Multilateral Cooperation," p. 67.

39. United States Congress, House Committee on Government Operations, *Government Programs in International Education,* 85th Congress, 2d Session, January 3, 1959, p. 204; see also Brzezinski, "Organization of the Communist Camp," p. 189, for listing of the dates of the agreements signed.

40. Frederick Barghoorn, *The Soviet Cultural Offensive* (Princeton: Princeton University Press, 1960), p. 84.

41. Cattell, "Multilateral Cooperation," p. 66, n. 8.

42. Aleksandr Kaznacheev, *Inside a Soviet Embassy* (New York and Philadelphia: J. B. Lippincott & Co., 1962), pp. 32–33.

43. Barnett, *Communist China,* p. 228.

44. M. S. Kapitsa, *Sovetsko-kitaiskie otnosheniia* (Moscow: Gosudarstvo izd-vo, 1958), p. 379.

45. Herbert Passin, *China's Cultural Diplomacy* (New York: Praeger, 1963), p. 6.

46. *Ibid.,* p. 5.

47. *Loc. cit.*

48. *Ibid.*, pp. 105–6.

49. Paige, "North Korea," pp. 250–51.

50. Fall, *The Two Viet-Nams,* pp. 185–86.

51. Rupen, "The Mongolian People's Republic," pp. 262–63. Rupen estimates also that, for 1960–1961, there were approximately 2,000 Mongols studying in the USSR, while fewer than 150 per year go to China for study. Further, many Mongols are fluent in Russian, while few know Chinese. *Ibid.,* p. 264.

52. *ACEN Survey,* p. 87.

53. It is reported that the January 12, 1961, agreement with Bulgaria allowed twenty Cuban students and one hundred workers to go to Bulgaria for training. It is estimated also that as of December 31, 1961, there were three hundred Cuban students in Romania and, as of October 1962, five hundred Cubans in Czechoslovakia; see Radio Free Europe, *Eastern Europe's Economic Commitments in Cuba,* November 12, 1962. Furthermore, Robert Scalapino has made the interesting point that North Korea has sought close cultural contacts with Cuba. It appears, he says, that: "Cuba, more than any single country, is a symbol to the North Koreans of the future triumphs of Communism over the United States": "The Foreign Policy of North Korea," *China Quarterly,* XIV (April–June 1963), 48.

54. United Nations Economic and Social Council (UNESCO), *Study Abroad,* XII (1960), 677; *ACEN Survey,* p. 140.

55. The complete data may be obtained from the Stanford Studies of the Communist System.

56. For this type of data see especially United Nations, *United Nations Demographic Yearbook* (New York, 1957), p. 621; and 1959, pp. 674 and 687. On this point, also see Arend Lijphart, "Tourist Traffic and Integration Potential," *Journal of Common Market Studies,* II, No. 3 (March 1964), 251–62.

57. Plurilateral treaties, in international law, are treaties which allow as signatories only a restricted number of parties. They are thus to be distinguished from multilateral treaties, which are generally open.

58. We must add one caveat about the data collected and employed. In dealing with the Soviet bilateral treaties, we used the systematic presentations of Jan F. Triska and R. M. Slusser, *A Calendar of Soviet Treaties, 1917–1957* (Stanford: Stanford University Press, 1959); R. M. Slusser and George Ginsburgs, "A Calendar of Soviet Treaties, January–December, 1958," *Osteuropa-Recht,* VII (June 1961), 120–31; for 1959, *Ibid.,* VIII (June 1962), pp. 132–64; for 1960, Ginsburgs, *Ibid.,* IX (June 1963), pp. 120–59; for 1961, *Ibid.,* X (June 1964), pp. 116–48; for 1962, *Ibid.,* XI (June 1965), pp. 129–60. In dealing with the agreements exclusive of the Soviet Union, however, there were no such systematic presentations available. We, therefore, were forced to use the *United Nations Treaty Series (UNTS),* Vols. 1–515 (but not including Vols. 504, 506, 508–10, and 512–13, which apparently were not distributed). The data here are not complete, for some agreements which we found elsewhere were not included in the *UNTS.* We have taken, however, what we hope is the first step toward construction of a systematic calendar of these treaties, to be fashioned along the same lines as those

calendars of Soviet treaties presented by Professors Triska, Slusser, and Ginsburgs. Copies of this appendix are available from The Stanford Studies of the Communist System.

59. One would initially be given to believe that there was a direct relationship between the increase in economic relations between the Soviet Union and Albania, so favorable for Albania, during the period 1958–1961, and the beginnings of Chinese success in weaning Albania away from the "Soviet orbit." This remains to be confirmed or rejected.

60. Except the Treaty of Friendship, Cooperation, and Mutual Assistance signed with East Germany only in June, 1964.

61. Not included in this total are technically specific agreements arrived at after regular COMECON meetings, e.g., on the standardization of machine tools, etc.

62. United Nations, *UNTS,* I. 5693, 396:63.

63. *Ibid.,* I. 6425, 448:67. But Albania also signed a number of bilateral agreements with other party-states in 1963. In February, she concluded a protocol on the exchange of goods with Hungary, a trade agreement with North Korea, an agreement regulating the exchange of goods and payments with Poland, and an agreement on the exchange of goods with East Germany. In March 1963, she concluded an agreement on the exchange of goods and payments with Czechoslovakia, and two agreements on the exchange of goods with Romania and North Vietnam; see *ACEN Survey,* p. 14.

64. United Nations, *UNTS,* I. 5702, 397:83. During 1963, however, Bulgaria signed three trade agreements: with China (March 5), with Cuba (January), and with East Germany (February 20). These agreements are noted in *ACEN Survey,* p. 22.

65. United Nations, *UNTS,* I. 5702, 397:83.

66. *Ibid.,* I. 7245, 219:45.

67. *Ibid.,* I. 6412, 447:75.

68. *Ibid.,* I. 6728, 209:34.

69. *Ibid.,* I. 5331, 374:101.

70. *Ibid.,* I. 7245, 219:45.

71. *Ibid.,* I. 7444, 95:156.

72. Noted in Randolph Braham, "Rumania: Onto the Separate Path," pp. 14–23.

73. Scalapino, "Foreign Policy," p. 37.

74. We should add here that we could find no evidence revealing the frequency or types of agreements concluded among or between the Asian members of the system. These, if there are any, are simply not reported to the UN.

75. On this point as it relates to the Soviet Union, see Jan F. Triska and R. M. Slusser, *The Theory, Law and Policy of Soviet Treaties* (Stanford: Stanford University Press, 1962), esp. pp. 9–48.

76. Brzezinski, "Organization of the Communist Camp," pp. 175–209.

77. From a study made by Jan F. Triska as part of preparing a textbook on Soviet foreign policy. We are grateful to Professor Triska for allowing us to use this information.

78. *Ibid.*

79. Professor Scalapino has also made similar calculations for the North Koreans. Scalapino, "Foreign Policy," p. 33.

80. Jan F. Triska, "Conflict and Integration in the Communist Bloc: A Review," *Journal of Conflict Resolution,* V, No. 4 (December 1961), 418–25.

81. Radio Bucharest, in replying on June 4, 1963, to a critical Soviet broadcast of May 30, 1964, defined "the basic principles of relations between the socialist countries" as being ". . . the principles of independence and national sovereignty, equality of rights, mutual advantage, comradely mutual aid, and noninterference in internal affairs. . . ," as quoted in *East Europe,* XIII, No. 7 (July 1964), p. 10. (See Chap. 1 above.)

82. Between May 1962 and June 1963, five Albanian delegations were in Moscow to participate in conferences sponsored by the system as a whole; see *ACEN Survey,* p. 91.

FIVE

PATTERNS OF SOVIET TREATY-MAKING
BEHAVIOR WITH OTHER COMMUNIST
PARTY-STATES

CHARLES D. CARY

An investigation of the interaction between and integration among the USSR and the thirteen other communist party-states in the period between approximately 1945–1962 is the object of this chapter. The method of investigation is the identification and analysis of the patterns in Soviet treaty-making behavior with these states. The underlying assumption is that the USSR leads the communist party-state system. This assumption implies that the USSR is responsible for the initiation of both bilateral and plurilateral treaties within the system.

METHODOLOGY

For source materials, we are relying on the series "Calendar of Soviet Treaties," which Professors Robert M. Slusser and Jan F. Triska initiated *(A Calendar of Soviet Treaties, 1917–1957)* and Slusser or George Ginsburgs has continued in *Ost Europa Recht* for the years 1958 through 1962. The title and/or short synopsis of each treaty entry in the "Calendars" provide the primary data. As the availability of documents has permitted, we have been reading the original treaty documents.

Professors Slusser and Triska offer a summary definition for the term "treaty" which constituted their basic criterion for the cataloguing of an international agreement in their "Calendar." A treaty is ". . . an agreement between two or more parties, usually states, usually embodied in a written document, establishing a relationship between the parties."[1] We have adopted this *generic* definition for use in our paper because of our reliance on the "Calendars." "In the Soviet view, the names given to the instrument—treaty, tractate, pact, convention, accord, declaration, exchange of notes, protocol, covenant, arrangement, resolution, compact, modification, supplement, regulations, etc.—are conventional rather than substantive denominations."[2] Since differing titles for treaties concerning similar subject matter may not represent substantive differences, it is necessary to compare the terms and conditions of the various treaties. For example, the USSR has concluded conventions and treaties concerning the consular relations with the other communist party-states and with other nations. A comparative examination of the terms of several of these conventions and treaties reveals a high degree of similarity.

Several recent studies have dealt with the subject of Soviet treaties in regard to interaction between the USSR and the other communist party-states. These investigations include Zbigniew K. Brzezinski's "The Organization of the Communist Camp" (*World Politics,* January 1961), Kazimierz Grzybowski's *The Socialist Commonwealth of Nations* (1964), Jan F. Triska's "Soviet Treaty Law: A Quantitative Analysis" (*Law and Contemporary Problems,* Autumn 1964), and Edward L. Miles's study with John S. Gillooly, "Processes of Interaction Among the Fourteen Communist Party-states: An Exploratory Essay" (Chapter 4 in the present volume).

Brzezinski, in his article, briefly surveys the institutional or organizational apparatus of the system, which plurilateral treaties have created, and selected bilateral treaty arrangements among system members. The Grzybowski book is the most comprehensive to date on treaty relations among the party-states. However, the focus is on the party-states' supranational organizations within the system and the framework of analysis is that of international law. The Triska paper and the Miles with Gillooly essay begin to explore the relationship between treaty relations and integration among the party-states.

Our study represents an expansion and refinement on the empirical and theoretical levels of these previous efforts. We concentrate on Soviet treaty-making behavior vis-à-vis the communist party-states in subject-matter areas. The basic technique of data aggregation of bilateral treaties which we employ in this paper is the following: Given a certain title and subject matter of a treaty, we ascertain with which party-states the USSR has concluded a treaty bearing this title and/or concerning this subject matter; then we attempt to compare the terms of the concluded treaties; finally, we determine with what other nations the USSR has concluded a similar treaty.

For example, Russia signed a treaty concerning consular relations with 12 out of the 13 other communist party-states between 1957 and 1960 (in 1957, East Germany, Hungary, Czechoslovakia, Romania, Bulgaria, Albania, and North Korea; in 1958, Poland and Outer Mongolia; in 1959, China and North Vietnam; and, in 1960, Yugoslavia). A comparison of several of these treaties with regard to language, content, and form reveals substantial similarities. The USSR concluded only two treaties concerning consular relations with other nations before 1962— Austria (1959) and the Federal Republic of Germany (1958).

Our reliance on the "Calendars" has introduced a problem which can affect the analyses in our investigation. This problem initially stems from presumed gaps in the "Calendars." We may assume that the USSR probably does not announce the conclusion of all of its treaties. Likewise, the authors of the "Calendars" in the process of their compilations may have missed some of the Soviet announcements of conclusions of treaties. Hopefully, our use of the "Calendars" has not contributed a third step to this filtering process; that is, we trust that we have not overlooked some of the entries in the "Calendars" in the course of our use of them.

On the basis of our method of aggregation of bilateral Soviet treaties, we might expect the conclusion of a particular treaty with a specific party-state; yet, we may not find that such a treaty has been drawn up. The problem is, then: To what factors can we attribute our failure to find the conclusion of a particular treaty with a specific party-state—is it the filtering process or is there no treaty?

THEORY

Richard A. Brody, in his paper "Cognition and Behavior: A Model of Inter-Unit Relations," suggests that "from our point of view the international system, like all social interaction systems, can be conceived of as a pattern of communication between units."[3] Identifiable and regular patterns of communication between units, that is, patterns of interaction and transactions, imply some sort of structural network of communication channels linking system members.

We may consider that treaties between two or more nations formalize or institutionalize such channels and establish communication networks. Undoubtedly, some interaction and transactions must precede the conclusion of a treaty between nations, but the formalization of the linking channel would affect the intensity and frequency of subsequent interaction and/or transactions.

At this point, we must make certain terminological distinctions in the context of our twofold focus on treaties and on communication channels and networks between nations. Karl Deutsch's book *The Nerves of Government* (New York, 1963) and his chapters in Philip E. Jacob and James V. Toscano's volume *The Integration of Political Communities* (Philadelphia, 1964) provide the basis for these distinctions. Interaction means interchange between nations which affects the nature of a particular communication channel linking them (such as decisions as to what the channel may carry). We use the term transaction to mean the flow of communications (goods, services, information) along a channel. Transactions can have both qualitative (referring to what is transmitted) and quantitative (referring to how much is transmitted) dimensions. The conclusion of a treaty is the manifestation of both interaction and transactions.

An examination of Article 7 of the treaty between the USSR and Romania concerning cultural cooperation (April 7, 1956) makes clear these distinctions:

> With a view to the application of this Agreement, a Mixed Soviet-Romanian Commission for cultural co-operation shall be set up, to which each party shall appoint three to five members.
>
> It shall be one of the tasks of the Commission to draw up annual plans for cultural co-operation, which shall be submitted to the Governments of the Contracting Parties for their approval.
>
> The Commission shall meet at least once a year, at Moscow and Bucharest in turn.
>
> Expenses connected with the meetings of the Commission shall be borne by the Party in whose capital the meetings of the Commission are held.
>
> In accordance with the annual plans agreed upon by the Mixed Commission and approved by the Governments of the Parties, the competent agencies of the Parties shall enter into direct consultation with each other with a view to the practical application of the measures for co-operation in the relevant cultural fields.[4]

At least once a year and subject to the approval of the respective governments, the Mixed Soviet-Romanian Commission determines the nature of the cultural link between the two countries. Such determination represents interaction. Transactions refer to the "measures for cooperation in the relevant cultural fields," which other articles in the same treaty have established for "application," that is, for determination by the Mixed Commission.

If there exists a leader of a system we would submit that it is the leader's responsibility to coordinate his system and standardize relations among system members.[5] Such coordination and standardization would involve the regulation of the channels of communications linking members and, subsequently, the flow of transactional communications. More specifically, coordination and standardization of relations among system members would involve the establishment by the system leader of communication channels of similar quality and caliber with system members. This establishment should manifest itself in recognizable patterns or networks of communication channels between the leader and the members of the system. Patterns in communication channels between system members should then tell us something about integration.

So far, political scientists have developed no independent measure of integration. Their analytical conceptualizations have centered on transactional and attitudinal variables.[6] One conceptual problem involves the separation of the process from the state of integration. Our concentration on the networks of communication channels which treaties formalize, that is, on treaty-networks, allows us some flexibility in our conceptualization of integration.

Our concern is the integration of the communist party-state system under Soviet leadership, as primarily evidenced by the treaty-making behavior and treaty networks of the USSR. Professors Triska and Slusser contend that "*international treaties* and *agreements,* ever since the first Soviet entry into foreign relations, have remained the fundamental source and *prima facie* foundation of relations between Soviet Russia and other governments."[7] One inference from their finding is that the existence of treaty relations between the USSR and the other communist party-states is necessary to the latter's integration under Soviet leadership. We associate the development of treaty-networks with the process of integration, and the character of the treaty-networks with the state of integration.

For the purposes of this chapter, integration of the communist party-states becomes the degree to which substantive treaty-networks within the system are complete and congruent. By a substantive treaty-network, we mean the pattern of treaty linkages or communication channels between nations in a subject-matter area (for example, consular relations).

A treaty-network is complete under the following two conditions:

1. For N members of a system, where N is greater than 1 and all members of the system and its leader are specified, then,

   (a) for a given subject-matter area, a system member tends to conclude bilateral treaties with only the $(N-1)$ other system members and, hence, $(N-1)$ two-way dyadic channels exist; or

   (b) for a given plurilateral treaty which includes the system leader, there tend to be only $(N-1)$ other signatories, all within the system, and hence $\dfrac{(N^2-N)}{2}$ two-way dyadic channels exist.

There are some exceptions to this first, or structural, condition. A particular subject matter of a treaty is sometimes not relevant to all system members. For example, we suggest that rescue-at-sea has little relevance to landlocked Czechoslovakia; yet, several plurilateral agreements on this subject exist among party-states with common seacoasts.

2. The quality and caliber of all channels for a given substantive treaty-network tend to be respectively the same.

This second or equivalent condition for completeness incorporates a comparison of the terms of treaties with regard to their effect on transactions and interactions.

Two or more treaty-networks (TN) are congruent under the following condition: The L_1 members $(2 < L_1 \leqq N)$ of TN_1, the L_2 members $(2 < L_2 \leqq N)$ of TN_2, and so on, tend to be the same members, where $L_1, L_2, \ldots$ are not necessarily equal. Thus, it is possible to compare the congruency between the various substantive treaty-networks of one party-state or between the treaty-networks in one subject-matter area of the various party-states.

The concepts of completeness and congruency of treaty-networks will prove useful in our analysis. At the outset, we assume a system leader (the USSR) and a certain set of nations (the thirteen other communist party-states). Our subsequent examination and comparison of the completeness and congruency of treaty-networks will indicate the degree of involvement of various system members. In addition, a longitudinal analysis of the completeness and congruency of treaty-networks would reveal any system transformation. For example, changes in the completeness and congruency of system treaty-networks over time could point out the formation or decomposition of possible subsets of party-states within the system.

We have assumed that the USSR is the leader among the communist party-states. However, a comparison of the treaty-making behavior of the various party-states with that of the Soviet Union is necessary for the establishment of the validity of our assumption. More specifically, we would suggest that the following evidence with regard to bilateral treaties would characterize the USSR as system leader:

1. the presence of a pattern of Soviet initiation in the conclusion of a particular bilateral treaty with the party-states and of their subsequent conclusion of similar bilateral treaties among themselves;

2. Soviet introduction of a new state into the system through the initiation with and extension to this nation of treaty relations.

In terms of our theory of communication channels linking system members, we must look at the substantive treaty-networks of the various communist party-states. It is necessary to compare the completeness of the treaty-networks of the system leader and the various party states in one subject-matter area. We would suggest that the Soviet treaty-networks of bilateral agreements with system members would tend to be more complete than the corresponding ones of the other communist party-states. N complete and congruent bilateral treaty-networks in one substantive area would seem to us different from one plurilateral treaty among the N members, although theoretically both incorporate $\dfrac{(N^2 - N)}{2}$ two-way dyadic channels.

The treaty-network approach involves both the transactional and the attitudinal variables of integration. In the first place, we ascertain to some extent the potentiality of nations for interaction and transactions.

For example, the presence or absence of communication channels between nations would certainly govern the possible intensity and frequency of transactions. Secondly, the extent of a communist party-state's treaty relationships with other members of the system, that is, its participation in treaty-networks, would constitute an indicator or measure of the attitudinal variable of integration at the level of the nation.

DISCUSSION AND ANALYSIS OF TREATY-NETWORKS

Data Problems

Before proceeding to our discussion and analysis of treaty-networks, we must point out several reservations about the nature of the data. First, it is difficult to ascertain which treaties remain valid and operative, unless the nations involved have formally abrogated them. Some treaties specify the duration of validity of the instrument with no provision for extension except renegotiation. Other treaties specify an initial duration and provide for their own automatic and subsequent renewal unless denunciation occurs. Where known, we incorporate abrogations into our analyses; otherwise, we are assuming the validity and operation of treaties during the time period under consideration in the paper.

Secondly, although our focus is on Soviet treaty-networks, we make comparisons with the treaty relations of the other communist party-states. No calendars as comprehensive (for instance, in terms of the number of years surveyed) and complete as the Slusser, Triska, and Ginsburgs series for the USSR exist for the treaties of the other communist party-states, with a possible exception of China.[8] Various sources provide our data on treaty relations of the other party-states. These include journal articles, an appendix in the Miles with Gillooly paper, "Calendar of System Bilateral Agreements Exclusive of the Soviet Union, Compiled from the *United Nations Treaty Series,* Volumes 1–449," and our own continuation of this system bilateral calendar through volume 503. Unfortunately, the scope of some of these sources does not encompass the treaty relations of the party-states with other, noncommunist nations. Thus, our comparisons with the treaty-networks based on these sources can only be suggestive in nature.

The fact that the composition of the system has not remained stable or constant during the time period under consideration can directly affect patterns of treaty-making behavior, and subsequent analyses of the treaty-networks. The later accession of the Democratic Republic of Vietnam or Cuba can affect any statements about the rapidity in the formation of a particular Soviet treaty-network and about the completeness of such a treaty network.

Soviet Bilateral Treaty-Networks

There seem to be two broad classifications of Soviet bilateral treaties. One class establishes collaborative channels through which transactions may pass. For example, the Soviet treaties concerning cultural cooperation envisage the exchange of personnel, publications, and information in various cultural areas such as education and the performing arts. The second class of treaties tends to establish guidelines for behavior of the signatories vis-à-vis one another. For example, Soviet treaties concerning the regulation of the question of citizenship of persons with dual citizenship create procedures for handling such questions of dual nationality by each signatory. Granted, Soviet treaties do not fall neatly into one or the other classification, particularly since "transactional" treaties involve some procedural articles which usually relate to the implementation of the transactional articles.

We suggest that those subject matters of a procedural nature are more susceptible to a plurilateral form of treaty instrument. The Soviet Union has concluded bilateral treaties concerning the procedural subject of friendship, collaboration, and mutual assistance with nine communist party-states (East Germany, Poland, Czechoslovakia, Hungary, Romania, Bulgaria, Outer Mongolia, China, and North Korea). Six of these nine (excluding Outer Mongolia, China, and North Korea) plus the USSR and Albania signed the Warsaw Pact (The Treaty of Friendship, Cooperation, and Mutual Assistance) on May 14, 1955. China was associated by a supporting statement with the Warsaw Pact, but did not sign the instrument. This plurilateral treaty ". . . laid down the basic aims and principles of cooperation of the signatories,"[9] and represents procedural coordination.

Table 5–2 at the end of the chapter gives us some idea of the completeness and congruency of Soviet bilateral treaty-networks. The criterion for the selection of subject-matter areas of treaties for this table was whether the subject was potentially relevant to the entire system. For example, we did not include treaties concerning border questions, or the settlement of claims resulting from the incorporation of Latvia, Lithuania, and Estonia into the USSR. We will discuss these treaties with relevance only to some subset of communist party-states later in the chapter.

An overall examination of this table reveals several patterns in Soviet treaty-networks. One pattern centers on the rapidity in the formation of the treaty-networks. During 1956, the Soviet Union concluded treaties concerning cultural collaboration with 11 out of the 13 other party-states. North Vietnam and Cuba, the two exceptions, entered the system later than the other members, but, nevertheless, respectively signed treaties on February 15, 1957, and December 12, 1960. North Vietnam and the USSR began active treaty relations in July 1956; their cultural treaty was the first nondiplomatic or noneconomic agreement between the two countries. The USSR and Cuba had *de facto* diplomatic relations since January 1959, but announced their agreement concerning the reestablishment of diplomatic relations *de jure* on the level of embassies on May 8, 1960.

In 1956, the USSR also signed cultural treaties with Syria (August 20, 1956), Norway (October 12, 1956), and Belgium (October 25, 1956). However, by the date of signing of the Soviet-Syrian agreement, the Soviet Union had already concluded in that year ten out of the eleven treaties with communist party-states. Thus, the USSR tended to establish the treaty-network concerning cultural collaboration with the party-states not only within a short period of time, but also previous to the incorporation of other states into the network.

In seven out of the twelve treaty-networks under consideration here, fifty per cent or more of the conclusions within the system took place within a given year (conditions of trade deliveries, 1952; atomic energy, 1955; cultural collaboration, 1956; legal aid and legal relations, 1957; dual nationality, 1957; consular relations, 1957; and training of _____ [e. g., Polish] citizens in Soviet civic institutes of higher learning, 1952).

With regard to the formation of the Soviet treaty-network concerning atomic energy, again we find that the USSR concluded seven out of the eight treaties within the system on this subject previous to extending the network to include the first non-member (Egypt, July 12, 1956). Also, the formation of the Joint Institute for Nuclear Research on March 26, 1956, with an initial membership of all party-states except Yugoslavia and Outer Mongolia, buttressed the Soviet network concerning atomic energy and preceded the conclusion of the Soviet-Egyptian treaty.

Thus, we are able to identify two patterns in Soviet treaty-making behavior at the bilateral level:

1. the tendency to conclude rapidly treaties within the system in one subject-matter area; and

2. the tendency to form the substantive treaty-network with the party-states previous to the incorporation of other states into the network.

Overall, we find a high degree of structural completeness in these Soviet treaty networks except for the area of social security. The degree of equivalent completeness—a comparison of the quality and caliber of the channels in each of the various substantive treaty-networks—requires more investigation. With regard to transactional treaty-networks, an analysis of flows through the channels would provide a necessary supplement to a comparative examination of the terms and conditions of the treaties. The four Eastern European party-states which border the USSR (Poland, Czechoslovakia, Hungary, and Romania) tend to form the consistent basis for congruent treaty-networks.

Comparison of the substantive treaty-networks of the individual communist party-states with those of the USSR yields several patterns. (See Table 5–3 at the end of the chapter.) First of all, in some substantive treaty-networks, it is possible to suggest Soviet leadership in the initiation of treaty relations. The leader nation with regard to the formation of a particular substantive treaty-network becomes that nation which signs first with the most party-states. Under this definition of leadership, it is not necessary for the leader to have the most complete treaty-network. (See Table 5–1.)

TABLE 5–1

Substantive Treaty-Network	Number of firsts in signing treaty with Eastern European party-states, including the USSR	Number of firsts in signing treaty with remaining party-states	TOTAL
Friendship, mutual assistance	3 (USSR)	3	6
(N = 11)	4 (Yugoslavia)	–	4
Scientific-technical	6 (USSR)	1	7
(N = 13)	3 (Poland)	–	3
Cultural collaboration	1 (USSR)	–	1
(N = 14)	1 (Poland)	1	2
	1 (Romania)	1	2
	5 (China)	2	7
Commerce[a]	5 (USSR)	4	9
(N = 12)	1 (Poland)	–	1
	1 (Czechoslovakia)	–	1
Legal aid and legal relations[b]	2 (USSR)	2	4
(N = 11)	4 (Czechoslo-vakia)	–	4
Dual nationality	7 (USSR)	2	9
(N = 10)			
Consular relations	4 (USSR)	4	8
(N = 13)	4 (East Germany)	–	4
Social security	4 (Czechoslo-vakia)	–	4
(N = 8)	2 (Poland)	–	2

[a] excluding Yugoslavia.
[b] excluding pre-war Yugoslavian agreements.

Consider the substantive treaty-network concerning consular relations. Thus, East Germany signed first with the USSR, Poland, Czechoslovakia, and Hungary—four party-states. The USSR signed first with four Eastern European party-states—East Germany, Romania, Bulgaria, and Yugoslavia—and four Asian party-states—Outer Mongolia, China, North Korea, and North Vietnam. The USSR was the leader, but shared its leadership with East Germany in Eastern Europe.

The data in this table show that in Eastern Europe, the USSR clearly initiated the conclusion of treaties among the Communist party-states only in three out of the eight cases. In one instance (cultural collaboration), China was the initiator. However, by combining the remaining party-states, where our data is probably not complete, with Eastern European states, the USSR emerges as system leader.

By comparing the first signatory of an Eastern European party-state across the substantive treaty-networks under consideration, we find that Bulgaria has signed first with the Soviet Union six out of the eight times; Romania, five times; and Czechoslovakia, Hungary, and Albania each four times. Given the unclear situation in Eastern Europe with regard to Soviet initiation of treaty relations, possibly the frequency of first signings with the USSR suggests a measure of legitimation of Soviet leadership in the integration of the system.

As we have previously stated, not all Soviet treaties seem to be relevant to all party-states. But, despite this lack of relevance to all, a pattern emerges of an attempt to coordinate relations in an equal and quick manner with the relevant subset of party-states. Treaties concerning border problems and Soviet troops stationed abroad illustrate this tendency. Within the six months from December 1956, to May 1967, immediately following the Polish and Hungarian revolts, the Soviet Union concluded bilateral treaties with Poland (December 17, 1956), East Germany (March 12, 1957), Romania (April 15, 1957), and Hungary (May 27, 1957) concerning the legal status of Soviet troops temporarily stationed in these countries. As Grzybowski has noted, "the three treaties [the Romanian treaty is no longer in force] are nearly identical, but with some important differences in detail, particularly as regards the movement of troops stationed in the respective countries."[10]

In the period 1948–1950, the USSR concluded two separate bilateral agreements with Poland (July 8, 1948), Romania (November 25, 1949), and Hungary (February 24, 1950) concerning their mutual border: (1) Treaty between the USSR and _____ Concerning the Regime on the Soviet-_____ State Border, with Final Protocol; (2) and Convention between the USSR and _____ Concerning Procedure for Settling Border Disputes and Incidents, with Related Documents. Then, in 1961, the USSR evidently renegotiated these border treaties and concluded a single treaty concerning Regimen of Soviet-_____ State Frontier, Co-operation and Mutual Aid in Frontier Questions with each of the three countries: Poland (February 15, 1961), Romania (February 27, 1961), and Hungary (October 3, 1961). Of the other party-states bordering on the Soviet Union, the USSR has concluded border treaties with Czechoslovakia and North Korea but not with Outer Mongolia and China during the time period under consideration: Treaty between the USSR and Czechoslovakia Concerning the Regime on the Soviet-Czechoslovakia Border and Procedure for Settling Border Incidents, with Related Documents (November 30, 1956); and Convention between the USSR and the Korean People's Democratic Republic Concerning Regulation of Border Questions (October 14, 1957).

With regard to non-system states with borders on the Soviet Union, the pattern for Finland is similar to that for Poland, Romania, and Hungary—an agreement in the late forties with renegotiation in 1960. Norway, Iran, and Afghanistan settled the question in 1949, 1957, and 1958, respectively, with one instrument.[11]

Transition from Bilateral to Plurilateral Instrument

Although our focus of concentration in this paper has not been on plurilateral agreements, some plurilateral agreements relate to the Soviet bilateral treaty-networks. More specifically, our concern here is with the transition from a bilateral to a plurilateral form of treaty instrument in a given subject-matter area.

The USSR has established a bilateral treaty-network concerning quarantine of agricultural plants and their protection from parasites and diseases. The primary impetus towards the conclusion of such treaties was the "Resolution of the First International Congress of Plant Pathology, Entomology, and Plant Protection" (August 4, 1949), although Soviet treaties with Iran (1935 and 1945), Czechoslovakia (November 28, 1947), and Poland (April 8, 1948) predate this resolution. The signatories of this resolution were the USSR, Albania, Bulgaria, Czechoslovakia, Hungary, Poland, and Romania. The nine Communist party-states which are in the Soviet treaty-network in this subject-matter area include the signatories of the resolution plus China, North Korea, and East Germany.

Again, we can suggest Soviet leadership in the initiation of treaty relations within the system in a subject-matter area. The USSR signed first with four Eastern European states (Czechoslovakia, Poland, Albania, and Romania) as opposed to three for Poland (Bulgaria, East Germany, and Hungary). (See Table 5–4 at the end of the chapter.)

The following quotation is from the text of the Romanian-Hungarian Convention Concerning the Protection of Agricultural Plants Against Pests and Diseases (December 14, 1953):

> In carrying out measures to destroy dangerous pests and diseases, the two Contracting parties shall make the fullest use of the experience, scientific findings and results of the plant protection service of the Union of Soviet Socialist Republics and the plant protection and quarantine services of the Romanian People's Republic and the Hungarian People's Republic.[12]

This reference to the expertise of the USSR with regard to plant protection arrangements between these two party-states lends support to our suggestion of Soviet leadership in the initiation of treaty relations among communist party-states in this subject-matter area.

It is possible that the nature of quarantine and protection of agricultural plants makes this subject matter only geographically relevant to subsets of the party-states, for example, Eastern European or Asian party-states. However, the eight members of the Council for Mutual Economic Assistance (USSR, East Germany, Poland, Czechoslovakia, Hungary, Romania, Bulgaria, and Albania) plus Outer Mongolia and North Korea signed a plurilateral Agreement Concerning Collaboration in the Field of Quarantine of Plants and Protection from Pests and Diseases (December 14, 1959). These nations concluded this treaty at the Twelfth Session of COMECON in Sofia at which Outer Mongolia and North Korea were observers. We suggest that the transition from a bilateral to a plurilateral form of treaty instrument can represent an attempt at a more efficient method of procedural coordination in this area.

Another example of the transition from a bilateral to a plurilateral instrument for treaties concerns veterinary medicine. (See Table 5–5 at the end of the chapter.) The Soviet Union has concluded only two bilateral treaties in this subject-matter area, with Czechoslovakia (May 18, 1957) and Finland (November 5, 1959). However, the other Eastern European states, with the exception of Albania, began concluding these treaties before the Soviet-Czechoslovakian treaty. Yet, on December 14, 1959, the eight members of COMECON plus Outer Mongolia and North Korea signed a plurilateral treaty, an Agreement Concerning Collaboration in the Field of Veterinary Medicine. This plurilateral treaty formed a treaty-network more complete than had existed previously for any single party-state. It is interesting to note that Yugoslavia and Poland signed a bilateral treaty subsequent to the plurilateral treaty. Why was Yugoslavia not incorporated into the plurilateral arrangement?

In 1956, the USSR and the various party-states with a common seacoast concluded plurilateral treaties concerning rescue-at-sea for their respective seas:

> USSR-China-North Korea: Agreement concerning collaboration between the shipwreck salvage services of the three states in saving human lives and aiding ships and airplanes wrecked in the waters of the Far Eastern Seas and the Pacific Ocean (July 3, 1956);
>
> USSR-East Germany-Poland: (July 7, 1956);[13]
>
> USSR-Romania-Bulgaria: Agreement concerning collaboration in saving human life and assistance to vessels and aircraft in distress on the Black Sea (September 11, 1956).

Grzybowski has determined that the "procedures set up in these agreements follow a single pattern for all three sea areas."[14]

With reference to our theory, all three of these rescue-at-sea treaties satisfy the structural condition of a complete plurilateral treaty-network, with one exception. This one exception is that North Vietnam, with a sea coast on the Pacific Ocean, is not a signatory of the USSR-China-North Korea treaty concerning this sea area. Otherwise, the respective party-states are all signatories to the plurilateral treaty revelant to rescue-at-sea operations of their common seacoast.

The Soviet Union has concluded several bilateral treaties concerning rescue-at-sea with non-member states which have a seacoast in common with the USSR and various ruling communist party states:

> BALTIC SEA
>
> USSR-Sweden: Agreement between the USSR and Sweden concerning cooperation for rescue in the Baltic Sea (September 29, 1954);
>
> USSR-Denmark: Agreement between the USSR and Denmark concerning saving human lives in the Baltic Sea (March 6, 1956), and
> Agreement between the USSR and Denmark concerning communications between the rescue services of the USSR and Denmark for collaboration in saving human lives in the Baltic Sea (June 14, 1956);
>
> USSR-Finland: Agreement between USSR and Finland concerning collaboration between rescue services in the Baltic Sea (December 7, 1956);
>
> PACIFIC OCEAN
>
> USSR-Japan: Agreement between the USSR and Japan concerning cooperation for the rescue of persons in distress at sea, with exchange of notes (May 14, 1956).

With regard to rescue-at-sea in both the Baltic Sea and Pacific Ocean, the three Scandinavian countries and Japan are not included in the relevant, geographically plurilateral treaty-networks of the party-states. Three of the four Soviet treaties with non-members on this subject predate the geographically plurilateral treaties among the communist party-states. We suggest that the geographically plurilateral treaties within the party-states system vis-à-vis the Soviet bilateral treaties with other nations imply the mutual identification dimension of the attitudinal variable of integration.

Yet another example of a geographically plurilateral treaty is the following:

> USSR-East Germany-Poland: Agreement concerning the load mark on vessels sailing under their flags and between their ports on the Baltic Sea (1961);

> USSR-Romania-Bulgaria: Agreement concerning the load mark on vessels sailing under their flags between their ports on the Black Sea (1960).

The geographically plurilateral treaty also illustrates the adaptability of subject-matter areas involving procedural planning to the plurilateral form of treaty instrument.

CONCLUSION

In this chapter, we have attempted to examine patterns in the treaty-making behavior of the Soviet Union with the other communist party-states, and then to make comparisons with such behavior on the part of the other party-states. Our focus has been on treaty-networks or on those channels of communication which link nations and are formalized by treaties. We contend that the concepts of complete and congruent treaty-networks, as developed in the section on theory, are useful approaches to the study of integration among the communist party-states.

Future investigation is necessary with regards to a more comprehensive, comparative examination of the terms and conditions of the treaties, and an analysis of relations among the party-states vis-à-vis the policies set forth in the treaties. Transactional data with which to assess the quality and caliber of transactional channels linking the party-states is sparse and not complete for all party-states or over a series of years.[15]

Treaties in various substantive areas require interaction(s) for implementation. For example, the provisions in the Soviet-party-state treaties concerning both scientific-technical and cultural collaboration establish mixed Soviet-party-state commissions in order to carry out the treaty and specify the frequency and location of commission meetings. Usually, the two treaty partners announce, via a joint communiqué or protocol, the sessions of the commission in the case of scientific-technical collaboration or the annual plan for cooperation based on a meeting of the mixed commission in the case of cultural collaboration. Thus, it becomes possible to keep a record of the presence of meetings of scientific-technical commissions or of annual plans for cultural cooperation, and

TABLE 5-2*

SUBJECT OF TREATY

COMMUNIST PARTY-STATE	Friendship, Mutual Assistance	Commerce	Condition of Trade Deliveries	Scientific-Technical Collaboration	Atomic Energy	Cultural Collaboration	Legal Aid and Legal Relations	Dual Nationality	Consular Relations	Training of Citizens in Soviet Civic Institutes	Social Security	Radio Broadcasting
East Germany	6–12–64ᵃ 10	9–27–57 7	3–16–51 2	9–27–51 6	4–28–55 5	4–26–56 3	11–28–57 3		5–10–57 1	5–12–52 6	5–24–60 3	1–13–53 5
Poland	4–21–45 3	7–7–45 2	2–29–52 4	3–5–47 1	4–23–55 2.5	6–30–56 9	9–28–57 2	1–21–58 2	1–21–58 8	5–19–52 7.5		10–22–49 2
Czechoslovakia	12–12–43 1	12–11–47 5	4–5–52 6	12–11–47 2	4–23–55 2.5	6–1–56 7	8–31–57 1	10–5–57 6	10–5–57 5	4–11–52 3	12–2–59 1	
Hungary	2–18–48 6	7–15–47 4	6–30–52 10	7–26–49 3	6–13–55 6	6–28–56 8	7–15–58 9	8–24–57 3	8–24–57 2	5–19–52 7.5	12–20–62 5	4–12–50 3
Romania	2–4–48 5	2–20–47 3	6–25–52 9	2–17–50 4	4–22–55 1	4–7–56 1	4–3–58 6	9–4–57 4	9–4–57 3	3–20–52 2	12–24–60 4	4–27–49 1
Bulgaria	3–18–48 7	4–1–48 6	6–16–52 8	2–18–50 5		4–28–56 4	12–12–57 4	12–12–57 7	12–12–57 6	3–7–52 1	12–11–59 2	
Yugoslavia	4–11–45 2 (denounced)	5–11–40 1		12–19–55 10	1–28–56 7	5–17–56 6	2–24–62 10	5–22–56 1	7–21–60 12			7–10–57 8

* For each cell in the table, there are two entries: date of signature and rank order of signing date in comparison with other ruling communist party-states.

TABLE 5-2 (Cont'd)

SUBJECT OF TREATY

COMMUNIST PARTY-STATE	Friendship, Mutual Assistance	Commerce	Condition of Trade Deliveries	Scientific-Technical Collaboration	Atomic Energy	Cultural Collaboration	Legal Aid and Legal Relations	Dual Nationality	Consular Relations	Training of Citizens in Soviet Civic Institutes	Social Security	Radio Broadcasting
Albania		2-15-58 9	4-19-52 7	2-19-52 7		5-3-56 5	6-30-58 8	9-18-57 5	9-18-57 4	7-5-52 9		6-27-50 4
Outer Mongolia	2-27-46 4	12-17-57 8	12-29-51 3	4-17-61 12		4-24-56 2	4-25-58 7	8-25-58 9	8-25-58 9	4-30-52 4		9-11-53 6
China	2-14-50 8	4-23-58 11	3-29-52 5	10-12-54 8	4-27-55 4	7-5-56 10			6-23-59 11	8-9-52 10		8-21-54 7
North Korea	7-6-61 9	6-22-60 12	10-5-50 1	2-5-55 9	9-7-59 8	9-5-56 11	12-16-57 5	12-16-57 8	12-16-57 7	5-6-52 5		
North Vietnam		3-12-58 10	4-8-57 11	3-7-59 11		2-15-57 12			6-5-59 10			
Cuba						12-12-60 13						
Total Party-State Signatories	10	12	11	12	8	13	10	9	12	10	5	8
Number of Other Signatories	1	6	1	2	7	19	—	—	2	—	—	—

SOURCE: "Calendars," except where noted: "Grzybowski, *Socialist Commonwealth*, p. 174.

TABLE 5-3*

SUBJECT OF TREATY

COMMUNIST PARTY-STATE	Friendship, Mutual Assistance	Scientific-Technical Collaboration	Cultural Collaboration	Commerce	Legal Aid and Legal Relations	Dual Nationality	Consular Relations	Social Security
East Germany	China(12-25-55)	Poland(6-6-50) Bulgaria(6-19-50) Czech.(6-23-50) Hungary(6-24-50) Romania(9-22-50) USSR(9-27-51) Albania(2-26-52) China(10-30-53) N. Korea(1-27-55)	China(10-9-51) Poland(1-8-52) USSR(4-26-56) Romania(7-15-58) Hungary(12-19-59) Cuba(3-29-61)	USSR(9-27-57) N. Viet.(3-7-59) Bulgaria(7-16-59) Albania(10-8-59) Czech.(11-25-59) China(1-18-60)	Czech.(10-11-56) Poland(2-1-57) Hungary(10-30-57) USSR(11-28-57) Bulgaria(1-27-58) Romania(7-15-58) Albania(1-11-59)		USSR(5-10-57) Czech.(5-24-57) Hungary(7-3-57) Poland(11-25-57) Romania(7-15-58)	Poland(7-13-57) Hungary(1-30-60) USSR(5-24-60)
Poland	USSR(4-21-45) Yugo.(3-18-46)[a] Czech.(3-10-47) Bulgaria(5-29-48) Hungary(6-18-48) Romania(1-26-49)	USSR(3-5-47) E. Ger.(6-6-50) Albania(1-25-51) China(7-20-54)	Albania(12-2-50) China(4-3-51) E. Ger.(1-8-52) N. Korea(5-11-56) USSR(6-30-56) Yugo.(7-6-56) N. Viet.(4-6-57) O. Mon.(12-23-58) Cuba(3-6-61)	Czech.(7-5-45) USSR(7-7-45)	Yugo.(prewar) Czech.(1-21-49) E. Ger.(2-1-57) USSR(9-28-57) Hungary(3-6-59) Bulgaria(12-4-61) Romania(1-25-62)	USSR(1-21-58) Hungary(7-5-61)	E. Ger.(11-25-57) USSR(1-21-58) Yugo.(11-17-58) Hungary(5-20-59) Czech.(5-17-60) Bulgaria(9-19-61)	Czech.(4-5-48) E. Ger.(7-13-57) Yugo.(1-16-58) Hungary(2-14-59) Bulgaria(7-12-61)
Czechoslovakia	USSR(12-12-43) Yugo.(5-9-46)[a] Poland(3-10-47) Bulgaria(4-23-48) Romania(7-21-48)	USSR(12-11-47) E. Ger.(6-23-50) China(5-6-52) Yugo.(7-3-56)	China(5-6-52) USSR(6-1-56) Yugo.(1-29-57) Romania(10-25-58) Cuba(12-22-60)	Poland(7-4-47) USSR(12-11-47) E. Ger.(11-25-59) Bulgaria(3-8-63)	Yugo.(prewar) Poland(1-21-49) Hungary(3-6-51) Bulgaria(4-13-54) E. Ger.(9-11-56)	USSR(10-5-57) Hungary(11-4-60)	E. Ger.(5-24-57) USSR(10-5-57) Albania(1-16-59) Hungary(3-27-59) Bulgaria(5-27-59)	Poland(4-5-48) Bulgaria(1-25-57) Romania(5-2-57) Yugo.(5-22-57) Hungary(1-30-59)

	Hungary(4-16-49) O. Mon. (4-8-57)	Hungary(2-24-61)		USSR(8-31-57) Romania(10-25-58) Albania(1-16-59)		China(5-7-60) Romania(5-12-60) N. Viet.(1-14-63) Yugo.(6-24-63) O. Mon.(11-8-63)	USSR(12-2-59)
Hungary	Yugo.(12-8-47)[a] Romania(1-24-48) USSR(2-18-48) Poland(6-18-48) Bulgaria(7-16-48) Czech.(4-16-49)	USSR(7-26-49) E. Ger.(6-24-50) China(10-3-53)	China(7-12-51) USSR(4-24-56) E. Ger.(12-19-58) Czech.(2-24-61)	USSR(7-15-47)	Yugo.(prewar) Czech.(3-6-51) Bulgaria(8-8-53) E. Ger.(10-30-57) USSR(7-15-58) Romania(10-7-58) Poland(3-6-59)	USSR(8-24-57) Bulgaria(6-27-58) Czech.(11-4-60) Poland(7-5-61)	E. Ger.(7-3-57) USSR(8-24-57) Hungary(3-18-59) Czech.(3-27-59) Poland(5-20-59)	Yugo.(10-7-57) Czech.(1-30-59) Poland(2-14-59) E. Ger.(1-30-60) USSR(12-20-62)
Romania	Yugo.(12-19-47)[a] Bulgaria(1-16-48) Hungary(1-24-48) USSR(2-4-48) Czech.(7-21-48) Poland(1-26-49)	USSR(2-17-50) E. Ger.(9-22-50) Bulgaria(9-29-50) China(1-9-53) Yugo.(10-27-56) N. Viet.(6-30-58)	China(12-12-51) Albania(2-14-53) USSR(4-7-56) O. Mon.(5-3-56) N. Korea(5-12-56) N. Viet.(10-12-56) Yugo.(10-27-56) E. Ger.(7-15-58) Czech.(10-25-58) Cuba(10-28-60)	USSR(2-20-47)	USSR(4-3-58) E. Ger.(7-15-58) Hungary(10-7-58) Czech.(10-25-58) Bulgaria(12-3-58) Poland(1-25-62)	USSR(9-4-57) Bulgaria(9-24-59)?	USSR(9-4-57) E. Ger.(7-15-58) Hungary(3-18-59) Bulgaria(4-23-59) Czech.(5-2-60) Yugo.(11-8-62)	Czech.(5-2-57) Bulgaria(9-14-60) USSR(12-24-60)
Bulgaria	Yugo.(12-27-47)[a] Albania(12-16-47) Romania(1-16-48) USSR(3-18-48) Czech.(4-23-48) Poland(5-29-48) Hungary(7-16-48)	USSR(2-18-60) E. Ger.(6-19-50) Romania(9-29-50) China(3-23-55) Yugo.(2-10-56)	China(7-14-52) USSR(4-28-56) Yugo.(12-24-56)	USSR(4-1-48) E. Ger.(7-16-59) Czech.(3-8-63)	Hungary(8-8-53) Czech.(4-13-54) Yugo.(3-23-56) USSR(12-12-57) E. Ger.(1-27-58) Romania(12-3-58) Poland(12-4-61)	USSR(12-12-57) Hungary(6-27-58) Romania(9-24-59)	Czech.(1-25-57) Romania(4-23-59) Czech.(5-27-59) Poland(9-19-61)	Czech.(1-25-57) USSR(12-11-59) Romania(3-14-60) Poland(7-12-61)

TABLE 5-3 (Cont'd)

SUBJECT OF TREATY

COMMUNIST PARTY-STATE	Friendship, Mutual Assistance	Scientific-Technical Collaboration	Cultural Collaboration	Commerce	Legal Aid and Legal Relations	Dual Nationality	Consular Relations	Social Security
Yugoslavia	USSR(4-11-45)[a] Poland(3-18-46)[a] Czech.(5-9-46)[a] Albania(7-9-47)[a] Bulgaria(11-27-47)[a] Hungary(12-8-48)[a] Romania(12-19-47)[a]	USSR(12-19-55) Bulgaria(2-10-56) China(2-17-56) Czech.(7-3-56) Romania(10-27-56)	USSR(5-17-56) Poland(7-6-56) Bulgaria(12-24-56) Czech.(1-29-57)	USSR(5-11-40)	Czech., Hungary, and Poland(prewar) Bulgaria(3-23-56) USSR(2-24-62)	USSR(5-22-56)	Poland(11-17-58) USSR(4-21-60) Romania(11-8-62) Czech.(6-24-63)	Czech.(5-22-57) Hungary(10-7-57) Poland(1-16-58)
Albania	Yugo.(7-9-47)[a] Bulgaria(12-16-47)	Poland(1-25-51) E. Ger.(2-26-52) USSR(4-19-52) China(10-14-54)	Poland(12-2-50) Romania(2-14-53) China(10-14-54) USSR(5-3-56)	USSR(2-15-58) E. Ger.(10-8-59)	USSR(6-30-58) E. Ger.(1-11-59) Czech.(1-16-59)	USSR(9-18-57)	USSR(9-18-57) Czech.(1-16-59)	
Outer Mongolia	USSR(2-27-46) Czech.(4-8-57)	USSR(4-7-61)	China(10-4-52) USSR(4-12-56) Romania(5-3-56) Poland(12-23-58)	USSR(12-17-57)	USSR(4-25-58)	USSR(8-25-58)	USSR(8-25-58) Czech.(11-18-63)	
China	USSR(2-14-50) E. Ger.(12-25-55)	Czech.(5-6-52) Romania(1-9-53) Hungary(10-3-53) E. Ger.(10-30-53) Poland(7-20-54) USSR(10-12-54) Albania(10-14-54) Bulgaria(3-23-55)	Poland(4-3-51) Hungary(7-12-51) Romania(12-12-51) E. Ger.(10-9-51) Czech.(5-6-52) Bulgaria(7-14-52) O. Mon.(10-4-52) N.Korea(11-23-53)	USSR(4-23-58) E. Ger.(1-18-60)			USSR(6-23-59) Czech.(5-7-60)	

(Yugo.)	Yugo.(2-17-56)				Albania(10-14-54) USSR(7-5-56)	
North Korea	USSR(7-6-61)	E. Ger.(1-27-55) USSR(2-5-55)	China(11-23-53) Poland(5-11-56) Romania(5-12-56) USSR(9-5-56) Cuba(8-29-60)	USSR(6-22-60)	USSR(12-16-57)	USSR(12-16-57) USSR(12-16-57)
North Vietnam		Romania(6-30-58) USSR(3-7-59)	Romania(10-12-56) USSR(3-7-59)	USSR(3-12-58) E. Ger.(3-7-59)	USSR(2-15-57) Poland(4-6-57)	USSR(6-5-59) Czech.(1-14-63)
Cuba			N. Korea(8-29-60) Romania(10-28-60) USSR(12-12-60) Czech.(12-22-60) Poland(3-6-61) E. Ger.(3-29-61)			

* Each entry in a cell consists of a CP state treaty partner in a substantive area and the date of conclusion of such treaty.

a no longer in effect

SOURCES OF DATA FOR TABLE 5-3

FRIENDSHIP, MUTUAL ASSISTANCE: Piotr S. Wandycz, "The Soviet System of Alliances in East Central Europe," *Journal of Central European Affairs*, XVI, No. 2 (July 1956), 177–81. *Die Verträge der Volksrepublik China mit anderen Staaten* (Frankfurt am Main: Alfred Metzner Verlag, 1957).

SCIENTIFIC-TECHNICAL COLLABORATION: Kazimierz Grzybowski, *The Socialist Commonwealth of Nations* (New Haven: Yale University Press, 1964), p. 27. Edward L. Miles, with John S. Gillooly, "Processes of Interaction Among the Fourteen Communist Party-States: An Exploratory Essay" (Stanford Studies of the Communist System, March 1965), Appendix B. *Die Verträge der Volksrepublik China mit anderen Staaten. United Nations Treaty Series*, Volumes 450–503.

CULTURAL COLLABORATION: "Processes of Interaction Among the Fourteen Communist Party-States: An Exploratory Essay." *United Nations Treaty Series*, Volumes 450–503. *Die Verträge der Volksrepublik China mit anderen Staaten.*

COMMERCE: *The Socialist Commonwealth of Nations. United Nations Treaty Series*, Volumes 450–503.

LEGAL AID AND LEGAL RELATIONS: Ulrich Drobnig, "Die Kollisionsnormen in den Rechtshilfeverträgen der Staaten des Ostblocks," *Ost Europa Recht*, VI (1960), 154–84.

DUAL NATIONALITY: Ivan Sipkov, "Settlement of Dual Nationality in European Communist Countries," *American Journal of International Law*, LVI (1962), 1010–19.

CONSULAR RELATIONS: "Processes of Interaction Among the Fourteen Communist Party-States: An Exploratory Essay." *United Nations Treaty Series*, Volumes 450–503.

SOCIAL SECURITY: Same as for Consular Relations. NOTE: In addition, all Soviet communist party-state treaties are from the "Calendars."

then to examine this record for patterns of interaction. The basis for one such pattern would be a comparison of the actual frequency of sessions of the scientific-technical commissions with the number stipulated in the treaty. We suggest that such patterns of interaction will reflect the stability or instability of Soviet-party-state relations and provide an empirical base for additional statements about integration within the system.

An intervening variable absent from our analyses thus far has been time. During the period under consideration, approximately 1945 until the end of 1962, the communist system experienced fluctuating composition and internal strife.[16] Yugoslavia withdrew and subsequently reentered; and East Germany, China, North Vietnam, and Cuba allied themselves. The events of internal discord include the Polish and Hungarian revolts of 1956, and deterioration of relations between the Soviet Union and both Albania and China.

An important question immediately arises: Does the treaty-making behavior of the system leader register the changing relations between the communist party-states? Essentially, the manifestations of changing relations between two nations are alterations in patterns of interactions and transactions between the respective countries. Given the formal nature of treaties, it seems probable that a change in Soviet treaty relations with the party-states would initially reflect changing patterns of interactions and transactions and subsequently affect internation behavior. Changes in patterns of interactions and transactions between two nations become a more sensitive indicator of international strife than changing treaty relations.

Yet, evidence for system transformation on the level of treaties can include abrogations and comparisons of completeness and congruency in treaty-networks. However, even in the presence of the acknowledged Sino-Soviet rift, the Soviet-Chinese friendship and mutual assistance treaty of 1950 endures.

An overall examination of Table 5–2 reveals the absence, since about 1960, of the formation of Soviet-party-state treaty-networks. On the basis of the "Calendars" for 1960–1962, Soviet treaty-making behavior has tended to involve specific transactional agreements with individual countries. This change in Soviet treaty-making behavior, that is, the curtailment in the establishment of system-wide treaty-networks and the emphasis on specific transactional agreements, might reflect mounting internal discord within the system.[17]

Our concern has been the integration among the communist party-states under Soviet leadership. We could make only tentative statements at this time about such integration because of our lack of comprehensive and complete data on treaty relations of the other party-states, particularly the Asian members. We must eventually synthesize our findings about the bilateral treaty-networks with an analysis of plurilateral arrangements within the system in order to discuss further the integration of the communist party-state system.

TABLE 5–4. QUARANTINE AND PROTECTION OF AGRICULTURAL PLANTS

USSR
  Czechoslovakia (11–28–47)
  Poland (4–8–48)
  Romania (5–27–50)
  Hungary (7–13–50)
  Bulgaria (8–25–50)
  East Germany (5–30–56)
  China (8–16–55)
  Albania (8–27–55)
  North Korea (11–30–55)

East Germany
  Poland (6–23–50)
  Romania (8–5–55)
  China (12–25–55)
  USSR (5–30–56)
  Hungary (10–25–57)

Poland
  USSR (4–8–48)
  Bulgaria (9–26–49)
  Hungary (10–29–49)
  East Germany (6–23–50)

Czechoslovakia
  USSR (11–28–47)
  Romania (10–31–52)
  China (8–18–53)

Hungary
  Poland (10–29–49)
  USSR (7–13–50)
  Romania (12–14–53)
  China (12–28–54)
  East Germany (10–25–57)

Romania
  USSR (5–27–50)
  Czechoslovakia (10-31-52)
  Hungary (12–14–53)
  Bulgaria (7–22–54)
  East Germany (8–5–55)
  Yugoslavia (9–25–56)

Bulgaria
  Poland (10–26–49)
  USSR (8–25–50)
  China (7–11–55)
  Romania (7–22–54)
  Yugoslavia (6–4–57)

Yugoslavia
  Romania (10–25–56)
  Albania (5–20–57)
  Bulgaria (6–4–57)

Albania
  USSR (8–27–55)
  Yugoslavia (5–20–57)

China
  Czechslovakia (8–18–53)
  Hungary (12–28–54)
  Bulgaria (7–11–55)
  USSR (8–16–55)
  East Germany (12–25–55)

Sources of data: USSR—"Calendars." China—*Die Verträge der Volksrepublik China mit anderen Staaten.* Other communist party-states—"Processes of Interaction Among the Fourteen Communist Party-States: An Exploratory Essay."

TABLE 5–5.   VETERINARY MEDICINE

USSR Czechoslovakia (5–18–57)	*Romania* Yugoslavia (8–4–56) East Germany (9–8–56)
East Germany Romania (10–8–56) Hungary (11–13–57) Czechoslovakia (3–12–58)	*Bulgaria* Poland (9–26–49) Yugoslavia (6–17–55) Czechoslovakia (6–3–57)
Czechoslovakia USSR (5–18–57) Bulgaria (6–3–57) East Germany (3–12–58)	*Yugoslavia* Bulgaria (6–17–55) Romania (8–4–56) Poland (5–5–60)
Hungary Poland (10–29–49) East Germany (11–13–57)	*Poland* Bulgaria (9–26–49) Hungary (10-29-49) Yugoslavia (5–5–60)

Sources of data: USSR—"Calendars." Other communist party-states—"Processes of Interaction Among the Fourteen Communist Party-States: An Exploratory Essay."

NOTES

1. Robert M. Slusser and Jan F. Triska, *A Calendar of Soviet Treaties, 1917–1957* (Stanford: Stanford University Press, 1959), p. iv.
2. *Loc. cit.*
3. Richard A. Brody, "Cognition and Behavior: A Model of Inter-Unit Relations" (mimeographed; Stanford, n. d.), p. 13.
4. *United Nations Treaty Series,* Vol. 259, No. 3698, p. 388.
5. See the following: Alex Bavelas, "Communication Patterns in Task-Oriented Groups," *Journal of the Acoustical Society of America,* XXII, No. 6 (November 1950), 725–30; and Harold Guetzkow and Herbert A. Simon, "The Impact of Certain Communication Nets upon Organization and Performance in Task-Oriented Groups," *Management Science,* I, No. 3–4 (April-July 1955), 233–50.
6. Maurice David Simon, in his paper "Communist System Interaction with Developing States, 1954–1962: A Preliminary Analysis" (Chapter 8 of the present volume), reviews the literature on integration.
7. Jan. F. Triska and Robert M. Slusser, *The Theory, Law, and Policy of Soviet Treaties* (Stanford: Stanford University Press, 1962), p. 26.
8. The compilation of Chinese treaties to which we refer was published by das Institut für Asienkunde in Hamburg under the title, *Die Verträge der Volksrepublik China mit anderen Staaten.*

9. Kazimierz Grzybowski, *The Socialist Commonwealth of Nations* (New Haven: Yale University Press, 1964), p. 178.

10. *Ibid.*, p. 205.

11. Another example of the rapid formation of a Soviet treaty-network with a subset of party-states is the following: The USSR concluded a Protocol Concerning Settlement of Mutual Property and Financial Claims Arising from the Incorporation of Lithuania, Latvia, and Estonia into the USSR with each of Bulgaria (January 18, 1958), Romania (March 7, 1958), Hungary (March 14, 1958), and Czechoslovakia (June 30, 1958).

12. *United Nations Treaty Series*, Vol. 342, No. 4906, p. 164.

13. Kazimierz Grzybowski, *Peaceful Settlement of International Disputes in the Communist Bloc* (mimeographed; Washington, D. C.: U. S. Arms Control and Disarmament Agency, 1953), p. 18.

14. Grzybowski, *The Socialist Commonwealth*, p. 171.

15. Statistics on foreign trade constitute a possible exception. For example, see Appendix A, "Tables on Trade Interaction within the Communist System," in the Miles with Gillooly Research Paper (No. 5 of the Stanford Studies of the Communist System, March 1965). Although we have not discussed treaty-networks concerning foreign trade in this chapter, Soviet treaty-making behavior in this area presents additional patterns of interaction, based on short-term trade agreements of five years or less, and yearly protocols.

16. W. W. Kulski, "Integrating the Communist Political Orbit," in Elmer Plischke (ed.), *Systems of Integrating the International Community* (Princeton: D. Van Nostrand Company, Inc., 1964).

17. The subsequent "Calendars," which updated the initial "Calendar" by Slusser and Triska, are the following: George Ginsburgs, "A Calendar of Soviet Treaties, January-December 1960," *Ost Europa Recht,* IX (1963), 120–59; George Ginsburgs, "A Calendar of Soviet Treaties, January-December 1961," *Ost Europa Recht,* X (1964), 116–48; George Ginsburgs, "A Calendar of Soviet Treaties, January-December 1962," *Ost Europa Recht,* XI (1965), 129–60; George Ginsburgs and Robert M. Slusser, "A Calendar of Soviet Treaties, January-December 1959," *Ost Europa Recht,* VIII (1962), 132–64; and Robert M. Slusser and George Ginsburgs, "A Calendar of Soviet Treaties, January-December 1958," *Ost Europa Recht,* VII (1961), 100–31.

SIX

THE DIVIDED NATIONS: INTERNATIONAL INTEGRATION AND NATIONAL IDENTITY

Patterns in Germany, China, Vietnam, and Korea

BRUCE R. SIEVERS

National division is one of the bizarre products of competition between communist and Western political systems. The "politics of division" that has brought about the division of four formerly national units and the subsequent incorporation of them into antagonistic international systems has been discussed at length in both scholarly and journalistic writings. Surprisingly little attention, however, has been paid to the fundamental political and social consequences these divisive processes have had for the new "national" environments. Such neglect is as regrettable as it is surprising, since these nations, aside from their vital role in international politics,[1] offer the best possible conditions for comparison of differing political systems.

This paper suggests that reflection upon observable tendencies in these cases may shed a great deal of light upon the integrative capacity of political communities, both national and international, because the divided nations offer a rare direct link between the two levels of integration and because they reveal, in an especially clear way, the crucial role of "national identity" in the integration process. The literature on integration theory focuses primarily on positive processes: In integrating communities, an increase of interaction leads to an increase in the "sense of political community," and so on in an upward spiraling process.[2] What happens, however, when a "sense of community" is already established and the transactions are cut off? Does the spiral start downward? Do the nations become increasingly divided? Two studies, one an investigation by Bruce Russett of trends in Anglo-American community relationships,[3] and the other, Oscar Jászi's analysis of the disintegration of the Austro-Hungarian empire,[4] give affirmative replies to these questions. Quite different answers are found below, yet the final results suggest an explanation of political disintegration which accounts for the differing outcomes of the cases studied by Russett and Jászi, on the one hand, and those of the divided nations on the other.

DIVIDED NATIONS AND THE INTERNATIONAL SYSTEMS

Since 1945, four national units have been divided between membership in the communist system and membership in the alliance system of the United States:[5] Germany, China, Korea, and Vietnam. Although these countries differ in many respects, they share at least one basic similarity: Each has undergone complete transformation from a single politico-cultural entity, which belonged to neither international system, into what are now two separate states, each of which has become fully a member of its respective system. These processes of division demonstrate several common characteristics: All involved a split between the communist and the Western systems; all took place, on the whole, without the consent of the populace; all caused subsequent economic disadvantages; none (with the possible exception of China) occurred along "natural" ethnic or linguistic dividing lines. There are also, however, certain obvious dissimilarities among the nations involved: They differ radically in size and population, in historical and cultural development, in stages of economic development, and in the specific ways in which each became divided.

Yet, in spite of these important differences, it is useful to look at the common process of political division and examine its effects upon the polities undergoing change. For this task, an important body of theory that has been recently developing in the field of political integration suggests its applicability. The theoretical work of Deutsch, Haas, and Etzioni has thoroughly explored the various aspects of national and international integration; Deutsch in particular, through a "communications" approach, suggests a method of linking various levels of integration on both attitudinal and interactional planes.

In the most schematic form, this process might be conceived of in terms of a broad definition of political integration suggested by Jacob and Teune in *The Integration of Political Communities* (1964):

> Political integration generally implies a relationship of *community* among people within the same political entity. That is, they are held together by mutual ties of one kind or another which give the group a feeling of identity and self-awareness.[6]

In terms of the definition, interaction in the form of "mutual ties" produces an integrative attitude in the form of a "feeling of identity" and the two combine in the form of "community" in the political entity. Presumably the reverse is also true: In the destruction of a political entity, the community will disintegrate when mutual ties are reduced and the corresponding identification and self-awareness disappear. At least such is the process suggested by Russett's research with repect to the "community" of Great Britain and the United States.

In terms of integration theory, then, the process of national division might be expected to take the following forms: (1) with the passage of time, each part becomes increasingly *tied* (interactionally) to its respective international system; (2) accordingly, with new socialization processes and absence of communication with its counterpart, each half becomes increasingly *isolated* from its opposite member; (3) accompanying the first two changes, as the more immediate problems of nation-building take over, *corresponding changes in attitudes occur,* that is, interest and identification increase with regard to the international system and decrease with regard to the other part of the old national unit.

On the first level (stage one above) the international transactions of the divided nations do not deviate from this pattern. An examination of ties on several levels of communication between these nations and the communist and western international systems reveals that the divided nations not only have a high level of transactions with the larger systems but that they have in fact the *highest* levels of all the members of the systems. Indeed, in purely transactional terms, the divided nations appear as a group to be the most highly integrated members of the two international systems.

This is most clearly illustrated by economic transactions. Table 6–1 indicates the dramatic increases in percentages of trade of each unit with its respective system in pre- and post-integration periods. Table 6–2 compares these percentages in specified years with those of the other members of the system. In the case of the communist system, the only nations whose trade with the system exceeds 75% and is rising are North Korea, North Vietnam, and East Germany—all divided. China for reasons peculiar to herself (her size and the Sino-Soviet split) forms an obvious exception here.

The trade percentages between Western parts of the divided nations and the Western system as a whole are all constant or rising, and South Korea, South Vietnam, and Taiwan hold the top three positions when ranked with all members of the system. West Germany ranks lower, but has shown the greatest rise of all relative to its prewar trading levels.

In terms of economic aid, too, the divided nations emerge, as a group, as the most "integrated members" of the two international systems. As is evident from Table 6–3, the amounts of aid given by the two system

TABLE 6–1. TRADE OF THE DIVIDED STATES WITH THEIR INTERNATIONAL SYSTEMS (AS PERCENTAGE OF COUNTRY'S TOTAL)

Year	1938	49	50	51	53	54	55	56	57	58	59	60	61	62	63
COUNTRY															
E. Ger.	18				77	88	72	73	73	74	76	75	76	79	79
N. Kor.	5 (est.)										98	96	96	97	
N. Viet.	5									80+		(80–90)			
C. Ch.	1	8	27		...avr. 75...					70	70	65	50	50	40
W. Ger.	32	60	50	46	44	43	44	45	46	45	47	48	49	52	53
S. Kor.				91	93	91	82	82	85	91	87	86	88	87	86
S. Viet.	66	79	81	81	81	79	77	86	83	81	81	77	79	79	75
Taiwan				65	72	81	80	73	66	72	74	74	74	74	71

Sources: *Directions of International Trade* 1950–64; *People's China*, III:7; *Peking Review*, June 17, 1958; "China's Economy and Its Prospects," by Yuan-Li Wu, *Current History*, May 1964, pp. 166–72; *Statistical Returns of the National Economy of the Democratic People's Republic of Korea* (1946–62); "Trade Patterns of the West, 1963" and "Trade of NATO Countries with Communist Countries, 1961–63," U.S. Department of State Research Memorandum (unclassified); *Statistisches Jahrbuch der Deutschen Demokratischen Republik 1958, 1965* (East Berlin: 1958, 1965); William Kaye, "A Bowl of Rice Divided: The Economy of North Vietnam," *The China Quarterly*, No. 9 (January-March 1962), pp. 82–93; Zwei entgegengesetzte Tendenzen der wirtschaftlichen Entwicklung in Vietnam," *Deutsche Aussenpolitik* (East Berlin: 1962), pp. 204–10.

TABLE 6–2. TRADE TRENDS WITHIN THE INTERNATIONAL SYSTEMS

Trade with Rest of Communist System				Trade with Rest of Western System			
Year	1955	1963	Trend		1955	1963	Trend
COUNTRY				COUNTRY			
E. Ger.	72%	79%	+	W. Ger.	44%	53%	+
N. Kor.	80+	96	+	S. Kor.	82	86	+
N. Viet.	70+	(85) (est.)	+	S. Viet.	76	76	n. c.
C. Ch.	75	40	−	Taiwan	80	74	−
USSR	79	72	−	USA	44	50	+
Czech.	64	74	+	France	43	51	+
Poland	64	64	n. c.	Italy	44	54	+
Hung.	60	69	+	Neth.	65	70	+
Bul.	86	82	−	B.-Lux.	61	74	+
Rom.	76	61	−	Can.	91	74	−
Yugo.	10	23	+	Japan	34	41	+
Alb.	95+	90+	−	Gr. Br.	28	34	+
Cuba	..	73	..				

Sources: See Table 6-1.

TABLE 6–3. FOREIGN AID (EXTENDED BY SYSTEM LEADER, 1945–1960)

Communist System			Western System		
Country	Total	per Capita	Country	Total	per Capita
N. Kor.	$ 750 mill.	$70	Taiwan	$1748 mill.	$166
E. Ger.	429 mill.	25	S. Kor.	2827 mill.	113
N. Viet.	365 mill.	23	S. Viet.	1290 mill.	91
C. Ch.	2500 mill.	4	W. Ger.	3664 mill.	66
Total Rest of System	1780 mill.	16		19190 mill.	57
All Other Develop. Countries	2648 mill.	2		14243 mill.	10

Sources: ECE *Economic Survey of Europe in 1957* (Geneva, 1958), pp. 55–58; UNESCO *World Economic Survey for 1960* (New York, 1961), p. 120; William Kaye, "A Bowl of Rice Divided: The Economy of North Vietnam," *China Quarterly,* No. 9 (January–March 1962), pp. 82–93; Kang Chao, "Pitfalls in the Use of China's Foreign Trade Statistics," *China Quarterly,* No. 19 (July–September 1964), pp. 47–65; A. Boone, "The Foreign Trade of China," *China Quarterly,* No. 11 (July–September 1962), pp. 169–83; Bernard Fall, *The Two Viet-Nams* (New York: Praeger, 1963), p. 175; David W. Chang, "U.S. Aid and Economic Progress in Taiwan," *Asian Survey,* III (March 1963), 152–60; Robert Rupen, "The Mongolian People's Republic and the Sino-Soviet Competition," in A. Doak Barnett (ed.), *Communist Strategies in Asia* (New York: Praeger, 1963), p. 268; U.S. Bureau of the Census, *Statistical Abstract of the United States 1961* (Washington, D.C., 1962), pp. 872–74; Frederic L. Pryor, *The Communist Foreign Trade System* (Cambridge: Massachusetts Institute of Technology Press, 1963).

leaders to the divided nations on each side far exceed that given to any of the other system members or nations outside either system, often by a factor as great as ten. In one sense, these significantly higher aid figures might be interpreted as the "price" (the concept suggested by Deutsch)[7] paid by the systems for the integration of the divided nations, as well as an economic indicator of the integration itself.

Another major indicator of international transactions is that of mail flow. Unfortunately, the data here is available only for the Western parts of the divided nations. As Table 6–4 shows, however, this data has a surprisingly high correlation with trade flows and, like the trade tables, reveals that the divided nations are, in general, the members with the strongest ties to their respective international systems. Figures available for

TABLE 6–4. MAIL FLOW (PERCENTAGE OF EACH COUNTRY WITH SYSTEM)
WESTERN SYSTEM ONLY IN 1958

Country	% with System	Trend*	Country	% with System	Trend*
S. Kor.	88	+	Bel.-Lux.	75	n. c.
S. Viet.	71	+	Neth.	65	n. c.
Taiwan	50	+	Italy	58	+
W. Ger.	47	+	Japan	55	+
			France	55	–
			Gr. Brit.	38	–

* "Trend" indicates growth or decline compared with prewar levels. The divided
nations have a much higher growth rate (avr. 20%) than the remaining system
members.
Source: Union Postale Universelle, *Statistique des Expeditions dans le Service
Postal International* (Berne: 1927–64).

Poland's mail flow suggest a similar correlation in the case of communist
countries and in turn suggest a similar degree of strength in communications ties.[8] These strong communications links in the form of mail flow
are highly significant; Deutsch, in fact, suggests that mail flow is one of the
most crucial indicators in a "performance approach in the study of integration."[9]

Finally, if we take treaties contracted as a relevant indicator of
political transactions on a different level,[10] the pattern again corresponds
to that which appears above. The divided states, communist and Western
alike, rank very highly in their international systems in the number of
treaties contracted with the system leader.

The pattern which emerges from examination of the trade, aid, mail
flow, and treaty indicators is clear: The divided states as a group have the
greatest number and the strongest ties of all the members to their respective international systems. While the evidence, due to the nature of the
data, is not entirely conclusive, it at least suggests the strong possibility
that the condition of "dividedness" may account to a significant degree for
the intensity of the new state's ties to its international system. Reasons
why this is so are suggested below.

WEAKENING NATIONAL TIES

We now turn to transactions between the two sectors of the divided
nations. The second stage of the pattern outlined above postulated that, as

TABLE 6–5. TREATIES WITH SYSTEM LEADER (TOTAL 1953–1961)

Communist System			Western System		
Country	*Total*	*Trend***	*Country*	*Total*	*Trend***
E. Ger.	39	+	W. Ger.	54	n. c.
C. Ch.	33	—	S. Kor.	33	n. c.
N. Kor.	32	+	Taiwan	26	n. c.
*N. Viet.	22	+	*S. Viet	10	n. c.
Bul.	40	+	UK	58	n. c.
Pol.	39	+	Japan	46	+
Mong.	37	n. c.	Canada	43	n. c.
Czech.	32	n. c.	Italy	32	n. c.
Yugo.	30	—	France	26	n. c.
Alb.	28	—	Neth.	23	—
Hung.	25	—	Bel.	17	n. c.
Rom.	24	—	Lux.	8	n. c.

* It is probable that not all of the Vietnamese treaties have been reported to the United Nations by the Soviet Union and the United States.
** "Trend" indicates a change in rank in the latter half of the period with respect to the former.
Sources: United Nations, *Treaty Series, Volumes 101–400* (New York: Secretariat, 1954–63); Edward L. Miles, with John S. Gillooly, "Processes of Interaction Among the Fourteen Communist Party-States: An Exploratory Essay" (March 1965), Chapter 4 in the present volume.

the new states became increasingly bound to their international systems, their ties with one another (those that were not summarily cut when the nation was divided) would drop off as they became preoccupied with building their own states anew. While strict governmental control is a very important factor here, the evidence suggests two trends: (1) Ties between the two parts of the divided nations have in fact relatively loosened, and (2) *even those ties which have remained more or less free of governmental control* have relatively loosened.

The herculean effort these states have put into nation-building is evident in the three sets of growth statistics given in Table 6–6 below. With respect to rates of growth in national income, industrial production, and education, the divided states are not only the highest in their systems, but are among the highest in the world. Moreover, various reports describing the progress of these countries all note an acute preoccupation with the attributes of nationhood, particularly with the rapid attainment of national economic strength.[11]

Corresponding to this intensive development of the new states, ties

TABLE 6–6. DEVELOPMENT FIGURES (PERCENTAGE INCREASE 1950–1960)

Communist System (official figures)			
Country	National Income	Indus. Prod.	Pupils
C. Ch.	300%	400%(1949–57)	250%
N. Kor.	228	500	28
N. Viet.	100 (1955–60)	600 (1955–62)	600 (1954 63)
E. Ger.	143	192	0

Western System			
Country	National Income	Indus. Prod.	Pupils
S. Kor.	500% (1953–62)	120%(1955–61)	51%
W. Ger.	200	180	6
Taiwan	200 (1953–62)	150	105
S. Viet.	12 (1960–62)	40 (1962–64)	350 (1953–62)

Sources: William Kaye, "A Bowl of Rice Divided: The Economy of North Vietnam," *China Quarterly,* No. 9 (January–March 1962), pp. 82–93; Bernard Fall, *The Two Viet-Nams;* Choh-Ming Li, *Economic Development of Communist China* (Berkeley: University of California Press, 1959); C. T. Hu, "Communist Education: Theory and Practice," *China Quarterly,* No. 10 (April–June 1962), pp. 84–97; David W. Chang, "U.S. Aid and Economic Progress in Taiwan," *Asian Survey,* III (March 1965), 152–60; U.N. *Statistical Yearbook* 1951, 55, 63; *Statistisches Jahrbuch der Deutschen Demokratischen Republik 1965* (Leipzig: Staatsverlag der DDR, 1965); U.N. *Economic Survey of Asia and the Far East 1964* (New York: 1965); *Statistical Returns of the National Economy of the Democratic People's Republic of Korea* (Pyongyang: Foreign Languages Publishing House, 1961); Ludwig Erhard, *Wohlstand für Alle* (Guetersloh: Signum, 1962); Joungwon A. Kim, "The Peak of Socialism in North Korea: The Five and Seven Year Plans," *Asian Survey,* V (May 1965), 255–68; Viet Nam Information Bulletin (August 31, 1963), p. 5.

with the other parts of the old nations have almost entirely dissolved. Table 6–7 indicates the degree to which flows of persons, trade, and mail have been cut off in all four cases. After the initial exodus of refugees has subsided, almost no movement of persons has taken place, and other forms of communication have fallen off concomitantly.

Germany's case is quite interesting here. Despite the Wall, communication does still go on in the forms of trade and mail. But, as Table 6–8 implies, both trade and mail flows have been relatively diminishing, and this regardless of an estimated forty per cent of the West German population who still have close relatives in East Germany. This is important

TABLE 6–7. SOCIAL COMMUNICATIONS BETWEEN THE DIVIDED STATES

Country	Persons		Trade	Mail
	1948–61	1961–65	1948–65	1948–65
Germany	3.7 mill.	sev. thou.	See Table 6–8	See Table 6–8
Korea	1.5 mill.	negl.	less than 1%	none reported since Korean war
Vietnam	1+ mill.	?	negl.	since 1954 small number of post cards
China	2 mill.	negl.	negl.	none since 1948

Sources: International Labor Office, *International Migration 1945–1957* (Geneva, 1959); Bernard Fall, *The Two Viet-Nams,* p. 182; Bernard Fall, "Sociological and Psychological Aspects of Vietnam's Partition," *Journal of International Affairs,* XVIII, No. 2 (1964), 173–87; Chong-Sik Lee, "Korean Partition and Unification," *Journal of International Affairs,* XVIII, No. 2 (1964), 221–40; *Far Eastern Economic Review,* issues January through June, 1964 (Hongkong); *China Quarterly,* No. 14 (April–June 1963), entire issue on North Korea, and No. 9 (January–March 1962), entire issue on North Vietnam; Paul Linebarger, "The Two Chinas," *Current History,* Vol. 47, pp. 162–66; *Statistisches Jahrbuch der Deutschen Demokratischen Republik 1955–1965* (Leipzig); *Statistisches Jahrbuch für die Bundesrepublik Deutschland 1955–1965* (Bonn); *The Flights from the Soviet Zone and the Sealing-off Measures of the Communist Regime of the 13th of August, 1961* (The Federal Ministry for All-German Questions, Bonn, 1962); and personal communications from the Ministry of Postal and Telecommunications, Taiwan and the Direction Generale des Postes et Telecommunications, Saigon.

because, while trade is entirely state controlled, mail is not. Additional evidence of dwindling postal communication is the decline, since 1950, both relatively and absolutely, in the number of letters from the East (including anonymous letters) received by Radio In the American Sector (RIAS), a West Berlin radio station which transmits programs primarily to the Soviet Zone.[12] A final significant indication of the natural abatement of social communication between the two parts of Germany is the gradual decline from 1950 to 1961 of attendance by East Berliners at the West Berlin theater.[13]

This evidence, based on all the available data, indicates that direct ties between the two parts of the divided nations are either declining or nonexistent. (There is a possible exception here with respect to listeners to interzonal radio broadcasts, which conceivably could be as popular as ever, but this is impossible to measure, and the RIAS figures above suggest the opposite conclusion.)

TABLE 6–8. SOCIAL COMMUNICATIONS
BETWEEN EAST AND WEST GERMANY

Year	1949	50	51	52	53	54	55	56	57	58	59	60	61	62	63	64
TRADE																
% of W. Ger.	4+	4	1.4	1.4	1.8	2	2	2	2.3	2.1	2.2	2.2	1.8	1.5	1.5	1.2
% of E. Ger.	20+	16	8	8	9	10	10	11	11	11	11	10	9	8	9	9
MAIL																
% to E. Ger.	—	—	—	15	12	5	5	5	5	4	4	4	—	—	—	—
% frm E. Ger.	—	—	—	12	10	6	6	6	6	7	5	4	—	—	—	—
PACKAGES (millions)																
tot. to E. Ger.	—	—	—	—	32	41	33	43	41	39	37	35	—	—	—	—
tot. frm. E. Ger.	—	—	—	8	9	7	7	7	8	7	—	—	—	—	—	—
RIAS																
% mail rec. from E. Ger.	—	38	38	23	18	27	23	27	21	21	18	19	11	—	—	—
THEATER																
% attend. by E. Berliners in W. Berlin	25	—	25	—	—	—	—	—	12	—	—	12	—	—	—	—

Sources: *Statistisches Jahrbuch der Deutschen Demokratischen Republik* 1961, 1965 (Leipzig: Staatsverlag, 1961, 1965); *Statisches Jahrbuch für die Bundesrepublik Deutschland 1964* (Bonn: Bundesdruckerei, 1964); *Probleme des Ost-West Handels* (West Berlin: Freie Universität, 1962); *Deutsches Bundespost einschliesslich des Landespostdirektion Berlin über das Rechnungsjahr (1953–59)* (Frankfurt/Main: Bundesdruckerei, 1954–60); *Deutsches Bundespost Geschäftsbericht über das Rechnungsjahr (1950–52)* (Frankfurt/Main: Bundesdruckerei, 1951–53); Richard L. Merritt, "Politics, Theater, and the East-West Struggle: The Theater as a Cultural Bridge in West Berlin," *Political Science Quarterly*, LXXX, No. 2 (1965), 186–215.

INTERNATIONAL AND NATIONAL ATTITUDES

Thus far, the pattern projected at first seems to hold. As the old political entity has been destroyed, the newly created states have become, in terms of mutual ties, very strong members of the international system of which they now form a part and, simultaneously, have almost eliminated, by compulsion or by atrophy, their association with the "other half." What, as a result, has happened to that additional essential element of political community—attitudes?

Here the results are surprising. If, according to the fundamental pattern suggested by integration theorists, "mutual ties . . . give the group a feeling of identity and self-awareness,"[14] we might expect an increase in positive identification when these ties are positively increased (as in a study by Merritt on integration of the American colonies[15]) and a decrease in identification when these ties are weakened (as in the study by Russett on the Anglo-American relationship). On the first count this pattern holds true in the divided states. Although judged on the basis of rather fragmentary data, positive identification on the part of both masses and elites of the divided nations with their respective international systems appears to have increased in accordance with the rapid growth in mutual ties noted above. In West Germany, in particular, there is available convincing data to support this contention. As Table 6–9 (based on mass opinion surveys) indicates, attitudes of the German population toward other members of the Western system have undergone a striking positive change as trade and mail flows have increased:

TABLE 6–9.   WEST GERMAN ATTITUDES TOWARD OTHER MEMBERS OF THE WESTERN SYSTEM

Question: Please tell me your feelings about these countries (Good, Neutral, Bad):

Date	U.S.			France			Italy			Great Britain		
	G	N	B	G	N	B	G	N	B	G	N	B
Oct 1954	61%	35%	4%	12%	48%	40%	15%	56%	29%	44%	51%	5%
Nov 1955				10	58	32				42	54	4
Apr 1956				11	62	27				35	59	6
Nov 1956	Not			11	51	38	Not			31	58	11
May 1957	Asked			10	45	45	Asked			14	48	38
Nov 1957				19	58	23				33	54	13
Oct 1958				19	54	27				32	61	7
Feb 1960				27	56	17				44	46	10
Jun 1961				25	58	17	33	55	12	35	54	11
Jun 1962				37	51	12	23	52	25	53	42	5
Feb 1963	73	25	2	37	49	14	25	54	21	53	42	5
Feb 1965				46	44	10	22	54	24	49	46	5

Source: Karl Deutsch et al., "Arms Control and European Integration."

Moreover, when German mass attitudes toward the West as a whole are compared with those in the other major Western powers, they appear to be significantly more favorable. (See Table 6–10). With respect to favorable opinions toward, and identification with, the Western system, German

TABLE 6–10. COMPARISON OF ATTITUDES TOWARDS THE WESTERN SYSTEM
Question: At the present time, do you think that (country) should be
on the side of the West, on the side of the East, or on neither side?

Percentage Saying "Side of the West"

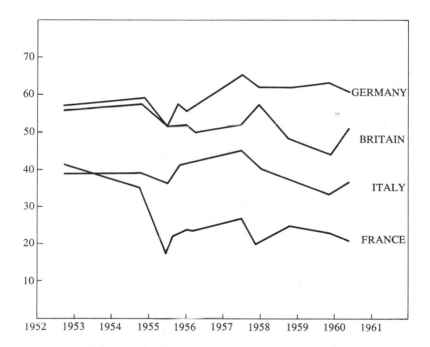

Illustration from Bruce M. Russett, *Trends in World Politics* (New York: The
Macmillan Co., 1965), p. 53. Copyright © 1965 by the Macmillan Company.
Reprinted by permission of the Macmillan Company.

mass attitudes have increased positively with increases in mutual ties and,
in fact, are among the highest in the Western system.

Evidence of a similar pattern of elite attitudes is equally convincing. In a study recently completed by Deutsch, intensive surveys of German and French elites provide some striking comparisons: 46% of the
German, but only 19% of the French, elite saw at least a moderate chance
for the success of European integration within the next ten years. Moreover, only 3% of the German, but 88% of the French, elite saw their foreign policy as increasingly nationalistic; 71% of the Germans as compared
with 45% of the French favor further limitations on national sovereignty

(in favor of increasing Western cooperation) in the coming years. On the whole, then, the German elite, as well as the mass, appears to identify highly with the Western system and favor further integration with it, to an even greater degree than do other European members of the system.[16]

Finally, "hand" content analysis of selected editorials in major national newspapers provided results which correspond to the attitudinal pattern seen in the surveys above. Unfortunately, this method of subjectively analyzing yearly editorials (on significant national dates) was the only truly comparable basis for evaluating attitudes in all of the divided nations. Because of the high correlation of newspaper with surveyed attitudes in the West German case, however, it was assumed to be a fairly reliable indicator. Admittedly, in the communist cases, newspapers are very much closer to the attitudes of the elite than those of the mass, yet the opinions of the two groups *on the issue of international identification* are probably quite similar. Indeed, East Germany might provide the only exception on this issue, but the author's experience there would suggest that this discrepancy is decreasing. Moreover, due to the high degree of social mobilization in the divided countries through intensive education, rapidly developing communication networks, and vast military conscription (as a group, the highest in the world),[17] it seems reasonable to assume some correspondence between actual mass attitudes and the positions expressed in the mass media. Most secondary sources also tend to support the findings below.

Table 6–11, therefore, is offered here as the primary indicator of international identification trends in each of the divided countries. As in the West German case, the correspondence is very close between the positive trends in mutual (systemic) ties (as indicated in Tables 6–1 to 6–5) and the increase in attitudes of positive identification with the international systems, although there is more change in the former than in the latter.

TABLE 6–11. POSITIVE IDENTIFICATION WITH INTERNATIONAL SYSTEM
(NEWSPAPER CONTENT ANALYSIS)

Year	E. Ger.	N. Kor.	N. Viet.	C. Ch.	W. Ger.	S. Kor.	S. Viet.	Tai.
1949	1, 2							
1950	2, 2			2,*2*	1,			
1951	2,			1, 2*	1, 0			
1952				1, 1*	1, 1			
1953				0,*1*	2,	, −1		
1954			0,	1,*1*	−1*	0, −1		0, 0
1955			0, 1	1,*1*	1, 1	−1, 1		1, 0

TABLE 6–11. (Cont'd)

Year	E. Ger.	N. Kor.	N. Viet.	C. Ch.	W. Ger.	S. Kor.	S. Viet.	Tai.
1956	2, 2		1, 1	2, 0*	1, 0	−1, 2	0, 0	−1,
1957	2, 3		0, 3	2,*0*	1, 2	1, 1	1, 1	0, 1
1958	2, 0		1, 3	, 1	1,	0, 2	1, 1	0, 2
1959	2, 2		0, 0	3, 3*	, 2	1,	2, 1	, 2
1960	3, 1		0, 0	2, 2	2, 0	2, 1	2, 1	2,
1961	3, 3		0, 1	3, 3	1, 2	2, 1	0, 3	2, 1
1962	2, 3	2, 2	0, 2	1, 1**	2, 0	2, 1	2, 0	1, 0
1963	2, 2	2, 2	2, 3	0, 1	3, 1	0, 2	2, 0	2, 1
1964	2, 2		3, 0	0, 0	1, 1	2,		1, 0
1965	3, 2	, 2			2, 2			2,

NOTES AND SOURCES: This table was constructed by "hand" content analyzing editorials from newspapers and weeklies on two significant annual dates in each country. The first figure in each column refers to the New Year's editoral, the second to the May Day (Germany) or "national day" (Korea, Vietnam, China) editorial. In the East German, North Korean, North Vietnamese, and Taiwanese publications in which there were no editorials, the front page feature story was used. Blank spaces indicate either no publication on that date or its unavailability to the author. The coding scheme was as follows:

−1: generally *negative reference* to the system ("socialist camp," "socialist brother countries," "free world," "Western alliance") or to the acknowledged system leader (Soviet Union, United States).

0: *neutral or no reference* made to system or leader.

1: *weak or moderate positive reference* made to system or leader.

2: *strong positive reference* made to system or leader or membership in system.

3: *very strong positive reference* and/or considerable editorial space devoted to membership in system.

The newspaper or weekly used for each country was the following:

East Germany: *Neues Deutschland* (daily, East Berlin)

North Korea: 1962–1963, *Korea News* (weekly); 1965, *Pyongyang Times* (weekly, published in Pyongyang)

North Vietnam: *Vietnam Information Bulletin* (weekly, published in Rangoon, Burma)

Communist China: *Renmin Ribao (People's Daily)*, except items marked (*), which are (1950–1957) editorials in *People's China* and (1959) in the *Peking Review*. All are published in Peking. Since 1962, indicated by (**), there has been a major discrepancy between negative reference to the Soviet Union and other "modern revisionists" and positive references to the "unity of the socialist camp." Only the latter were coded.

West Germany: *Frankfurter Allgemeine Zeitung* (daily, Frankfurt am Main)

South Korea: *The Korean Republic* (daily, Seoul)

South Vietnam: *The Times of Vietnam* (weekly, Saigon)

Taiwan: 1954–1958, *China News;* 1959–1965, *China Post* (dailies, Taipei)

As noted above, the first figure in each column refers to the New Year's edition of the publication, the second to the respective "national" day. These are: East and West Germany—May 1; North Korea—August 15; South Korea—August 15; North Vietnam—September 2; South Vietnam—October 27; Communist China—October 1; Taiwan—October 10.

But now we have arrived at the crucial question: Has the growth in positive identification with the new international system been accompanied by a decline in identification with the old national unit, as the weakening of ties suggests? Here the answer seems to be a surprising *no*—the evidence of surveys and content analysis indicates no abatement whatever in national identification, and, in some cases, even shows an *increase* in emphasis upon the old nationality.

Again, West Germany provides the best-documented example. Table 6–12 reveals the consistent and significant rise in concern from 1951 to 1965 about the issue of German reunification. This, when viewed in comparison with the above data on German international attitudes pre-

TABLE 6–12.   WEST GERMAN ATTITUDES TOWARDS REUNIFICATION
Question: What is the most important question for people in West Germany to be concerned with?

	Percentage of All Respondents Saying:					
Date	German Reunification	Berlin Problem	Total I & II	Econ. & Domestic	All Other	Don't Know and No Reply
Oct. 51	18	—	18	45	46	5
July 52	23	—	23	33	55	5
July 53	38	—	38	25	44	6
Jan. 55	34	—	34	28	44	7
Feb. 56	38	—	38	22	47	7
Jan. 57	43	—	43	18	42	8
Jan. 59	45	16	61	15	31	8
Jan. 60	38	6	44	27	33	7
Feb. 61	35	4	39	23	37	8
Aug. 61	19	37	56	13	31	6
Feb. 62	30	23	53	20	47	6
Jan. 63	31	11	42	28	36	8
Jan. 64	41	7	48	32	21	8
Jan. 65	47	4	51	33	19	8
Jan. 65 (Age 16–29 only)	50	6	56	26	19	8

Source: *Informationsdienst*, Institut für Demoskopie, Allensbach am Bodensee, May 1965 and reprinted in Karl Deutsch *et al.*, "Arms Control and European Integration." Columns total over 100% in some cases because of overlapping answers.

sents a paradoxical situation: While West Germans have tended to identify more and more closely with the Western international system, they appear to have in no way relinquished identification with that part of their former nation which has become a member of the opposing international system. Even more surprising is the fact that the younger people, who would, on the face of it, seem to have the weakest attachment of all to the separated part of the nation, show even a stronger interest in reunification than the older age groups.

The paradox is even clearer in the case of the elite. According to the Deutsch study, a large part (54%) of the same West German elite which thinks that European unification is likely to occur in the next ten years also believes that German reunification is likely to be achieved within the coming twenty-five years; indeed, only 2% of the German elite think that reunification will never be achieved. Finally, 89% of the elite (as opposed to 29% of the French elite) favor eventual German reunification, and 55% of these feel quite strongly about the issue.[18]

This same pattern emerges, from the content analysis, in all of the divided nations. Neither the emphasis upon nor identification with the larger national entity shows any sign of diminishing in either the communist or the Western parts of the country. This is the more remarkable for the fact that one would expect the elites of the new states, particularly of the communist states, to emphasize construction of the new (socialist) nation and attempt to suppress any association with the former national identity. However, as Table 6-13 indicates, the communist states, no less than the Western ones, show an undiminishing attachment to the concept of the larger undivided national unit.

Other sources, too, supply convincing evidence of the continuation and even the growth of mass identification with the traditional national units. In the West German case, survey data has already been cited. In addition, a parliamentary "Report on Youth" from a 1965 study of West German youth noted that "approximately 80% of the young people consider reunification as a necessary and urgent political obligation."[19] This is a striking expression of a strong underlying identification with the traditional German nationality. Likewise, the preoccupation of the West German government with the reunification issue is a basic theme of postwar European politics; recent German election campaigns (1963-66) only make this clear once again. In East Germany, on the other hand, one might suspect a possible major discrepancy between elite and mass attitudes on the nationality issue. Yet, in spite of the regime's strenuous efforts to legitimize the "German Democratic Republic" domestically and internationally, the East German government has never relinquished its claim to represent "ganz Deutschland." The Wall and border towers seem to symbolize for Germans on both sides of the line the division of what is ultimately a whole

TABLE 6–13.   NATIONAL THEMES IN NEWSPAPERS

Year	E. Ger.	N. Kor.	N. Viet.	C. Ch.	W. Ger.	S. Kor.	S. Viet.	Tai.
1949	3, 2							
1950	2, 2		3,*2*	1,				
1951	3,		2, 0*	0, 2				
1952			1, 1*	1, 1				
1953			0,*1*	1,	3,			
1954			0,	0,*2*		2, 3		3, 3
1955			1, 2	1,*0*	2, 3	3, 3		2, 3
1956	2, 2		2, 2	0, 0*	2, 0	3, 2	2, 1	1,
1957	1, 2		3, 2	0,*0*	1, 2	3, 3	0, 2	3, 3
1958	1, 2		2, 2	, 2	1, 2	3, 2	0, 2	0, 3
1959	2, 2		3, 3	2, 0*	1, 2	3,	1, 0	, 3
1960	2, 2		2, 1	2, 2	0, 3	2, 3	0, 1	0,
1961	3, 2		1, 2	0, 2	3, 1		0, 1	1, 3
1962	3, 2	2, 3	1, 2	0, 2	3, 3	, 3	1, 2	3, 2
1963	3, 2	2, 2	2, 3	1, 2	3, 2	0, 3	0, 2	3, 3
1964	2, 2		2, 3	0, 2	3, 1	2,		2, 3
1965	3, 2	, 2			2, 3			3,

NOTES AND SOURCES: For sources and dates see Table 6–11. This table, like Table 6–11, was constructed on the basis of "hand" content analysis of editorials in the major newspapers or weeklies of the various countries. The coding scheme was as follows:

For sources and dates see Table 6–11.

> 3: national theme (national reunification, "our suffering brethren in the north," transitoriness of national division, recounting of the history of division, and so on) is the *primary topic* of the editorial.
> 2: national theme is *one of several major themes* of the editorial.
> 1: national theme is *mentioned* or referred to.
> 0: *no reference* made to national theme.
> −1: national theme is *rejected* or declared hopeless (this did not occur in any of the material read).

—their common nationality. As the East Germans press analysis shows, the nationality theme, far from being relegated to the background by the regime, has received more emphasis there than in any other of the eight divided states.

In North Korea, there has been intensified emphasis during recent years (since 1960) on the idea of "one Korea." This has been constantly stressed in all North Korean literature, that intended for domestic as well as for international audiences. M. T. Haggard describes reunification as "the overriding aim of North Korean foreign policy."[20] The intense propaganda drive carried out on all fronts for the attainment of this goal is a direct indication of the importance which North Koreans attach to the national entity.

South Koreans are hardly less insistent in stressing the underlying existence and need for ultimate restoration of the true national unit. One South Korean writer remarks:

> The seemingly detached and disengaged attitude of the world leaders on the Korean question, however, is not, and cannot be, shared by the Koreans, either North or South. To them, the issue of Korean unification is a burning one, a matter of life and death, although the intensity of heat generated by the issue varies from period to period and region to region. No other issue is capable of arousing more passion and emotion among the Korean population than that of unification.[21]

It is significant that, in 1960, Korean students in Japan formed an organization which has since been gaining strength, dedicated to the reunification of the country. This coincided with a student upsurge at home in South Korea and the subsequent formation of the National Unification League. This group has developed as the only truly effective organization of all those which sprang up during the 1960 student revolt. William Douglas comments that the League "represented on the national scene the opinions of the large portion of Korean students, whether League members or not, who were intensely nationalistic."[22] Chong-Sik Lee notes the same result of the 1960 revolt and maintains, in addition, that it has had a continuing effect upon the population at large by generating renewed concern with the issue of reunification.[23]

Little needs to be said about the commitment to a national ideal in Vietnam. Although war has intensified the issue, Bernard Fall and other commentators have made it clear that commitment to an independent national entity has been a widespread and deep-rooted phenomenon in Vietnamese history, particularly since the outbreak of World War II.[24] The apparent success of propaganda pitched to nationalist themes in both north and south reveals the very basic nature of the nationalist appeal and its ability to instill unsurpassable faith in the minds of the populace. The fact that the present conflict takes the form of a civil war in the south makes the nationalist theme all the more paramount. Moreover, the unwillingness of leaders on either side to accept the legitimacy of the 17th parallel as a final boundary, even in the face of the enormous costs of the war, is a sign that for elites as well as for the population as a whole the acceptance of divided status is very far from being considered a satisfactory long-term solution.

China, although disproportionally divided, shows the persistence of national attachment no differently than the other nations. Communist China's national consciousness is legend. An interesting example of this is provided in a series of open-ended interviews in a mainland Chinese village recently compiled by Jan Myrdal.[25] Beyond local village problems, the major preoccupation of the villagers and the general subject on which their thought focuses, particularly in the case of the younger and more educated inhabitants, is the creation of "the *Chinese nation's* new society." The fundamental identification, even on the lowest levels, that of the local Labor Brigade and the People's Militia (of which all inhabitants between 16 and 45 are members), is with "China." The local structures are seen as parts contributing to the whole. The comments of two teachers in the community school clearly demonstrate this:

> Because we explain to the children that the purpose of their studying is to make them fit to build up their country, our pupils now work with great enthusiasm. . . . Our aim is to turn the children into healthy bearers of culture, willing to work with others and loving their socialist country. . . .
> They [the school children] will be good builders of their country. I have a very strong sense of this. . . . Some time ago, I gave them a composition to write: "What are you going to be when you grow up?" Some said they were going to join the Chinese People's Liberation Army. A couple wanted to be airmen in order as they said to "defend China's wide frontiers."[26]

It is quite evident in all party doctrine that "China" is considered to be traditional China, including Taiwan and other disputed border areas.

Taiwan likewise attempts to maintain an identity inseparable from that of greater China. Beyond the legalistic position that Taiwan consists only of an administrative unit of the Chinese Republic which is to be restored in the future, government leaders on the island are no less adamant than their mainland counterparts in insisting on the indestructible unity of all China. Moreover, although there persists an historical dispute as to the cultural autonomy of the eighty per cent of the present Taiwanese who inhabited the island before Chiang Kai-shek took refuge there, even this distinction seems to be dissolving (one major indication of this is the recent return of the major leader of the separatist movement to Taiwan and his reconciliation with the regime[27]) in favor of a common front for the rescuing of China from the communist "usurpers."

Ironically, it would appear that if any of the divided states had a legitimate basis for an identity apart from that of the former national unit, it would be Taiwan. The island's physical separation from the mainland and its long period of Japanese occupation would seem to provide it with some degree of cultural autonomy and a reason for regarding itself not as a divided nation, but as a newly independent state. The evidence is insufficient to justify a final judgment on this point; but, if one may assume even a moderate effectiveness of government propaganda (through educational institutions, press, radio, and so forth) one would have to conclude that the population does identify on a very fundamental level with greater China. The government itself is relentless on this point. As an eminent Asian specialist notes:

> The most unsettling factor on the Chinese scene is the presence of two different Chinese governments, each claiming to be the only "China" and each possessing strong military forces and valid political leadership. Transcending the vulgarized Western conception of Chinese "face," there is a deep level of feeling in both the Chinese governments that identity itself is at stake.[28]

And it is exactly this issue of *national identity* which emerges as the crucial factor for all of the divided nations.

THE ROLE OF NATIONAL IDENTITY

The evolution of the divided states thus presents something of a paradox. In terms of mutual transactions, these states have become closely tied to the communist and Western international systems, in fact, *the most closely bound of all the system members*. Accordingly, as might be expected from integration theory, with the increase of such systemic ties on both mass and elite levels, favorable attitudes toward and identification with the respective systems have also increased. However, we also saw that, as mutual ties between the two parts of the former nation were broken off or weakened of their own accord, elite and mass attitudes apparently *did not* correspondingly change; if anything, mutual (national) identification has tended to *increase*.

This does seem to be a peculiar phenomenon. Why should the divided states continue to cling, for as long as twenty years, to images of themselves which would seem to have outlived their relevancy as well as lost any basis in positive mutual reinforcement? Why have they not gradually lost interest in one another and ceased mutually to identify (as happened in the case of Britain and America) when social communications between them gradually diminished or disappeared? Indeed, one might expect that the elites especially, for a variety of reasons—requirements of membership in the international system, desire for stability, demands of nation-building, need for legitimacy—would want to leave the old images behind and create new ones of their own.

One reason which might be suggested why the people do not abandon the former national images might be because the ties between the parts of their nations were cut forcibly and against their will. Yet this is doubly untenable: Neither were all ties forcibly cut (some have dwindled off spontaneously), nor were the elites innocent bystanders to the process. The same elites who today refuse to abandon the larger national identity had an active hand in dividing their nations. A second possible reason is that either masses or elites or both are just shamming—the citizenry on both sides pay lip service to nationalist phases but "underneath it all" they really do not believe in them. Yet, not only does the above evidence discount this, but such an answer simply begs the question. Even if it were a sham, why the need to sham?

Rather, the essential explanation, I suggest, lies in the nature of "national identity" itself. In early psychological processes of self-conceptualization, the formulation of a national identity plays a vital role. This is a basic social insight that political science is gradually learning from social psychology: that not only in the pathologies of extreme nationalism, but in all political attitude formation, the development of national identity is of absolutely fundamental significance. Erikson and Doob have demonstrated this in their classic studies of the psychology of identity; Pye and Verba have expanded on this work in the area of political development.[29] It is the theoretical and empirical findings of these investigations that have profound significance for exactly the problem which emerges in the case of the divided nations.

Certainly, in the situation of a divided nation, the identity which was formerly associated with that national unit is called into question. When a basic national identity is disturbed or unsettled, Erikson maintains, the entire process of personality development is correspondingly adversely affected. A new "search for identity" begins and an anomic rootlessness ensues, which may, if serious enough, end in a new "total solution in life" as a replacement for the lost or undeveloped "wholeness":

> [A positive sense of identity] depends on the support which the young individual receives from the collective sense of identity characterizing the social groups significant to him: his class, his nation, his culture. Where historical and technological developments severely encroach upon deeply rooted or strongly emerging identities on a large scale, youth feels endangered, individually and collectively, whereupon it becomes ready to support doctrines offering a total immersion in a synthetic identity (extreme nationalism, racism, or class consciousness) and a collective condemnation of a totally stereotyped enemy of the new identity.[30]

Doob and Pye examine basic manifestations of these different levels of identity crisis. Doob, investigating a case in which the new "total solution" has been found, suggests that patriotic characteristics are associated with general personality traits similar to those associated with prejudice, that is, rigidity, intolerance, authoritarianism, moralism, and aggressiveness.[31] Pye's study, which concerns people who have had their original sense of identity shaken, but who have not yet seized upon a new "synthetic identity," indicates very different personality traits. His findings reveal characteristics in the Burmese "modal personality" almost polar opposites of those above; instability rather than rigidity, goallessness rather than authoritanianism, amoralism rather than moralism, passivity rather than aggressiveness. Both of these conditions are found in the divided nations.

Thus the psychology of identity provides a clue to the remarkable tenacity of national attachment in the divided nations and its continued existence in company with a seemingly incompatible measure of enthusiasm for international system affiliation. National identification, as an essential part of the elemental process of self-identification, appears, once established, to fulfill a psychological function quite apart from the mutual social ties which served to create it. If this is so, then belief in national identity does not depend upon the continued existence of positive interaction or even communications with the rest of the nation. This accounts for the vitality of belief in the old nationality in spite of the absence of continued social communication. However, there emerges pressure for creation of a new identity, because, although the breaking of mutual ties does not destroy the subjective basis for national identity, it does put the reality of its objective existence into question. Faced with this form of an identity crisis, the members of the divided nations continue to maintain their original national identity in spite of the challenge to it, yet seek new "synthetic identities" or "total solutions" in the form of international identifications and ideologies.

Convincing evidence supports this explanation of the behavior of the divided nations. Not only, as we have seen, do the members of these nations persistently retain their old national identities, but they also appear to be engaging in widespread searches for "synthetic identities" in the form of extreme ideological affiliations with their international systems and in the behavior described below. Particularly in the communist parts of the nations, this search for totality takes the form of ideological fervor. As Table 6–14 shows, two of the divided states rank at the top of the system in percentage of party membership. Of the other two, China has the largest total party membership and the Vietnamese membership is unknown, but China and North Vietnam might be thought of as leaders of the entire system in terms of ideological enthusiasm.

In the cases of the three Asian members of the Western system, the elites exhibit a similar kind of ideological devotion, but, here, to an "anticommunist" dogma. The degree to which this is shared by their populations is difficult to determine, but these peoples exhibit other indications of "total solutions" to the identity crisis. In South Korea, there has

TABLE 6–14. COMMUNIST PARTY MEMBERSHIP, 1965

Country	As % of Population	Total
No. Kor.	ca. 12	1,600,000
E. Ger.	10.1	1,610,679
N. Viet.	ca. 3.7	700,000
C. China	2.4	18,000,000+
Czech.	12	1,684,416
Rom.	6.6	1,450,000
Bul.	6.5	550,384
Yugo.	ca. 5.5	1,030,041
Hung.	5.2	540,000
USSR	5	13,000,000
Poland	4.8	1,725,521
Mong.	4.5	46,000
Alb.	3	53,000
Cuba	1	60,000

Source: Jan F. Triska, "The World Communist System," Chapter 1 in the present volume, Table 1–1.

in recent years occurred an inexplicably rapid increase in the number of religious sects, many of them nationalistic.[32] Further, the latent student ideologism and nationalism which burst forth in the 1960 revolution remain an ever-present potentiality.[33] The Vietcong, fanatical Buddhist sects, and extremist political groups are manifestations of such total ideological commitment in South Vietnam. In Taiwan, the ideological fervor of the Kuomintang is maintained, most evidently in the army, which is the largest per capita of any nation in the world.[34] Only in West Germany does ideological enthusiasm seem to be lacking, but there the often-mentioned youth's search for identity seems to take its place. Aside from the eighty per cent of the West German youth described in the parliamentary "Report on Youth" as considering reunification to be "a necessary and urgent political obligation," the young are pictured as looking for identity through fadism and excitement. In the description of the *Frankfurter Allgemeine Zeitung,*

> German youth present a picture of "lonely and insecure young people straining for some sort of inspiration."[35]

More recently this inspiration seems to have been found in part in the form of millenarian doctrines which are gaining increasing support among German students, particularly in Berlin where both emotionalism and the dilemma of identity are at a peak.

Thus the characteristics described by both Pye and Doob appear in the divided nations: goallessness and instability of those in search of an identity, ideological fanaticism of those who have found a new "synthetic" one. It is significant that these characteristics seem more pronounced in the youth who have grown up in the days since division; rather than a natural abatement in the identity crisis as the division is forgotten, there is present a persisting and even increasing awareness of national incompleteness, together with its accompanying psychological symptoms. In sum, the factor of national identity seems to explain a great deal in the cases of the divided nations. That attitudinal changes in these countries have not corresponded to their reorientations in social communication is accountable to the pervasive quest for identity. Likewise, the ideologism and anomic behavior found in each state seem to be the recurrent symptoms of identity crises.

If such an interpretation is basically correct, it could have important implications for integration theory in general and for an evaluation of the integrative capacity of international systems in particular. The fundamental upshot is this: In any large-scale process of political integration, national identity is an absolutely crucial factor. Recent work in integration theory, in stressing the importance of social communication, seems at the same time to have generally neglected the vital psychological function fulfilled by national identity. The divided nations clearly indicate that identity can persist despite silenced communications; while populations have been cut off from one another and have even lost interest in each other as individuals, they have not at all lost interest in the national unit or ceased to identify with the traditional nationality. Indeed, this suggests that because of its psychological importance, a national identity, once established, could conceivably continue to exist in the absence of *any* social communication between divided parts.

This assertion would seem to contradict the findings of Russett and Jászi in their analyses of disintegrating political communities: Decreases in communications ties have not led here, as they found, to decreased feelings of community identity. But the disagreement is only an apparent one, because the weakening of ties and attitudes in the larger communities they studied (Anglo-American and Austro-Hungarian, respectively) took place precisely in favor of the strengthening of *national* identities. While in the present cases national identity has been challenged by division, in their cases national identity was challenged by inclusion. In both instances, the result has been the same: the vigorous perpetuation of identification with the national units.

Thus, national identity does, indeed, emerge as the crucial limiting factor upon the integrative capacity of international systems. In one sense, this is saying nothing new. Deutsch, in his study of the North Atlantic communities, has pointed out that those international systems which have been the most successful in maintaining stability have been those which have stopped short of total integration and have accommodated national units within loose bonds.[36] And many writers have recently theorized that both communist and Western systems seem to be moving toward such "polycentrist" kinds of communities. In another sense, however, this is saying something rather novel. For it is suggested here that the integrative capacity of international systems is limited not only by the autonomy of the national units, but by the nature of national identity within the units as well. That is to say, an international system will hardly be successful in accommodating its national units if the units themselves are in a state of flux.

This observation provides a somewhat unorthodox view of the relations between the divided states and their international systems. The creation of stable international political communities presupposes the existence of stable national identities, but it is precisely these which the divided states lack. Therefore, while they are in one sense the most "integrated" members of their respective systems, these states are in another sense the ones *least* securely attached. For psychological reasons, old national identities do not disappear with the abolition of social communications between the new states. For the same psychological reasons, ideological identifications with the new international systems are high. Thus, the integration of the divided states into the international systems, while superficially successful, has taken place only at the expense of creating and perpetuating fundamental identity crises within these states.

What does such a view mean for the role of the divided states in the future development of the communist and Western international systems? While comments here must remain purely speculative, at least one major consequence seems implied from the above analysis. Due to the crucial psychological role of national identity, identification with the traditional national units seems unlikely to diminish in *any* of the divided states in the foreseeable future. This means that the predictions by those who expect a gradual reduction of interest in national reunification questions "as time goes on and national memories are forgotten" are based on a false premise that identity is a function of interaction; these predictions are therefore fundamentally wrong. In fact, the identifications of peoples in the divided nations with their traditional nationalities show no signs of withering away—indeed, they are probably rising.

The two great international systems thus find themselves in a common dilemma. It is clearly in the interest of each system to have well-defined and stable boundaries. Yet it is exactly in the areas in which it would be most desirable to create stable borders (in the divided nations) that the people involved refuse to abandon the idea of the undivided nation. Since the systems will not give up the states, and the peoples will not relinquish their national identities, the situation remains in a state of perpetual strain. This analysis suggests that these national identities will continue to refuse to "fade away." If so, then one can expect that the divided nations will remain in the future, as they have been in the past, the focal points of international tension and the most destabilizing elements of the communist and Western international systems.

NOTES

1. That the divided nations continue to be the primary points of tension between the communist and Western systems was highlighted in a major policy speech delivered by Brezhnev on the eve of the anniversary of the Bolshevik revolution. Four of the five issues listed by the Party Secretary as "among the unsolved problems causing instability in the world" were the undetermined situations of the four divided nations (*New York Times,* November 7, 1964, p. 8). Although this paper is not primarily a policy-oriented one, it does deal with social factors that ultimately have very deep implications for exactly the policy concerns dealt with by Brezhnev.
2. This is the basic model, in its most elemental form, developed by Karl Deutsch in his *Nationalism and Social Communication* (New York: Wiley, 1953). It appears in a more general theoretical form in *The Nerves of Government* (New York: The Free Press, 1963), particularly pp. 178–80, and in its most recent and most schematic form in "Communication Theory and Political Integration," Chapter II of *The Integration of Political Communities,* Philip Jacob and James Toscano (eds) (New York: Lippincott, 1964), pp. 46–74. In the latter essay Deutsch notes: "The next line of development is the crude modeling of this process of the learning of habits of community perceptions, community identification, community compliance, and community support. What is proposed is a primitive theory of the methods of learning to form a market for common political institutions" (p. 56).
3. Bruce Russett, *Community and Contention: Britain and America in the Twentieth Century* (Cambridge: MIT Press, 1963).
4. Oscar Jászi, *The Dissolution of the Hapsburg Monarchy* (Chicago: University of Chicago Press, 1929). Jászi analyzes in a broad historical sweep what Russett studies in terms of communications and integration theory: the slow disintegration of a "sense of community" in an international setting. Both writers trace a gradual drop-off in "mutual relevancy" between nations and a resulting decline in mutual sympathy, thus implying the reversibility of the integration process.
5. The term "communist system" here designates the fourteen states in which the communist party is the ruling party; actually, it is a subsystem of the larger communist system with which our project, the Stanford Studies of the Communist System, is concerned. The term "Western

system" simply signifies here, for convenience, thirteen of the major nations in the broad Western alliance system which clusters around the United States: the European Economic Community countries (West Germany, France, Italy, The Netherlands, Belgium, and Luxembourg); Great Britain, Canada, Japan, South Korea, South Vietnam, Taiwan, and, of course, the United States. They were selected on the basis of their geographic, economic, or political importance in the alliance.

6. Philip E. Jacob and Henry Teune, "The Integrative Process: Guidelines for Analysis of the Bases of Political Community" in Jacob and Toscano, *Integration,* p. 4. They go on to suggest that "integration" is really a "dispositional" term and that "definitions of dispositional terms . . . will appear to be indicators" (p. 10). Thus, the indicators of mutual ties (for example, transactions) and integrative attitudes (for instance, survey data) can themselves define the degree of integration in a given political community.

7. Deutsch in Jacob and Toscano, *Integration,* Chapter VI, "The Price of Integration," pp. 143–78, ff.

8. In 1958, the proportion of Polish mail which was sent to the communist system was 50 per cent; the proportion of trade was 58 per cent. *Statistique des Expeditions dans le Service Postal International* (Berne: Bureau international de l'Union postale universelle, 1960).

9. Deutsch in Jacob and Toscano, *Integration,* pp. 76–82 and 97.

10. Jan F. Triska suggested in personal discussions concerning this study that treaty-making might be a revealing indicator of *committed* interaction.

11. See, for instance, Joungwon A. Kim, "The 'Peak of Socialism' in North Korea: The Five and Seven Year Plans," *Asian Survey,* V, No. 5 (May 1965), 255–69; Yoon T. Kuark, "North Korea's Industrial Development during the Post War Period," *China Quarterly,* No. 14 (April–June 1963), pp. 82–93; David W. Chang, "U.S. Aid and Economic Progress in Taiwan," *Asian Survey,* V, No. 3 (March 1963), 152–90; Kang Chao, "Growth of the Construction Industry in Communist China," *China Quarterly,* No. 22 (April–June 1965), pp. 125–42; Ralph L. Powell, "Commissars in the Economy: 'Learn From the PLA' Movement' in China," *Asian Survey,* V, No. 3 (March 1965), 125–38; Bernard Fall, *The Two Viet-Nams* (New York: Praeger, 1963); *Sudostasien zwischen gestern und morgen,* special issue of *Deutsche Aussenpolitik* (East Berlin, 1962), particularly "Zwei entgegengesetzte Tendenzen der wirtschaftlichen Entwicklung in Vietnam," pp. 204–10; and Ludwig Erhard, *Wohlstand für Alle* (Gütersloh: Signum, 1962).

12. For this information and the mail figures which appear in Table 6–8, I am indebted to Richard Merritt, who generously allowed me to use material he gathered in Berlin.

13. Richard L. Merritt, "Politics, Theater, and the East-West Struggle: The Theater as a Cultural Bridge in West Berlin, 1948–61," *Political Science Quarterly,* LXXX, No. 2 (June 1965), 186–215.

14. See the definition cited on page 6, above.

15. Richard L. Merritt, "Symbols of American Community, 1735–1775" (Ph. D. thesis, Yale University, 1962), to be published in a revised form.

16. These figures are taken with the permission of the author from an unpublished study carried out by Karl Deutsch *et al.,* "Arms Control and European Integration" (Yale University, 1965). The surveys of West

German and French elites were conducted by Lewis Edinger and Roy Macridis, respectively.

17. Bruce Russett *et al., World Handbook of Political and Social Indicators* (New Haven: Yale University Press, 1964), pp. 72–75. The average of those in military service as a percentage of the total population for the divided nations is 2.14, as compared with a .85 for the entire world (median .6). This is all the more significant when one considers that military conscription, in a way unlike that of any other form of social mobilization, offers an excellent opportunity for ideological indoctrination.

18. Deutsch *et al.,* "Arms Control and European Integration."

19. "Report on Youth" as described in the *Frankfurter Allgemeine Zeitung,* June 22, 1965, pp. 1, 7.

20. M. T. Haggard, "North Korea's International Position," *Asian Survey,* V, No. 8 (August 1965), 375.

21. Chong-Sik Lee, "Korean Partition and Unification," *Journal of International Affairs,* XVIII, No. 2 (1964), 221.

22. William A. Douglas, "Korean Students and Politics," *Asian Survey,* III, No. 12 (December 1963), 584–95.

23. Lee, "Korean Partition," p. 229.

24. Fall, *The Two Viet-Nams,* pp. 9–130.

25. Jan Myrdal, *Report From a Chinese Village,* trans. Maurice Michael (New York: Random House, 1965). Obviously, these interviews are not rigorously systematic and they were mediated through a translator, but as an indication of basic concerns and orientations on the grass roots level, they are extremely revealing.

26. Myrdal, *Report,* pp. 309–10. An intelligent young peasant who liked to read expressed in his own way thoughts on national identity: "This book is good. The heroes are very well described and they are all so courageous. They want to defend their country and are prepared to sacrifice their own lives for it. Reading such a book helps me to raise my ideals" (p. 194).

27. The return of Thomas Liao, longtime leader of the "Taiwan Independence Movement," to Taiwan in the summer of 1965 was heralded with great fanfare by the government. His reconciliation was seen as a major step in the final uniting of Taiwanese with Chinese from the mainland in the crusade to regain the homeland. Liao was quoted as saying, "Blood is thicker than water and nobody in the world can ever create dissension between us by any means." The report concludes with the assertion that, "All the people in Taiwan today are strongly for the same unique goal–the recovery of mainland China." *China Youth,* III, No. 4 (June 15, 1965), 1.

28. Paul M. Z. Linebarger, "The Two Chinas," *Current History,* XLVII (September 1964), 162. Another writer makes this point even more explicit: "Within the Chinese leadership there may be going on an authentic search for a separate and distinct identity"; A. M. Halpern, "Communist China's Foreign Policy: The Recent Phase," *China Quarterly,* No. 11 (July–September 1962), p. 92.

29. Erik H. Erikson, *Childhood and Society* (New York: Norton, 1950); Leonard Doob, *Patriotism and Nationalism: Their Psychological Foundations* (New Haven: Yale University Press, 1964); Lucien Pye,

Politics, Personality, and Nation Building (New Haven: Yale University Press, 1962); and Sidney Verba and Lucien Pye (eds.), *Comparative Political Culture* (Princeton: Princeton University Press, 1965), particularly Verba's concluding essay.

30. Erik H. Erikson, "Wholeness and Totality—A Psychiatric Contribution" in Carl F. Friedrich (ed.), *Totalitarianism* (Cambridge, Mass.: Harvard University Press, 1954), p. 170.
31. Doob, *Patriotism and Nationalism,* p. 127.
32. Ji Won-Yong, "Christian Church and Sects in Korea," *Korea Journal,* V, No. 9 (September 1965), 4–11.
33. Douglas, "Korean Students," pp. 585, 594–95.
34. Russett *et al., World Handbook*, p. 74.
35. "Report on Youth," p. 7.
36. Karl Deutsch, *Political Community at the International Level* (New York: Doubleday, 1954), Chapter 3, pp. 39–45.

SEVEN

CUBA'S INTEGRATION INTO THE WORLD COMMUNIST SYSTEM, 1962-1966: A PRELIMINARY ASSESSMENT

DAVID RONFELDT
DANIEL TRETIAK

INTRODUCTION

Conceptual Framework

Since 1960, Cuba has entered into a pluralistic security community relationship with the communist system.[1] In general terms, such relationships proceed primarily along political, economic, and military dimensions; often the rate and level of achievement along one dimension may differ from that along another. For assessing the development of integration along any or all such dimensions, the use of two key variables has been suggested: value-sharing and mutual responsiveness by the actors involved.[2] The effect of any act on overall integration thus depends on its consequences in terms of these two variables. Analytically, political acts may be more closely related to value-sharing than to mutual responsiveness, while economic and military acts may pertain more to mutual responsiveness than to value-sharing.

The development of a security community is seen as dynamic, occurring unevenly in accordance with the relationship between both value-sharing and mutual responsiveness. To distinguish between less and more developed security communities and to chart changes in community relationships, an analytic field based on the two variables may be constructed, as shown:

189

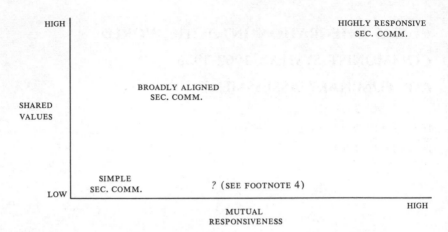

Security communities which simply met the minimal requirements would lie at or near the point of intersection. Security communities in which value-sharing and mutual responsiveness are both high would be situated toward the upper-right area and may be termed "highly responsive security communities."[3] Between these two types would fall security communities in which there has appeared more value-sharing than in a simple security community, yet fewer indications of mutual responsiveness than are required for a highly responsive one. Such security communities may be referred to as "broadly aligned."[4]

While the above framework permits an assessment of any integration relationship between national actors, the case of Cuba applies particularly to relationships between a community of more developed nations and a less developed one (or ones). Even though shared values may be moderately high on both sides, the capabilities for mutual responsiveness may be inadequate (that is, the costs may be excessive) to permit sustained side-payments essential for consolidation of the new member's integration into a given community.[5] By the same token, such membership may require that the new member subordinate various goals to those of the community. This may seem an excessive price to pay for less developed nations anxious to protect their independence from any foreign influence.

During the post-World-War-II period, several integrative efforts have failed or have not fulfilled initial goals for either or both of the above reasons. For example, three East African new nations were unwilling to accept associate status in the Common Market, fearing that a position of inferiority would exist between themselves and the more developed Western European nations.[6] Furthermore, in the late 1950's, the Soviet Union showed that Albania was no longer needed by the communist system if Albanian demands (e.g., for economic aid) were to prove excessive in relation to the diminishing benefits (e. g., military support) it brought to the system.[7] Also, concurrently, the communist system was either unable or unwilling to expand the size of the system to include Guinea. In this instance, the Russians were reluctant to make sustained payments sufficient to support Guinean developmental goals in exchange for its membership in the communist system. Sékou Touré, of course, was unwilling to join Guinea to the communist system.[8]

With Albania and Guinea, there was a relatively high degree of value-sharing with the members of the communist system (more, perhaps, than seen in the East Africa-Common Market case). Yet, neither side was sufficiently willing or capable of stimulating relationships beyond a certain point. One important reason for this has been the fact that the Soviet Union has invariably given priority to maintaining its coalition with the relatively developed Eastern European nations, and has not wished to jeopardize that coalition by supporting even such small, but underdeveloped, nations as Albania and Guinea.

Historical Background:
Cuba's Entry into the Communist System

Cuba's demands on the communist system, and especially the Soviet subsystem, came at a time (1959–1961) when the latter had taken up measures designed to strengthen Eastern European-Russian integration, rather than to encourage expansion of the system or pay excessive costs to maintain the system (with increased payments to Albania and China). It seemed hardly likely that the Soviet subsystem would respond rapidly to the diverse needs of the Cuban revolutionary elite both before and during the period under study.

Cuba's drive to enter the communist system was greatly motivated by military needs arising out of her perceptions of threats from the United States. At the same time, Cuba hoped to gain economic support for her developmental goals from the communist system. Little early concern was manifested among the noncommunist radical Cuban elite that Cuba would be required to meet certain conditions of the communist system in return for the system's support. The Cubans quickly and unhappily realized that their association with the communist system would require Cuba's favorable response to certain demands of the system, in exchange for its support. The lack of extensive relations between the Cuban revolutionary elite and the communist system prior to 1959, the presence of unshared (as well as shared) values and perceptions of the environment, differing stages of economic development, all were conditions which intrinsically militated against Cuba's rapid integration into the communist system after 1961.[9]

Yet, by then, Cuba had explicitly opted out of the United States-led international system and implicitly considered itself and was considered to be aligned with the communist system. The relationship between Cuba and the communist system had passed the stage of a simple security community, and also possessed elements of an alliance, but no formal military treaty existed. The military responsiveness of the communist system, especially its leader, the Soviet Union, had not been tested fully under threats to Cuba, such as the missile crisis in 1962. Cuba did not have to call on communist military support during the Bay of Pigs invasion in 1961. Nor had Cuba's responsiveness to various Russian demands been determined, such as those concerning the planning of Cuban economic development.

During the years 1961–1962, transactions between Cuba and the communists increased substantially, in comparison with those extant hitherto. Notwithstanding, the actual level of integration increased only slightly. Various events required each side to reevaluate the other. The Bay of Pigs and the October 1962 missile crisis; the dispute over the course of Cuban economic development; the Cuban revolutionary elite's reluctance to become publicly involved in the Sino-Soviet dispute; the elite's commitment to expansion of revolution in Latin America; all were areas of discord in a relationship initiated under less than ideal conditions.

By the end of 1962, however, at least one issue had evidently been resolved: The Russians showed, especially in the missile crisis, that the communist system would not go to war for Cuba against the United States, but that it might be able to deter the latter from attacking Cuba. Still, only an unofficial defensive alliance existed. Russia continued to persevere against Chinese and Cuban demands (sometimes partially coordinated) that Russia give greater support to armed struggle in Latin America. The Soviet subsystem continued to exert pressure on Cuba to modify its economic goals and enter into an as yet undetermined relationship with international communist economic planners. Also, Cuba was asked to align itself politically with the Soviet Union against the Chinese.

CUBAN PARTICIPATION IN COMMUNIST INTERNATIONAL ORGANIZATIONS

During the period from the latter part of 1962 through early 1966, efforts were made to integrate Cuba into the communist system. As a result, Cuba gradually began to participate in the international organizations which order the political, economic, military, and communications activities of the communist system: the fronts (in which party-states, nonruling parties, and others participate); and essentially regional party-states organizations, for example, the Council for Mutual Economic Assistance (COMECON) and the Warsaw Treaty Organization (WTO). The fronts are intended to be the principal organizations for maintaining the integrity of the system *as a whole,* while the regional organizations involve multi-lateral coordination and cooperation by the party-states. The importance of such organizations derives from the fact that:

> Sustained efforts at persuasion have to be organized, maintained, paid for, and protected against violent disruption. It is not surprising, there-fore, that there appears to be no case of a security-community which was established solely by the appearance of a sense of community or by persuasion unaccompanied by the growth of institutions and or-ganizations which sustained the "we-feeling" and channeled it into activities of group living.[10]

In other words, to the extent that a member is integrated into a system, it can be expected to participate in the organizations designed to sustain that system. Consequently, participation indexes are used as indi-cators of integration; for, while transactional data (trade, mail flow, visit-ors exchange, and so forth) may suggest something about the level of interaction, these data may, nevertheless, lead one to exaggerate the level of integration present in a given relationship. Here, Cuban involvement in communist international organizations serves as a guide to both the extent and quality of overall integration into the communist ruling-party system and will enable us to assess the state of Cuban integration in terms of the analytic field presented above. Cuban behavior at front meetings marked by Sino-Soviet conflict indicates the degree of Cuban alignment (or value-sharing) with one subsystem or the other. In addition, the extent of Cuban pro-Soviet alignment is further verified by examining Cuban participation in other organizations that are predominantly controlled by the Soviet subsystem. In regard to those other organizations, Cuban rela-tions with COMECON and the WTO are particularly suggestive of the level of mutual responsiveness.

Political Organizations

Introduction. Several political organizations referred to as "fronts" or "front organizations" have existed since before World War II; others were founded after the war, frequently as noncommunist bodies that were later taken over by communist functionaries. While often not under explicit Soviet communist control, they generally followed the Soviet "line" on international political issues; hence the name "front."

In the past few years, the fronts have assumed an increasingly im-portant function in the communist international system: aggregating the political views of all communists, since no formal or informal mechanism exists now for bringing communists of all persuasions together (as did the Comintern and Cominform previously). Thus, meetings of such front or-ganizations as the World Peace Council (WPC), World Federation of

Democratic Youth (WFDY), the Women's Democratic International Federation (WDIF), and the International Union of Students (IUS) have been the only regular occasions for feuding communists to meet multi-laterally. Such meetings reinforce positions held by those already committed to the communist value system, as well as further the socialization of others not yet so committed.

Since 1963, the harmony which hitherto prevailed at front meetings has been replaced by the increasing appearance of Sino-Russian debates. Delegates attending the meetings—when speaking and/or voting —have often been required to declare themselves on issues dividing the two leading communist party-states. Therefore, delegate behavior at front meetings has been a particularly good indicator of how party-states, non-ruling communist parties, and noncommunist nations are aligned politically with either Russia or China on major issues within the communist system.[11] For that reason, in this section we will examine Cuban participation in these international organizations.

Cuban Behavior at Front Meetings.   Cuba has been represented at meetings of various front organizations for many years, formerly by members of the old Cuban communist party—the *Partido Socialista Popular* (PSP)—and currently by delegations of Cuban mass organizations affiliated with the fronts. In the early 1960's, as the PSP became an integral partner in the Cuban government and as Cuba became a quasi-party-state within the international communist system, the Cuban delegations to front meetings began semiofficially to represent the Cuban party-state, rather than just the PSP. Cuba's revolutionary elite was quite reluctant to align itself publicly with either Russia or China during most of the late 1962–1965 period; nevertheless, from our investigation into Cuban delegates' actions at front meetings, a clear behavioral pattern has emerged as to how the Cubans supported either Russia or China.

We examine Cuban behavior only at meetings in which Sino-Soviet conflict was clearly manifested; that is, at three front meetings in 1963; ten in 1964, eleven in 1965, and four in 1966 (8 months). (The total in 1963 comes to four with the addition of the International Red Cross Congress, a noncommunist meeting at which the Soviet Union and China quarreled.) Table 7–1 reveals the scope of Cuban participation in these front meetings, across dimensions derived from the following four questions: (1) Were the Cubans present at the meetings? (2) Who reported their presence: the Cubans and/or either (or both) subsystem leader(s)? (3) How did Cuba speak and/or vote on issues over which Russia and China clashed? (4) Who reported the speeches/votes: Cuba, China and/or Russia?[12]

A *scoring system* was devised for awarding scores to the Cubans for their behavior at each meeting as reported by themselves and by the two subsystem leaders competing for their allegiance.

(1) If any of the three nations reported the Cubans present, the Cubans were given one point; if the reportage of that country shows high salience between Cuba and the system, an extra point is added. The sum of the points provides an index of the mutual salience between Cuba and the communist system. The score could be a maximum of six. Column Four gives the total score per meeting.

(2) In order to determine toward which subsystem leader Cuba showed greater affect, scores for each meeting were allocated to Cuba according to reports (by any or all actors) on Cuban speaking and/or voting behavior.

A. If any actor's report showed that Cuba voted in support of either subsystem leader, Cuba was given two points, positive if pro-USSR, negative if pro-China.

OR

B. Cuba was given one point if an actor's overall reportage only suggested—in the researchers' judgment—that a Cuban speech at a given meeting paralleled that of one subsystem leader or the other, positive if for the Soviet Union and negative if for China.

Adding those points for any given meeting provides an index of overall affect regarding Cuban alignment with one subsystem leader or the other. The maximum possible score is six; conflicting reports can and do affect the scoring. Column Seventeen shows the final tally for each meeting.

From the separate indexes of *salience* and *affect,* a composite index was constructed in order to provide an assessment of overall Cuban alignment with either subsystem leader for a given meeting. This index enables us to chart, over time, the shifting Cuban performance at meetings. Two assumptions were made:

1) The more salient Cuba's presence, the more significant is its alignment with a given subsystem.

2) The higher its positive or negative affect, the more aligned Cuba is with the respective subsystem leader. Thus, the more or less salient (to the system-leaders and Cuba) is the (Cubans') affect toward the leaders, the higher the alignment with a given subsystem leader.

Consequently, the overall index is constructed by *multiplying* the salience by the affect scores; a maximum of 36 could be attained, plus or minus. The outcome is given in Column Eighteen, and graphed in Figure 7–I. That figure shows the plot of two curves: One represents the index for meetings held under China's auspices (the 1964 and 1965 Ban-Atomic-Hydrogen Bomb Conferences, held in Japan, and the Peking Scientific Symposium); the second represents the index for all other meetings (including the noncommunist International Red Cross Congress).

Table 7–1 and Figure 7–I reveal that in an overwhelming majority of the cases considered, Cuba was aligned with Russia, not China. Yet, pro-Soviet alignment generally was of an implicit nature only. The Soviet

Table 7-1 CUBAN BEHAVIOR IN COMMUNIST INTERNATIONAL POLITICAL ORGANIZATIONS

MEETINGS	Rus rept Cub pres	Chi rept Cub pres	Cub rept Cub pres	SALIENCE	Rus say explicitly Cub pro-Rus	Rus say implicitly Cub pro-Rus	Rus say explicitly Cub pro-Chi	Rus say implicitly Cub pro-Chi	Chi say explicitly Cub pro-Rus	Chi say implicitly Cub pro-Rus	Chi say explicitly Cub pro-Chi	Chi say implicitly Cub pro-Chi	Cub say explicitly Cub pro-Rus	Cub say implicitly Cub pro-Rus	Cub say explicitly Cub pro-Chi	Cub say implicitly Cub pro-Chi	AFFECT TOWARD S.U.	ALIGNMENT WITH S.U.
1963																		
World Congress of Women (June)	1	2	1	4		1				1		−1					1	4
Student Seminar (Aug)	1	2	1	4													0	0
Int'l Red Cross (Aug–Sept)	1	1	1	2						1	−2						−1	−2
Int'l Org of Journalists (IOJ) (Sept)	1		1	2		1								1			2	4
1964																		
Int'l Union of Students (IUS) (Feb)		2	1	2						1		−½					½	1
Int'l Lawyers (Mar–Apr)		2		2		1				1		−1				−1	0	0
IOJ (Apr)	1			2						1				1			2	4
Women's Problems (May)		2	1	3										1			1	3
10th A-H Bombs* (Aug)	1	1	1	3			−2				−2						−4	−12
Peking Science Symposium (Aug)			1	2								−1				−1	−2	−4
World Youth Forum (Sept)	1	1		3		1				1		−1		1			2	6
IUS (Nov–Dec)	1	1	1	2						1							1	2
Exec Cmte 8th Congress	1	2		3						1		−1		1			1	3

Table 7-1 (cont'd) CUBAN BEHAVIOR IN COMMUNIST INTERNATIONAL POLITICAL ORGANIZATIONS

1965													
Moscow CP Meeting (March)	1	1	1	3			1		1		1	3	9
Teachers' Int'l (Apr)		2	1	2				2				2	4
Vietnam Support (June)	1			2		−½			−½			−1	−2
World Peace Council (July)	1	1		3			1	2		1		4	12
Youth Festival** (July)	1	1		3			1	2		1		4	12
WFTU Exec Cmte (July)	1	1		1					1			1	1
11th A-H Bombs***(Aug)	1	1		3	1		1			1		1	3
Food Workers (Sept)	1	1		2			1		1	1		2	4
IOJ Exec Cmte (Sept)	2	1		3			1		1	1		2	6
WFTU Cong (Oct)	2	1	1	4			1		1	1		2	8
WIDF Council (Oct)		2	2	2			1		1	1		2	4
1966													
Tri-Continental Conference (Jan)	2	1	1	4			1		1	1		2	8
WFDY Congress (June)		1	1	1			1		1	1	−1	1	1
WPC Council (June)		1	1	1	1		1		1	1		3	3
Latin American Students (July–Aug)	1	1	2	2			2		1	1		3	6

* A Cuban came to the conference and remained even after the Russians and their followers departed; the Russians charged that the Cuban and others at the Chinese-sponsored meeting were fraudulent delegates. Then, the Cuban branch of the World Peace Council issued a statement disclaiming that a Cuban was at the meeting; this statement did not appear in *Hoy*, but was in both *Pravda* and *Prensa Latina diario*. Notwithstanding, the Cuban stayed at the Chinese meeting and no Cuban went to the Russian "rump" session.
** Cuban elites strenuously joined the Russians in postponing a Youth Festival scheduled for Algiers; the Chinese were opposed to postponement.
*** At the 1965 meeting, no Cuban or Russian delegates attended: tacit Cuban support for the Russians.

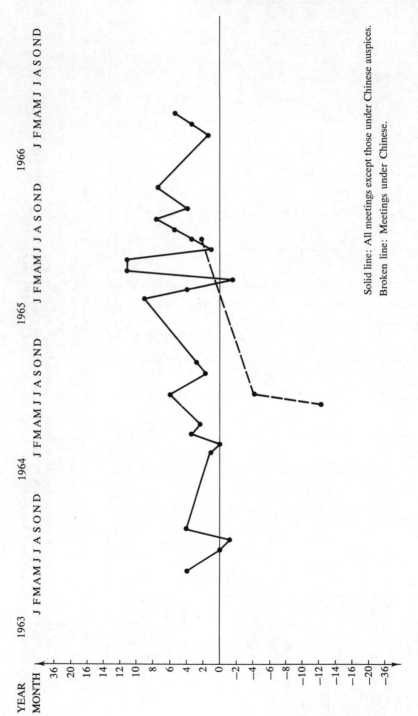

YEAR 1963 1964 1965 1966
MONTH J FMAMJ J ASOND J FMAMJ J ASOND J FMAMJ J ASOND J FMAMJ J ASOND

Solid line: All meetings except those under Chinese auspices.
Broken line: Meetings under Chinese.

FIGURE 7–I.

reports examined rarely emphasized Cuba's pro-Soviet alignment; Chinese sources more than Cuban ones implied the pro-Soviet direction in which Cuban alignment was proceeding. All evaluations concur in that at nearly all system-wide meetings, the Cubans were at least implicitly pro-Soviet. In Cuban and Chinese reports, implicit references to pro-Chinese Cuban behavior virtually ceased after 1964.

While an alignment score of 36 (plus or minus) could have been attained for a meeting, at no time does the Cuban level reach more than one-third that amount. Pro-Soviet alignment was lowest in 1963 (highest score: four), and one case of negative alignment is listed. In 1964, the highest score was six, but there were two cases of negative alignment. In 1965, the highest positive alignment score was twelve (two instances), and there was only one case of negative alignment; in 1966, the highest score was eight and no negative cases were offered. The data thus suggest that pro-Soviet alignment increased over time, albeit within fairly narrow limits (minimum, one; maximum, twelve).[13] One reason why the alignment index is not higher is that the Cubans irregularly reported their pro-Soviet positions between 1963 and 1965, in accordance with Cuba's avowed policy of nonalignment in the Sino-Soviet dispute.

The pro-Chinese plot deserves several substantive comments concerning the specific meetings. It should be pointed out that both the USSR and Cuba went to the Tenth Hiroshima Atomic-Hydrogen Bomb Conference in August 1964, but that the USSR walked out while a Cuban delegate remained at the Chinese-sponsored meetings and voted with China. Later in the same month, the Cubans attended the Peking Scientific Symposium, to which the Soviet Union was not invited and which it criticized. In 1965, however, neither Cuba nor the Soviet Union sent representatives to the Eleventh Hiroshima Atomic-Hydrogen Bomb Conference; such Cuban behavior clearly suggests pro-Soviet alignment.

The relatively strong increase in the level of political alignment between Cuba and the Soviet subsystem from 1963 to early 1966 correlates with known political developments in relations between Cuba and the communist system during that period. Ernesto "Che" Guevara, the primary Cuban advocate of "the Chinese way," disappeared in early 1965 from Cuba; Sino-Cuban economic and political friction developed, being publicly revealed in early 1966; some Russo-Cuban mutual accommodation was reached over support for armed revolutions in Latin America; and, in accordance with advice from the Soviet subsystem, Cuba continued to effect a moderate economic development strategy, deemphasizing industrialization in favor of increased agricultural production.

Given a continued willingness of both the Soviet subsystem and Cuba to share similar values and respond to various needs of each other, we would expect that the degree of Cuba's pro-Soviet political alignment would continue to increase from one year to another. However, the progression will not be steady, but, rather, will continue to fluctuate.

The examination of Cuban behavior at meetings of the communist international political organizations shows the increase of Cuba's political alignment with the Soviet-led subsystem; that is, an increase especially in the value-sharing component of Cuban integration into the communist system. Since the development of pluralistically integrated relationships involves more than political alignment, we will next investigate Cuba's willingness to participate in the communist international organizations that may functionally channel and regulate economic, military, and communications transactions between party-states. Cuban participation in these organizations provides a good indicator of the level of mutual responsiveness, as well as of shared values, between Cuba and the system. This aspect of the inquiry also adds to our understanding of the degree of pro-Soviet political alignment, which would be enhanced by Cuban participation in other Soviet-dominated functional organizations.

We will discuss Cuban relations with eight communist international organizations: an economic organization, the Council for Mutual Economic Assistance (COMECON); two dealing with communications, the International Organization for Radio and Television (OIRT) and the Organization for the Cooperation of Socialist Countries in Telecommunications and Posts; a military one, the Warsaw Treaty Organization (WTO); and five others, the Joint Institute for Nuclear Research at Dubna, the Organization for Railway Cooperation, the Danube Commission, the Mixed Commission for Danube Fisheries, and the Control-Regulation Office. Of these, Cuba has participated in the first three, as well as had informal relations with the Warsaw Treaty Organization.

Economic Organization

The Council for Mutual Economic Assistance (founded in 1949) organizes the economic integration of the communist ruling parties; its effectiveness may affect their level of political integration. At the highest level, COMECON is governed by decisions taken at the infrequent Meetings of Representatives of Communist Parties of COMECON Member Countries. The next level is the Session of the Council, which convenes approximately once every year and has occasionally permitted observers. Below is the Executive Committee, which meets several times a year and sometimes invites observers. On the working level, COMECON members and observers frequently meet in permanent commissions which discuss economic collaboration and development in different fields. Since June 1963, there have been twenty-one such commissions in operation. Of the fourteen ruling party-states, the Soviet Union, Mongolia and all Eastern

European nations (except Yugoslavia) hold member status; Yugoslavia obtained associate status in late 1964. China, North Korea, and North Vietnam received observer status during the 1956–1958 period.

Cuba first began participating as an observer in meetings of the permanent commissions in late 1962.[14] The first instance of her attendance at a regular meeting of the Executive Committee apparently occurred in October 1963.[15] She first attended a Council Session in February–March 1965. However, Cuba probably has never signed any documents formalizing her association with COMECON.[16]

Cuban leaders have rarely discussed the Council. However, two comments by Prime Minister Fidel Castro and Ernesto "Che" Guevara have revealed their attitudes toward integration into the organization. Their remarks combined with the absence of comments by other leaders suggest a policy decision to participate cautiously in COMECON activities. In August 1963, Guevara (former Minister of Industries, who had been one of the two or three most influential and powerful figures in the government before his disappearance in early 1965) replied to a question about whether Cuba would enter COMECON, stating:

> At the present time, we are not interested in Comecon. We will be in it as observers. We have connections with this organization, but we are too far from Europe and its specific problems to enter now.[17]

This negative evaluation, coming at an early stage of Cuba-COMECON relations, was followed in September 1964 by a similar comment by Premier Castro. During an impromptu press conference, according to a report in *Hoy,* Castro answered a question about the Council in this manner:

> ". . . There is nothing concrete about relations with Comecon . . . but that in principle products will not be produced in Cuba which may be more easily and economically acquired in other countries."
>
> Fidel added that Cuba is far from Europe, but that it could coordinate its industries with countries like Mexico and expressed [the view] that there will be coordination of production with all of Latin America when political conditions change.[18]

Hence, Guevara and Castro seemed to persist in an uncommitted attitude toward COMECON, both before as well as after the 1964 upsurge in Cuban participation in the organization (see below); and both leaders stressed geographic obstacles.

Cuban Participation in COMECON Commissions. While the above comments provide some insight into Cuban policy toward economic integration into the communist system, more rigorous data comes from a record of Cuba's participation at COMECON meetings and reportage of COMECON events in various Cuban publications. The level of Cuban participation in COMECON is revealed by an extensive examination of reports of commission meetings.[19] The extent of Cuban attendance from July 1963 through May 1966, is recorded in Table 7–2, which shows both the total number of attendances for each six-month period and also the percentage ratio between that total and the total number of all COMECON meetings reported during the specified period. Before July 1963, Cuba is known to have observed only three commission meetings, one of them in 1962. Thus the data indicate that Cuban participation increased steadily during 1963; by mid-1964 it had risen to a high level, at which it remained until mid-1965. The rate of Cuba's attendance declined remarkably and inexplicably in late 1965, when Cuba did not appear at commission meetings attended previously. Then, during early 1966, Cuban participation attained an extremely high level.

Table 7–2 also offers comparative data for North Korea, North Vietnam, and the Chinese People's Republic. North Korea's pattern of participation closely resembles Cuba's, both in terms of temporal shifts and the general rate. Korea's rate of attendance also dropped during late 1965—but not so severely—and then returned to a high level. China, as might be expected, had a rate of participation much lower than that of the other observers. Yet, like Cuba's and North Korea's, it increased to a high level in early 1964 and stabilized there until mid-1965. This increase put China on the same level as North Vietnam for that period. Afterward, Chinese participation declined steadily but did not rise in early 1966, as did Cuba's and North Korea's.

North Vietnam's record ranks above China's, but below Cuba's and North Korea's. However, the figures for North Vietnam suggest a curve much different from that of the other observers, one that shows a slight decline from July 1963 until June 1965, and then moves sharply upward to a higher level for the period from July 1965 until May 1966. Indeed, the rise in North Vietnam's participation during July–December 1965 is as striking as the decline experienced by the other three observers. Undoubtedly the increase in Vietnam participation is related to issues bearing upon the war in Vietnam.

The table suggests several conclusions about Cuban relations with COMECON: (1) Cuba did not begin participating substantially until early 1964; (2) Since then, Cuba has been the first or second most active of the four observers, except during the latter part of 1965; (3) The low level of Chinese involvement suggests that Cuba's relations with COMECON have meant greater economic integration into the Soviet-led subsystem than into the Chinese-led one.

Cuba is known to have observed at meetings of nineteen of COMECON's twenty-one permanent commissions since October 1962.[20] While very little is known about what takes place at these meetings, the frequency of Cuban participation and the names of the commissions provide

TABLE 7–2. REPORTED ATTENDANCE AT COMECON COMMISSIONS BY CUBA AND OTHER OBSERVERS[a]

	1963 July–Dec.		1964 Jan.–June		1964 July–Dec.		1965 Jan.–June		1965 July–Dec.		1966 Jan.–May		TOTAL	
	actual no.	as % of all	actual no.	as % of all	actual no.	as % of all	actual no.	as % of all	actual no.	as % of all	actual no.	as % of all	actual no.	as % of all
Cuba	7	22%	17	42%	14	40%	15	42%	3	13%	12	75%	68	37%
North Korea	8	25%	17	42%	13	37%	17	47%	7	30%	8	50%	70	38%
North Vietnam	9	28%	12	29%	9	26%	8	22%	9	39%	6	37%	53	29%
China	5	16%	12	29%	9	26%	10	28%	3	13%	0	0%	39	21%
All Meetings for which Attendance was Published	32		41		35		36		23		16		183	

[a] Figures are for number of meetings at which Cuban attendance was reported. Cuba *may* have attended others, without reports appearing.

some indication of the types of information and cooperation which have most interested the Cubans. Thus, Cuba has observed eight times at meetings of the Foreign Trade Commission; six times each at meetings of the Transportation Commission, the Oil and Natural Gas Commission, the Machine Industry Commission, and the Non-Ferrous Metallurgy Commission; five times each at meetings of the Ferrous Metallurgy Commission, the Currency and Finances Commission, the Chemistry Industry Commission, and the Agriculture Commission; four times each at meetings of the Standards Commission,[21] the Geology Commission, and the Construction Commission; three times each at meetings of the Commission for Coordination of Scientific and Technical Research, the Light Industry Commission, and the Food Industry Commission; twice at the Statistics Commission; and once each at meetings of the Electric Power Commission, the Economic Questions Commission, and the Radiotechnology and Electronics Commissions. Cuba is not known to have ever attended meetings of the Coal Commission or the Commission for Peaceful Uses of Atomic Energy.[22] The commission meetings which Cuba attended were mainly those concurrently frequented by the other observers: the Agriculture, Ferrous Metallurgy, Foreign Trade, and Oil and Gas Commissions. The major exception is the Economic Questions Commission.

   COMECON in Cuban Elite Publications.   Additional information about Cuban integration into COMECON comes from qualitative data from selected Cuban publications that reflect attitudes of the Cuban economic and political elites. Discussions in *Comercio Exterior* suggest the level of interest in COMECON by some elements of the economic elite concerned with Cuban relations with the Council and Cuba's position in the international division of socialist labor, which COMECON is intended to implement.[23] The journal gave moderately high attention to the organization, in terms of a pattern which parallels that of actual attendance, except in early 1966. (See Table 7–3, based on frequency of mention of the word "COMECON" per given time period; and compare with the level of salience in *Cuba Socialista,* given in Table 7–5.) The comments about COMECON in *Comercio Exterior* were neutral or only mildly positive in content; at no time did the Council receive strong, sustained praise. Moreover, little was said about Cuban relations with the organization.

   From the content of remarks in articles authored by Cubans, the impression is given that the Cubans were uncertain about the extent of economic integration which should take place between Cuba and the organization. During late 1963 and early 1964, the importance of participation in COMECON for Cuba's development was recognized, along with the fact that integration was adversely affected by distance from Eu-

TABLE 7–3.   ATTENTION TO COMECON IN <u>COMERCIO EXTERIOR</u>

	Frequency of Mention of COMECON			
Year	Jan.–Mar.	Apr.–June	July–Sept.	Oct.–Dec.
1962			n.p.	n.a.
1963	n.a.	1	24	3
1964	7	16	11	0
1965[a]	10	10	3	6
1966	2			

[a] Only one issue, rather than the customary two, was published for the period January–June 1965. This single issue mentioned COMECON twenty times. Thus the chart shows ten references for each quarterly period.
n.a.=not available
n.p.=not published

rope, the "imperialist" blockade, Cuba's limited resources, and the lack of trained personnel.[24] During mid-1964, emphasis was given to the benefits that underdeveloped nations in general might obtain from association with COMECON, although Cuban relations with the organization were not used as an example.[25] Since then, no article written by a Cuban has advocated participation in COMECON by Cuba or any developing nation not already associated with the organization. On the contrary, there is some evidence that Cubans were questioning the value of the relationship. An important article in late 1964 on the long-range planning of Cuban trade and development points out specifically that there are limits and shortcomings to trade with and aid from the communist countries; that participation in any international division of labor should be planned differently for both imports and exports; that it is necessary to remain alert to the best markets for Cuba's needs; that greater attention should be given to prospects for expanding trade with capitalist markets; and that Cubans might study the development plans of certain noncommunist countries, such as Japan.[26] In overview, then, the Cuban writers have viewed Cuban involvement in COMECON with caution.

The political elite appears to have had much less interest than the economic elite, as indicated by the level of salience of COMECON in the two primary organs of Cuba's political party, *Hoy* (later, *Granma*) and *Cuba Socialista*.[27] Both publications demonstrate a generally low level of attention.[28] (On *Hoy* and *Granma*, see Table 7–4, based on square inches of coverage; on *Cuba Socialista*, see Table 7–5, based on frequency of mention of the word "COMECON.") In both publications there is extensive, though declining, attention from June 1962 until the end of 1963, after which it becomes quite low during 1964. The level of salience then rises in *Hoy* and *Granma* during 1965 and 1966,[29] but remains at a very low level in *Cuba Socialista*.

The initial outburst in salience in June 1962 is the result of enthusiasm about the Council Session taking place then, which revised the structure and operating principles of COMECON, and whose decisions opened the door to Cuban involvement and to greater participation by the other observers. The low salience during 1964 may derive both from Cuban disappointment with the benefits of participation and from such intra-COMECON problems as Romanian dissent from Soviet planning goals and the repercussions of the Sino-Soviet conflict.[30] As with front organization meetings, the Cuban press chose to omit reportage of such disaccord, rather than make a negative comment or expose discord within the communist system. The increase in attention to COMECON in *Hoy* in early 1965 is explained by good coverage of the important Executive Committee and Council Session meetings being held then, which Cuba attended.

TABLE 7–4. ATTENTION TO COMECON IN HOY AND GRANMA

| | Square Inches | | | |
Year	Jan.–Mar.	Apr.–June	July–Sept.	Oct.–Dec.
1962		340[a]	63	78
1963	58	16	72	37
1964	0	2	30	0
1965	35	13	20	16
1966	13[b]			

[a] June only.
[b] January–February only.

TABLE 7–5. ATTENTION TO COMECON IN CUBA SOCIALISTA

| | Frequency of Mention of COMECON | | | |
Year	Jan.–Mar.	Apr.–June	July–Sept.	Oct.–Dec.
1962			16	54
1963	4	0	39	1
1964	1	0	0	3
1965	2	1	0	0
1966	0[a]			

[a] January only.

Very few articles in *Hoy* and *Granma* discussed Cuban relations with COMECON. On only three occasions did these newspapers refer to Cuba's attendance at commission meetings: twice in 1964 and once in 1966. None of the articles in *Cuba Socialista* mention Cuban association with the organization. Not one of the three major articles on COMECON in that journal was written by a Cuban.

In summary, we see that while indicating increased integration during the 1962–1966 period into the communist system and the Soviet-led subsystem in particular, these various sets of behavioral and attitudinal data show that Cuba's integration into COMECON has been limited and has proceeded with hesitation and difficulty. Although Cuba participates to a greater extent than the other observers mentioned, her status is still that of an observer and not that of a member. While nothing in the COMECON charter would prevent more active cooperation, Cuba's involvement has remained essentially passive.[31] Moreover, the relationship with COMECON may not be entirely stable, as the downturn in late 1965 suggests.

Certainly, the Cuban political elite has maintained a rather ambivalent attitude toward participation in the organization. Economic and geographic obstacles have also hindered the attainment of higher levels of integration. Prospects for increased integration will depend greatly on raising the productivity of the Cuban economy so as to diminish the load which Cuba has imposed on the Soviet subsystem, and on the resolution of conflicts among COMECON members.

The Soviet Union appears to have had greater interest in promoting Cuba-COMECON relations than have had the other members of its subsystem. Misgivings about Cuban participation in COMECON are found not only among the Cubans but also among the Eastern Europeans. Possibly the best substantiated incident of Cuban-Eastern European conflict occurred during an early stage in Cuba-COMECON relations. In October 1963, the *Financial Times* and, later, *Der Spiegel*,[32] printed reports—rapidly picked up by the Chinese communist newspaper in Hong Kong, *Ta Kung Pao*[33]—that at a special COMECON meeting in Prague at that time the Cubans were severely reprimanded by certain delegates of Eastern European countries. According to the reports, after turning down an extra request by Cuba for financial aid to repair damage from a recent hurricane, certain delegates proceeded to chastise the Cubans for wasting aid, for not following advice from COMECON advisers, for not ridding the party of pro-Chinese elements, and for not undertaking some improvement of relations with the United States.

The Soviet press ultimately denied the reports, but not until October 24. Cuba media basically reprinted the Tass release.[34] That no Cuban statement was issued denying the validity of the articles suggests that the

Cuban political elite was displeased with the actions of the Eastern Europeans and that the reports were, in fact, true.[35]

Communications Organizations

The International Organization for Radio and Television (OIRT) embraces the Eastern European countries (except Albania and Yugoslavia, which observes occasionally), the Soviet Union, China, Mongolia, North Korea, North Vietnam, Finland, Mali, the United Arab Republic, Iraq, and Cuba. OIRT promotes the exchange of radio and television programs and gives advice on broadcasting problems. Cuba joined the organization at the 1961 meeting of its Technical Committee, and Cuban participation has been channeled through the Instituto Cubano de Radio Difusion. In general, the Cuban press rarely discusses OIRT meetings.

The Nineteenth Session of the Technical Committee was held in Havana in March 1965, the first not to take place in continental Europe. It was attended by the Soviet Union, the Eastern European members, and North Korea, according to the good coverage in Cuban press reports. For Cuba, one of the most important results was the prospect that within two or three years television programs could be received directly from European transmitters; further, a Cuban was designated to occupy the vice-presidency of the organization.

The organization is essentially controlled by the Soviet-led subsystem. While China had attended most past meetings, no representative was sent to the March 1965 conference. Moreover, the Cuban press made no reference to the absence of a Chinese delegate.

In contrast, at a September 1963 OIRT meeting in Bucharest at which both China and Cuba were present, the Cuban delegates' behavior was similar to that at front meetings during the same period. At that meeting, China attacked the Soviet Union and the representatives of other nations regarding participation by the OIRT administrative council in the Moscow Congress for Peace and Disarmament. As a result, the meeting was recessed by its chairman; thereupon, all delegations left the room, with the exception of the representatives from China, North Korea, and Cuba. Nevertheless, apparently neither Cuba nor Korea joined China on the final vote on the issue.[36]

The International Organization for Telecommunications and Posts is similiar to the five other regional postal unions of the world which are included within the Universal Postal Union. All the party-states except Yugoslavia have belonged since its inception in 1958; Yugoslavia entered in late 1964. Cuba joined in July 1965 at a meeting of Ministers of Communications in Peking; *Hoy* did not publish this news.[37] *Hoy, El Mundo,* and *Prensa Latina diario* have rarely mentioned this organization.

Military Organization

The Warsaw Treaty Organization (WTO) includes the Soviet Union and the Eastern European countries, with the exception of Yugoslavia. There is no evidence that Cuba has ever either applied for admission or been present at meetings of the secretive Economic Commission of the WTO.

Nevertheless, Cuban leaders and the Cuban press have always maintained a high interest in the organization and its activities. It is likely that from 1962 to 1964 the Cuban leaders would have welcomed an opportunity to become a signatory to the mutual defense treaty. Under such an arrangement, Cuba's military defenses would have been far more secure *vis-à-vis* the United States and the Cuban exiles than through bilateral pledges of assistance. However, in light of the outcome of the October 1962 missile crisis, Cuban membership in the WTO would have entailed grave and undesirable risks not only for the Soviet Union but also for the Eastern European nations. The latter apparently preferred to dispatch quantities of military goods and advisers to the exposed and distant island, without offering any specific mutual defense pledge.

Cuban interest in relations with the WTO was favorably discussed in a commentary in *Hoy,* entitled "The Warsaw Treaty,"[38] which pointed out that the Warsaw Treaty is "an agreement of friendship, cooperation, and mutual assistance, concluded by the European socialist countries, in order to defend the peace and security of Europe." The key statements with regard to Cuba's possible membership were contained in the final paragraphs:

> Although all those that compose this treaty at present are European socialist countries, nonsocialist and non-European countries could integrate themselves into it; that is to say, countries on other continents and with different socioeconomic regimes . . . could form part of the pact.
>
> The fact that Cuba is an American country does not prevent it from being a member of the Warsaw Treaty.
>
> Although Cuba does not form part of that Treaty, it counts on the support and the unrestricted solidarity of the Soviet Union, which has, more than one time, warned the U.S. imperialists that in case of armed attack from the United States on our country, the Soviet Union will come to our help with all its power.
>
> The rest of the socialist countries will not fail either to give their solidarity to our country.

While this statement is not a definitive expression of attitude and policy toward the WTO, it does make several important points. First, Cuba approves of the organization. Second, the organization could accept new members. Third, Cuba's geographical situation should not prevent it from being accepted. Fourth, although there is no statement that Cuba would like to join, there is also no statement that Cuba would not like to join. Fifth, reliance on pledges of assistance and solidarity by the Soviet Union and the other socialist countries provides some substitution for the benefits that might be derived from formal membership in the WTO.

The para-editorial refers to the "support and unrestricted solidarity" of the Soviet Union but only to "solidarity" from the other socialist countries. This phrasing suggests a less decisive commitment on the part of Eastern Europe to defend Cuba militarily, and implies some reservation about mutual defense arrangements with the beleaguered island.

During the two years following the *Hoy* discussion, international tensions over Cuba were markedly reduced. Perhaps because Cuba had become less of a military risk for the communist system than it had been in 1962–1963 and had strengthened its political alignment with the Soviet subsystem, Cuban Vice-Premier and Minister of Defense Raúl Castro was invited to attend military maneuvers of the WTO in Eastern Europe in late October 1965—the first time a Cuban had been so honored.[39] During his visit Castro discussed the current relationship between the WTO and Cuba, saying:

> The members of the Revolutionary Armed Forces of Cuba feel themselves broadly and indissolubly tied with the friendly armies of the Warsaw Pact. Our country does not belong formally to that pact, but this does not mean that we would be indifferent to an aggression of the revanchists and North Americans against the socialist countries. In the first place, because of the solidarity of proletarian internationalism, we would regard it as an aggression on our country; and in the second place, in reality, if the member countries of the Warsaw Pact are attacked, surely we would be attacked simultaneously. Then we would have to fight together against the common enemy. That is to say, Revolutionary Cuba is indestructibly tied to the fate of the countries of the socialist camp.[40]

Unlike the 1963 commentary in *Hoy*, Raúl Castro suggested that informal relations had developed between Cuba and the WTO. He did not mention obstacles to Cuban participation in the WTO (such as geographic distance, closed membership). His remarks did not focus on what the socialist countries would do for Cuba if it were attacked, but rather emphasized what would be Cuba's reaction to aggression against the socialist camp and Eastern Europe in particular.

Cuba's military relationships with the party-states continue to be based on bilateral relations. We would expect that Cuban integration along the military dimension would continue to be slow, although there might be more evidence for informal relations in the future than has hitherto been the case.

Other Organizations

Cuba has virtually no relations with the remaining communist international organizations (see p. 200, above). Nevertheless, the Cuban press occasionally reports on their activities, referring to them as significant examples of the operation of "the principles of equality, mutual gain, and respect for sovereignty" amongst the communist nations.

SUMMARY AND CONCLUSION

In the introduction, the position was taken that the general level of integration among national actors could be assessed by considering political, economic, military, and other activities in terms of their contribution to value-sharing and mutual responsiveness. These two dimensions delineate an analytic field upon which may be charted given and changing levels of integration (whether overall, or political, economic, or military alone). The terms "simple security community," "broadly aligned security community," and "highly responsive security community" were used to describe different sectors of the analytic field.

Quantitative and qualitative data on Cuban participation in communist international organizations have been used as indicators of integration. The research in the section on Cuban participation in those organizations has shown that: (1) politically, there has been a substantial rise in the level of alignment between Cuba and the Soviet subsystem, although the fluctuation present suggests a somewhat unstable relationship; (2) economically, with the exception of the decline from July–December 1965, Cuba became one of the most active observers in COMECON, but there is no indication that there has been enthusiasm amongst either the Cuban elite or COMECON members for engaging in a significant increase in economic integration; (3) despite recent attempts to improve Cuba's relations with the WTO, military integration between Cuba and that organization remains quite limited; (4) the level of integration obtaining along the communications and other dimensions has increased only slightly since 1963.

Therefore, we arrive at several major conclusions of this inquiry: (1) Cuba increased its alignment with the communist system during the entire period under consideration; (2) by mid-1966, Cuba's alignment with the Soviet subsystem had surpassed that of late 1962, after having followed a mildly pro-Chinese or nonaligned policy in late 1963 and part of 1964; (3) notwithstanding, overall integration into the ruling party system has proceeded with hesitation and difficulty, although it has con-

siderably increased since late 1962; (4) Cuba has overwhelmingly preferred integration into the Soviet-led subsystem to integration with the
Chinese one; it even engaged in pro-Soviet integrative acts while evincing
fluctuating alignment during 1963 and 1964.

There has been an increase in the number of shared values and in
the level of mutual responsiveness, especially across political and economic dimensions. In terms of the analytic field proposed earlier, Cuban
integration into the communist system has advanced in the following manner from late 1962 to spring 1966:

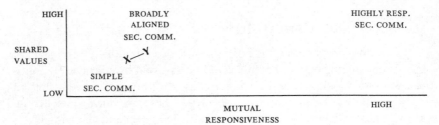

X: Cuba and communist system, late 1962
Y: mid-1966

In sum, Cuba may now be entering a "broadly aligned security community" relationship with the Soviet-led subsystem, but yet remains very
distant from a highly responsive security community relationship.

NOTES

1. The minimum requirements for the existence of a security community
   are said to be an assurance of peaceful change for some time and some
   sense of community. See Karl Deutsch, Sidney A. Burrell *et al., Political Community and the North Atlantic Area* (Princeton: Princeton
   University Press, 1957), pp. 5–6.
2. See Karl Deutsch *et al., Political Community,* pp. 123–33. Also, compare with Bruce Russett, *Community and Contention* (Cambridge,
   Mass.: Massachusetts Institute of Technology Press, 1963), Chapters
   2 and 12. Russett emphasizes mutual responsiveness; value-sharing fits
   into the concept of mutual identification and becomes a capability for
   responsiveness. However, it is not clear that the concept of value-sharing
   may be subsumed under the concept of mutual responsiveness; consequently, we have chosen to keep the two concepts separate here.
3. As suggested by Russett, *Community and Contention,* pp. 214–16.
4. While we have no specific term for the lower-right area, examples of
   security communities involving relatively high responsiveness but low
   value-sharing might be certain military alliances (in which the members

agree on few issues, but respond quite well to each others' needs against a common enemy), and possibly the relations between Cuba and Spain or Russia and Ethiopia. Historically, integrative efforts based primarily on a military alliance—essentially negative in purpose—have generally not survived beyond the usefulness of the alliance; see Deutsch *et al., Political Community,* pp. 44–46, 156–57, 190–91; and Russett, *Community and Contention,* pp. 196–98.

5. William H. Riker, *The Theory of Political Coalitions* (New Haven: Yale University Press, 1962).

6. Joseph S. Nye, Jr., *Pan-Africanism and East African Integration* (Cambridge, Mass.: Harvard University Press, 1965), pp. 219–35.

7. William E. Griffith, *Albania and the Sino-Soviet Rift* (Cambridge, Mass.: Massachusetts Institute of Technology Press, 1963), Chapter 1. Moreover, while the differences in China's relations with the Soviet Union cannot be solely accounted for by Soviet unwillingness to support Chinese goals, this clearly was an important reason. See Donald S. Zagoria, *The Sino-Soviet Conflict, 1956–1961* (Princeton: Princeton University Press, 1962), especially pp. 152–221.

8. Richard Lowenthal, "China," in Z. K. Brzezinski (ed.), *Africa and the Communist World* (Stanford: Stanford University Press, 1963), pp. 190–92.

9. For good treatment of post-1959 Cuban political and economic development, see Theodore Draper, *Castro's Revolution: Myths and Realities* (New York: Frederick A. Praeger, 1962), and *Castroism: Theory and Practice* (New York: Frederick A. Praeger, 1965); also Richard Fagen, "The Cuban Revolution: Enemies and Friends," in David Finley, Ole Holsti, and Richard Fagen, *Enemies in Politics* (Chicago: Rand-McNally, forthcoming); Antonio de la Carrera, "Fidel Castro's New Phase," *New Leader,* XLVIII (October 25, 1965), 3–12; and Daniel Tretiak, "Cuba and the Soviet Union: The Growing Accommodation," RM–4935–PR (July 1966), RAND Corporation, Santa Monica.

10. Karl Deutsch, "Security Communities," in James Rosenau (ed.), *International Politics and Foreign Policy* (Glencoe: Free Press, 1961), p. 100.

11. By now it should be clear that the term "fronts" may be somewhat out-of-date, since delegates to meetings of several organizations discussed here often arrive at decisions only after bitter debate. Notwithstanding, for the sake of convenience, we continue to use the term "fronts."

12. Unfortunately, as far as we know, there are no central archives in which are logged the attendance, votes, and activities of the delegations at the various front meetings. Consequently, large circulation, elite publications were used to ascertain the answers. For the Soviet Union, *New Times* (a weekly, the translated *Novoe vremia*), *Pravda,* and *Izvestiia* (daily newspapers); for Cuba, *Noticias de Hoy* (pre-1961, daily organ of the old PSP; post-1961, unofficially of the ORI, then the PURS; hereafter, *Hoy*), *Granma* (successor to *Hoy* and *Revolución* after October 1965), and *Prensa Latina diario* (the daily news release of Prensa Latina, the Cuban news agency, as distributed from Mexico City, D.F.); for China, the English language weekly *Peking Review* and *Jen-min Jihpao* (*People's Daily,* the party organ). Occasionally, *El Siglo,* the daily of the pro-Soviet Chilean communist party, was also examined.

13. On the basis of somewhat limited data, Cuba was not as staunchly aligned with Russia as the Eastern European party-states (including Romania but excluding Albania), but was decidedly more aligned than either North Korea or North Vietnam.

14. See *East Europe,* January 1963, p. 40; this seems to pre-date the March 1963 figure in Michael Kaser, *Comecon* (London: Oxford University Press, 1965), p. 91.

15. See *El Mundo,* June 25, 1963, p. 1; compare Kaser, *Comecon,* p. 90, with *Quarterly Economic Review,* Annual Supplement (June 1965), p. 10; also *El Mundo,* June 23, 1963, p. 1.

16. Compare Kaser, *Comecon,* p. 91; *Quarterly Economic Review,* Annual Supplement (June 1965), p. 10.

17. *Hoy,* August 21, 1963, p. 5.

18. *Hoy,* September 18, 1964, p. 8.

19. This data was collected from the following newspapers: *Nepszabadsag* (July 1963–May 1966; Budapest daily and organ of Hungary's communist party); *Pravda* (July 1963–May 1966); and *Izvestiia* (July 1963–May 1966). *Nepszabadsag* seems to be the best single source of information about COMECON commission meetings. Data from Cuban sources were not included in this sample because they provide inadequate comparative data on North Korea, North Vietnam, and China. Data from *Hoy, Granma, Prensa Latina diario,* and *El Mundo* (considered to be under less control than *Hoy* and *Granma*) would add six meetings not reported in the other sources, and would yield a sample having this pattern:

CUBAN ATTENDANCE AT COMMISSIONS

1963	1964	1965			1966	
July–Dec.	Jan.–June	July–Dec.	Jan.–June	July–Dec.	Jan.–Feb.	Total
4	8	2	1	1	1	17

20. These data were gathered from the aforementioned issues of *Nepszabadsag, Pravda,* and *Izvestiia,* as well as from earlier issues of *Nepszabadsag* (June 1962–June 1963); from those Cuban sources already mentioned; and *International Affairs* (January 1963–December 1965; the English-language edition of the Russian monthly journal of political analysis, *Mezhdunarodnaia zhizn*); from *East Europe* (June 1962–March 1966; published monthly in New York), and Kaser, *Comecon.*

21. Cuba is a member of the Institute of Standards, which is connected with the Standards Commission.

22. The Cubans would seem to have an interest in the peaceful uses for Cuba of nuclear technology. (For example, *Hoy,* June 28, 1963, referred to a small conference in Havana on applications of nuclear energy.) Also, Cuban leaders and economists have occasionally alluded to economic benefits from peaceful application of atomic energy. See, for example, Pedro Rios, "Notas sobre planificación perspectiva," *Comercio Exterior,* III (October–December 1964), 70; *El Mundo,* January 25, 1966, p. 4.

23. *Comercio Exterior* is the quarterly journal of the Ministry of Foreign Trade and carries articles by foreigners as well as Cubans.

24. Pedro Rios, "Reflexiones sobre politica comercial," *Comercio Exterior,* I (October–December 1963), 42; Julio Gonzales Noriega, "Las in-

versiones desde el punto de vista del comercio exterior," *Comercio Exterior*, II (January–March 1964), 82–83.

25. "El Comercio exterior de los paises socialistas," *Comercio Exterior*, II (April–June 1964), 24–35; and "La experiencia de Cuba on comercio exterior," *Comercio Exterior*, V (April–June 1964), 50–98.

26. Pedro Rios, "Notas sobre planificación perspectiva," *Comercio Exterior*, III (October–December 1964), especially pp. 64–72.

27. All issues of *Cuba Socialista*, the monthly theoretical publication of the Cuban Party organization, the PURS(C), now called the Cuban Communist Party.

28. That is, generally low both as to actual coverage and in comparison with the attention in two other Cuban publications, *El Mundo* and *Prensa Latina diario*, neither of which is as closely identified with Cuban party policy as are *Hoy, Granma*, and *Cuba Socialista. El Mundo*, in particular, gave considerable attention to COMECON and other international communist organizations.

29. The decline in Cuban attendance at COMECON commission meetings noted earlier is not matched by a decline in attention to COMECON in *Hoy* and *Granma* during the July–December 1965 period.

30. See Kaser, *Comecon*, pp. 91–107.

31. See A. Bykov, "CMEA: International Importance of its Experience," *International Affairs*, February 1965, p. 18.

32. *Financial Times* (London), October 10, 1963; *Der Spiegel* (West Germany), October 16, 1963, pp. 97–98.

33. Reuters report of October 10, printed in *Ta Kung Pao* (Hong Kong), October 11, 1963, p. 2.

34. *Pravda*, October 24, 1963, p. 3; *El Mundo*, October 24, 1963, pp. 1–2; *Prensa Latina diario*, October 24, 1963, p. C–1. Compare these with *Hoy*, October 24, 1963, p. 3, which omitted the passage, "according to reliable information received by Tass the reports . . . concerned fabrications and falsifications."

35. For additional information about tension between Cubans and Eastern Europeans, as well as Russians, see Anthony Sylvester, "East Europeans in Cuba," *East Europe*, XIV (October 1965), 2–8.

36. *Neues Deutschland* (East Berlin), September 17, 1963.

37. *Pravda*, July 16, 1965, p. 5.

38. *Hoy*, August 27, 1963; in answer to a reader's question about whether Cuba, now that it has been "separated from" the OAS, could enter the Warsaw Pact, even though Cuba was an American nation.

39. This indication of a slight increase in Cuba's military integration does not correlate with the decline in COMECON participation noted above; while we do not weight either indicator, the Castro trip does seem to support the view that the commission participation decline was not caused by any sudden erosion in Cuban relations with the Communist system.

40. *Hoy*, October 28, 1965, p. 1.

EIGHT

COMMUNIST SYSTEM INTERACTION WITH DEVELOPING AFRO-ASIAN STATES, 1954–1962: A PRELIMINARY ANALYSIS

MAURICE D. SIMON

INTERACTION AND POLITICAL INTEGRATION

The proliferation of economic, diplomatic, and socio-cultural contacts between members of the communist system and the developing Afro-Asian states in the last decade has been the subject of numerous scholarly studies.[1] Although many of these analyses are well-documented and valuable for their descriptive detail, a major shortcoming has been their persistent tendency to focus on single functional areas of interaction, that is, trade, economic aid, technical assistance, personal diplomacy, student exchange, and the like, instead of systematically examining the relationships between transactional behavior in several of these categories. Therefore, the task of this chapter is to analyze and measure the *overall* dimensions of communist system interaction with twenty-six developing Afro-Asian states during the period 1954 to 1962.[2]

The quantitative analysis of interstate transactions is one way of approaching the subject of political integration.[3] At present, there is great semantic confusion surrounding this concept; definitional statements are abundant; and the theory itself can properly be described as low-level or middle-range.[4] For these reasons, it is necessary at this point to offer a brief review of some of the literature dealing with this subject and to present an interpretation of the relationship between interaction and political integration.

Among theorists of international affairs, Karl Deutsch, Bruce Russett, Amitai Etzioni, and Ernst Haas have utilized data on transactional flows as operational indicators of political integration. Although their definitions of political integration differ, all of these theorists suggest that a considerable amount of interunit transactions must take place before a particular integrative threshold (unification, community, or viable international organization) can be reached. Deutsch indicates that integrated units must be mutually relevant; that is, they must devote a significant proportion of their time and resources to one another (salience). He concludes, "Transactions are therefore the first step to salience. The study of quantitative densities of transactions is the first step toward estimating the degree to which people are connected with each other."[5] Both Deutsch and Russett contend that there must occur a significant amount of interunit communication before states can attain the integrative threshold called community.[6] In a similar vein, Haas argues, "If the present international scene is conceived of as a series of interacting and mingling national organizations, then integration would describe the process of *increasing* the interaction so as to obscure the boundaries between the system of international organizations and the environment provided by their nation-state members."[7] Etzioni also postulates that there is a link between transactions and political integration, claiming that efforts toward the unification of states gain momentum when ". . . the flow of people, goods, and communications across [the] national boundaries increases."[8]

While all of these theorists recognize that interaction is a key general variable with respect to political integration, they also emphasize that a set of attitudinal variables is associated with politically integrated units. A major attitudinal variable that is discussed by all of these theorists is mutual identification. For Etzioni, a political community must be ". . . the dominant focus of political identification for the large majority of politically aware citizens."[9] According to Deutsch, integration involves the ". . . increasing acceptance and use of the same or equivalent patterns of living, thinking and feeling among the individuals who are members of the various political units . . . so as to produce either a common 'we-feeling' among them, or a devotion of most of them to some symbol or symbols . . . or to a shared image of its population."[10] Russett also is concerned with mutual identification and taps this variable by studying political socialization practices and public opinion data.[11] Finally, Haas points out that the transfer of certain political loyalties or identifications from the nation-state to supranational organizations could promote international integration.[12]

A second major attitudinal variable examined by these theorists is mutual responsiveness. Russett states, "Formally, responsiveness is the *probability* that the demands of one party will be met with indulgence rather than with deprivation by the other party. Responsiveness is a general term giving us, in the specific case, only a probability statement."[13] This suggests that prior to the voluntary adhesion of an independent state to an existing supranational unit, such as the communist system, that state would have to have strong expectations that the larger unit would be responsive to its demands.

In this chapter, political integration is viewed as a set of political relationships reflecting the dispositions described above; that is, the attainment of political integration (community) is equated with the expression of these attitudinal variables in concrete political forms. In a recent theoretical work, Philip E. Jacob and Henry Teune imply that political integration can be conceptualized in this manner. They define political integration, roughly, as ". . . a state of mind or disposition to be cohesive, to act together, to be committed to mutual programs. . . ."[14] This definition might be refined in terms of operational indicators that demonstrate two or more states' disposition to be cohesive.[15] One indicator might be a measure of the degree to which political units have developed, or do develop, substantially similar value systems, internal structures, infrastructures, and processes.[16] Content analysis could be employed to determine the focus of elite political identifications, while survey research might determine the nature of mass political loyalties.[17] An indicator of mutual responsiveness might be a measure of the degree to which political entities develop domestic and foreign policies that are either conflicting, compatible, or supportive.[18] This list of potential operational indicators of political integration certainly is not exhaustive. The purpose of the discussion is to stress that political integration can be conceptualized as a set of specific political relationships expressing two or more states' disposition to be cohesive in their dealings with one another.

This conceptualization would facilitate a more precise explanation of the relationship between interaction and political integration. In a recent volume, Haas points out why there has been considerable confusion about this relationship in the past:

> The leading exponent of the transactional approach to integration is Karl Deutsch. The flow of transactions in terms of volume—i.e., a process—constitutes one dimension of his analysis. But at the same time Deutsch defines integration as a condition under which "integrated" states have foregone the use of violence as a means of settling their differences. Thus some of the indicators by which the final condition can be identified also serve as a definition of the process; ranges of transactions as well as the presumed result of the transactions constitute integration. This manner of conceptualizing the phenomenon makes it exceedingly difficult to isolate cause and effect.[19]

If political integration is conceptualized as a set of specific political relationships, it becomes a dependent variable; transactions can be considered as an independent variable associated with politically integrated units. In this way, it is possible to avoid the temptation to argue that the high volume of transactional flows between national units means that they are politically integrated.[20] This is, incidentally, a temptation many political scientists have succumbed to in the past.

Deutsch currently argues that high interaction between states can lead to political integration only if these transactions produce significant joint rewards or expectations of mutual benefits. He asserts, "The second step in measuring the degree to which people are linked is the study of covariance, that is, the study of joint rewards and penalties."[21] Deutsch's tentative hypotheses on the relationship between transactions and integration are based on the classic reinforcement or learning theory. He postulates that transactions which produce joint rewards can lead to mutual identification between the states experiencing these benefits: "When these transactions are highly visible, easy to identify and differentiate, people may form images of the community or of the group involved in the transactions. If these transactions were rewarded, the image of a community may be strongly positive. Linking this kind of community, people may say: We belong together."[22] *Therefore, it is necessary to study both the qualitative and the quantitative aspects of interaction before inferences about political integration can be made.*

Even the relationship between high interaction and positive covariance (joint rewards) is not necessarily symmetrical. There are numerous factors which can explain high levels of interaction. The close proximity of two states might make a high degree of interaction between them inevitable even though past transactions had resulted in joint penalties. Since the human memory is selective, dissociative, and combinatorial, there may be a multiplicity of transactions between highly unlikely partners at any given point in time;[23] for example, the political elites of one state may recall historical periods of cooperation with another state instead of years of conflict when they formulate policies that will accelerate the number of transactions between them. High interaction may be the result of a choice between the lesser of two evils; the Soviet Union chose to become a German ally in 1939 despite memories of past penalties and forebodings of the potential dangers involved in associating with the Nazi government. Finally, there is no guarantee that joint expectations of rewards will be fulfilled. Cooperative ventures may be undertaken with great optimism, yet terminate in failures which produce joint penalties.[24]

There are also tremendous complexities involved in assessing the relationship between high interaction and positive covariance, on the one hand, and political integration, on the other. Transactions and joint rewards are associated with two levels of society: the mass and the elite. Indexes demonstrating that there are extensive transactions and (inferentially) joint rewards between two states at the mass level may or may not tell us how far the process of political integration has progressed. Much depends on the responsiveness of the political elites of the two countries to mass demands and attitudes. In the case of France, for example, de Gaulle may resist societal pressures in favor of political integration with other member states of the Common Market. However, mass indicators are more meaningful when the communist system is examined. Since mass transactions are regulated and controlled by the party and governmental elites, the quantitative densities of transactions give a more accurate indication of the elite posture toward political integration.

In this chapter, it is postulated that there are regular, patterned methods of interaction between the communist system and the developing states. Thus, when the latter are placed on interactional scales according to the quantitative densities of their transactions with the communist system, there should be a high degree of association between the rank orders for the various indexes. It should be possible to identify specific developing states which, over time, have a wider scope and a higher intensity of interaction with the system than do others. Furthermore, it should be possible to build a composite index that will characterize the overall transactional relationships of these developing states to the communist system.[25]

For the reasons outlined above, it is not implied in this study that high interstate transactional flows constitute political integration. *Instead, it is proposed that high interaction between states on the political, economic, and social levels is a necessary, but not sufficient, prerequisite for the attainment of a particular integrative threshold (community, unification, or, in this case, voluntary membership in the communist system).*[26]

Aggregate figures reveal the burgeoning size and scope of communist system economic programs directed toward the Afro-Asian developing states; they do not, however, provide an accurate comparative measure of the degree of interaction between the communist party-states and specific Afro-Asian countries. When absolute measures are employed, it is logical to expect the largest countries (particularly India and Indonesia) to appear at the top of interaction scales. Therefore, in this study, measures that correct for the "relative weight" of the developing states have been used whenever possible.

Four summary measures have been used to tap the dimension of economic interaction for the period 1954 to 1962. Two of these measures concern economic aid. The developing states have been ranked according to cumulative communist system economic aid commitments (1954 to 1962) as a percentage of their 1961 gross national product and according to cumulative party-state aid per capita (1962 population) (see pp. 229–30). The summary measure for trade interaction is average annual trade with the system (1954 to 1962, or, in the case of former colonies, post-independence to 1962) as a percentage of average annual trade turn-over (see p. 231). With respect to technical assistance, the developing states have been ranked according to the average annual number of party-state technicians they have hosted (since 1957 or post-independence) per 100,000 1962 population[27] (see p. 232).

Spearman's rank correlation method ($p = 1 - \dfrac{6\Sigma d^2}{N(N^2 - 1)}$) was employed to test the statistical degree of association between the four indexes of economic interaction.[28] The results are presented in the following correlation matrix:

TABLE 8–1

		I.	II.	III.
Cumulative aid commitments as % of 1961 GNP	I.			
Cumulative aid per capita (1962 population)	II.	.936		
Average annual trade with communist system as % of average annual turnover	III.	.554	.514	
Average annual number of system technicians hosted per 100,000 1962 population	IV.	.855	.888	.608

This statistical test demonstrates that there is a very strong relationship between the rankings for the various economic indexes. The correlations are all significant at the .001 level.[29] This suggests that over the nine-year time period there has been a single underlying dimension of communist economic interaction with the developing states; thus, it should be possible to make predictions about a developing state's general ranking on one scale, such as trade, by determining its ranking on another scale, for example, economic aid or technical assistance.[30]

Since correlation coefficients are summary statistics which hide a great deal of the data, for the purpose of visual illustration the developing states have been placed into contingency tables, according to whether their interaction with the communist system in the various categories has been high, medium, or low. The assignment of a particular developing state to a high, medium, or low classification is, of course, arbitrary. A rule of thumb has been followed in arriving at the distinctions: An attempt has been made to keep the number of states in the high, medium, and low groups roughly equal, while seeking to avoid violation of the internal clustering patterns that appear in the data. The fact that the developing states cluster around the high-high, medium-medium, and low-low diagonal merely provides a visual, but not statistical, confirmation of the strong correlations which emerged when Spearman's rank order method was applied to the data.[31] The contingency tables are presented in Tables 8–2 through 8–7.

TABLE 8–2. AID AS PERCENTAGE OF GROSS NATIONAL PRODUCT

	High	*Medium*	*Low*

Aid Per Capita *High*	Afghanistan
	Guinea
	Iraq
	Mali
	Somali
	   Republic
	Syria
	UAR (Egypt)
	Yemen
	            100%
		Ghana
		
		11.1%	

Medium		Burma Cambodia Ceylon Ethiopia India Indonesia Nepal Tunisia 88.9%	
Low			Iran Israel Jordan Lebanon Morocco Pakistan Sudan Thailand Turkey 100%
Totals:	100%	100%	100%

Spearman Coefficient: .936

TABLE 8–3.   AID AS PERCENTAGE OF GROSS NATIONAL PRODUCT

		High	Medium	Low	
Average Annual Trade *High*		Afghanistan Guinea Mali Syria UAR (Egypt) Yemen 85.7%	Burma 12.5%	Turkey 11.2%	
Medium			Cambodia Ceylon India Indonesia 50%	Iran Jordan Morocco Sudan 44.4%	Spearman Coefficient: .554
Low		Iraq 14.3%	Ethiopia Ghana Tunisia 37.5%	Israel Lebanon Pakistan Thailand 44.4%	Not available (trade data): Nepal Somali Republic
Totals:		100%	100%	100%	

The contingency tables reveal that six of the developing states—Afghanistan, Guinea, Mali, Syria, the United Arab Republic (Egypt), and Yemen—maintained a consistent pattern of intense economic interaction with the communist system from 1954 to 1962; all of these states appear in the high-high category in each of the tables. The two sub-Saharan African states and Afghanistan received aid commitments equivalent to more than 35% of their 1961 gross national products, while communist system pledges to the three Middle Eastern states ranged from 26.1% to 19.4% of their 1961 GNP. In terms of cumulative aid per capita, Syria, Guinea, the UAR and Afghanistan fared best; they were all above the $29 level. In contrast, Mali and Yemen were assured they would get $22 and $14 per capita, respectively. Afghanistan, Guinea, and the UAR conducted from 39.8% to 28.2% of their total trade with the system, while Yemen, Mali, and Syria were considerably below this mark—between 17.4% and 12.1% of their average annual trade was with the party-states.[32] Among the six states, Guinea, Yemen, Afghanistan, and Syria were the leaders in hosting communist system technical assistance personnel, receiving an annual average of between 13.2 and 7.4 technicians

TABLE 8–4. AID AS PERCENTAGE OF GROSS NATIONAL PRODUCT

	High	Medium	Low	
Economic Technicians *High*	Afghanistan Guinea Iraq Mali Syria UAR (Egypt) Yemen 87.5%	Cambodia Ghana 22.2%		
Medium	Somali Republic 12.5%	Burma Ceylon Ethiopia India Indonesia Nepal Tunisia 77.8%	Iran Turkey 22.2%	Spearman Coefficient: .855
Low			Israel Jordan Lebanon Morocco Pakistan Sudan Thailand 77.8%	
Totals:	100%	100%	100%	

per 100,000 1962 population. Mali and the UAR lagged far behind the four others in this category, registering annual averages of 2.3 and 2.2 party-state technicians per 100,000 1962 population.

The Somali Republic and Iraq had economic interaction patterns which were not wholly consistent, but which placed them in the high-high group in most of the tables. The communist system established notable economic connections with the Somali Republic in the period immediately following its achievement of independence in 1960. By 1962, communist system aid commitments amounted to 106.5% of the African state's 1961 GNP and were equal to $36.44 per capita. Trade statistics were not available, but the strong correlations between economic indexes would suggest

TABLE 8–5. AID PER CAPITA

	High	Medium	Low	
Average Annual Trade *High*	Afghanistan Guinea Mali Syria UAR (Egypt) Yemen 75%	Burma 28.6%	Turkey 11.1%	
Medium		Cambodia Ceylon India Indonesia 57.1%	Iran Morocco Sudan 33.3%	Spearman Coefficient: .514
Low	Ghana Iraq 25%	Ethiopia Tunisia 14.3%	Israel Jordan Lebanon Pakistan Thailand 55.6%	Not available (trade data): Nepal Somali Republic
Totals:	100%	100%	100%	

that the Somali Republic either has developed or will develop strong foreign trade ties with the party-states. Communist technical assistance to the fledgling state was not particularly impressive (medium category —.8 technicians per 100,000 1962 population), but given the large aid commitments, it should be expected that the number of party-state personnel working in the country will multiply rapidly in future years; this number more than doubled from 1961 to 1962. Iraq appears in the high-high category in the three tables which do not involve trade; system economic aid amounted to 15.4% of its 1961 GNP or $32.10 per capita, while the annual average figure for communist system technicians hosted per 100,000 population was 5.3. The trade percentage for the period (3.1%-low category) was inconsistent with Iraq's high interaction on the other indexes, but after the 1958 revolution the annual average was much higher (6.1%). Thus, since 1958, Iraq has steadily increased its economic interaction with the communist system in all four categories.

Cambodia and Ghana had economic interaction profiles which

TABLE 8–6. AID PER CAPITA

	High	Medium	Low	
Economic Technicians High	Afghanistan Ghana Guinea Iraq Mali Syria UAR (Egypt) Yemen 88.9%	Cambodia 12.5%		
Medium	Somali Republic 11.1%	Burma Ceylon Ethiopia India Indonesia Nepal Tunisia 87.5%	Iran Turkey 22.2%	Spearman Coefficient: .888
Low			Israel Jordan Lebanon Morocco Pakistan Sudan Thailand 77.8%	
Totals:	100%	100%	100%	

indicate they were progressively accelerating their financial transactions with the party-states. Both countries received aid commitments equal to about 10% of their 1961 GNP, but Ghana ($21.38) surpassed Cambodia ($11.48) on a per capita basis. The Southeast Asian state had greater trade interaction with the system (an annual average of 10.0% to 4.4% for the period), but Ghana was moving upward on this scale; in 1958, the African state's trade with the system represented only 1.5% of its total turnover in contrast to the 7.6% recorded in 1962. Both states were in the high group for technical assistance, with Cambodia ranking above Ghana (they hosted respective annual averages of 2.4 and 1.5 party-state technicians per 100,000 1962 population).

TABLE 8–7. AVERAGE ANNUAL TRADE

	High	Medium	Low	
Economic Technicians *High*	Afghanistan Guinea Mali Syria UAR (Egypt) Yemen 75%	Cambodia 12.5%	Ghana Iraq 25%	
Medium	Burma Turkey 25%	Ceylon India Indonesia Iran 50%	Ethiopia Tunisia 25%	Spearman Coefficient: .608
Low		Jordan Morocco Sudan 37.5%	Israel Lebanon Pakistan Thailand 50%	Not available (trade data): Nepal Somali Republic
Totals:	100%	100%	100%	

TABLE 8–8

Developing state's rank on interactional index:		×	*Average of the correlations between that index and the other indexes:*		
I. Aid as % GNP (Afghanistan)	3	×	.782 (average of .936, .554, .855)	=	2.3
II. Aid per capita (Afghanistan)	6	×	.779 (average of .514, .936, .888)	=	4.7
III. % Total Trade (Afghanistan)	1	×	.559 (average of .554, .514, .608)	=	.6
IV. Economic Tech. (Afghanistan)	3	×	.784 (average of .608, .855, .888)	=	2.4
			Total	=	10.0
			COMPOSITE SCORE (average of scores above)	=	2.5

In order to summarize the material presented above and to simplify the later discussion, a composite scale of economic interaction has been devised. Each developing state was ranked according to its composite score for economic interaction, derived as shown in Table 8–8.[33] The composite scale (with high, medium, and low distinctions) is presented in Tables 8–9 through 8–13.

TABLE 8–9.   COMPOSITE ECONOMIC SCORES 1954–1962

Ranking	Developing State	Composite Score
	HIGH INTERACTION	
1.	Guinea	1.5
2.	Afghanistan	2.5
3.	Syria	3.1
4.	Somali Republic	3.6
5.	United Arab Republic (Egypt)	3.7
6.	Yemen	4.1
7.	Mali	4.4
8.	Iraq	6.4
9.	Cambodia	7.1
	MEDIUM INTERACTION	
10.	Ghana	8.0
11.	Indonesia	9.0
12.	Ceylon	9.2
13.	Burma	9.5
14.	Nepal	9.6
15.	Tunisia	10.4
16.	Ethiopia	11.4
17.	Turkey	11.9
18.	India	12.2
	LOW INTERACTION	
19.	Sudan	13.0
20.	Morocco	14.1
21.	Iran	14.4
22.	Pakistan	14.8
23.	Lebanon	15.5
24.	Jordan	16.3
25.	Israel	17.4
26.	Thailand	17.7

TABLE 8–10.   CUMULATIVE ECONOMIC AID COMMITMENTS FROM
COMMUNIST SYSTEM, 1954–1962, AS A PERCENTAGE OF 1961
GROSS NATIONAL PRODUCT

Ranking	Developing State	Aid as % 1961 GNP
	HIGH INTERACTION	
1.	Somali Republic	106.5
2.	Guinea	58.4
3.	Afghanistan	46.5
4.	Mali	37.0
5.	United Arab Republic (Egypt)	26.1
6.	Syria	25.7
7.	Yemen	19.4
8.	Iraq	15.4
	MEDIUM INTERACTION	
9.	Ethiopia	13.0
10.	Indonesia	12.7
11.	Nepal	10.7
12.	Ghana	10.3
13.	Cambodia	10.0
14.	Burma	9.1
15.	Ceylon	8.1
16.	Tunisia	6.1
17.	India	3.0
	LOW INTERACTION	
18.	Sudan	1.8
19.	Morocco	.6
20.5	Pakistan	.4
20.5	Turkey	.4
22.	Lebanon	.3
24.5	Iran	0
24.5	Israel	0
24.5	Jordan	0
24.5	Thailand	0

LEGAL AND MILITARY INTERACTION

It is a difficult task to find quantitative or "hard" data pertaining
to communist system political interaction; very few social scientists have
made detailed compilations that "map" communist system political transactions, such as official interstate visits by party and governmental dele-

TABLE 8–11.   CUMULATIVE ECONOMIC AID PER CAPITA (1962 POPULATION)
FROM COMMUNIST SYSTEM, 1954–1962

Ranking	Developing State	Per Capita Aid in $
	HIGH INTERACTION	
1.	Syria	41.78
2.	Somali Republic	36.44
3.	Guinea	35.10
4.	United Arab Republic (Egypt)	32.24
5.	Iraq	32.10
6.	Afghanistan	29.95
7.	Mali	22.07
8.	Ghana	21.35
9.	Yemen	14.00
	MEDIUM INTERACTION	
10.	Cambodia	11.48
11.	Ceylon	11.02
12.	Indonesia	10.89
13.	Tunisia	10.76
14.	Nepal	6.05
15.	Burma	5.39
16.	Ethiopia	5.14
17.	India	2.48
	LOW INTERACTION	
18.	Sudan	1.76
19.	Lebanon	1.10
20.	Morocco	.97
21.	Turkey	.76
22.	Pakistan	.31
24.5	Iran	0
24.5	Israel	0
24.5	Jordan	0
24.5	Thailand	0

gations or nation-to-nation communications.[34] Therefore, in this section the focus is upon legal and military interaction, both of which have an important bearing upon political relationships between states.

Jan F. Triska, Robert Slusser, and George Ginsburgs have charted the treaty-making behavior of the system leader, the Soviet Union, providing the data which will be used in this study to measure legal inter-

TABLE 8–12. AVERAGE ANNUAL TRADE WITH COMMUNIST SYSTEM
(1954–1962) AS A PERCENTAGE OF AVERAGE TOTAL TURNOVER

Ranking	Developing State	% Trade With System
	HIGH INTERACTION	
1.	Afghanistan	39.8
2.	Guinea	29.2
3.	United Arab Republic (Egypt)	28.2
4.	Yemen	17.4
5.	Turkey	15.6
6.	Mali	14.8
7.	Syria	12.1
8.	Burma	11.2
	MEDIUM INTERACTION	
9.	Iran	10.8
10.	Cambodia	10.0
11.	Ceylon	8.3
12.	Sudan	7.6
13.	Indonesia	6.6
14.	Jordan	5.1
15.	India	5.0
16.	Morocco	4.8
	LOW INTERACTION	
17.	Ghana	4.4
18.	Pakistan	4.3
19.	Lebanon	3.9
20.	Tunisia	3.3
21.	Iraq	3.1
22.	Israel	2.2
23.	Ethiopia	1.8
24.	Thailand	.8

Not available: Somali Republic, Nepal.

action.[35] Triska has emphasized that treaties, agreements, and conventions
are significant types of interactions directed to the "hard core" of Soviet
foreign policy, that is, ". . . that component of policy which expresses
articulation and normalization of relationships, commitments, stability,
conservation of forces but assimilation to change and concession to progress, resolution of conflicts, and attempt for creation of more favorable
situations. . . ."[36] Although the treaty data presented in this study are

TABLE 8–13. AVERAGE ANNUAL NUMBER OF COMMUNIST SYSTEM
ECONOMIC TECHNICIANS (1957–1962) WORKING IN DEVELOPING
STATES PER 100,000 1962 POPULATION

Ranking	Developing State	Average Annual # Technicians per 100,000 pop.
	HIGH INTERACTION	
1.	Guinea	13.2
2.	Yemen	11.6
3.	Afghanistan	9.0
4.	Syria	7.4
5.	Iraq	5.3
6.	Cambodia	2.4
7.	Mali	2.3
8.	United Arab Republic (Egypt)	2.2
9.	Ghana	**1.5**
	MEDIUM INTERACTION	
10.	Tunisia	.8
11.	Somali Republic	.8
12.	Nepal	.5
13.	Ceylon	.3
14.	Burma	.3
15.	Indonesia	.2
16.	Turkey	.2
17.	Ethiopia	.2
18.5	Iran	.1
18.5	India	.1
	LOW INTERACTION	
20.5	Morocco	.02
20.5	Pakistan	.02
22.	Sudan	.01
24.5	Israel	0
24.5	Jordan	0
24.5	Lebanon	0
24.5	Thailand	0

concerned only with the Soviet Union, in the future it may be possible to
gather information about the treaty behavior of the other party-states and
to present a more accurate profile of this important type of system interaction with the developing states.[37]

In the legal interaction category, the developing states were scaled

TABLE 8–14. AVERAGE ANNUAL NUMBER OF TREATIES CONCLUDED
BETWEEN 26 DEVELOPING STATES AND THE SOVIET UNION, 1954 OR
POST-INDEPENDENCE TO 1962

Ranking	Developing State	Average # Treaties
	HIGH INTERACTION	
1.	Afghanistan	5.4
2.	India	5.0
3.	Guinea	4.4
4.	UAR (Egypt)	4.2
5.	Indonesia	3.7
6.	Ghana	3.5
7.	Iran	2.8
8.	Mali	2.7
9.	Syria	2.5
	MEDIUM INTERACTION	
10.	Somali Republic	2.3
11.	Cambodia	2.1
12.	Burma	2.0
13.	Iraq	1.7
15.	Ceylon	1.6
15.	Morocco	1.6
15.	Sudan	1.6
17.	Tunisia	1.4
18.	Ethiopia	1.3
	LOW INTERACTION	
19.	Yemen	1.1
20.	Nepal	1.0
21.	Lebanon	.8
22.	Turkey	.7
23.	Pakistan	.4
24.	Israel	.2
25.	Thailand	.1
26.	Jordan	0

according to the frequency of their treaty engagements with the Soviet Union[38] (see Table 8–14). The application of Spearman's rank correlation method once again confirmed the hypothesis that there are regular, patterned modes of interaction between the communist system and the developing states. There was found a strong statistical relationship between the rankings for the legal and economic variables, as evidenced by the following matrix in which all of the correlations are significant at the .001 level:

	Frequency of treaty interaction (average annual number of treaties with the Soviet Union):
Cumulative system aid as a percentage of 1961 GNP	.630
Cumulative system aid per capita (1962 population)	.646
Average annual trade with system as percentage of total turnover	.640
Average annual number of system technicians working in state per 100,000 1962 population	.591

The correlation between the composite economic rankings and the treaty interaction rankings was even stronger—.692. The relationships between the rankings on these two scales are visually illustrated in Table 8–15.

The table indicates that five of the states which appeared in the

TABLE 8–15

		High	*Medium*	*Low*
Treaty Interaction	*High*	Afghanistan Guinea Mali Syria UAR (Egypt) 55.6%	Ghana India Indonesia 33.3%	Iran 12.5%
	Medium	Cambodia Iraq Somali Rep. 33.3%	Burma Ceylon Ethiopia Tunisia 44.5%	Morocco Sudan 25%
	Low	Yemen 11.1%	Nepal Turkey 22.2%	Israel Jordan Lebanon Pakistan Thailand 62.5%

highest category for overall economic transactions with the communist system also had the most frequent treaty interaction with the system leader. On the average, Afghanistan, Guinea, and the United Arab Republic concluded more than four treaties a year with the Soviet Union, while the comparable figure for Mali and Syria was more than 2.5. Three states which had high composite scores for economic interaction—Iraq, the Somali Republic, and Cambodia—fell into the medium category for treaties, but all three signed an average of more than 1.7 agreements a year with the Soviet Union. Yemen was the only developing state that had a high economic interaction, but a low frequency of treaty engagements; this deviant case warrants further study.

Although Ghana, India, and Indonesia were in the medium category for overall economic transactions with the system, their high frequency of legal interaction with the Soviet Union (an average of more than 3.5 treaties were concluded annually) was not unexpected. All of these states demonstrated consistently positive trends in their economic interaction with the system. In fact, Ghana already fell into the high category for aid per capita and technical assistance, while India and Indonesia would have ranked near the top of the economic interaction scale if absolute measures had been employed.[39]

The available data on communist system military assistance suggests that there is also a strong association between this type of political interaction and the intensity of economic relations.[40] According to State Department estimates, six of the nine states which ranked highest on the composite economic scale received substantial amounts of military aid from the communist system prior to 1961.[41] The United Arab Republic (Egypt) received $315 million in military aid, Iraq $188 million, Syria $128 million, Afghanistan $38 million, Yemen $17 million, and Guinea $1 million. Indonesia, which had intense economic interaction with the system in absolute economic terms, was given $506 million. Only two states in the low economic category, Morocco ($4 million) and Sudan $100,000), were given military aid; it should be noted that, among the members of the low group, these two states demonstrated the most positive trends in their economic interaction with the communist system.

It has been established above that there is great consistency in the communist system's economic, legal, and military interactions with the developing states. In the following section, the relationship between social interaction and the intensity of legal and economic transactions will be examined.

SOCIO-CULTURAL INTERACTION

In order to properly assess the degree of interaction between states at the mass level, it is necessary to collect and analyze quantitative data pertaining to socio-cultural transactions. Unfortunately, there is a dearth of such information about the communist system. For example, accurate and comprehensive figures on mail flow and tourist travel are currently unavailable.

It is possible to ascertain which developing states have concluded cultural and educational agreements with the communist party-states. According to the Department of State, fifteen of the developing states under examination had signed cultural and educational agreements with members of the communist system by the close of 1962.[42] The pattern of interaction was consistent with the economic and legal trends: The developing states which had signed cultural and educational agreements with the party-states generally clustered around the high and high-medium positions on the legal and economic scales. The treaty relationships are summarized below:

Ghana: with Albania, Bulgaria, China, Czechoslovakia, East Germany, Hungary, Romania, and the Soviet Union.

Guinea: with Bulgaria, China, Czechoslovakia, East Germany, Hungary, North Korea, North Vietnam, and the Soviet Union.

Mali: with Bulgaria, Czechoslovakia, Mongolia, North Korea, Poland, and the Soviet Union.

Syria: with Bulgaria, Czechoslovakia, East Germany, and the Soviet Union.

UAR: with Hungary, Poland, and the Soviet Union.

Indonesia: with Czechoslovakia, Hungary, and the Soviet Union.

Ethiopia: with China, Czechoslovakia, and the Soviet Union.

Afghanistan: with Czechoslovakia and the Soviet Union.

India: with Romania and the Soviet Union.

Iraq: with Hungary and the Soviet Union.

Cambodia: with Czechoslovakia and the Soviet Union.

Sudan: with the Soviet Union.

Ceylon: with the Soviet Union.

Nepal: with the Soviet Union.

Somali Republic: with the Soviet Union.

In the future it would be useful to analyze the terms of these agreements and to examine the number and quality of cultural transactions that have been planned.

A future study of communist system interaction with the developing states might also deal with transportation and communications transactions. The Soviet Union has signed air service agreements with Afghanistan, Ghana, Guinea, Indonesia, India, Iraq, Morocco, Sudan, the UAR (Egypt), and Turkey.[43] With reference to social interaction, it would be interesting to know how many weekly flights take place over these routes and how many passengers utilize the service.

In this study, it was necessary to use State Department data on student exchanges to tap the dimension of socio-cultural interaction.[44] In order to establish a control for the educational development of the states under examination, each state was ranked according to the following measure: average annual number of higher education students studying in the communist system (1956–1962) per 1,000 higher education students (Table 8–16).

TABLE 8–16. AVERAGE ANNUAL NUMBER OF HIGHER EDUCATION STUDENTS FROM DEVELOPING STATES STUDYING IN COMMUNIST PARTY-STATES, 1956–1962 (PER 1,000 HIGHER ED. STUDENTS)

Ranking	Developing States	Average # Students
	HIGH INTERACTION	
1.	Somali Republic	510.2
2.	Yemen	81.6
3.	Iraq	32.8
4.	Mali	31.1
5.	Ghana	25.9
6.	Guinea	21.9
7.	Cambodia	14.3
8.	Sudan	13.5
	MEDIUM INTERACTION	
9.	Ethiopia	10.8
10.	Syria	7.9
11.	Afghanistan	7.6
12.	Morocco	6.3
13.	Nepal	3.6
14.	Indonesia	2.6
15.	Tunisia	2.4
16.	UAR (Egypt)	1.1
17.	Ceylon	1.0
18.	Burma	.8
	LOW INTERACTION	
19.	India	.2
20.	Turkey	.1
23.5	Iran	0
23.5	Israel	0
23.5	Jordan	0
23.5	Lebanon	0
23.5	Pakistan	0
23.5	Thailand	0

As anticipated, there was a strong statistical relationship between the rankings for the composite economic interaction and student exchange scales. When Spearman's rank order method was applied, it was found that there was a .766 correlation (significant at the .001 level) between these rankings.[45] Thus, the consistent pattern of communist system interaction cited in the preceding sections was repeated once again. The contingency table (8–17) illustrates the similarity in the rankings.

Six of the nine states which ranked highest on the composite economic scale—Cambodia, Guinea, Iraq, Mali, the Somali Republic, and Yemen—occupied the top positions for student exchanges. During the 1956 to 1962 period, an average of 510.2 to 14.3 students out of every 1,000 enrolled in higher education in these countries did academic work within the communist system. The comparable figures for Syria and Afghanistan, which had intense economic relations with the party-states, were 7.9 and 7.6, respectively (medium category). Among the major economic partners of the party-states, only the UAR, with its relatively advanced higher education system, had low student interaction (1.1 stu-

TABLE 8–17.   COMPOSITE ECONOMIC RANKINGS

Student Exchanges	High	Medium	Low
High	Cambodia Guinea Iraq Mali Somali Republic Yemen	Ghana	Sudan
Medium	Afghanistan Syria UAR (Egypt)	Burma Ceylon Ethiopia Indonesia Nepal Tunisia Turkey	Morocco
Low		India	Iran Israel Jordan Lebanon Pakistan Thailand

dents per 1,000 at the university level). Ghana, which had the highest overall economic score in the medium economic category, was one of the leaders for student exchanges (25.9 students per 1,000).

There was a lower degree of association between the rankings for legal interaction and student exchange; however, the Spearman correlation coefficient for this relationship was .470, still significant at the .001 level. The states which were in the high and medium positions on the student exchange scales clustered into these same categories for treaty interaction. These relationships are summarized in Table 8–18.

The analysis of data has confirmed the major hypothesis of this study, namely, that there are regular, consistent patterns of the interaction between the communist system and the developing states. In the final section of the essay, this patterned activity will serve as the basis for a set of hypotheses and conclusions.

HYPOTHESES AND CONCLUSIONS

The steady expansion of communist system interaction with the developing states seems to support a stimulus-response or "multiple symmetry" model of East-West relations proposed by Jan F. Triska and David D. Finley. They suggest that in the cold war context ". . . unilateral

TABLE 8–18. STUDENT EXCHANGES

Treaty Interaction	High	Medium	Low
High	Ghana Guinea Mali	Afghanistan Indonesia Syria UAR (Egypt)	India Iran
Medium	Cambodia Iraq Somali Republic Sudan	Burma Ceylon Ethiopia Morocco Tunisia	
Low	Yemen	Nepal	Israel Lebanon Jordan Pakistan Thailand Turkey

initiation of a novel course of action which effectively unbalances the conflict between antagonists, novel either in nature or in magnitude, must elicit a compensating response from the target if the system of which the opponents are part is to recover its previous equilibrium." They do not claim that the restoration of equilibrium is historically inevitable, but contend that ". . . maintaining and perhaps modifying the nature of the conflict system obliges a nation to meet and match its opponent in some fashion along every dimension into which the conflict is carried."[46] In terms of the "multiple symmetry" model, the rapid acceleration of communist system political, economic, legal, military, and socio-cultural transactions with the developing states since 1954 can clearly be interpreted as an attempt to counteract Western programs designed to win the allegiance of the uncommitted Afro-Asian nations.

The degree of party-state participation in the interaction programs seems to be a function of the level of economic development. The more advanced Eastern European subsystem has been far more active in establishing formal ties with the developing states. In 1961, the Eastern European subsystem (including Mongolia, excluding Albania) had signed 81.9% of the trade agreements in existence between the system and the developing states; in the same year, the Soviet Union and other Eastern European party-states provided 89.3% of the system technicians serving in these countries.[47] More than 92% of the economic aid extended by the system during the 1954–1962 period emanated from the Eastern European subsystem. The Eastern European subsystem also played host to the great majority of exchange students; in 1963, 97.7% (12,510) of the foreign students studying in communist countries were concentrated in Eastern Europe.[48]

As might be expected, the Soviet Union was the most active party-state in establishing cooperative relations with the developing states. In 1961, it had signed more trade agreements (22) with the Afro-Asian nations than had any other member of the system, and it provided 69.9% of the communist technicians serving in the developing states. During the nine-year span under examination, the Soviet Union accounted for 71.4% of the economic assistance extended by the system to the Afro-Asian states. In the socio-cultural realm, the Soviet Union hosted 60.3% (7,720) of the foreign students studying in communist countries during 1963.

Among the other Eastern European party-states, Czechoslovakia, East Germany, and Poland had the most intense relations with the developing nations. In 1961, Czechoslovakia had signed 21 trade agreements with them, only one less than the Soviet Union; Poland was close to this mark with 18 agreements in effect. Czechoslovakia and Poland also provided substantial amounts of economic assistance to the developing states: Czechoslovakia accounted for 9.8% of system aid during the period and Poland for 5.7%. Although no specific figures are available, East Germany and Czechoslovakia are believed to be the two Eastern European party-states (excluding the Soviet Union) most active in the technical assistance and student exchange categories.[49]

China is the only member of the Asian subsystem which had a high degree of interaction with the developing states. In 1961, China had thirteen effective trade agreements with the Afro-Asian nations under consideration, while North Korea and North Vietnam had both signed only six such agreements. China was the sole member of the Asian subsystem which extended aid to the developing states under examination; Chinese aid during the 1954–1962 period amounted to $402 million or 7.9% of the economic assistance given by the system as a whole. The Chinese also made a concerted effort in the technical assistance category; in 1961, 10.7% of the system technicians working in the developing states were Chinese. According to State Department data, the Chinese were less active in the student exchange category; in 1963, only 290 foreign students were being educated in China, 2.3% of the system total.

From the composite scores for the 1954–1962 period (see Table 8–19) eleven of the developing states—Guinea, Afghanistan, the Somali Republic, Mali, Syria, Ghana, Iraq, the United Arab Republic, Yemen, Cambodia, and Indonesia, in that order—can be identified as having had the highest frequency, intensity, and scope of interaction with the communist system. Although none of these states have reached the levels of interaction characteristic of system members (described in Chapter 4 of the present book), their transactional profiles make them potential candidates for system membership.

It was postulated earlier that high interaction between states is a necessary, but not sufficient, prerequisite for political integration. If that is true, it should be expected that, in general, the eleven states named above have demonstrated a stronger disposition toward cohesion with the communist system than have the fifteen remaining countries. There are several ways in which this hypothesis could be tested. A comparison of United Nations voting records on cold war issues could be made.[50] If the hypothesis is valid, it should be found that the majority of states which voted frequently in favor of the communist system also ranked highest on the overall interactional scale. Content analyses could be made to evaluate the attitudes of the leaders of the developing states. The expectation would be that leaders who displayed the most positive orientations toward the party-states would represent the countries which had the highest densities of transactions with the communist system. Survey research could be employed to measure mass attitudes; again, the hypothesis would be confirmed if the results showed a strong correlation between positive affect and high interaction. It would also be necessary to examine communist system orientations toward the developing states. There is already some evidence that the countries which ranked highest on the interactional scale enjoyed higher status among the communist leaders. For example, Ghana, Guinea, and Mali, often described as "progressive" states by communist theoreticians, were in attendance at the Twenty-second Congress of the Communist Party of the Soviet Union in October 1961.

It is also postulated that the major transactional partners of the communist system share a set of common economic, political, and social characteristics which make them the focus of party-state interaction programs. Although it will be the task of a future paper to isolate these specific characteristics, three broad statements can be made at this time:

(1) With a few exceptions, the states which clustered at the top of the composite scale were the smallest and least developed of the twenty-six countries under examination.[51] This lends support to David Beim, who argues in "The Communist Bloc and the Foreign Aid Game" that, in its dealings with the uncommitted nations, the system is primarily motivated by a desire to bring them into a state of dependence;[52] by concentrating on the smallest and most backward states, the communist system can gain considerable political influence with limited financial inputs. As Herbert Dinerstein put it:[53]

> The attraction of Soviet [communist system] attention to the smallest and least developed countries is understandable. Even comprehensive aid could be relatively inexpensive and the political pay-off could be a new socialist state. At the same time, investment in countries with well developed middle classes seems to promise only modest gains and may even lead to the consolidation of capitalism. The small countries seem to offer the possibility of spectacular success at cut prices.

According to the data presented in this chapter, the concentration upon the smallest and least developed of the uncommitted nations can be expected to continue.

(2) A majority of the states which had the highest interaction were not geographically contiguous to the communist system. Furthermore, the transactional trends suggest that there is a growing emphasis on involvement with non-neighbors, namely, the newly emerging African states. Perhaps this can be explained by the historical experience of the developing states. System neighbors may be wary of intimate relations with the party-states, recalling imperialistic ventures of China and the Soviet Union which directly affected them. On the other hand, the states

which are not geographically contiguous to the system may not have as many reservations; the communist system can approach them with a relatively clean slate (especially in comparison with the West). This interactional trend seems to dispel the notion that the communist system will expand by osmosis, adding members which lie on its periphery. The system now possesses modern economic, political, and technological capabilities that make integration by osmosis alone unnecessary.

(3) A combination of strategic and tactical factors may explain the high interaction of certain developing states. Many of the states which rank highest on the transactional scales experienced short-term crises or long-standing strategic disputes which permitted the communist system to initiate intensive interaction programs. For example, system interaction with Egypt and Syria accelerated after a period of high tension with Israel and following the Suez crisis. Close relations with Iraq developed following the 1958 revolution. When Guinea withdrew from the French Union and was isolated by both its neighbors and the former mother country, the communist system moved quickly to establish important ties with the African state. The communist system has been able to capitalize on the Somali Republic's disputes with Ethiopia and Afghanistan's problems with Pakistan. As Beim points out, the strategic position of some countries makes them attractive transactional partners for the communist system.[54] The communist system's strong relationships with Syria and Iraq were designed to offset Western involvement in Turkey, Iran, and Pakistan; the party-states' bid for the support of Egypt and Yemen in an effort to counter Western influence in Lebanon, Israel, Jordan, and Saudi Arabia. Given the cold war context, it can be predicted that strategic and tactical considerations will continue to be numbered among the key determinants of communist system interaction with the developing states.

The remarkably consistent pattern of interaction between the communist system and the developing states described in this study yields one final conclusion. Since all transactions are controlled and regulated by party-state officials, the communist system can effectively coordinate its relations with the developing states. Once a political decision has been made to seek close ties with a particular Afro-Asian country, all functional areas of interaction can be activated immediately; that is, the communist system can quickly initiate trade programs, extend economic and technical aid, sign cultural agreements, and so forth. This means that the system can manipulate its transactions with the developing states in a way that permits it to achieve maximum political impact at any given moment. This is an important asset in this era of cold war, an era in which the communist system and the West are vying for the approval and support of the developing states.

TABLE 8–19.   OVERALL INTERACTIONAL SCORES, 1954–1962

Ranking	Developing State	Overall Score
1.	Guinea	2.1
2.	Afghanistan	2.9
3.	Somali Republic	3.1
4.	Mali	4.1
5.	Syria	4.5
6.	Ghana	4.6
7.	Iraq	5.1
8.	UAR (Egypt)	5.3
9.	Yemen	5.5
10.	Cambodia	5.8
11.	Indonesia	6.5
12.	Sudan	9.2
12.	Burma	9.2
14.	Nepal	9.3
14.	Ceylon	9.3
16.	India	9.9
17.	Tunisia	10.0
18.	Morocco	10.2
19.	Iran	11.3
20.	Ethiopia	11.7
21.	Turkey	12.5
22.	Lebanon	14.5
23.	Pakistan	14.6
24.	Israel	15.6
25.	Jordan	15.7
26.	Thailand	16.0

NOTES

1. This chapter is a shortened version of an earlier paper: Maurice D. Simon, "Communist System Interaction with the Developing States, 1954–1962: A Preliminary Analysis" (Stanford Studies of the Communist System, January 1966). For an extensive bibliography of major source material, see footnote 1, p. 46, of the earlier paper.
2. The criterion for selection of the developing states was availability of data. The communist system refers to all party-states except Cuba and Yugoslavia; they were excluded due to lack of data.

3. Footnote 3, p. 46, of Maurice D. Simon, "Communist System Interaction," offers a bibliography on this topic.
4. Perhaps the writings on this subject might be called "pre-theories." James N. Rosenau has used this term in the following manner: "Briefly, by pre-theory is meant both an early step toward explanation of specific empirical events and a general orientation toward all events, a point of view or philosophy about the way the world is. Ideally, pre-theories would be limited to the former meaning, but this requires that a field be in general agreement about the 'proper' orientation towards its subject matter, a situation which the field of foreign policy research is far from even approximating." Quoted from "Pre-Theories and Theories of Foreign Policy," a paper prepared for the Panel on Intra- and International Politics at the Conference on Comparative and International Politics, Northwestern University, April 2–4, 1964, p. 19.
5. Philip E. Jacob and James V. Toscano (eds.), *The Integration of Political Communities* (New York: Lippincott, 1964), p. 51.
6. Bruce M. Russett, *Community and Contention: Britain and America in the Twentieth Century* (Cambridge, Mass.: Massachusetts Institute of Technology Press, 1963), pp. 217–221.
7. Ernst B. Haas, *Beyond the Nation-State: Functionalism and International Organization* (Stanford: Stanford University Press, 1964), p. 29.
8. Amitai Etzioni, *Political Unification: A Comparative Study of Leaders and Forces* (New York: Holt, Rinehart and Winston, Inc., 1965), p. 52.
9. *Ibid.,* p. 4.
10. Jacob and Toscano, *Integration,* p. 36.
11. Russett, *Community and Contention,* pp. 128–43.
12. Haas, *Beyond the Nation-State,* pp. 49–50.
13. Russett, *Community and Contention,* p. 29.
14. Jacob and Toscano, *Integration,* p. 10.
15. Jacob and Toscano imply that they expect their definition to be refined in terms of operational indicators: "Political integration . . . refers to more than one aspect or dimension of behavior. It has no one best indicator. Despite these various facts about definitions of political integration, indicators are often used as definitions." They add, "Full agreement on a definition is neither likely nor necessary, but it is essential that there be understanding of the different usages of the term 'integration.' . . ." *Ibid.,* pp. 10–11.
16. Jan F. Triska has stated that two of the principal unifying [integrative] elements of the communist world are: "The *communist parties* ruling the fourteen states and creating thereby fourteen quasi-identical political, economic, social, and legal systems." "The acceptance by the fourteen communist party elites of *the Marxist-Leninist belief system* as a common source of present and future political, economic, social, and legal systems." See *The Rift in the Communist World* (Stanford: Stanford Studies of the Communist System, 1964), p. 2.
17. The Stanford Studies in International Conflict and Integration has been engaged in an exploratory piece of research which includes an automated content analysis of the major public addresses of Nehru, Sukarno, and Nasser at the international Afro-Asian conferences held at Bogor (1954), Bandung (1955), and Belgrade (1961). See Nazli Choucri and John Osgood Field, *Afro-Asian Study Propositions and Procedures*

—*Part I,* June 1965. Some survey research has been done pertaining to attitudes of foreign students towards the communist system. See, for example, a public opinion poll conducted among three hundred students from French-speaking African states in *Jeune Afrique,* No. 7 (June 4–10, 1962), pp. 16–17.

18. When most analysts speak about the "disintegration" of the communist system, they refer to the incompatible foreign and domestic policies of the Soviet Union and China.

19. Haas, *Beyond the Nation-State,* p. 27.

20. One can, of course, refer to transactions as elements associated with the *process* of political integration. When I refer to political integration, I am speaking about the set of relationships associated with the *attainment of an integrative threshold* (community, unification, or, as in this paper, voluntary membership in the communist system).

21. Jacob and Toscano, *Integration,* p. 53.

22. *Ibid.,* p. 54.

23. *Ibid.,* pp. 61–63.

24. Both the Soviet Union and the United States have been criticized by developing states which were dissatisfied with the administration of economic assistance programs.

25. The value of a composite index is demonstrated in Frederick Harbison and Charles A. Myers, *Education, Manpower, and Economic Growth* (New York: McGraw-Hill Book Company, 1964). The authors use a composite index of human resource development to rank a representative list of seventy-five countries and to group them into four levels of human resource development. This facilitates their discussion of strategies of human resource development.

26. I cannot think of any cases where states generally considered to be "integrated" have had low interaction. I can think of cases where states have had high interaction, but are not generally considered to be "integrated."

27. In the category of technical assistance, I would have preferred to use the number of native engineers, instead of population, as a control, but these data were unavailable.

28. See George A. Ferguson, *Statistical Analysis in Psychology and Education* (New York: McGraw-Hill Book Company, 1959), pp. 179–83.

29. The critical values for the Spearman coefficients are found in Ferguson, *Statistical Analysis,* p. 316.

30. This is an important finding, especially when one considers the difficulties involved in data on the communist system.

31. The percentage figures that appear in the tables also confirm the strong correlations. For example, 85.7% of the countries which appeared in the high category for aid as a percentage of GNP had high average trade with the system; 50% of the states in the medium category for aid as a percentage of GNP were in the medium category for trade; and 44.4% of those in the low category for aid as a percentage of GNP were in the low category for trade.

32. Pre-independence trade was not calculated in arriving at these averages.

33. Although more sophisticated means are available to achieve such a composite index, it was felt that, due to the nature of the research, such a simple scaling technique was justified. The underlying assumption of

this simplified weighting of each variable is similar to that of the more complicated mathematics of factor analysis and of part-whole correlation. The assumption is simply that the average relationship of a given variable with all other variables in the scale is some index of its relative importance to the principal component measured by the scale.

34. Zbigniew Brezezinski has mapped such transactions in *The Soviet Bloc: Unity and Conflict* (New York: Frederick A. Praeger, Inc., 1961), pp. 445–79. The State Department has also made compilations that map governmental delegation interaction. When I compared the governmental delegation rankings for 1957–1958 with the economic rankings for this period, I found that there was a high correlation between these scales. This suggests that governmental delegation interaction might be a good indicator of political interaction and could be used in future studies—if the State Department data for the years 1954–1956 and 1959–1962 are available. See United States Department of State, *The Soviet Bloc Exchange Program in 1957* (Office of Intelligence Research and Analysis: Report 7657, January 31, 1958) and *The Soviet Bloc Exchange Program in 1958* (Bureau of Intelligence and Research, Report 7937, January 30, 1959).

35. See Robert M. Slusser and Jan F. Triska, *A Calendar of Soviet Treaties 1917–1957* (Stanford: Stanford University Press, 1959); Robert M. Slusser and George Ginsburgs, "A Calendar of Soviet Treaties, January–December 1958," 7 *Ost Europa Recht* (1961), pp. 100–131, and "A Calendar of Soviet Treaties, January–December 1959," 8 *Ost Europa Recht* (1962), pp. 132–164. See also George Ginsburgs, "A Calendar of Soviet Treaties, January–December 1960," 9 *Ost Europa Recht* (1963), pp. 120–159; "A Calendar of Soviet Treaties, January–December 1961," 10 *Ost Europa Recht* (1964), pp. 116–148; and "A Calendar of Soviet Treaties," 11 *Ost Europa Recht* (1965), p. 129–160.

36. Jan F. Triska, "Soviet Treaty Law: A Quantitative Analysis," *Law and Contemporary Problems* (Autumn 1964), p. 896.

37. See, for example, the calendar of communist system bilateral agreements contained in Chapter 4 of the present book.

38. Complete data appear in the appendix of my earlier paper. Pre-independence years were not used in deriving the annual averages. In the case of Syria, the years 1958–1960 were not used in deriving its average frequency. These were the years it was a member of the United Arab Republic.

39. These three states have all signed agreements with the Soviet Union concerning collaboration on the peaceful uses of atomic energy (Indonesia in 1960, India and Ghana in 1961). Only two other developing states have signed such agreements—the UAR in 1956 and Iraq in 1959.

40. Robert Loring Allen has stated: "Arms shipments constitute a heavy burden upon the economies receiving them. The transactions commit a substantial proportion of experts for many years to come." *Middle Eastern Economic Relations with the Soviet Union, Eastern Europe, and Mainland China* (Charlottesville: University of Virginia Press, 1958), p. 55.

41. U. S. Department of State, *The Sino-Soviet Economic Offensive through 1960* (Bureau of Intelligence and Research: Research Memorandum RSB–43, June 18, 1964), p. 9.

42. U. S. Department of State, *Compilations of Cultural and Educational Agreements and Exchanges between Communist Countries and the Free World in 1963* (Bureau of Intelligence and Research, September 1964). For Soviet cultural agreements, the sources in footnote 35 were used.

43. See sources in footnote 35.

44. U. S. Department of State, *Bloc-Free World Cultural and Educational Exchanges in 1962* (Bureau of Intelligence and Research: Research Memorandum RSB–46, March 29, 1963), pp. 4–5.

45. The correlation coefficient for student interaction and aid as a percentage of gross national products was .808; for student interaction and aid per capita it was .785; for student interaction and trade it was .306; and for student interaction and economic technicians it was .705. All of these correlations were significant at the .001 level except the .306 for trade and student interaction. This indicates that the communist system has high trade with some countries with which it had little social interaction in terms of student exchanges. This may reflect the dependence of certain of the party-states and the developing countries upon one another for specific goods.

46. Jan F. Triska and David D. Finley, "Soviet-American Relations: A Multiple Symmetry Model," *Journal of Conflict Resolution,* IX, No. 1 (March 1965), 44.

47. See appendix in my earlier article.

48. See U. S. Department of State, *The Communist Economic Offensive through 1963* (Bureau of Intelligence and Research: Research Memo randum RSB–43, June 18, 1964), p. 16.

49. See U. S. Department of State, *A Comparison of United States and Soviet Bloc Aid Personnel* (Bureau of Intelligence and Research: Report No. 7998, April 16, 1959), p. 2; and U. S. Department of State, *Sino-Soviet Bloc Exchanges with the Free World in 1960* (Bureau of Intelligence and Research: Report 8401, February 1961), p. 9.

50. This was done for a two-year period (1961–1962) in an earlier paper. See Jan F. Triska with David O. Beim, Noralou Roos, and Maurice D. Simon, *The World Communist System* (Stanford: Stanford Studies of the Communist System, 1965), pp. 43–64.

51. The United Arab Republic and Indonesia are the two major exceptions.

52. David Beim, "The Communist Bloc and the Foreign Aid Game," *Western Political Quarterly,* XVII, No. 4 (December 1964), 790.

53. Herbert S. Dinerstein, "Soviet Doctrines on Developing Countries: Some Divergent Views," in Kurt London (ed.), *New Nations in a Divided World* (New York: Frederick A. Praeger, Inc., 1963), p. 87.

54. Beim, "The Communist Bloc," p. 790.

NINE

SOCIOECONOMIC DEVELOPMENT AND POLITICAL ACCESS IN THE COMMUNIST PARTY-STATES

DENNIS C. PIRAGES

One of the most interesting and useful hypotheses that can be drawn from contemporary theoretical literature in comparative politics is that the level of socioeconomic development or modernization is an important factor in determining the nature of a political system. Seymour Lipset has found that industrialization, urbanization, wealth, and education form one major factor which is highly correlated with democracy.[1] Karl Deutsch suggests that social mobilization resulting from rapid industrialization increases the salience of a political system for a large part of the population and therefore seriously affects the rules of the political game.[2] Daniel Lerner relates political instability in the Middle East to problems of modernization.[3] The precise nature and the general dynamics of this relationship remain to be clearly explicated, however, as few attempts have been made to integrate the rapidly expanding relevant literature on individual countries into a more general theoretical framework.

In attempting to extract maximum value from pertinent empirical studies, it is helpful to use the framework for political analysis suggested by David Easton.[4] Within this framework, the system of political elites or leaders is analytically separated from the "environment" with which it must deal.[5] In terms of attitudinal problems of socioeconomic development, the relevant part of the environment is society or human beings. The model emphasizes the flow of demands and supports from the environment (society) to the political system (leaders).[6] The key to successful maintenance of political power, in Easton's terminology, lies in balancing the demands and supports coming from the citizens. Elites try to meet citizen demands to insure a balance of supports, for if demands begin to greatly exceed the support level and cannot be suppressed, the leaders risk the loss of their positions. The problem is to identify alterations in the political orientations of individuals in the environment that cause modifications in the types of demands and supports transmitted to the political system at various levels of socioeconomic development. These changes, in turn, have an effect on the composition and structure of the political system.

When speaking of such changes, it is necessary to abstract those that are of chief political interest as, in reality, a variety of complex changes occur. Arthur S. Banks and Phillip M. Gregg, through a process of factor analysis of the data from *A Cross Polity Survey,* have isolated one key dimension of political systems that they have called access. The attributes that cluster along this dimension refer to what we more commonly call elite responsiveness or use of coercive methods against citizens.[7] Political systems can be ranged along this dimension according to the elites' distance from the citizens or, in other words, their "accessibility" to citizen demands. Elite systems that are very accessible to demands are usually described as "democratic" and those that are more distant as "dictatorial" or "totalitarian." When speaking of changes in the political system resulting from changes in socioeconomic developmental level, the emphasis is on movement along the access dimension.

Socioeconomic development refers to the movements occurring in the economic and social systems of a society as a concomitant of industrialization or modernization and generally implies massive changes in a cluster of closely related variables including increases in urbanization, in the general level of educational attainment, in exposure to mass communication, and in wealth available for distribution among the members of the society.[8] All indicators in each of these areas are closely connected and it is their joint upward movement that signifies a change in the level of socioeconomic development.[9]

When dealing with the relationship between development and movement along the access dimension of the political system, the analysis is made on a macro level. When working on this level, concern is allotted to the aggregate of all demands and supports coming from the citizens as well as to the overall accessibility of the elites. To formulate statements about the aggregate of demands and supports requires an examination of the effects of development on the micro level; that is, on the individuals composing this aggregate. It must be kept in mind that the analysis proceeds on two distinct planes and there will be occasion to jump from one analytical level to another in attempting to answer the questions previously posed.

When referring to the total performance of a society and the demands and supports given to the political system, it is useful to visualize that society as being composed of individuals occupying various "political status positions." To occupy a "political status position" means to enjoy an economic, educational, or communicating position in a society that is associated with certain orientations toward the political system. In less developed societies, the majority of the population occupies no political status position at all, as the political elites are not considered salient. In highly industrialized countries, on the other hand, the population is highly differentiated and many types of political status positions are occupied. When speaking of the effects of developmental level on the balance of demands and supports, the reference is to the number of individuals in the society who occupy political status positions from which evidence indicates that certain types of demands and supports can be expected. It has recently been shown that individuals enjoying similar socioeconomic status positions in different societies have similar political status positions; the political orientations of individuals exhibiting similar socioeconomic characteristics in different societies are more alike than the political orientations of individuals possessing different socioeconomic characteristics in the same society.[10]

Socioeconomic development implies the constant movement of individuals into new political status positions. Thus more people will be exposed to education, mass media, modernity, and so forth, and will have more leisure to devote to other than strictly occupational activities. In less developed countries, most of the population is engaged in subsistence activities and has little time to indulge in political pursuits. In these societies, tradition dictates that the majority of the individuals will not concern themselves with happenings outside their daily sphere of existence. Daniel Lerner, in his study of the Middle East, observed that the individual in less developed societies has a constrictive psychological outlook. He has a very narrow range of opinions, cannot imagine himself in the role of others, and claims no knowledge of or concern for the political system.[11] Lerner also found that, as societies develop, there occurs a rapid movement into new political status positions as a result of increasing education and media exposure, these processes being highly correlated with the emergence of the "empathetic" individual capable of imagining himself in the place of others, including the political elites.[12] The empathetic individual expects the political elites to respond to his demands. Lerner noted that this movement to new political status positions, as indexed by urbanization, literacy, and media exposure, was indicated by the close relationship between these indicators and political participation for fifty-four nations reporting the relevant statistics.[13]

Karl Deutsch has discovered a close link between what he refers to as "social mobilization" and the expansion of the political horizons of a large section of the population. Social mobilization is the name given to the overall process of change that happens to a substantial part of the population in moving from traditional to modern ways of life.[14] The process is indexed by changes in the developmental level and is highly correlated with movement into new socioeconomic and political status positions.

Both Lerner and Deutsch, concentrating on the less developed societies emerging from traditional into more modern ways of life, note that the chief effect of socioeconomic development is a mass movement from political status positions in which the political elites are not salient for the individual to new positions in which citizens voice demands and give support to the political system. The political system becomes more salient for greater numbers of individuals and the volume of potential demands and supports greatly increases. An inert political system can survive at low levels of development, but empirical evidence suggests that political elites involved with a more developed society must be very careful in efforts to balance demands and support and should develop an adequate feedback system for keeping in touch with the much more complex human environment.

Data from Gabriel Almond and Sidney Verba's *The Civic Culture* confirm that the portion of the citizens for whom the political elites are salient continues to expand as higher developmental levels are reached. Information provided by survey research in five countries distributed in the upper half of the world developmental continuum indicates that the salience of the political system as indexed by discussion of political issues and estimation of the impact of the national government on daily life continues to increase for greater numbers of individuals with developmental level right to the top of the developmental continuum.[15]

In summary, individuals having more education, media exposure, and psychic and physical mobility are more likely to place demands upon and give support to the political system. The data illustrate that socioeconomic status is a major determinant of political orientations in the countries studied, and that between country differences in political orientations are largely the result of the differing numbers of higher political status positions available to be filled.[16] People with similar socioeconomic standing in different societies have similar orientations toward their political systems.[17]

The political system is established to meet certain types of demands growing out of basic human needs, not the least of which is a necessity for some order in what otherwise would be that condition of social chaos which theorists have referred to as a "state of nature." Abraham Maslow offers a set of five basic goals, or needs, that he finds dominate the conscious life of humans. These are for physical comforts, safety, love, esteem, and self-actualization. They are related to each other "in a hierarchy of prepotency . . . [which] means that the most prepotent goal will monopolize consciousness . . . [while] the less prepotent needs are minimized, even forgotten or denied. When a need is fairly well satisfied, the next prepotent need emerges, in turn to dominate the conscious life and to serve as the center of organization of behavior, since gratified needs are not active motivators."[18] Fitting these human needs to a typology of demands that can be made to the political system, it is clear that the physiological and safety needs lead to material demands, the needs for love and esteem lead to participatory demands, and the need for self-actualization can be expected to lead to demands for effective political participation and access to political elites.

Individuals in the lower political status positions of all societies devote most of their time and energy to meeting Maslow's more elementary, or lower level, needs for physical comforts, including food, clothing, shelter, and safety from the pressures of the natural environment. As the political status structure begins to change in a society, citizens moving up from lower positions realize the importance of the political system and look to it to fulfill demands for material comforts arising from the daily struggle for existence. One of the key problems for the elites in developing countries is meeting these demands for material benefits with the small amounts of resources available. The nature of the contemporary political world encourages rapid large-scale changes in the political status structure, the result being that pressures on the elites for material benefits arise unexpectedly and create very unstable situations.[19] As the proportion of individuals having their more basic needs satisfied increases, a greater number concentrate on fulfilling social needs for citizenship and political participation. Demands for the franchise and other forms of participation come from those who occupy political status positions in which they are free from basic material demands and who have been educated to feel worthy of expressing a voice in political decisions. In general, the more developed societies have more occupants of these higher political status positions and, therefore, a high correlation exists between indicators of economic development and political awareness and participation.[20]

T. H. Marshall, reviewing the history of English political development, calls attention to the order in which demands made themselves felt in British political history. He points out that these have been of three types: civil rights, political rights, and social rights. As different segments of the British population moved into new political status position as the result of continuing economic development, they first voiced demands of a civil nature, including liberty of person, the right to justice, freedom to own property, and, in general, safety from the arbitrary actions of political elites. As more individuals moved to higher status positions, demands for effective political participation were voiced. Finally, demands were made for a just share of the economic product for all, including a guaranteed modicum of economic welfare and security, as well as equal opportunities for self-actualization through access to political decision-making.[21] In the British case, the movement to higher political status positions was gradual and orderly, and the political system could easily accommodate the new kinds of demands.

In the contemporary world, demands made upon the political elites are multiplied many times over because of the feeling of relative deprivation introduced by contacts with much more developed societies. Political development is unpredictable and various techniques of demand suppression are used by the elites to maintain a balance between demands and supports. In most of the less developed countries and the communist party-states, the political elites do not have the benefit of a reservoir of supports built up over past generations. Tremendous political upheavals have taken place in these countries in the last twenty years as the elites have struggled with momentous problems of meeting heavy material demands from the citizens with very limited resources. Responsiveness to all demands has not been feasible and the elites have usually been compelled to rely upon some type of forced demand reduction to keep a disgruntled population from overthrowing the political system.

As a society becomes more developed, the elite system has access to more material resources that can be distributed among the citizens in attempts to build more support. Political elites are held responsible for economic progress and, as the economy develops in these countries, more individuals see it in their interest to support the established political elite. As individuals move into higher political status positions, demands arise for effective political participation. If these demands are met, new quantities of supports are generated in the relevant part of the society. Over time, the political system can build a fund of support by meeting the demands of those in different political status positions with appropriate responses. The longer an elite system persists and the more developed a country becomes, the more likely it is that a large reservoir of citizen supports is available to the elites.

Starting with the basic human needs with which the political system must deal, it has been found that the quantity of citizen demands increases and the type of demands changes as more individuals move into political statuses in which the lower level needs are no longer pressing. The quantity of potential support also increases as more material and social resources are available to the elites to meet demands. The key to building support to balance increasing citizen demands is to meet the demands with the appropriate responses. It is important to remember that the above developmental dynamics grow out of needs that are common to all people. These dynamics should therefore be universal, and all political systems in societies at approximately the same developmental levels are faced with similar sets of problems.

The effects of development on movement by the political system along the access dimension, discussed above, should now be apparent. With increasing levels of development, demands change from material to participatory in nature, and the elites acquire more resources of all types to use in building citizen support. It is only natural that access to the political elites should increase in response to participatory demands from the citizens. At lower developmental levels, it is often necessary to keep the political compliance structure somewhat coercive (reliance on physical force to maintain citizen compliance). It becomes much more difficult, however, for elites in countries at higher levels of development to do likewise. It is not only "cheaper," but necessary, for elites in advanced societies to insure that a good portion of the citizens complies with political directives for calculative or normative reasons.[22] In order to insure the latter type of citizen compliance, it is imperative that elite responsiveness to citizen demands be perceived by the citizens to be at a high level.

If the above theoretical framework has any validity, it must be supported by empirical evidence. Aggregate statistics denoting political system performance are rare, but a recent effort by Arthur S. Banks and Robert Textor to codify political, economic, and social attributes of nation-states provides a few gross indicators that permit a tentative check to be made.[23] Assuming that most political elites are of rational individuals who have chosen not to ignore demands for increased responsiveness, *the socioeconomic developmental level of nation-states should be positively correlated with greater access to elites. The responsiveness of the decision-making structure should be greater and the political compliance structure should be less coercive at higher developmental levels.*

In order to test this theoretical deduction, thirty-five countries for which the relevant data are available have been ranked according to gross national product per capita, which is highly indicative of level of socioeconomic development.[24] An aggregate index has been constructed using ten political system attributes, all highly loaded on the access factor, to test the relationship between developmental level and the access dimension for the available sample of noncommunist political systems. Four of the indicators denote type of compliance structure and the other six index elite responsiveness.[25] The *higher* the aggregate score, the more coercive and less responsive are the political elites. (See Table 9–1.)

This tentative check on the theoretical framework reveals the expected relationship between developmental level and the access dimen-

TABLE 9–1. DEVELOPMENTAL LEVEL RELATED TO THE ACCESS DIMENSION*

Gross National Product per Capita	Compliance Structure	Responsiveness
More than $1000 United States, Canada, Sweden, Australia, New Zealand, United Kingdom, Belgium, Norway, Denmark.	0.00	0.00
$500–$1000 France, West Germany, Finland, Netherlands, Austria, Israel, Ireland, Venezuela, Italy, Argentina.	1.35	0.70
$300–$500 Malaya, South Africa, Lebanon, Japan, Greece, Spain, Colombia, Mexico.	2.81	2.85
Less than $300 Turkey, Tunisia, Portugal, Nicaragua, Honduras, El Salvador, Ecuador, Algeria, United Arab Republic.	6.89	6.08

* Only the average scores for the groups of countries are reported, but the statistics for *each* country reveal a very remarkable correlation between developmental level and access.

sion. With very few exceptions, a higher level of development, as indexed by gross national product per capita, means a more responsive and less coercive system of political elites. At higher levels of development, elites generally choose, or are forced, to respond to demands for effective political participation. As citizens become more educated, mobile, and communicative, they demand an effective voice in political affairs and access to the political system. It becomes prohibitively expensive for elites to use force to suppress these demands. As demands are met, a reservoir of supports and an effective political communication system are established which permit the elites to analytically balance demands and supports. Hence, greater access to political elites, as well as political stability, is associated with higher developmental levels.

THE COMMUNIST SYSTEM: HYPOTHESES

The world communist system is composed of states at very different levels of socioeconomic development. The Asian states are among the least developed in the world, the Balkan states are at intermediate levels, and the Eastern European states rank among the world's more developed countries. If a normal course of political development had been followed in this sample of states, it could be expected that they would roughly resemble Western political systems at the same developmental levels. Semicompetitive political systems had developed in the Eastern European states prior to World War II, and there is no reason to doubt that access would have slowly increased in each of these countries.[26] The political intrigues and dislocations that occurred in Eastern Europe during the interwar period are very similar to those now taking place in the developing nations, as occupants of new political status positions attempt to force the political elite to become more responsive to their demands.[27]

The disruptions resulting from World War II and the following takeover by communist parties closely connected with Moscow resulted in the establishment of nearly identical political systems in the European party-states and eventually in the Asian states. The nature of these political systems, stressing limited access to small groups of ruling elites and a coercive compliance structure made necessary by the "class struggle," is too familiar to bear repetition here. The essential point is that nonresponsive, coercive political systems were installed in countries at very different levels of economic development. Stalin was able to maintain control over this empire by liberal use of armed force, secret police, and loyal followers in leadership positions, and the citizenry had little chance to make demands upon the political leaders. The social disorganization following the war and the systematic elimination of potential opposition by the elites served to maintain these political systems.

The death of Stalin and the disintegration of centralized control have resulted in the emergence of somewhat independent political elites in each of the party-states. De-Stalinization was brought on largely by Khrushchev's understanding "that Soviet society could not develop further without a drastic change in the methods of governing it—a renunciation of mass terrorism involving a major reduction in the role of police coercion in daily life and a major increase in the role of material incentives for the ordinary worker and peasant."[28] The renunciation of mass terror by the system leader resulted in its abrogation by followers in other socialist countries, a process that has led to reemergence of political elites relying less upon the use of terror and more upon the approval of their respective citizenries for maintenance of power.[29] Now that the monolithic Stalinist system of centralized control has been abandoned, each of the party elite systems is faced with the task of dealing with the demands from a more organized and communicative populace. As the developmental level of the society with which the political elite must deal is of key importance in determining the proper amount of access to the political system, those party-state political elites embedded within more developed societies should by now have become much more accessible to citizen demands than those communist political elites involved with less developed societies.

As Khrushchev realized, the economy suffers if the political elites do not establish a relationship with the citizens that is appropriate to developmental level. It can be expected that those systems, if any, that have failed to develop adequate access channels and elite responsiveness are now faced with problems of stagnation in the party directed economy and slowdowns in output per man hour. This output lag stems from resentment by citizens who feel that the political system is not meeting their needs or demands, and who, therefore, are not willing to support the economy with their best efforts. Similarly, it can be expected that this has curtailed innovation in these economies and, consequently, the rate of economic growth, as no one is willing to take chances when it is safer to continue to use accepted methods of production and distribution. Finally, if the political leaders have established the proper responsive relationships with their citizens, they should also have established an effective political communication network enabling them to anticipate the effects of the actions they take and thus avoid outbursts of anomic violence against the political system.

Party-state elites, like other elites, desire to develop some semblance of responsiveness and less coercive compliance structures. The CPSU's 1961 program admits that the party is consciously attempting to change the political compliance structure when it posits two main goals for the future. The first is indicative of attempts to respond to material demands from the citizens by attempting to create the "material and technical basis of communism within the next two decades."[30] The appeal is made for calculative involvement by citizens when it is promised that "in the current decade . . . everyone will live comfortably. . . . The demand of Soviet people for well appointed housing will in the main be satisfied; hard physical work will disappear; the USSR will have the shortest working day."[31] With the more distant future in mind, the aim is to construct "a communist society" where distribution will be made on the basis of one's needs.

The party's program acknowledges the existence of citizen demands for better material conditions springing from physiological needs and promises that these demands will be met, while bearing in mind that it is ultimately hoped that moral involvement can be created by increasing access for those citizens who are now only calculatively involved with the political system. The party recognizes the importance of permitting at least some type of citizen access to the political system as it stresses the importance of the systematic renewal of the membership of leading bodies so that "more hundreds of thousands and millions of working people may learn to govern the state."[32] While much of the party program is written for propaganda purposes, the concerns voiced therein demonstrate that the political elites are aware of citizen demands and are attempting to respond to them.

The Soviet party program is closely studied and imitated by the other party elites. They, too, are faced with citizen demands corresponding to their social and political status structures. Steps have been taken in most party-states to meet demands for more consumer goods that stem from the simplest type of human needs. The vast structure of youth groups, party auxiliary organizations, and other bodies concerned with politics that has arisen under party auspices in each of the party-states indicates that leaders are aware of demands for participation and access arising from social and psychological needs. In the face of continuing socioeconomic development, the party elites have been forced to make a choice between maintaining a coercive compliance structure with minimum elite access and responsiveness and facing the consequences, or developing communication with the citizens and responsiveness to their demands. If the aforementioned hypotheses are valid, those elites that have taken the former alternative are condemned to economic stagnation and political frustration, while those taking the latter can expect a normal course of economic progress and the development of substantial support from citizens who see the political leaders attempting to meet their demands. Large scale changes in political systems do not always occur suddenly, however, and subtle shifts in access to elites can take place almost unnoticed, a fact that complicates the testing of these hypotheses.

A summary of the interrelated hypotheses generated in the theoretical discussion follows:

1. The speed with which the party-state elites have become more responsive to citizen demands and have attempted to shift the political compliance structure from a coercive to a normative basis should be related to socioeconomic developmental level. At this point in time, a decade after the collapse of Stalinist system, the more developed party-states should be characterized by greater citizen access to political elites and greater elite responsiveness to citizen demands.

2. Those party-states which have deviated significantly from the order predicated above, in a more coercive, less responsive direction, should be characterized by slowing or decreasing individual and systemic indicators of economic progress, as well as pressure for liberalization.

These deviant party-states should also be characterized by imperfect political communication between the political elites and the citizens. The leadership might be out of step with public opinion on key issues and changes in elite positions are likely to be forced by violence from the citizens or unusual manifestations of political unrest.

THE COMMUNIST SYSTEM: EMPIRICAL DATA

Indicators of socioeconomic development have been selected with two criteria in mind. First, they have been selected with a view toward minimizing the possibility that they have been distorted for propaganda purposes. It must be remembered that the indicators used are for comparisons between communist countries; only very general comparisons with western countries are attempted. It is hoped that, if any of these indicators are distorted, the falsification is systematic for the party-states and will not really make a serious difference in comparing their developmental levels. In the effort to avoid distortion, prestige statistics such as gross national product per capita have been neglected in favor of indicators that are less publicized but just as indicative of socioeconomic development.

The second criterion for the selection of indicators is the fact that these aggregate statistics should be helpful in indicating the composition of the political demand structure in the society. Most writers venturing to equate these economic indicators with the emergence of certain types of political systems in the aggregate or with the emergence of certain political orientations in individuals stress the importance of urbanization, the development of mass communications, education, and general societal wealth.[33] Attempts have been made here to collect statistics under each of these headings to give a picture of the developmental level of each of the party-states in these vital areas. (See Table 9–2.) Since adequate indicators of urbanization for key party-states are not available, four indicators have been averaged under each of the three remaining headings to yield a figure indicative of the developmental level of each of the party-states. Development within these three areas has again been averaged and a summary figure hopefully representative of overall level of socioeconomic development follows. It is impossible to average one type of indicator with another, and the figures representing developmental level are scaled figures based on one hundred points for the best performance by any of the party-states in a particular area of interest and no points for the worst performance. The other party-states have been assigned values between zero and one hundred for each indicator in ratio to their performance in comparison with the highest and lowest party-states. In arriving at the overall developmental score, corrections have been made to assure that each of the categories is given equal weight. No country has an index number one hundred in any category, as no country consistently appears close to the top.

The indicators used to index communications development are the number of telephone subscribers per thousand people, newspaper circulation per thousand, radio receivers per thousand, and annual per capita consumption of newsprint. The level of educational development is demonstrated by averaging statistics showing the number of persons in advanced schools per ten thousand people, number of school teachers on all levels per ten thousand people, per cent of children aged five to nineteen in school, and literacy figures for those fifteen and over. Societal wealth and industrialization is indexed by statistics showing annual per capita energy consumption, per cent of the population not dependent on agricultural occupations, number of physicians per ten thousand inhabitants, and number of hospital beds per ten thousand persons.

The overall rankings reveal that East Germany and Czechoslovakia are nearly even in level of development and are followed by Hungary, the USSR, Bulgaria, and Poland, all of whom are bunched together considerably below the level of the leaders. As each of the three indicators forms part of the cluster of variables referred to as modernization or development, they all correlate highly with each other and with the final average.[34] Table 9–3 illustrates the correlation between these variables for the party-states.

TABLE 9–2. SCALED SCORES SUMMARIZING DEVELOPMENTAL LEVEL

	Communication	Education	Wealth	Average
East Germany	89	44	71	68
Czechoslovakia	66	64	68	66
Hungary	56	40	41	46
USSR	33	43	54	43
Bulgaria	36	55	29	40
Poland	27	45	41	38
Mongolia	16	38	35	30
Romania	26	29	27	27
Yugoslavia	21	36	09	22
North Korea	13	—	00	07
Albania	06	05	04	05
North Vietnam	—	—	00	00
China	00	00	00	00

TABLE 9–3.   CORRELATIONS BETWEEN DEVELOPMENTAL VARIABLES*

	Wealth	Education	Average
Communication	.89	.71	.94
Wealth and Industry		.78	.96
Education			.87

* Pearson product moment correlations.

Some interesting deviations from the expected pattern occur. The summary score best predicts the level of wealth and industry and also does very well at predicting the development of mass communications. Education development does not correlate as highly with the summary score as could be expected, and correlates much less perfectly with wealth and communications development. The fact that *education* developmental levels seem to be somewhat independent of other indicators in the party-states and least highly correlated with *communications* development gives rise to a hypothesis that the balance between these two variables is indicative of developing elite responsiveness and less coercive compliance structures. A glance at the country profiles reveals that East Germany and Hungary stand out in the degree to which the development of mass communications exceeds development in other sectors. Romania and Czechoslovakia display rather balanced profiles, while the rest of the non-Asian party-states display more zeal for development of the educational system.

If the first hypothesis is substantiated, East Germany and Czechoslovakia should permit the greatest access to political elites, followed by Hungary, the USSR, Bulgaria, and Poland, each of which could be expected to have slightly less responsive elites. Romania, Yugoslavia, and Albania should be characterized by little elite responsiveness to citizen demands, or, at least, lack of access to elites in these countries would not be inconsistent with economic development or political stability.

Access Indicators

In looking for variables indicative of a changing access structure, it is important to remember that one of the key attributes of the political systems in question is the emphasis placed on the erection of "iron curtains" between the party-states and other political systems. Such isolation from contact with other political systems is essential to the existence of a coercive compliance structure in political systems dealing with societies that are developed enough to be affected by contact with other political ideas. In this situation, "the impact of the outside universe is inevitably disruptive and dangerous to the totalitarian regime."[35]

Under Stalin, the flow of political information and the generation of new political demands was carefully controlled. Travel abroad was forbidden for both tourists and students. Foreign newspapers and books, sources of potentially revolutionary ideas, were suppressed. Attempts to control the introduction of political ideas from abroad were complemented by efforts to diminish the possibility of generation of new political ideas and demands internally. In short, the responsiveness of elites to citizen demands was at a minimum during this period and this was reflected in a coercive political compliance structure created to keep access to the elites at a minimum. The movement away from nonresponsiveness on the part of the elites since the break with Stalinist methods and the subsequent attempts to reduce the coercive aspects of the compliance structure are suggested both by changes in indicators of internal control as well as indicators of isolation from the outside world.

The number of students that each party-state sends to study in western countries is indicative of elite response to demands for contact with people in other societies. The presence of large numbers of students abroad suggests that the political elite is responsive to this type of demand and that it feels safe in allowing students to leave the country. If very few students are sent abroad, they can be carefully screened and pressures against relatives might be sufficient to insure the student's return. If many students are sent abroad, careful screening of each applicant becomes impossible. The ability of a political system to absorb many students exposed to different political ideas gives evidence of an elite that has acquired enough support from the citizens so that its position is not so weak as to make citizen contact with other political systems dangerous.

The number of students permitted to study abroad should be one indicator of each country's position on the access dimension and, according to the first hypothesis, should be closely related to socioeconomic developmental level. As virtually no students were allowed abroad prior to 1954, the speed with which elites have moved with response to this type of demand is indexed by the current figures. Table 9–4 contains two measures of this type of interaction. The first column shows the number of students actually sent abroad, and the second is a weighted figure showing the ratio of domestic students to students sent to the West. The second indicator is obviously the more significant as it takes into account the differences in student population among countries. The number of students sent abroad is very significant in Hungary, where one of every twenty-four university students studies in a Western country. Yugoslavia, Poland, and Bulgaria send significant numbers of students West, but, contrary to expectations, Czechoslovakia and the USSR do very poorly in

TABLE 9–4. STUDENTS STUDYING IN 15 SELECTED DEMOCRACIES

	Number Studying in the West	Number of Domestic Students per Student in the West
Hungary	1681	24
Yugoslavia	647	248
Poland	427	449
Bulgaria	114	539
Albania	12	975
Romania	86	1150
Czechoslovakia	64	1994
USSR	164	14607
Mongolia	0	infinite

SOURCE: *UNESCO Statistical Yearbook, 1964.*

this category. Statistics are not available for highly developed East Germany. Only one of the four most developed countries ranks high on this variable; the Spearman rank order correlation with developmental level is —.07. (Unless otherwise specified, all correlations cited in the remainder of this chapter are Spearman rank order correlations.)

Works of Western social scientists, when translated into native languages, are a source of new ideas that the nonresponsive coercive elite cannot be expected to tolerate. As elites become more responsive and build more supports for themselves by increasing citizen access, their ability to tolerate social science translations from Western languages should increase. More accessible political elites should be indicated by more social science translations from Western languages. Table 9–5 shows the number of social sciences translations from Western languages as well as the percentage of all social science translations that is Western.

For most of the party-states, there are two main sources of social science literature to translate: the Soviet Union and the Western countries. The USSR, however, can only translate from Western languages as, until very recently, few works in the social sciences were produced in the other socialist countries. Thus, the Soviet Union's translation figure is highly inflated. There is only a very weak correlation of .15 between this variable and socioeconomic development. Yugoslavia, Poland, and Hungary are most liberal in translating from Western languages, as they are in sending students abroad. The rankings on these first two indicators of access correlate .53, demonstrating that these two activities are closely related. The party-states that send students abroad also translate more foreign social science literature.

TABLE 9–5. SOCIAL SCIENCE TRANSLATIONS

	1952		1960		1962	
	No.	Percentage	No.	Percentage	No.	Percentage
USSR	14	52	64	51	60	52
Yugoslavia	9	17	16	34	14	50
Poland	33	10	30	32	24	31
Hungary	5	6	2	12	10	19
Czechoslovakia	12	5	4	6	11	13
Bulgaria	8	4	3	6	7	9
East Germany	7	13	6	11	5	8
Romania	—	—	2	5	5	8
Albania	1	6	0	0	0	0

SOURCE: *Index Translationum,* 1952, 1960, 1962.

Obviously, quantity of translations does not necessarily mean that the works translated are of high quality or always contain social ideas that may in some ways be hostile to a totalitarian political elite. In this case, however, a glance at the titles translated in 1962 reveals that those states translating the highest percentage of social science literature from Western sources also translated material of good quality, while those countries translating very few works relied mainly on matter written by fellow travelers or books portraying Western social systems in a bad light.[36] It is also interesting to note that all the party-states except East Germany have greatly increased the percentage of translations from Western sources since the Stalinist era. Yugoslavia and Poland show the most rapid increases, followed by Hungary and Czechoslovakia.

The growing preoccupation with Western literature is not restricted to the social sciences, but spills over into all areas of literary activity. Table 9–6 indicates the party-states' translation activities for 1959 and 1961. Literary interest is an important transactional indicator and the implications of this type of data are very important.[37] Note the tremendous difference in the translations balance between Yugoslavia, Poland, and Hungary on one hand, and Bulgaria, Czechoslovakia, and Romania on the other. The latter three seem to be tightly anchored to the communist system, while the former resemble Western states in their translational activities.

External indicators of change are easy to locate because the data on this type of activity is available from Western sources. Information on internal liberalization comes from the party-states themselves and good, comparable data are very difficult to find. The following indicators repre-

TABLE 9–6. PARTY STATE BOOK TRANSLATIONS

	1959 Russian	1959 Western	1961 Russian	1961 Western
Yugoslavia	89	356	140	392
Poland	137	286	184	392
Hungary	92	136	107	162
Bulgaria	277	52	363	56
Czechoslovakia	376	263	447	249
Romania	201	59	329	80
Albania	20	13	74	24
USSR		864		778

SOURCE: *UNESCO Statistical Yearbook, 1964.*

sent attempts to use the available sources in determining changes in elite responsiveness and compliance structure, both components of the access dimension.

The number of university level students that are permitted to study social sciences or humanities is closely regulated in the party-states. For the world as a whole, the number studying in these fields is not closely related to developmental level.[38] Countries at lower levels of socioeconomic development are almost as likely as those at higher levels to have a large proportion of their college students studying in the humanities and social sciences. There is a key difference, however, between party-states and other states. While the average enrollment in these educational areas for noncommunist countries is thirty-two per cent, the only party-state to approach this figure is Yugoslavia.[39] The communist countries concentrate their efforts in the scientific and technical fields and channel students away from studies in the politically sensitive social sciences and humanities. This imbalance in the educational system, in at least one case, has led to demands for a change in the excessive emphasis placed upon the sciences and engineering.[40] The correlation between developmental level and students studying in social sciences and humanities for the party-states is —.30. (See Table 9–7.)

Both the absolute figure and the direction of change denote elite responsiveness to long ignored latent demands for an increase in the number of students permitted to study in these areas. A familiar pattern emerges for this variable as Czechoslovakia, East Germany, and the USSR fall far below their predicted position. Yugoslavia and Poland, joined by Bulgaria, are the most liberal states according to this indicator. Poland is the only party-state that shows a really significant increase in

TABLE 9–7. PERCENTAGE OF STUDENTS STUDYING SOCIAL SCIENCES
AND HUMANITIES

	1956 or Earlier	Since 1960
Yugoslavia	41	32
Bulgaria	24	24
Poland	15	23
Albania	—	20
Romania	14	18
Hungary	—	11
East Germany	15	9
Czechoslovakia	17	9
China	12	8
USSR	7	7

SOURCE: *UNESCO Statistical Yearbook, 1964.*

social sciences and humanities emphasis, while Czechoslovakia, East Germany, and China have become much less liberal. Correlations between this variable and the two indicators of external liberalization show that it correlates .48 with social science translations and .62 with students studying in the West. It is clear that the three indicators are closely linked, as more liberal party-states rank high on all indicators, while the less liberal party-states rank consistently low.

One of the most important attributes of a coercive nonresponsive political elite is reliance upon the use of force to keep citizens disciplined. Indicators of such a factor are difficult to find. The percentage of the population aged 15 through 64 in the armed forces yields some indication of the amount of military force that the elites feel is necessary to maintain political power. The armed forces act as a disciplinary unit, as well as a political socialization force. It can be argued that military forces are a function of perceived outside threats to the political elite. Whereas this might hold true for the Soviet Union, the system leader, it is doubtful that this holds for the rest of the party-states. There is no reason, for example, why the political elites of Yugoslavia should feel much less threatened by outside force than the elites in Czechoslovakia. Obviously, some portion of the variance is due to fear of outside threats, but the data reveal that the size of the military installation thus indexed is closely related to the other three liberalization indicators. This variable correlates —.15 with the developmental level, but is highly negatively correlated with students studying abroad (—.62), social science translations (—.80), and social sciences and humanities students (—.59). As on the other indicators,

Yugoslavia, Poland, Hungary, and Bulgaria prove most liberal, while Czechoslovakia, the USSR, East Germany, and Albania seem to be most coercive. (See Table 9–8.)

TABLE 9–8. POPULATION AGED 15–64 IN MILITARY FORCES (PERCENTAGE)

	Paramilitary	*Total Forces*[11]
China	.1	1.4
Yugoslavia	—	1.5
Poland	.5	3.8
Romania	1.0	4.7
Hungary	1.1	5.7
Bulgaria	.5	5.8
Czechoslovakia	.8	6.2
North Vietnam	.9	6.3
USSR	.5	6.8
East Germany	1.4	7.5
Albania	2.3	9.4
North Korea	—	11.7

SOURCE: "The Military Balance, 1964–65" (London: Institute for Strategic Studies, 1964).

The next internal variable of concern is communist party membership. The developmental dynamics predict that the more developed societies contain many citizens occupying higher political status positions and demanding access and effective political participation. In the party-states, there is only one way to effectively participate in politics legally: to join the communist party. Raw party membership statistics do not reveal much about the responsiveness of party elites. Party membership alone does not guarantee effective political participation, as even the larger parties can be composed of nonaccessible elites and apathetic members. The *rate* at which the party-states are recruiting new members into the party, however, gives some indication of elite willingness to expand the party in deference to demands for participation. While a high rate of increase in party membership does not guarantee increased elite responsiveness, it does testify to an elite that realizes the importance of permitting more people to participate in politics through party membership.

Table 9–9 reveals that Romania, Poland, the USSR, Mongolia, China, and Hungary have rapidly expanding communist parties. Czechoslovakia and East Germany are again notable for deviance from their

TABLE 9–9. COMMUNIST PARTY MEMBERSHIP

	Prior to 1960		After 1961		Yearly Increase
Romania	720,000	1958	1,240,000	1964	12.0%
Poland	1,023,577	1958	1,614,237	1964	9.6
USSR	8,366,000	1959	12,000,000	1965	7.2
Mongolia	36,333	1958	46,000	1963	5.3
China	13,960,000	1959	18,000,000	1965	4.8
Hungary	437,956	1959	520,000	1963	4.7
Yugoslavia	899,310	1959	1,030,041	1964	2.9
Czechoslovakia	1,500,000	1959	1,676,509	1964	2.4
Bulgaria	484,000	1958	528,674	1962	2.3
North Vietnam	620,000	1959	570,000	1963	2.2
East Germany	1,472,930	1958	1,610,679	1963	1.9
Albania	48,644	1956	53,000	1962	1.5
North Korea	1,164,251	1956	1,300,000	1964	1.5

SOURCE: "World Strength of the Communist Party Organization" (Washington: Department of State, 1960, 1965).

expected position and are largely responsible for the low (.15) correlation between rate of party expansion and developmental level. In general, the greater the increase in party membership, the smaller is the size of the military establishment in relation to the population (.77), and the greater is the percentage of social science literature that is translated from Western sources (.51). There is almost no relationship between this indicator and the other two variables (students abroad and humanities emphasis), which indicates that this may be the weakest of the access indicators.

In centrally planned economies, increases in salaries occur somewhat apart from actual increases in productivity. While productivity increases impose parameters within which salary increases can take place, it can be argued that capital investment procedures can be altered or inflationary wage increases granted if the political elites are concerned about meeting demands for higher wages. While this relationship is somewhat contaminated by the parameters set by productivity increases, it is safe to assume that willingness to increase the level of workers' salaries is demonstrative of elite attempts to build supports and that this variable should be highly correlated with the other indicators of increasing elite responsiveness.

The less developed party-states show the greatest yearly increases in nominal wages, while the more advanced system members, Czechoslovakia and East Germany, have been very hesitant in this respect.

TABLE 9–10.   AVERAGE NOMINAL WAGE INCREASES

	1961	1962	1963	Average
Romania	5.0	6.0	—	5.5
Poland	4.4	3.6	4.6	4.2
Bulgaria	5.0	2.4	3.4	3.6
USSR	1.0	4.0	—	2.5
Hungary	1.2	2.0	4.0	2.4
East Germany	3.9	0.9	—	2.4
Czechoslovakia	2.4	0.6	—	1.5

SOURCE: *Economic Survey of Europe, 1963.*

Yearly wage increases correlate negatively (—.94) with developmental level, but correlate well with four access indicators.

The degree of freedom given the press in each country is indicative of position on the access dimension. A free press is dangerous for nonresponsive, coercive political elites, as it can be a source of disruptive political ideas. Well-chosen editorials can spark revolution among a disgruntled citizenry. A free press can act as a channel for political communication between elites and citizens. Thus, degree of press freedom should be closely related to the other access indicators and, if the first hypothesis is valid, to socioeconomic developmental level.

The data in Table 9–11 are reproduced from a study by five experts on the world's press that have recently ranked all national press systems on a freedom scale running from one, completely free, to nine, totally

TABLE 9–11.   PRESS FREEDOM, RANKED ON A NINE-POINT SCALE

Yugoslavia	6
Poland	7
Hungary	7
Bulgaria	8
Czechoslovakia	8
East Germany	8
Romania	8
USSR	8
Albania	9

SOURCE: Raymond B. Nixon, "Freedom in the World's Press: A Fresh Appraisal with New Data," *Journalism Quarterly*, XLII, No. 1 (Winter 1965), 3–14.

TABLE 9–12. CORRELATION MATRIX FOR ACCESS INDICATORS

	2	3	4	5	6	7	Dev.
1. Students abroad	.14	−.17	.62	.62	.64	.72	−.07
2. Wage Increases		.67	.65	.66	−.10	.31	−.94
3. Party Membership			.77	−.16	.51	.52	.15
4. Military Forces				.59	.80	.83	−.15
5. Soc. Science & Hum. Studies					.48	.43	−.30
6. Social Science Translation						.94	.06
7. Press Freedom							.10

Average Correlation .50

controlled. Yugoslavia proves to be the most liberal party-state, with a ranking of six, followed by Hungary and Poland with a ranking of seven. As on the other indicators, the remaining party-states trail these three countries.

The pattern is now clear. The first hypothesis must be rejected, as the most developed party-state elites are not establishing a responsive relationship with their citizens more quickly and are not striving to build a less coercive compliance structure. The correlation between developmental level and the summary measure of access is —.27. The two most developed party-states rank near the bottom on all the indicators. On the other hand, three of the less developed states, Yugoslavia, Romania, and Poland, seem to be evolving less coercive compliance structures and elite responsiveness at a much faster rate than the rest of the party-states. Yugoslavia's position as the most responsive and least coercive party-state lends credence to the often expressed opinion that Yugoslavia actually resembles a Western developing nation rather than a communist party-state. The continuing friction between Yugoslav and Romanian elites and the system leadership seems indicative of the desire on the part of the party leaders of these countries to break away from Soviet domination and follow their own ideological and developmental paths. The developmental dynamics discussed above portend that these three political systems probably fall closest to an "expected" position along the access dimension and, therefore, have the best chance of any of the party-states to follow a developmental path leading to the establishment of more normal citizen-elite relationships.

Czechoslovakian and East German elites have not been very willing to become more responsive to the demands of their citizens, according to the data. These countries rank consistently lower than expected on all the indicators and are largely responsible for the poor correlations be-

TABLE 9–13.   AVERAGE RANK ON ALL DEPENDENT VARIABLES[42]

Yugoslavia	1.83
Poland*	2.36
Hungary	3.71
Romania	4.14
Bulgaria	4.57
USSR	6.16
Czechoslovakia*	6.28
East Germany	6.75
Albania	7.33

* As the theory predicts, recent intense pressures for liberalization have moved Czechoslovakia to a somewhat more "normal" position on this dimension. On the other hand, less industrialized Poland is sinking to a much lower rank, a change apparently linked to continuing student unrest.

tween level of socioeconomic development and these variables. If the theory discussed above is valid, the elites in these countries should be faced with problems of economic stagnation, disorganization, low productivity, and increasing pressures for elite responsiveness. Furthermore, the channels of political communication between the political elites and the masses should prove to be underdeveloped and largely responsible for anomic outbursts of violence against political decisions.

While only one of the variables correlates significantly with developmental level (yearly wage increases, —.94), it is obvious that the indicators are measuring activity along at least one key dimension. Each of the variables, taken as an indicator of movement along an access continuum, is highly correlated with the other variables. The data indicate that percentage of population aged 15–64 in the military yields the best prediction of position on this dimension as the average correlation between this and the other variables is .71. The second best indicator is freedom of the press (average correlation, .63), followed by percentage of social science translations from Western languages (.55), social science and humanities students (.44), percentage of third level students studying abroad (.44), yearly wage increases (.39), and, finally, yearly party membership increases (.36).

In general, the data show that the more coercive and less responsive political elites, that is, Czechoslovakia, East Germany, and Albania, have greater investment in military force per adult, lower yearly wage increases, a smaller proportion of students studying in Western countries, fewer students studying in the social sciences or humanities, fewer translations of Western social science literature, more restrictive press systems, and party membership that is increasing very slowly. The less coercive and more responsive party elites, that is, Yugoslavia, Poland, Romania, and Hungary, show smaller amounts of military force per adult, higher annual increases in wages, a greater proportion of students studying in the West, a greater concentration on studying the social sciences and humanities, more translation of Western social science literature, free press systems, and rapidly expanding communist parties. These indicators should be closely related to more difficult to obtain measures along this dimension. It is interesting that the three most coercive and least responsive political systems emphasize the development of the mass communication sector instead of the educational system; this being some empirical verification of the proposition that development and control of communication is emphasized by more coercive political elites.[43]

Alternate Hypotheses

The empirical data indicate that the first hypothesis developed from the theoretical model must be rejected for the communist system. Contrary to expectation, the party-state elites in the most socioeconomically developed countries have not developed less coercive and more responsive relations with their citizens at a faster pace than the less developed countries. The two most developed party-states, Czechoslovakia and especially East Germany, have been conspicuous in their failure to become more responsive to citizen demands. If the theoretical model has validity, hypotheses two and three predict that these two party-states should exhibit evidence of economic stagnation and faulty political communications networks.

It is always difficult to pinpoint cause and effect in problems of economic advancement or quiescence. There are a host of variables that can have great effect on economic progress. The theoretical model posits that one cause of economic stagnation is the failure of political elites to establish the proper responsive relationship with the citizens. If the political leaders are perceived by the citizens to be ignoring what they consider to be proper demands, they are likely to react silently by not performing well in their economic roles. This is especially true in economies where credit for economic progress through centralized direction is claimed by the political elites. If the elites depend upon coercion to force economic progress in a well-developed country, the citizens are likely to do enough to keep from getting into trouble, but yet not be likely to exert themselves for the sake of an elite from whom they are alienated. Economic waste, duplication, unproductive investments, and lack of innovation are likely to occur in this type of society, as no one is willing to go out of his way to correct wasteful situations or innovate new procedures for meeting production problems. This is especially true in complex developed economies where administrative responsibility must be decentralized and progress often depends on the performance of many key individuals at all levels of responsibility. Realizing that no data can "prove" exactly what causes economic quiescence in any particular case, Tables 9–14, 9–15, and 9–16 are presented in support of the hypothesis that the establishment of an elite-citizen relationship proper for the level of socioeconomic development has much to do with economic progress.

The tables reveal that Czechoslovakia has been beset by serious economic problems. National income increased by only one per cent in 1962 and declined four per cent in 1963. Output per man in industry declined one per cent in 1963, while the rest of the party-states displayed healthy increases in productivity. Industrial production also declined in 1963 in Czechoslovakia, but increased in all the other party-states. This economic setback led President Novotny to declare in December 1964 that "responsible economic organizations cannot persist any longer in their lack of decision when it comes to stopping unwanted production, reducing stocks, closing uneconomical plants and concentrating production in modern enterprises."[44] In short, as predicted, the Czechoslovak economy has suffered from disorganization caused by the lack of incentive to innovate, as well as lack of worker concern for increasing productive efforts which in turn has lead to pressures for economic and political reforms. Key personnel and workers must develop some sort of moral commitment to the economic and political systems built up as a result of proper elite responses to their more sophisticated political demands.

Industrial production in East Germany has risen at the same rate as in Czechoslovakia since 1958. These two states show the slowest growth rate of any of the party-states for this period. While East Germany's national income did not decline in 1963, as did Czechoslovakia's, it increased more slowly than the national incomes of all the other party-states. These figures cannot prove that the overly coercive political compliance structure was responsible for this economic stagnation, but they do confirm the theoretical predictions that these two party-states would show the poorest records of economic progress. The evidence is convincing and begs further testing of hypotheses of this nature.

The third hypothesis predicts that those states whose elites have been less responsive to citizen demands than their developmental level indicates they should, have poorly established political communication networks, an elite that is out of touch with public opinion, and frequent outbursts against unpopular actions taken by political leaders. It is difficult to measure the frequency of outbursts against political decisions as there are not enough observers to adequately report such outbreaks of violence in the party-states, and there is no accurate collection of recent statistics of such a nature available. It is also difficult to determine whether

TABLE 9–14. OUTPUT PER MAN IN INDUSTRY

	1960	1961	1962	1963 (plan)	1963
Bulgaria	2.3	9.2	7.8	6.1	4.6
Czechoslovakia	7.0	5.1	3.1	0.7	−1.0
East Germany	7.4	5.3	6.6	7.2	6.5
Hungary	5.9	7.0	4.4	5.5	3.2
Poland	10.7	6.7	3.2	3.2	2.7
Romania	11.1	6.5	6.5	9.3	7.2
USSR	4.5	3.6	6.2	5.6	5.0

SOURCE: Data represent percentage increase over previous year, *Economic Survey of Europe in 1963*.

TABLE 9–15. NATIONAL INCOME

	1960	1961	1962	1963 (plan)	1963
Albania	3.0	5.8	8.0	11.0	8.0
Bulgaria	6.8	2.8	6.2	—	6.0
Czechoslovakia	8.0	7.0	1.0	—	−4.0
East Germany	4.6	3.7	4.2	3.0	2.5
Hungary	5.9	7.0	4.4	5.5	3.2
Poland	4.5	7.2	2.0	5.2	6.0
Romania	11.0	10.0	4.5	13.0	7.0
USSR	8.0	7.0	6.0	7.0	4.0

SOURCE: Percentage increase over previous year, *Economic Survey of Europe in 1963*.

TABLE 9–16. INDEX OF INDUSTRIAL PRODUCTION

	1956	1957	1958	1959	1960	1961	1962	1963
Bulgaria	78	87	100	129	146	161	178	196
Czechoslovakia	81	90	100	111	124	135	143	142
East Germany	84	90	100	112	122	129	137	142
Hungary	78	89	100	111	125	139	149	159
Poland	83	91	100	109	122	134	145	152
Romania	84	91	100	110	128	148	168	189
USSR	82	91	100	111	122	133	146	158
Yugoslavia	77	90	100	113	130	139	148	171

SOURCE: *Yearbook of Labor Statistics, 1964*, p. 606.

elite decisions are out of step with public expectations, as no one has undertaken survey research to determine public desires in the party-states.

To help surmount these observational difficulties, public and elite reaction to one political event has been selected as indicative of the development of a successful communications network. Nikita Khrushchev's ouster as First Secretary of the Communist Party of the Soviet Union caught ail of the party-state leaders by surprise. In the more developed states, where the theoretical model predicts public opinion is an important factor to be considered by the elites, there is no doubt that there were public demands for explanations of the removal of the man who had done so much to reduce the burdens of the average citizen by abolishing many of the terroristic aspects of the Stalinist system. In the less developed states (that is, Albania, Bulgaria, Romania) the model predicts that the political elites are not salient for the majority of the citizens and do not have to worry about public reaction to their decisions on such an issue. An analysis of the varying elite responses to Khrushchev's ouster and the events that followed in the party-states provides evidence of the structure of the political communication network in each of the party states.

The three less developed countries are all at a level of development where the establishment of an effective communication network is not difficult, as only a small portion of the citizens normally make any demands on the political system. As could be expected, the Bulgarian party dutifully approved the exclusion action.[45] There were no subsequent reports of any violence arising from this decision. The Albanians, on the other hand, hailed Khrushchev's downfall as a "heavy blow to American imperialists."[46] As there was no report of any resulting citizen unrest, it can be assumed that the Albanian elite operated somewhat apart from the inert masses. The Albanian attitude toward Khrushchev is indicative of the elite's view concerning evolution of a less coercive political compliance structure. As the empirical data indicate, the Albanian leadership exhibits no desire to change the political compliance structure. Romania responded to the dismissal in a manner similar to the Bulgarians. Gheorghiu-Dej sent perfunctory greetings to the leaders and expressed hope for flourishing relations.[47] There was no suggestion of any opposition to the action. In all three cases, it must be assumed that the elites had at least developed a political communication network commensurate with the socioeconomic developmental level, which, in this instance, means almost no communication network at all.

Yugoslavia at first deleted some of the harshest criticism of Khrushchev from the party journal.[48] This was followed by printing of numerous favorable accounts of his activities. The party took no official position.[49] The Yugoslav reaction was primarily the result of its distance from the ideological center of the communist system. The Yugoslavs are not much concerned with happenings in the Soviet Union, as they have carved out their own course of political development. The elite is fairly free from pressures from the citizens, as the society is not very developed. There was no extensive public response to the ouster.

Reaction was similar in both Hungary and Poland. Kadar proved to be in touch with the masses from the very beginning, as he approved the merits of Khrushchev and promised that his government would continue the policies inaugurated while the latter had been in office.[50] He never retracted his stand on the ouster and the fact that he was in touch with public opinion allowed him to exploit the issue and reach "the zenith of his popularity."[51] Gomulka responded to the announcement by paying the first public tribute to the fallen leader.[52] He also seemed able to correctly gauge public opinion on this issue and gain popularity because of his position. In both Hungary and Poland, the political elites had developed effective political communication permitting them to make popular decisions and avoid mass unrest.

The reactions of the leadership of Czechoslovakia and East Germany are of greatest interest. If the hypothesis is correct, the political elites, due to their lack of responsiveness, have not established an effective communications network. The data seem to verify this hypothesis. The East German party elite first issued a Politburo statement combining "limited" praise for Khrushchev with pledges of confidence in the new leadership.[53] This statement did not seem to meet with citizen approval, as visitors to East Germany reported that there was extensive questioning of party officials about the ouster.[54] It was stated that local party meetings were disrupted when officials were unable to control members demanding explanations for the Moscow power switch. Eventually, the East German communists were forced to call top-level meetings with all noncommunist parties and mass organizations in an apparent effort to quell widespread agitation.[55] The Czechoslovak reaction to the dismissal was similar. The presidium issued a statement saying that the party and people had learned of Khrushchev's release with "surprise and emotion." It went on to say that the party and the people had appreciated his policies.[56] The Czech leadership refused to participate in the downgrading of Khrushchev, but on the other hand no responsible officials outside the presidium ever made any original comments, indicating that there was great indecision on the handling of the issue.[57]

The evidence suggests that the party-states fall into three groups when their political communication networks are examined. The elites of the less developed states have not yet found it necessary to worry too much about public reaction to political decisions. Political elites in these countries made immediate decisions on how to react to the ouster and no opposition was voiced. The Polish and Hungarian party leadership was able to correctly gauge public feeling on the matter and to exploit it for their own benefit. This indicates the development of at least a rudimentary feedback network. As predicted, the regime in East Germany was not in contact with the masses as its decision on this issue led to massive unrest. Meetings had to be called to calm the political storm. In Czechoslovakia, the communications network proved to be no more developed, as the leadership never could take a clear position on the dismissal, although it was able to avoid extensive unrest. While the evidence is not overwhelming, it is clear from this one example that the hypothesis should not be rejected and warrants further testing.

CONCLUSION

Taking into consideration a hierarchy of human needs that should be common to all men regardless of the cast of their political systems, a set of related hypotheses has been deduced from some of the more important findings of recent studies in comparative politics regarding the effects of socioeconomic development on relations between political elites and their citizens. These hypotheses were then tested against recent empirical data from the countries composing the communist system. The data have tentatively verified the hypotheses.

It is hoped that this study will stimulate new inquiries into the nature of each of the party-state political systems. A search through the literature reveals a dearth of good objective studies of citizen access within the party-states. It is becoming increasingly obvious since the dissolution of the Stalinist system of centralized control that each of the party-state elites has become much freer to determine its own relationship with the masses. As of now, we know very little about the complexities of these developing relationships or their likely effect on the future organization of the communist system. It is obvious that the party-states are not going to become liberal democracies with competing political parties in the near future. Political change takes place very slowly. The data indicate, however, that citizen access to decision-making structures is increasing and elite responsiveness to citizen demands is evolving within the single party frameworks in some of the party-states, just as such responsiveness is found within the Mexican single-party system. Perhaps the main barrier to our perception of these changes is the fact that the single party goes by the title "communist," instead of by some more ideologically acceptable name.

It is suggested that the access dimension, indexed by measures of elite responsiveness and use of coercion to maintain citizen compliance, might be a useful tool in classifying party-state political systems. The use of such indicators as mentioned above, and more refined indicators should they become available, permits meaningful differentiations to be made between the party-states rather than simple classification of them all as "totalitarian" political systems. The opportunities that the objective study of these political systems and their performance offers to the student of political development should no longer be ignored.

NOTES

1. Seymour Martin Lipset, *Political Man* (Garden City: Doubleday and Company, Inc., 1960), p. 42.
2. Karl Deutsch, "Social Mobilization and Political Development," *American Political Science Review,* LV, No. 3 (September 1961), 493–514.
3. Daniel Lerner, *The Passing of Traditional Society* (New York: Free Press of Glencoe, 1958).
4. See David Easton, *A Framework for Political Analysis* (Englewood Cliffs: Prentice-Hall, Inc., 1965), for a more complete explication.
5. *Ibid.,* pp. 66ff.
6. *Ibid.,* pp. 112ff.
7. Arthur S. Banks and Phillip M. Gregg, "Dimensions of Political Systems: Factor Analysis of a *Cross Polity Survey,*" *American Political Science Review,* LIX, No. 3 (September 1965), 602–615.
8. See Lerner, *Passing,* Chapter 2, and Lipset, *Political Man,* pp. 32ff.
9. For precise correlations between developmental variables of this nature, see Bruce M. Russett, *et al., World Handbook* of *Political and Social Indicators* (New Haven: Yale University Press, 1964), p. 12.
10. Norman Nie and Kenneth Prewitt, *Economic Development and Political Culture* (Stanford University, Institute of Political Studies, Feb. 1965 [mimeo.]), p. 12.
11. Lerner, *Passing,* p. 131.
12. *Ibid.,* Chapter 3.
13. *Ibid.,* p. 63.
14. Karl Deutsch, "Social Mobilization and Political Development."
15. Gabriel Almond and Sidney Verba, *The Civic Culture* (Princeton: Princeton University Press, 1963), pp. 80 and 116.
16. *Ibid.,* Chapter 3.
17. Nie and Prewitt, *Economic Development,* p. 13.
18. Abraham Maslow, "A Theory of Human Motivation," in Philip I. Harriman (ed.), *Twentieth Century Psychology* (New York: The Philosophical Library, 1946), pp. 11–12.
19. One of the major reasons for the predominance of dictatorial forms of government in states at lower developmental levels.
20. See Russett *et al., World Handbook* (in general).
21. T. H. Marshall, *Class, Citizenship, and Social Development* (Garden City: Doubleday and Company, Inc., 1964), Chapter 3.
22. For a complete discussion of the various types of compliance structure in all types of organizations, see Amitai Etzioni, *A Comparative Analysis of Complex Organizations* (New York: The Free Press of Glencoe, 1961), Chapter 1.

23. Arthur S. Banks and Robert Textor, *A Cross Polity Survey* (Cambridge, Mass.: Massachusetts Institute of Technology Press, 1963).

24. For exact relationship between gross national product per capita and the other developmental indicators see Russett *et al., World Handbook,* pp. 261ff.

25. Andrew C. Janos, "Eastern Europe: The Politics of Economic Mobilization," Paper presented at the annual meeting of the Far Western Slavic Association, Seattle, Washington, April 11, 1965, pp. 26–29.

26. See Hugh Seton-Watson, *The East European Revolution* (New York: Frederick A. Praeger, 1951), Chapter 2.

27. R. Lowenthal, "The Prospects for Pluralistic Communism," *Dissent,* XII, No. 1 (Winter 1965), 109.

28. See "International Communism: The End of an Epoch," *Survey,* No. 54 (January 1965) (whole issue).

29. Jan F. Triska (ed.), *Soviet Communism: Programs and Rules* (San Francisco: Chandler Publishing Co., 1962), p. 71.

30. *Ibid.,* p. 70.

31. *Ibid.,* p. 99.

32. Witness the large forced turnouts and mobilization activities that take place before every election. The elites obviously hope that this type of participation will meet the individual participation needs.

33. See Lerner, *Passing,* Chapter 2, and Lipset, *Political Man,* Chapter 2.

34. See Russett *et al., World Handbook,* pp. 261ff., for examples of correlations of this type for all the nations of the world.

35. Ivo K. Feierabend, "Expansionist and Isolationist Tendencies of Totalitarian Political Systems: A Theoretical Note," *Journal of Politics,* XXIV (1962), 737.

36. See *Index Translationum,* 1962 (Paris: UNESCO, 1964), for a complete list of translated works.

37. See Karl Deutsch, "Transaction Flows as Indicators of Political Cohesion," in Philip Jacobs and James Toscano, *The Integration of Political Communities* (New York: J. B. Lippincott Company, 1964), pp. 75–97.

38. Available statistics show that there is only a very slight positive correlation between developmental level and numbers of students in social sciences and humanities.

39. This average is computed from data available from twenty-one countries with a gross national product per capita greater than $250 and a population larger than five million.

40. Frederick Harbison and Charles Meyers, *Education, Manpower, and Economic Growth* (New York: McGraw-Hill Book Co., 1964), p. 116.

41. This figure includes Soviet troops stationed in Poland, Hungary, and East Germany.

42. The available data permit only determination of rankings for these countries.

43. See above p. 419, and Zbigniew Brzezinski and Carl Friedrich, *Totalitarian Dictatorship and Autocracy* (New York: Frederick A. Praeger, 1961), Chapter 11.

44. Antonin Novotny, former President of Czechoslovakia, Speech reported in *Rude Pravo,* Dec. 13, 1964.

45. *New York Times,* October 21, 1964, p. 3.

46. *Loc. cit.*

47. *Ibid.,* October 18, 1964, p. 32.
48. *Loc. cit.*
49. *Ibid.,* October 21, 1964, p. 3.
50. *Loc. cit.*
51. *Ibid.,* October 26, 1964, p. 11.
52. *Ibid.,* October 18, 1964, p. 1.
53. *Ibid.,* October 19, 1964, p. 12.
54. *Loc. cit.*
55. *Ibid.,* October 22, 1964, p. 15.
56. *Ibid.,* October 20, 1964, p. 8.
57. Radio Free Europe, "Communist Reaction to the Khrushchev Ouster" (Munich: Research Department Radio Free Europe, November 12, 1964), p. 4.

TEN

EMPIRICAL SOCIOLOGY IN THE EASTERN EUROPEAN COMMUNIST PARTY-STATES

JOHN S. SHIPPEE

I. INTRODUCTION

Until 1956, empirical sociology was a "forbidden science" in all the communist party-states except Yugoslavia. Since then, this field has been revived in the Soviet Union and most of Eastern Europe. In more recent years, Western scholars have interested themselves in Eastern European empirical sociology primarily as it has developed in Poland and the Soviet Union. A number of brief, descriptive articles have been published in Western journals since 1958. Recent studies reflect a growing interest in the subject.[1] Thus far, little comparative, empirically based research on Eastern European sociological developments has appeared. This study was undertaken to partially remedy that lack.

The term "empirical sociology" will be used here to denote sociological research based on or using quantitative or observed data. It should not be understood to include specifically demographical, historical, or anecdotal-anthropological work. Rather, the term describes work based on data taken from the observation, questioning, or interviewing of sample populations, however unsophisticated the methodology. Unfortunately, a detailed comparison of empirical sociological methodology in Eastern Europe is beyond the scope of this study.

The countries included in the study are the Union of Soviet Socialist Republics, Poland, Yugoslavia, Hungary, Bulgaria, Czechoslovakia, East Germany, and Romania. There has been no evidence of a sociological revival of any sort in Albania. This nation has therefore been omitted from consideration.

The main obstacle facing a study of this nature involves the quality, availability, and usefulness of primary and secondary source material, which varies greatly from country to country. When this study was undertaken in late 1965, a comparatively large amount of material in Western languages was available on the history and current developments in Soviet, Polish, Yugoslav, and East German sociology. The opposite is true for Czechoslovakia, Hungary, Bulgaria, and Romania. Limitations of time and linguistic versatility prevented the employment of indigenous source materials, except when procurable in translation. A secondary obstacle stems from the varying degrees of reliability of the many sources, both Eastern and Western, utilized in this paper.

Nonetheless, the data obtained from this material is sufficient to allow useful, if preliminary, comparisons of the different levels of sociological development in Eastern Europe.[2]

From the communist viewpoint, empirical sociology has dangerous implications for the Marxist-Leninist belief system as it was officially interpreted prior to 1956; various authorities, including Bezeredz, Chalasinski, and Ahlberg cite this as the explicit rationale for its suppression under the influence of Stalinism.[3] Orthodox pre-1956 Marxism-Leninism raised the general theory of society contained in the doctrine of "historical materialism" to the level of irrefutable dogma. This theory still remains a central tenet of the communist political belief system as it is variously interpreted today. It holds that the development of any society is predicated on the economic conditions prevailing within it. Socialist societies, by definition, cannot foster the social ills (poverty, crime, alcoholism, discrimination, oppression, economic breakdowns, prostitution, and the like) which are the natural corollaries of capitalism. Further, the contradictions inherent in all economic systems are held to drive them inevitably toward communism.[4]

If this were actually the case, the empirical sociological study of socialist societies would be unnecessary, and the study of sociology might be replaced by historical materialism. This in fact took place in the Soviet Union in 1924, and in Poland and East Germany as part of the general suppression of Eastern European sociology between 1950 and 1952.[5] Sociology is taught under faculties of historical materialism in East Germany and the Soviet Union. Much of the sociological material published since 1956 in Eastern Europe has appeared in philosophical (that is, ideological) journals.[6]

Evidence of Soviet sociologists' continued dependence on historical materialism was presented in a paper read at the Fifth World Congress of Sociology, held in the United States in 1962. In it, two of the USSR's leading social scientists stated that,

> Marxist sociology employs the theory and method of scientific sociology, i.e., historical materialism, in specific sociological research in order to understand the inner mechanism of social events and the laws

of their development and to analyze specific social situations that arise in the process of social life.[7]

Ahlberg points out that the primary Soviet criticism of Western or "bourgeois" sociology continues to be directed toward its lack of such a unifying general theory.[8]

Disinterested, objective, and empirical study of social behavior might prove politically dangerous to communist regimes. The results of such sociological analysis might contradict official pronouncements and propaganda concerning the state of public opinion, society, or the reasons for social problems. Thus, the continued existence of sociology as a discipline provided a potential focal point, however weak, for "counter-revolutionary forces" in communist nations. In Stalin's Soviet Union, and in Eastern Europe after 1950, this risk was deemed too great by communist elites. By 1952, empirical sociology had officially ceased to exist in all of Eastern Europe except Yugoslavia.

Two assumptions can be made concerning the revival and reinstitutionalization of empirical sociology in Eastern Europe. The formal development of empirical sociology in communist party-states can be supposed to depend directly on the degree to which it is tolerated by their respective political elites. Secondly, the rapidity and scope of sociological development is approximately inversely proportional to official reliance on historical materialism as a tool for the analysis of social behavior.

In making comparisons of the rebirth and development of empirical sociology in each of the eight countries under study, several *a priori* distinctions prove quite useful. In the first place, it is helpful to distinguish sociology as it has developed in these nations into two categories, as follows:

1) *Instrumental* sociology. In this form, empirical sociology is, limited in its evolution to use as a tool for applied research into current problems. Instrumental sociology is primarily a useful adjunct to other disciplines and methods of gathering information. It is strictly limited and controlled in development and in the areas of research to which it is applied.

2) *Autonomous* sociology. This definition characterizes the evolution of empirical sociology as a separate academic discipline. Where sociology is an autonomous discipline, the course of its development, the questions it asks, and the methods it uses are primarily determined by its own needs. This is not to imply that autonomous sociology is not often largely dependent on instrumental research. It simply means that sociology is recognized as a separate discipline, the physical and human resources of which are under its own control.

These distinctions provide the basic criteria for comparative measurement and evaluation of sociological development in Eastern Europe. Autonomous empirical sociology is considered more highly developed than its instrumental counterpart. These classifications depend, in turn, on the degree of development of the institutional manifestations of empirical sociology.

These independent "institutional" variables may be roughly categorized according to function. Those employed in this study comprise the institutional manifestations of sociological research, teaching and publication. Institutions responsible for these functions may be distinguished into two groups, which will be designated "formal" or "informal" sociological institutions. In general, "formal" sociological institutions are those explicitly and primarily devoted to the discipline of sociology. The second designation will be applied to sociological appendages of other disciplines and to nonacademic organizations.

Formal sociological research institutes are those whose *raison d'être* is to formulate and carry on empirical sociological research which is principally evaluated according to criteria of scholarly merit, rather than the current demands of ideology or propaganda. Sociological research conducted under the auspices of other disciplines (pedagogy, economics, statistics, and so forth) and institutions, designed to produce more or less predetermined results, comes under the "informal" classification.

Similarly, nations which have established at least one university chair in sociology are engaging in formal sociological teaching. Those countries in which instruction in sociological theory and methods is under the jurisdiction of other faculties teach sociology informally.

Scholarly journals provide a good indication of the comparative state of sociological publication in each country. The existence or absence of a regularly published journal in the field of sociology serves to distinguish countries which engage in formal sociological publication from those which do not. Devotion of resources on a regular basis to one or more such journals indicates continuing interest in sociology as a discipline. The appearance of occasional articles in newspapers and journals of other fields does not.

These institutional distinctions provide a means for determining the state of development (autonomous, instrumental, or between the two) which empirical sociology has attained in each of the eight countries being studied. Where formal institutions have developed in all three areas, empirical sociology is autonomous almost by definition. Conversely, a complete lack of formal sociological institutions indicates that if it exists at all, empirical sociology has been limited to instrumental functions.

The existence of formal sociological research institutions is a necessary criterion for the development of an autonomous sociological discipline. In the absence of formal facilities for sociological teaching and publication, however, these latter can be devoted to purely instrumental ends. This appears to have occurred in the Soviet Union and East Germany.[9] On the other hand, the ongoing devotion of resources to empirical sociology itself, implicit in the establishment of formal teaching and publication facilities, indicates that it has achieved legitimacy as an autonomous discipline. Therefore, the formal institutionalization of sociological teaching and publication will be considered evidence that empirical sociology has achieved autonomous status.

This set of variables proves quite useful in clarifying the patterns which have characterized the revival, development, and applications of empirical sociology in Eastern Europe. Thus far, this has not been attempted on any kind of methodologically consistent, comparative basis in the Western literature.[10] It is apparent from this material that sociological development in Poland and Yugoslavia took place quite rapidly and that it quickly freed itself from many ideological and political restrictions. It is equally clear that sociological development in the Soviet Union and East Germany occurred more slowly and under greater limitations. Information concerning sociological developments in the other four countries is less organized and more difficult to find and interpret. The variables discussed above provide a framework for the isolation of specific factors relevant to the detection of sociological development patterns.

To facilitate the comparison of such patterns as might emerge, the rebirth and development of empirical sociology in the Soviet Union may be used as the point of reference. The suppression of the discipline in Eastern Europe was due largely to Soviet instigation.[11] Using its own behavior as a benchmark, it is possible to assess the ability of the Soviet Union to influence the course of sociological revival. This approach also allows a preliminary comparison of Soviet innovative potential in ideologically sensitive areas with that of other Eastern European nations.

The study will focus on several questions concerning the nature of Eastern European sociological development. These are:

1) What patterns, if any, are apparent in the rebirth, institutional development, and application of empirical sociology in Eastern Europe? Are they consistent for all three aspects of this sociological "renaissance"?

2) Has sociological development in Eastern Europe been primarily instrumental or autonomous? How has this varied from nation to nation?

3) To what extent was the early (that is, pre-Soviet) revival of sociology in Poland and Yugoslavia dependent on the existence of a strong, pre-communist sociological tradition?

4) Does the early and rapid development of empirical sociology correlate with its widespread and flexible employment in behavioral research?

5) What is the relationship between the development and official sanction of empirical sociology, in both its instrumental and autonomous forms, to the role of historical materialism?

6) How is sociological development in Eastern Europe related to sociological interaction with the West?

7) What future developments are likely to occur with regard to empirical sociology in Eastern Europe?

These questions will receive more detailed examination in sections dealing with the revival of sociology, its institutional development, areas of research and application, and international sociological interaction.

Before proceeding further, it may be helpful to discuss the pre-communist development of sociology in each of the nations being considered. This may be accomplished by comparing the years in which sociology was first recognized as an academic discipline, and the degree to which it had been institutionalized prior to World War II. These comparisons are summarized in Appendix A. In addition, estimates have been made of the amount of sociological activity in each country between 1945 and its official suppression.

Appendix A indicates that sociological studies were initiated prior to World War I in Russia, Czechoslovakia (that is, Prague), Romania, and Yugoslavia. Polish sociology was founded in 1918, as was the Polish state. Though it was the victim of early suppression in the Soviet Union, sociology survived World War II in all the other nations mentioned above. Though sociological studies originated as late as 1940 in Hungary, they appear to have continued fairly strongly after the war. Bulgaria never developed sociology as a formal discipline.

Between world wars, strong and active sociological institutions were developed in Czechoslovakia, Poland, Romania, and Yugoslavia. With the possible exception of Czechoslovakia, it is difficult to single out leaders within this group. The prominence of her two leading sociologists, Masaryk and Beneš (who were the first and second presidents of the Czechoslovak Republic), combined with a somewhat higher degree of institutionalization, suggests that the discipline was somewhat stronger in Czechoslovakia than in the other three nations.

After the war, however, the resurgence of sociology in Czechoslovakia was weaker than in Poland, Hungary, and Yugoslavia. Though teaching and publication were reinstituted on a small scale, they apparently died out quite rapidly after the communists took over.[12]

In Poland, on the other hand, sociological teaching, research, and publication revived quite strongly after the war ended. Sociological instruction continued there, though under increasing handicaps, for over five years. In 1951, chairs in sociology were abolished and replaced with chairs in the history of social thought or in Marxism.[13] Research was carried out in rural sociology and in a number of other fields.[14] Toward the end of 1951, all activity in sociology was officially suppressed in Poland.

The official ban on Hungarian sociology was promulgated in 1950. Prior to its enforcement, a comparatively large amount of empirical sociological inquiry into problems of industry and argiculture was carried out.[15]

Yugoslav sociologists were more fortunate. Tito never chose to enforce a complete suppression of sociology. At least two of the faculties of sociology established before World War II continued to function after the war and throughout the period of sociological suppression in the rest of Eastern Europe.[16] Sociologists were allowed to publish the results of studies in rural and industrial sociology as early as 1953.[17]

Very little information exists concerning the postwar revival of sociology in Romania. Some research into living standards was initiated in 1948, and may have been continued informally following official suppression.[18]

No available evidence indicates that sociology developed to any degree in Bulgaria following the war.

Sociology was suppressed in the Soviet Union during the 1920's, and was not revived there until 1958.

It is practically impossible to evaluate East German sociology according to the criteria employed in the above discussion. East Germany did not become a separate national entity until 1949. From 1933 to 1949, Germany was subject to Nazi rule, war, and reconstruction, none of which were conducive to sociological development. There is evidence, however, that some sociological research was carried out prior to 1950.[19]

Only Yugoslavia and Poland, of the four nations in which sociology was strongly developed before 1940, appear to have revived it in any strength after the war. Polish sociology was not completely suppressed until 1951. Sociology continued to exist as an autonomous discipline in Yugoslavia in the years during which it was banned in the remainder of Eastern Europe (1951–1956).

II. THE REVIVAL OF EMPIRICAL SOCIOLOGY IN EASTERN EUROPE AND THE SOVIET UNION

The first hints of a revival of interest in empirical sociology in Eastern Europe reached the West in 1956. Delegations from each nation involved in this study attended the Third World Congress of Sociology held that year in Amsterdam.[20] In 1957, an entire issue of the *International Social Science Journal* was devoted to current work of Polish sociologists.[21] The first article on Soviet sociology appeared in *Survey* the following year.[22] Since then, evidence of the rebirth of empirical sociology in each of the countries of Eastern Europe except Albania has become available. Some of the more important aspects of this material are summarized and compared in the tables comprising Appendix B.

The development of empirical sociology vis-à-vis the regime of each country shows approximately the same pattern. This may be broken down into three stages, as follows:

1) Revival (or clandestine continuation) of interest;

2) Official recognition of the existence and necessity of empirical sociology; and

3) Official acceptance and approval of sociology as an indispensable source of information (that is, instrumental) or as an autonomous and legitimate social science.

Appendix B reflects this pattern. The first manifestation of the rebirth of empirical sociology in Poland, Romania, Yugoslavia, and East Germany was a revival of informal research. The Yugoslav sociologists worked openly and published their results soon after completing their projects.[23] The Polish and Romanian projects were both carried out in 1952.[24] However, due to the official ban on sociology in force in both countries, both projects were clandestine and informal. The first informal sociological research in East Germany was carried out in 1956.

The first sign of sociological revival in the USSR, Czechoslovakia, Hungary, and Bulgaria was these countries' attendance at the Third World Congress of Sociology. The Soviet Union did not initiate informal empirical research until 1958, two years later. The other three countries were even slower in this respect.

Informal sociological research, attendance at international conferences, or both together do not indicate more than revived interest in the applications of empirical sociology. Neither can be taken to signify official tolerance or acceptance of sociology in any form.

This contention is supported in that both occurred prior to the establishment of national sociological associations or coordinating bodies in each country. Table 10–3, in Appendix B, suggests that the time differential between indications of revived interest and the founding of such professional bodies was usually on the order of several years. Their establishment constituted official recognition of the nature of sociological research as a separate, necessary and, in some ways, novel entity. Thus, national sociological associations may be included in the definition of formal sociological institutions. By themselves, these associations did not imply the official acceptance and approval of empirical sociology, only recognition of its existence.

Four nations, Yugoslavia, Poland, East Germany, and Romania, preceded the Soviet Union in initiating informal empirical sociological investigations. Only Poland and Yugoslavia founded formal national sociological associations prior to similar Soviet action. Czechoslovakia, Hungary, and Bulgaria followed Russia in both informal interest and formal recognition of empirical sociology. This relationship is tentative evidence of a distinct leadership-followership pattern in the development of sociology in Eastern Europe. Within this pattern, four variations may be distinguished. Poland and Yugoslavia constitute the first of these, having initiated both informal empirical research and formal sociological institutions prior to the Soviet Union. The second includes East Germany and Romania, in which informal sociology preceded its manifestation in the Soviet Union. These countries appear to have awaited Soviet initiatives before allowing formal sociological institutionalization. Sociological development in the USSR, selected as the point of reference, constitutes the third variation. The fourth includes Hungary, Bulgaria, and Czechoslovakia, which, until 1964, undertook neither formal nor informal steps in the initiation and development of empirical sociology prior to Russia.

Indicators of official approval of empirical sociology are more difficult to isolate. Such approval has been explicitly granted in Poland, the USSR, and East Germany by party or governmental action. Table 10–4 shows similar approval implicit in the provision of funds for autonomous sociological journals by Czechoslovakia and Yugoslavia. There is no evidence of official approval of empirical sociology in Romania, Hungary, or Bulgaria. This conforms closely to the leadership-followership pattern outlined above. Official acceptance and approval was first accorded empirical sociology by Polish and Yugoslav elites in 1956, five years before similar Soviet action. In the USSR sociology was given official approval in a formal CPSU protocol. This was followed in 1963 by formal party action calling for sociological research in East Germany. The official Czech approval of empirical sociology, implicit in permission for publication of a sociological journal, was accorded in 1965. The latter constitutes a partial break with the leadership pattern, insofar as it implied the recognition of sociology as an autonomous discipline, a step which has been discussed, but not yet taken in the Soviet Union.[25]

Public opinion surveying is another aspect of empirical sociological revival in which Polish and Yugoslav leadership is clearly evident. Both countries began to undertake "Gallup-type" informal surveys in newspapers and periodicals in 1956. Table 10–5 shows that Romania followed in 1959 with some informal consumer polls that have not been fully reported.[26] The Soviet Union set up a polling organization as part of *Komsomolskaya Pravda* in 1960, following which the remaining four countries began to employ public opinion sampling. Once again, the pattern of leadership suggested above is roughly confirmed. In this case, East Germany is the single exception to the pattern.

In each of the five countries for which there is evidence, informal public opinion surveying has been closely connected to mass communications media. This has facilitated its instrumental employment in several ways. It has allowed rapid distribution and widespread response for given sets of questions (at the expense of scientific selection of sample groups). This method also helps to focus public interest on opinion polls. In this way, it heightens the propaganda value of their results. In a number of cases, such polls have been designed to inspire heavy responses favorable to the political and normative goals of national political apparatuses.[27] Publication of statistics and individual responses obtained from such surveys is a useful propaganda device. Deviant and nonconforming responses have been published as examples of incorrect attitudes.[28] The periodic use of such surveys is a relatively easy means of determining the general values and opinions of broad (if unselected) segments of the population. They have a high instrumental potential, but are extremely informal and haphazard in their utilization of empirical sociological technique.

Consumer opinion surveying has been employed in Yugoslavia, Poland, Hungary, Czechoslovakia, and Romania.[29] This type of polling has a high instrumental payoff in helping to determine a distribution of economic resources that will result in minimal waste.

Poland and Yugoslavia are the only Eastern European nations which, as of 1965, have engaged in formal public opinion research (utilizing preselected sample groups, objective question techniques, full data analysis, nonnormative interpretation of results, and so forth). Poland established the Public Opinion Research Center under the auspices of Polish Radio in 1958. It is the only research institute in Eastern Europe wholly dedicated to the scientific sampling and measurement of public opinion.[30] The methodological shortcomings and propagandistic nature of the opinion surveys undertaken so far by the opinion polling organizations attached to *Komsomolskaya Pravda* (USSR), *Sonntag* (East Germany), and *Narodna Mladezh* (Bulgaria) indicate that they remain informal sociological research organizations.

Poland and Yugoslavia have led in the revival of each aspect of empirical sociology considered in this section. The earlier developments in Yugoslavia may well be due to her freedom from the monolithic Soviet control prevailing elsewhere in the communist system before 1956. Polish sociology revived quite rapidly and soon exceeded its Yugoslav counterpart in scope. By 1958, as the following section will show in more detail, both had allowed empirical sociology to become an autonomous discipline. In the same year, sociological research began in the USSR. It is highly probable that the functional leadership exercised by Poland and Yugoslavia in the rebirth of Eastern European empirical sociology is partially due to its comparative strength prior to World War II. Polish sociologists whose reputations were well established before the war, such as Stanislaw Ossowski and J. Chalasinski, played a major role in its early revival following de-Stalinization. Prewar sociologists may have contributed to the early revival of sociology in Yugoslavia. The comparatively low level of sociological development in Bulgaria at present may be partially attributed to the lack of a prewar sociological discipline. Insofar as Romania and Czechoslovakia did not share in this leadership, prewar sociological strength was a necessary but not sufficient condition for early and rapid sociological development under communist rule.

Other than in Poland and Yugoslavia, the early manifestations of the Eastern European sociological revival were principally of an instrumental nature. This is true both of early research attempts and the later beginnings made in public opinion research.

Appendix B shows clearly that none of the manifestations of sociological revival occurred at the same time throughout Eastern Europe. As nearly as can be determined, the starting dates for empirical research vary over an eight-year period, from 1952 to 1960. The first sociological association was set up in Yugoslavia in 1954; the latest in Czechoslovakia ten years later. Public opinion surveying began in 1956 in Poland, but was not attempted in Bulgaria until 1963. These time differentials indicate that the renaissance of empirical sociology, unlike its suppression, can be accounted for primarily by national needs and circumstances rather than external pressure.

The next section indicates the degree to which the institutional development of empirical sociology in Eastern Europe conforms to the patterns detected in its revival.

III. SOCIOLOGICAL INSTITUTIONALIZATION

This section is based on data concerning the institutionalization of empirical sociological teaching, research, and publication in Eastern Europe. Tables 10–6 and 10–7 summarize the available material on sociological teaching institutions. Tables 10–8 and 10–9 deal with persons engaged in sociological research. Tables 10–10 and 10–11 indicate the kinds of journals in which empirical sociological material is published in Eastern Europe. These tabulations were made from data available in early 1966; additional data may have become available since.

These data may be analyzed employing the distinctions made above between formal and informal manifestations of sociological institutionalization. The data concerning sociological research and teaching in Romania, Czechoslovakia, Hungary, and Bulgaria are, however, inadequate for such analysis. The almost total lack of evidence concerning sociological institutionalization in these countries makes it difficult to draw meaningful conclusions concerning its current level of development.

Table 10–6 indicates that Poland and Yugoslavia are the only Eastern European countries in which empirical sociological instruction has been formally institutionalized. Several of Poland's fourteen chairs of sociology were reestablished in 1957. In Yugoslavia, formal sociological instruction was never completely interrupted. Since 1958, instruction in empirical sociology has been resumed informally (that is, not under separate faculties) in the USSR, East Germany, and Romania. Its institutional status in the remaining three countries is unknown.

The Soviet Union, Romania, and East Germany (and, in all likelihood, Hungary, Czechoslovakia, and Bulgaria) had not, as of 1965, allowed the teaching of sociology as a separate discipline. Subordination to faculties of philosophy, historical materialism, economics, and statistics restricts its development according to the instrumental needs of these institutions. Restriction of sociological instruction to preexisting faculties may impair the flexibility of sociological research by limiting it to certain areas of inquiry. Thus, formal sociological teaching institutions appear to be a necessary condition for the existence of empirical sociology as an autonomous discipline. Such institutions were found to exist only in Poland and Yugoslavia.

The apparent absence of formal teaching institutions in Romania, East Germany, Hungary, Czechoslovakia, and Bulgaria conforms to the pattern of innovative leadership proposed in the previous section.[31] All of these countries continue to follow the Soviet example in this respect. By contrast, sociological teaching in Poland and Yugoslavia developed its own facilities quite rapidly.

Table 10–8 shows that formal sociological research facilities have developed more rapidly in Eastern Europe than have teaching institutions. It is evident that of all the nations of Eastern Europe, Poland has devoted the greatest amount of resources to formal sociological research and teaching. In addition to 14 university chairs previously mentioned, she has at least 18 formal sociological research institutes. East Germany has at least 31 institutions which engage in sociological teaching and research. Ludz makes it quite clear that most of these take up sociological research as an informal adjunct to their principal functions.[32] The USSR has also engaged in formal sociological research. Appendix D suggests that though formal institutionalization of sociological research began comparatively early in Yugoslavia, it has not developed as rapidly as in Poland.

Institutes devoted principally to formal sociological research indicate a greater development of sociological autonomy than those in which it is a secondary and informal activity. In Poland, 18 of the 21 institutes engaged in empirical sociological research (nearly 90 per cent) are of the former variety as of 1965. This can be said of slightly less than half the institutes in both Yugoslavia (3 out of 7) and the USSR (7 out of 16). This is true of only 30 per cent, or 8 out of 27, of the East German institutes which are known to have carried out sociological investigations.

Formal institutionalization of sociological research is clearly more acceptable to ruling communist elites than formal sociological instruction. Sociological research, formal as well as informal, has a higher potential short-term payoff in terms of accurate information concerning communist society and social behavior. In addition, its applications are more amenable to direct control through allocations of funds and resources.

Tables 10–8 and 10–9 also show that chronologically the institutionalization of empirical sociological research is consistent with the cross-national leadership pattern developed earlier.[33] Poland and Yugoslavia exercised functional leadership in the development of both informal and formal sociological research institutions in Eastern Europe. In the second subpattern, Romania's Economic Research Institute has engaged in informal sociological research since 1954.[34] The first informal sociological research in East Germany was carried out by the German Central Pedagogical Institute in 1956.[35] East Germany did not formally institutionalize sociological research until four years after similar Soviet action in 1959. No evidence is available indicating that Romania has taken like steps. Sociological research in Hungary and Czechoslovakia is, from all indications, exclusively informal. This situation may now be changing. Recent information from Bulgaria indicates that limited formal sociological research is being planned there.[36]

The evidence concerning institutionalization of sociological publication presented in Tables 10–10 and 10–11 shows a recent and significant variation in pattern. Yugoslavia and Poland began formal sociological publication comparatively early, instituting regularly published sociological journals in 1956 and 1957, respectively. They were joined in 1965 by Czechoslovakia. Sociological publication remains informal in the USSR, East Germany, Hungary, Romania, and Bulgaria. In these nations, material relating to empirical sociology usually appears in newspapers or those journals principally concerned with philosophy, party affairs, and economics. Regular employment of philosophical journals for the publication of sociological research results shows the continuing relationship of historical materialism and empirical sociology in most of Eastern Europe.

The limitation of sociological publications to the journals of those fields may well be evidence of relatively strict official supervision. Such articles are more likely to be judged by standards of instrumental value and ideological orthodoxy than would be the case if a separate journal, formally devoted to questions of sociology and its empirical applications, were available.[37]

The recent establishment of formal sociological publication in Czechoslovakia constitutes the first case in which a nation other than Poland or Yugoslavia has preceded the Soviet Union in any aspect of formal sociological institutionalization. This may indicate that Czechoslovakia has decided to follow their example by allowing empirical sociology to develop as an autonomous discipline. In addition, this development is evidence that Soviet influence over sociological developments in Eastern Europe is waning.

Recent information indicates that sociological publication is becoming formal in the USSR as well. A trial issue of a new periodical, *Social Research (Sotsialnye issledovania)* appeared late in 1965. Regular publication, according to George Fischer, was scheduled to begin in 1967.[38]

The early and continuing existence of formal sociological institutions devoted to teaching, research, and publication in Poland and Yugoslavia is clearly evident. Empirical sociology has definitely become an autonomous and self-perpetuating discipline in these nations. The situation in Czechoslovakia and the USSR is doubtful, although empirical sociology appears to be progressing toward a similar status in both countries. Empirical sociology in the remaining five countries appears instrumental and directly subordinate to official control.

Poland and Yugoslavia have clearly allowed significant revision of certain aspects of the Marxist-Leninist belief system by permitting empirical sociology to become autonomous. Historical materialism has been replaced by empirical investigation as the principal means for the analysis of social problems, behavior, and change. Instrumental sociology, as permitted in East Germany, Hungary, Romania, and Bulgaria, is supplementary to historical materialism. This suggests that, having allowed the revival of empirical sociology, these nations have not yet resolved the ideological question concerning its role vis-à-vis that of historical materialism. Czechoslovakia and the Soviet Union, however, appear to be moving in this direction.

These conclusions are supported by comparing the sociological literature published in Poland, Yugoslavia, and the Soviet Union. Much Polish and Yugoslav research and analysis is neither hampered nor limited by ideological requirements. The questions studied, however, have often had ideological aspects. By contrast, empirical sociological investigation in the Soviet Union has, until quite recently, been explicitly governed by ideological considerations.[39] Since late in 1964, there has arisen evidence of increasing pressure within the Soviet intelligentsia to grant autonomous status to empirical sociology.[40]

IV. APPLICATIONS OF EMPIRICAL SOCIOLOGICAL
RESEARCH IN EASTERN EUROPE

Over the past decade, empirical sociological research has been undertaken in all eight of the Eastern European nations included in this study. The areas of human behavior subjected to such study have varied in number from country to country. Comparative analysis of the applications of empirical investigation allows a preliminary assessment of the functional flexibility permitted empirical sociology in each.

To facilitate this analysis, twenty-seven major areas of possible sociological investigation have been distinguished. They are listed in Table 10–12. Empirical research has been undertaken in at least one Eastern European nation in each area listed except that of "Alcoholism, drug use, and so on" (Category X).

The listing in Table 10–12 is, of necessity, preliminary. It was compiled from material available in early 1966. The areas open to sociological investigation in each country are increasing with the passage of time. Further, it is probable that available sources concerning the applications of empirical sociology are incomplete. Again, much more is known about Poland, the USSR, Yugoslavia, and East Germany than is known about the remaining four nations. The comparatively narrow range of empirical sociological research found in Romania, Czechoslovakia, and Hungary is due in part to a paucity of available data. For these countries, the admittedly questionable assumption that little available data indicates limited development must be utilized.

Empirical sociological investigation has usually been instrumentally motivated in Eastern Europe. Empirical research into economy-related areas has been initiated in nearly all of Eastern Europe. Many other studies involve individual and group behavior that is not directly amenable to state control. Empirical studies of ideologically relevant questions have been fairly numerous.

Empirical investigations of standards of living, industrial sociology, rural and agricultural sociology, and consumer behavior have been widespread in Eastern Europe. All are clearly related to economic development and control. Each of these areas has been the subject of empirical sociological research in at least six Eastern European nations. Such research has provided information increasingly necessary to economic planners in Eastern European governments. It makes possible more efficient solution of economic problems, greater accuracy in the analysis of economic needs, and informed decisions regarding changes in economic policy. Empirical investigation also provides a basis for the analysis of worker dissatisfaction and for improving methods of influencing and controlling behavior on the job.

The other most commonly investigated areas of behavior involve youth, family life, the role of women, cultural activities, and propaganda effectiveness. Each of these has been empirically studied in at least five Eastern European nations. Behavior in each of these areas is only partially subject to direct governmental control. In the majority of cases, it is also ideologically relevant.

The present generation of Eastern European youth is the first (outside the Soviet Union) to have been socialized entirely under communist control. Empirical studies of its values, attitudes, and motivations have been carried out in Poland, Yugoslavia, the Soviet Union, East Germany, Hungary, Romania, and Bulgaria.[41] They have provided direct information on the effect of government-controlled and informal (that is, family, group interaction, and the like) socialization processes on the behavior and opinions of the younger generation. Empirical research is also valuable in detecting shortcomings in educational and training programs, and in suggesting efficient means of instituting social controls that will result in the efficient production of "new communist men."

Marriage and family life comprise an institution which is highly resistant to formal, centralized control. Empirical sociological investigations in this area may be ideologically instrumental by showing how the changes in family life following the introduction of communist rule have conformed to Marxist predictions.* Kharchev's studies of Soviet family life have focused on this theme.[42] Empirical study of family life is also highly instrumental in pointing up familial influences not in conformity with elite-determined societal needs, and suggesting means of counteracting these influences.

A major goal of the Marxist belief system is complete female equality. Empirical research has been employed to determine the factors impeding its realization and to suggest means for overcoming them.*

Empirical investigations of culture have concentrated on the analysis of leisure-time use.* In one sense, this is consumer research, instrumental for the efficient planning of cultural facilities (plays, sporting events, music, radio, television, and so forth). This kind of study is also useful in suggesting methods for maximizing the "socially useful" employment of leisure time.[43]

Sociological research into the penetration and effectiveness of propaganda techniques is of obvious instrumental value to Eastern European governments.* The effectiveness of governmental communications monopolies and the techniques they employ can be efficiently tested by this method.

The empirical study of religion, subject to government restriction or control throughout Eastern Europe, is also fairly widespread.* This aids elites in determining the tenacity and social roots of religious practices.

Western scholars have criticized Soviet sociologists (and, by implication, those in other Eastern European nations) for abstaining from the study of the communist party, national leaders, the military, and other politically sensitive phenomena.[44] The lack of such studies is partially due to the criteria of instrumentality. These areas are more amenable to direct political control than those discussed above. The instrumental value of sociological investigation is therefore not as high. As a result, only in Poland, and in some cases, Yugoslavia, have the communist party, the military, local governments, and voter motivation been subjected to empirical investigation. These nations share the common Eastern European interest in instrumental sociology, but have not confined empirical research within its limits.

A comparison of the number of areas investigated empirically in each country emphasizes this further. For reasons discussed above, the figures given in Table 10–13 are approximations.

TABLE 10–13. MAJOR AREAS OF HUMAN BEHAVIOR SUBJECTED TO
EMPIRICAL SOCIOLOGICAL RESEARCH AS OF 1966

	Number	Rank
Poland	26	1
Yugoslavia	20	2
USSR	15	3
East Germany	12	4
Romania	9	5
Czechoslovakia	7	6
Hungary	6	7
Bulgaria	5	8

They show, however, that Polish and Yugoslav sociologists have undertaken research on a far wider selection of questions than have their colleagues in the remaining six countries. Thus, Table 10–13 reveals a definite relation between sociological autonomy and functional flexibility.

In addition, Table 10–13 approximates the leadership pattern discussed in Section II. The functional leadership in sociological development exercised by Poland and Yugoslavia extends to new areas of research application. Table 10–12 indicates that areas open to sociological research in East Germany, and, to a lesser degree, in Romania, conform fairly closely to those studied in the Soviet Union. Very little information was available concerning sociological research in Hungary, Czechoslovakia, and Bulgaria. Existing evidence indicates that these countries have limited sociological research to areas in which it is relatively widespread throughout Eastern Europe.

In comparison with Poland and Yugoslavia, the other six nations of Eastern Europe have until recently imposed rigid limits on sociological research. It is utilized only in cases where a high payoff in terms of information relevant to problem-solving, economic efficiency, or social control is perceived. This situation is likely to continue as long as each country subordinates empirical sociology to the ideological requirements of historical materialism.

Once again, this situation appears to be on the verge of important modification in the Soviet Union. Recent articles have urged wider application of empirical sociological research with unprecedented enthusiasm.[45]

V. INTERNATIONAL SOCIOLOGICAL INVOLVEMENT AND EXCHANGE

Before 1960, the main sources of information concerning sociological developments in Eastern Europe were World Congresses of Sociology. Other forms of sociological interaction between communist nations and the West have included publication and comment on sociological material and exchanges of scholars.

It is more difficult to compare sociological interest and sophistication on the basis of international interaction than by the methods used in previous sections. The only available basis of direct comparison consists of attendance data from the five World Congresses of Sociology. This data is summarized in Table 10–14.

All of the nations involved in the study have sent delegations to these Congresses since 1956.[46] (Yugoslavia was the only Eastern European nation represented at the Second World Congress, held in 1954.) Removal of the Soviet-inspired ban on sociology was partially responsible for this sudden and universal renewal of interest. Delegation size has varied considerably from country to country. The Soviet Union has sent the largest delegation of any communist nation to each of the three World Congresses of Sociology held since 1956. Maintenance of symbolic leadership within the communist system may have necessitated this. Poland and Yugoslavia, which have exercised functional leadership in the revival of Eastern European sociology, have consistently sent the second and third largest delegations. Representation from the remainder of Eastern Europe has remained at a low level. The comparatively large Czech delegations at the Fourth and Fifth Congresses may be symptomatic of the pressures that have resulted in the recent rapid increase of sociological institutionalization in Czechoslovakia.

The Fourth World Congress, held in 1959, emphasized the differences in sociological development between Poland and Yugoslavia and

TABLE 10–14. SIZE OF DELEGATIONS TO WORLD CONGRESSES OF SOCIOLOGY

	1st (1950)		2nd (1954)		3rd (1956)		4th (1959)		5th (1962)	
	NO.	RANK	NO.	RANK	NO.	RANK	NO.	RANK	NO.	RANK
Soviet Union	0	—	0	—	13	1	27	1	18	1
Poland	4	1	0	—	10	2	26	2	10	2
Yugoslavia	0	—	2	1	8	3	21	3	7	3
East Germany	0	—	0	—	3	5	15	4	3(?)	6
Romania	0	—	0	—	4	4	7	6	4	5
Czechoslovakia	0	—	0	—	3	5	11	5	7	3
Hungary	0	—	0	—	2	7	3	7	2	7
Bulgaria	0	—	0	—	1	8	2	8	0	8

SOURCES: *ISSJ* II, No. 3 (1950), p. 15; and the appendices of the *Transactions* of the (2nd–5th) *World Congress(es) of Sociology* (London and Louvain: International Sociological Association, 1954, 1956, 1959, 1962).

the other six countries. The Soviet, East German, Romanian, and Bulgarian delegations confined their contributions to polemics against "bourgeois" (that is, Western) sociology.[47] Papers presented by the Polish and Yugoslav delegations minimized the role of ideological assumptions, while emphasizing the empirical nature of their sociological undertakings.[48]

A similar dichotomy is reflected in Eastern European publications concerning Western sociology. In most of Eastern Europe, a survey of the *Index Translationum* shows that, until 1963, very few Western works had been translated.[49] Firsthand knowledge of Western developments, until recently, has been limited to scholars equipped to study them in their original languages. Polish, Yugoslav, and, quite recently, Soviet sociologists have had access to increasing amounts of translated Western material. In addition, Ludz indicates that East German sociologists maintain a continuing interest in the work of their West German colleagues.[50] Outside Yugoslavia and Poland, most Eastern European commentary on Western sociology has consisted of ideologically based polemic. The usual criticism of Western empirical sociology includes its lack of a general, all-embracing social theory (that is, historical materialism) and its employment as an instrument of capitalist rule.[51] This type of polemic may be a device for inquiring into Western sociological developments without incurring political disapproval.

Polish, Yugoslav, Soviet, and Romanian sociologists have published articles in international and Western sociological journals. This was initiated in 1957, with the publication of an issue of the *International Social Science Journal* devoted to current Polish sociology.[52] The Polish Academy of Sciences began publishing the *Polish Sociological Bulletin* in 1960, in which much current Polish sociological research and thought appears in English translation. Continued publication of this journal shows the strong interest of Polish sociologists in exchanging research results with their Western counterparts. Since 1961, Yugoslav sociologists have published several articles in Western periodicals, including the *International Social Science Journal* and *Public Opinion Quarterly*.[53] Three Soviet articles, dealing with techniques and results of empirical research, have appeared in Western journals.[54] The first was published in 1962. With the exception of Romania, none of the other five countries have attempted to initiate sociological publication in Western languages. Romania published a single issue of the English-language *Romanian Journal of Sociology* just prior to the Fifth World Congress of Sociology in 1962.[55] It has not appeared since. Recently, however, a report of a Romanian youth opinion poll appeared in *UNESCO Features*.[56]

Poland and Yugoslavia are the only Eastern European nations to have allowed Western sociologists to carry on empirical research. This was started in 1957 in Poland and three years later in Yugoslavia. Sociologists from both these countries have studied, lectured, and carried on research in Western nations for several years. Very few Western sociologists have visited the other six nations. Most of these have gone to the Soviet Union. None, so far as can be determined, have been allowed to engage in empirical research.

All eight nations being studied have engaged in some form of international sociological interaction. Poland and Yugoslavia are more deeply involved in it than are the other six in terms of shared publications and research. The Soviet Union is also slowly improving its communication with the West in these areas. The official control exercised over sociology in the other five countries has limited international contact. In these nations, international sociological interaction has been sporadic and usually polemical.

VI. CONCLUSION

Since 1956, some degree of sociological development has occurred in each of the eight countries examined in this study. Albania is the only European communist nation which has shown no interest whatsoever in empirical sociology. Yugoslavia and Poland are clearly the functional leaders in the development of the discipline. Yugoslavia, not subject to Stalinist repression, led the other nations in several aspects of sociological institutionalization. Empirical sociology has been allowed to develop more rapidly and strongly in Poland than elsewhere in Eastern Europe.

It may be helpful to focus on the questions posed in the opening section in summarizing the results of this study.

The first of these asked if any consistent patterns marked sociological development in Eastern Europe. In Section II, a three-stage pattern of sociological revival characterizing all eight nations was distinguished. The first stage, revival of interest, was marked by attendance at international sociological conferences or resumption of informal (and occasionally clandestine) sociological research. All eight nations had achieved this level of development by 1956. Official recognition of empirical sociology, usually signified by the establishment of national sociological associations, has occurred in all eight countries. The final level, official acceptance and approval of empirical sociology, either on an instrumental or autonomous basis, has been reached only in Poland, Yugoslavia, East Germany, the USSR, and Czechoslovakia. Table 10–15 gives the approximate dates at which each stage was attained.

That the length of time between these stages varies from country to country demonstrates that sociological development has not been subject to effective international control. Each country has, instead, determined its own rate of development.

TABLE 10–15. STATUS OF SOCIOLOGICAL REVIVAL IN EASTERN EUROPE

	Interest	Official Recognition	Official Approval
Yugoslavia	Continuous	1954	1956
Poland	1952	1957*	1956
USSR	1956	1958	1961
East Germany	1956	1961	1963
Czechoslovakia	1956	1964	1965
Hungary	1956	1961	—
Romania	1952	1959	—
Bulgaria	1956	1966	—

* The Polish Sociological Association was formed a year after the resumption of empirical sociology was granted official approval. An informal national sociological group had been founded in 1955, however.

A separate pattern of sociological leadership and innovation has also become clear. Using Soviet sociological development as a base, it remains relatively consistent for sociological revival, institutionalization, and application in all eight countries. Four subpatterns include:

1) Development of both formal and informal aspects of empirical sociology prior to the Soviet Union. This variation characterizes Poland and Yugoslavia.

2) Informal sociological development prior to that of the USSR, combined with reluctance to exceed the limits placed on formal sociology by the latter. East Germany and Romania fit this subpattern.

3) Soviet sociological development.

4) Formal and informal sociological development both occurring after similar developments in the Soviet Union. The nations included here are Hungary, Bulgaria, and, until recently, Czechoslovakia.

The second question asked whether sociological development in each nation was instrumental or autonomous. All eight countries share an interest in the instrumental aspects of empirical sociology. Poland and Yugoslavia have been the only Eastern European nations in which it has become an autonomous discipline. Material presented throughout the study supports this conclusion. Quite recently, Czech sociology also began moving in the direction of autonomy. Recent Soviet publications indicate that this may soon occur in the USSR.

The current stage of empirical sociological development in each of the eight nations is schematically summarized in Table 10–16.

Table 10–16 indicates that official approval of empirical sociology

TABLE 10–16.   EASTERN EUROPEAN SOCIOLOGICAL DEVELOPMENT AS OF 1966

Leadership Subpattern	Nation	Status	Development
1.	Poland	officially approved	autonomous
	Yugoslavia	officially approved	autonomous
2.	East Germany	officially approved	instrumental
	Romania	officially recognized	instrumental
3.	U.S.S.R	officially approved	semiautonomous
4.	Hungary	officially recognized	instrumental
	Bulgaria	officially recognized	instrumental
	Czechoslovakia	officially approved	semiautonomous

is a necessary but not sufficient condition for its development as an autonomous discipline. The recent developments in Czechoslovakia, discussed in Section III, may signify that the leadership pattern which held for the first decade of sociological development in Eastern Europe is now breaking down.

The relation between pre-communist sociological development and its early revival was the subject of the third question. Sociology was highly developed in Poland, Yugoslavia, Romania, and Czechoslovakia prior to World War II. Of these nations, Poland and Yugoslavia pioneered in the post-Stalin revival of empirical sociology. The availability of sociologists trained before the war played a major role in this. Thus, a strong pre-communist sociology appears to have been necessary but not sufficient for its early development under communism. The absence of prewar sociology in Bulgaria coupled with its comparatively late development under communism provides further support for this contention.

Section IV answered the fourth question by showing a clear relationship between the early development of empirical sociology in Poland and Yugoslavia, and its widespread application in research. However, this may be due primarily to the autonomous nature of sociology in these countries, rather than its early development. Continued autonomous development of Czech sociology may soon allow this to be determined more precisely.

Question five concerned the relationship of empirical sociology and the doctrine of historical materialism. Before 1956, the two were officially considered to be in irreconcilable conflict. Any formal sociological development whatsoever shows a revision in this viewpoint. The comparative levels of sociological development in Eastern Europe nations thus reflect each country's potential for ideological innovation. Both autonomous and instrumental sociology signify dissatisfaction with the limitations imposed on behavioral analysis by the traditional interpretation of historical materialism. The discussion in Section III indicated that autonomous sociology shows greater ideological revisionism than its instrumental form. Section IV supported this conclusion by showing that sociological research has been far more flexible in Poland and Yugoslavia than in the remaining six countries. Adoption of instrumental sociology in the latter reflects implicit doubt concerning the analytical value of historical materialism. By allowing empirical sociology to become an autonomous discipline, Poland and Yugoslavia have gone further. There, empirical sociology has been allowed to replace ideological doctrine as the principal accepted means for analyzing social behavior and change.

These conclusions indicate that among the nations of Eastern Europe, Poland and Yugoslavia have the greatest potential for rapid ideological innovation. Currently, Czechoslovakia has the next highest capability in this area. Ideological innovation occurs more slowly in the Soviet Union, East Germany, Romania, Hungary, and Bulgaria (in that approximate order). Albania has exhibited no potential whatever for such change.

Material related to the sixth question, which dealt with international sociological interaction, was presented in Section V. It showed a strong relationship between the degree of such interaction and the type of sociological development in each country. In general, only Poland and Yugoslavia have allowed strong and continuing exchanges of research results and sociologists with Western nations. Lately, the Soviet Union has strengthened its activities in these areas also. The remaining five nations, however, have usually limited their contacts with Western sociologists and their work to attendance at international congresses and conferences. Poland and Yugoslavia are the only nations which have allowed Western sociologists to engage in empirical research.

The final question dealt with future developments in Eastern European empirical sociology. It is difficult to make predictions on this score based on present knowledge. However, a few educated guesses may be hazarded. In the first place, it is extremely unlikely that empirical sociology can again be successfully suppressed throughout Eastern Europe. The monolithic Soviet domination of Eastern Europe which made this possible after World War II no longer exists. In addition, empirical sociology appears to have proven itself of great value to national development in all of Eastern Europe except Albania. Secondly, it is probable that Czechoslovak sociology will soon achieve fully autonomous status. Sociology in the Soviet Union has also begun to move in this direction. This, in turn, may inspire similar action in the remainder of Eastern Europe.

Empirical sociology in Poland and Yugoslavia will probably increase in flexibility and sophistication with the passage of time. Nothing short of a major change in official attitudes can prevent this. Empirical sociology in these countries is so strongly institutionalized that any significant reduction in its scope could be accomplished only by drastic governmental measures.

In the other six countries, the role of empirical sociology vis-à-vis historical materialism is still in question. Two, Czechoslovakia and the Soviet Union, appear to be resolving this issue in favor of sociological autonomy. This will probably occur sooner or later in the other Eastern European nations as objective behavioral data becomes increasingly necessary for efficient national development. However, as long as empirical sociology remains at the purely instrumental stage, it is not likely to be applied to the study of politically sensitive questions. Such studies will begin to appear only as sociology in each country achieves a continuing and autonomous base of institutional strength. Even then, it is unlikely that sociologists will be allowed to publicly challenge official policy in areas of great political sensitivity.

Sociologists are playing an ever larger role throughout Eastern Europe. Their work may yet suffer setbacks in individual nations, but their importance in the future development of communist societies can no longer be dismissed.

APPENDIX A

TABLE 10–1. SOCIOLOGY IN EASTERN EUROPE PRIOR TO ITS SUPPRESSION

	1. Sociological Studies Initiated	2. Sociology Suppressed
USSR[1]	1910(?)	1924
Bulgaria[2]	Between World Wars (never institutionalized)	1950(?)
Czechoslovakia[3]	1882(approx.)	1949(approx.)
Hungary[4]	1940	1950
East Germany[5]	NR	1950(?)
Poland[6]	1918	1951
Romania[7]	1910	NDA
Yugoslavia[8]	1906	never completely suppressed

TABLE 10–1. (Cont'd)

	3. Chairs of Sociology and date first founded		4. Prewar Sociological Journals and date first published	
	No.	*Date*	*No.*	*Date*
USSR	1	1919	0	—
Bulgaria	0	—	NDA	—
Czechoslovakia	8	1913(?)	3	1930
Hungary	1	1940	1	1940
East Germany	NR	—	—	—
Poland	6	1919	1	1932
Romania	2	1910	2	1935
Yugoslavia	6	1906	None	

	5. National Sociological Association Founded	6. Post-World-War-II Revival	
USSR	None	USSR	NR
Bulgaria	None	Bulgaria	None
Czechoslovakia	1925	Czechoslovakia	Weak
Hungary	None	Hungary	Strong
East Germany	NR	Poland	Strong
Poland	1921	Romania	Weak
Romania	1918	Yugoslavia	Strong
Yugoslavia	NDA		

1. Data on USSR from source No. 6. (Throughout Appendices A-F, italicized numbers refer to the items in the Notes to Tables.)
2. Data on Bulgaria from source No. 7
3. Data on Czechoslovakia from sources Nos. *12–14*
4. Data on Hungary from source No. *34*
5. Data on East Germany from source No. *23*
6. Data on Poland from sources Nos. *17, 18*
7. Data on Romania from sources Nos. *11, 15*
8. Data on Yugoslavia from source No. *16*

NR Not Relevant
NDA No Data Available

APPENDIX B

Aspects of the Revival of Empirical Sociology in Eastern Europe and the Soviet Union

TABLE 10–2.   FIRST MANIFESTATIONS OF THE REVIVAL OF SOCIOLOGICAL
RESEARCH IN EASTERN EUROPE

	(1) Date of 1st Post-Suppression Empirical Research	(2) Nature of (1)	(3) Chronological Rank
Poland	1952[1]	rural	1
Romania	1952[2]	leisure-time use	1
Yugoslavia	1952–53[3]	rural, industrial	3
East Germany	1956[4]	youth	4
USSR	1958[5]	industrial and leisure-time use	5
Czechoslovakia	1958(?)[6]	work attitudes	6
Hungary	1960(?)[7]	education	7
Bulgaria	NDA	—	—

(?) indicates that these are the earliest studies detected, not necessarily the first done.

NDA No Data Available

1. *30*, p. 230
2. *57*, p. 81
3. *7*, p. 959
4. *23*, pp. 379–80
5. *62*, Vol. XV, No. 33, 1963, p. 3
6. *22*, p. 67
7. *26*, p. 50

TABLE 10–3.   FOUNDING OF NATIONAL SOCIOLOGICAL ASSOCIATIONS OR
COORDINATING BODIES

	(1) Year Founded	(2) Chronological Rank	(3) Year Affiliated with ISA	(4) Chronological Rank
Yugoslavia[1]	1954[2]	1	1956(?)	1
Poland[3]	1957[9]	2	1958(?)	2
USSR[4]	1958[2]	3	1958	2
Romania[5]	1959	4	1959	4

TABLE 10–3. (Cont'd)

	(1) Year Founded	(2) Chrono- logical Rank	(3) Year Affiliated with ISA	(4) Chrono- logical Rank
East Germany[6]	1961	5	1963	5
Hungary[7]	1961	6	NDA	—
Czechoslovakia[8]	1964	7	NDA	—
Bulgaria	NDA			

1. *78*, p. 201
2. United into Society of Sociology and Philosophy in 1956; split off again in 1960. *78*, p. 201; *81*, p. 9
3. *1*, p. 48
4. *29*, p. 53
5. *9*, p. 128; (*42*) p. 225
6. *23*, p. 335
7. *27*, pp. 46–47
8. *22*, p. 62
9. This was preceded by a less formal organization founded in 1955.

TABLE 10–4. FIRST EXPLICIT OFFICIAL APPROVAL GIVEN EMPIRICAL SOCIOLOGICAL RESEARCH

	(1) Year	(2) Form	(3) Chrono- logical Rank	(4) 1st Empirical Study
Poland[1]	1956	Sociologists asked for expert testimony at Poznan trials	1	1952
Yugoslavia[2]	1956	Journal started	2	1952–53
USSR[3]	1961	Statement of the XXII Congress of the CPSU	3	1958
East Germany[4]	1963	Social Research Program outlined by SED central committee	4	1956
Czechoslovakia[5]	1964–65	Formation of a sociological association and publication of a sociological journal supported	5	1959

TABLE 10–4. (Cont'd)

	(1) Year	(2) Form	(3) Chrono- logical Rank	(4) 1st Empirical Study
Hungary	No similar evidence of official acceptance			
Romania	No similar evidence of official acceptance			
Bulgaria	No similar evidence of official acceptance			

1. *28*, p. 144
2. *7*, p. 959
3. *23*, pp. 330–31
4. *23*, p. 328
5. *22*, pp. 62–63

TABLE 10–5.   FIRST PUBLIC OPINION POLLS UNDERTAKEN

	(1) Year	(2) Sampling	(3) Subject	(4) Chrono- logical Rank
Poland[1]	1956	Newspapers	Several subjects	1
Yugoslavia	1956[2]	Youth newspapers	Youth attitudes	2
USSR	May 1960[3]	*Komsomolskaia pravda*	Peace	4
Romania[4]	1959	NDA	Consumer research	3
Hungary[5]	1961	NDA	Workers' attitude on Berlin crisis	5
East Germany[6]	1961	*Sonntag* (newspaper)	Rural, cultural	5
Bulgaria[7]	1963	Bulgarian youth research center (and newspaper)	Youth opinions on questions asked Marx	7
Czechoslovakia[8]		Though opinion polling has been done there was not enough data to determine when it was begun.		

1. *33*, p. 84
2. *86*, p. 104
3. *62*, XII, No. 20 (1960), 24
4. *55*, p. 154
5. *26*, p. 45
6. *24*, p. 530
7. *19*, pp. 29–30
8. *22*, pp. 62–63

APPENDIX C

Formal and Informal Institutionalization of Sociological Training

TABLE 10–6. DATA SUMMARY

	(1) Number of higher educational institutions offering training in sociology	(2) Number of university chairs in sociology
Poland	8 (6 universities)	14
Yugoslavia	5 (3 universities)	3
USSR	at least 4	0 (taught under chair of historical materialism at Moscow, Leningrad)
East Germany	4	0 (taught as part of philosophy and economics)
Romania	2	0 (taught as part of statistics)
Czechoslovakia	NDA	—
Hungary	NDA	—
Bulgaria	NDA	—

	(3) Year sociological teaching resumed	(4) Rank in strength of teaching sociology
Poland	1957	1
Yugoslavia	Not interrupted	2
USSR	NDA	4
East Germany	1958	3
Romania	NDA	5
Hungary	—	—
Czechoslovakia	—	—
Bulgaria	—	—

TABLE 10–7. SOCIOLOGICAL TEACHING IN EASTERN EUROPEAN NATIONS

I. **Poland**

    A. *University chairs*

        1. University of Warsaw (*44*)

          a) Sociology (1957)*

          b) Sociography (1957)

          c) Sociology of Political Relations (date undetermined)

          d) History of Social Thought (date undetermined)

          e) History and Theory of Moral Values (date undetermined)

        2. University of Lodz

          a-d) 4 chairs, the first of which was established in 1957 (*23, 48*)

        3. University of Kraków

          a) General Ethnography and Sociology (1957) (*10, 51*)

          b) Sociology and Demography (1957) (*10, 51*)

        4. University of Wroclaw

          a) 1 chair established in 1957 (*29*)

        5. University of Poznan

          a) 1 chair established in 1958 (*10, 44*)

         6. Catholic University of Lublin

          a) Christian Sociology (established by 1959) (*48*)

    B. *Other teaching institutions*

        1. Institute of Sociological Studies of the Higher School of Social Sciences of the Central Committee of the Polish Workers Party (1958) (*10*)

        2. Sociology Department of the State Military Academy (date undetermined) (*48*)

II. **Yugoslavia**

    A. *University chairs*

        1. University of Belgrade (never discontinued) (*7, 93*)

        2. University of Zagreb (date undetermined) (*2, 86*)

        3. University of Ljubljana (1960) (*87*)

    B. *Other teaching institutions*

        1. Advanced School for Political and Behavioral Sciences (1960) (*85*)

        2. Higher School for Personnel and Social Services (1960) (*82*)

III. **USSR**

    A. *Sociology is principally taught in the departments of historical materialism of the universities of Moscow, Leningrad, Kiev and Gorki and in the various sociological research institutes. It was resumed around 1959. (65, 66)*

TABLE 10–7. (Cont'd)

IV. East Germany

A. *Sociological instruction given principally under the following faculties and institutions (23)*
1. Humboldt University (Berlin)
   a) Faculty of Philosophy
   b) Faculty of Economic Science
2. E. M. Arndt University (Greifswald)
3. Schiller University (Jena)
4. Karl Marx University (Leipzig)
(So far as is known, none of the above has established chairs of sociology.)

V. Romania

A. *No known chairs of sociology (60)*
B. *Institutions teaching sociological research methods (60)*
   1. Lenin Institute of Economic Science, Chair of Statistics
   2. Bucharest Polytechnic Institute, Chair of Statistics

VI. Czechoslovakia

No data available

VII. Hungary

No data available

VIII. Bulgaria

No data available

*Dates in parentheses indicate when (where known) the teaching institutions were founded.

APPENDIX D

Institutionalization of Sociological Research

TABLE 10–8.   QUANTITATIVE AND CHRONOLOGICAL INDICATORS[1]

	(1) Number of sociological research institutes	(2) First institute founded	(3) Chrono-logical rank
Poland	18	1956	1
USSR	7	1958	3
East Germany	8	1963(?)	4
Yugoslavia	3	1957	2
Romania	NDA	—	—
Hungary	NDA	—	—
Czechoslovakia	NDA	—	—
Bulgaria	at least 2	1966	5(?)

	(4) Other institutes engaging in sociological research
Poland	2
USSR	9
East Germany	19
Yugoslavia	4
Romania	at least 2
Hungary	number undetermined
Czechoslovakia	at least 1
Bulgaria	at least 1

	(5) Total number of institutions, faculties and chairs engaging in sociological research and teaching	(6) Rank
Poland	37	1
East Germany	31	2
USSR	21	3
Yugoslavia	11	4
Romania	at least 4	5(?)
Hungary	impossible to estimate	—
Czechoslovakia	impossible to estimate	—
Bulgaria	at least 2	6(?)

TABLE 10–8. (Cont'd)

	(7) Years of most rapid early development	(8) Rank
Poland	1956–1958	1
Yugoslavia	1957–1960	2
USSR	1960–1962(?)	4
East Germany	1962–1963	4
Romania	impossible to estimate	—
Hungary	1963–present(?)	5
Czechoslovakia	1963–present(?)	6
Bulgaria	1965–66	7

1. The information for this table was derived from numerous sources and combined. A list of the sociological research institutes and institutes engaging in sociological research known to the author is given in Table 10–9 of this Appendix.

TABLE 10–9. INSTITUTES ENGAGING IN EMPIRICAL SOCIOLOGICAL RESEARCH

SYMBOLS:

1. Date indicates year institute founded, where known.
2. Italicized number indicates numbers of references in Notes to Tables mentioning or describing the institute in question.
3. Asterisk denotes institutes primarily engaged in sociological research of an empirical nature, so far as can be determined.

I. Poland

1. *Department of Sociological Studies of the Institute of Philosophy and Sociology of the Polish Academy of Sciences (1956) (*10*)
   Divisions:
   a) *Philosophy and Sociology (1956) (*10*)
   b) *Sociology and History of Culture (1956) (*10*)
   c) *Institute of the Sociology of Labor (*48*)
   d) *Institute of Urban Sociology (*48*)
   e) *Institute of Labor Cultural Research (*48*)
   f) *Institute of Mass Cultural Research (*44*)
   g) *Rural Sociology (*44*)
   h) *Basic Sociological Research (*44*)
   i) *Section of Sociology of Political Relations (1962) (*44*)
   j) *Section of Medical Sociology (1964) (*44*)
2. *Institute of Rural Sociology of the Institute of Agricultural Economics (1957) (*47*)

TABLE 10–9. (Cont'd)

---

3. *Public Opinion Research Center of the Polish Radio and Television Service (1957) (*33, 45*)
4. *Sociology Center of the Institute of Social Economy (1958) (*44*)
5. *Sociological Section of the Silesian Science Institute (*48*)
6. *Sociology and History of Cultural Center, Lodz (*44*)
7. *Sociology Section of the Institute of Work Protection (1956) (*44*)
8. *Sociology Section of the Western Institute of Poznan (*44*)
9. Center for Research on Higher Education (1960) (*44*)
10. Institute of Town Planning and Architecture (*44*)

II. East Germany

1. *Division of Sociological Research of Institute of Social Sciences of the Central Committee of the Socialist Unity Party (1964) (*23*)
2. *Sociological Section of the Union of Philosophical Institutions of the D.D.R.
3. Humboldt University (Berlin)
   - a) *Sociological Commission of the School of Social Sciences
   - b) *Interfaculty Research Group "Sociology and Society"
   - c) Institute for Political Economy
   - d) *Sociological Working Group of the Institute of Philosophy
   - e) Division of Systematic Pedagogy
   - f) Division of the Subject of Pedagogy (*Fachpädagogie*)
   - g) Institute of Pedagogical Psychology
   - h) Institute of Psychology of the Faculty of Mathematics and Natural Sciences (?)
   - i) Institute of Music Science
   - j) Institute of Art History
   - k) Institute of Hygiene of the Faculty of Medicine
4. Working Group of the Research Division "Professional Education with Matriculation" of the German Institute for Professional Education
5. Research Group "Day Schools" of the German Central Institute of Pedagogy
6. Technical University of Dresden
   - a) Institute for Marxism-Leninism
   - b) Division of Psychology of the Pedagogical Institute
7. *Sociological Commission of Martin Luther University (Halle-Wittenberg)
8. Psychological Institute of the Friedrich Schiller University (Jena)
9. Institute of Psychology of the Karl Marx University (Leipzig)
10. *Sociological Research Group of the Institute of Philosophy of the Karl Marx University
11. Institute of Pedagogy of the Karl Marx University
12. Institute of Pedagogy of the German Higher School of Physical Culture

TABLE 10–9. (Cont'd)

13. University of Rostock
    a) *Institute of Marxism-Leninism
    b) Institute for High School Pedagogy
14. Chair of Psychology of the Pedagogical Institute of Karl-Marx-Stadt

III. USSR

1. *Section for Social Research of the Institute of Philosophy of the Soviet Academy of Sciences (1959) (*68*)
2. *Laboratory of Sociological Studies attached to the Institute of Philosophy of the University of Moscow (*62, 68*)
3. *Laboratory of Sociological Studies of the University of Leningrad (*62, 68*)
4. *Leningrad Institute of Human Studies (*68*)
5. *Sociological Research Laboratory of Sverdlovsk University (*62, 64*)
6. Public Opinion Institute of *Komsomolskaia pravda* (*62, 64, 72*)
7. Moscow Labor Research Institute (*67*)
8. Institute of Economics of the University of Novosibirsk (*62, 64*)
9. Central Statistical Board (*72*)
10. University of Gorki (*62*)
11. Laboratory of Economic and Mathematical Studies at the University of Novosibirsk (*62*)
12. Social Economics Department of the Leningrad Mechanics Institute (1965) (*62*)
13. Leningrad Electro-Technical Institute (1965) (*62*)
14. *Leningrad Public Institute for Social Research (1963) (*62, 64*)
15. Economics Institute of the Siberian Divison of the Soviet Academy of Sciences (*62*)
16. Pedagogical Institute at Krasnoyarsk (*62*)
17. *Sociological Laboratory at the University of Kiev (*62*)

IV. Yugoslavia

1. *Sociological Department of the Institute of Social Sciences (1957) (*84, 87*)
2. *Institute of Sociology at Ljubljana (1959) (*84, 87*)
3. Legal and Political Science Department of the Institute of Social Sciences (*84*)
4. *Zagreb Institute of Social Management (1957) (*87*)
5. Rural Institute of the Serbian Academy of Sciences (*2*)
6. *Institute for Social Problems of Serbia (*76*)

V. Romania

1. Economics Research Institute of the Romanian Peoples Republic (*58*)
2. Agricultural Economics Section of the Lenin Institute of Economic Science (*58*)

TABLE 10–9. (Cont'd)

VI. Hungary

1. Karl Marx University of Economic Science (*2*)

VII. Bulgaria

1. Bulgarian Youth Research Center (*19*)
2. Methodological Research Center of Bulgarian Radio (*20*)

VIII. Czechoslovakia

No information available

APPENDIX E

TABLE 10–10. PERIODICALS PUBLISHING SOCIOLOGICAL MATERIAL[1]

	(1) Nature of Periodicals	*(2) Number of Sociological Journals*	*(3) Date Sociological Journal First Published*
Poland	Legal, philosophy, sociology	5 (4 Polish, 1 English)	1957
Yugoslavia	Social policy, philosophy, sociology, etc.	1	1956[2]
Czechoslovakia	Philosophy, sociology	1	1965
USSR	Philosophy, party, university journals, sociology (planned)	0	1959[3] 1965[4] 1967[4]
Romania	Party, social science	0	1962[3]
Hungary	Philosophy, party, university journals	0	—

TABLE 10–10. (Cont'd)

	(1) Nature of Periodicals	(2) Number of Sociological Journals	(3) Date Sociological Journal First Published
East Germany	Philosophy, party	0	—
Bulgaria	Philosophy	0	—

1. Data for this table obtained from 8, pp. 69–93. Periodicals known to be publishing sociological material are listed in Table 10–11.
2. This periodical dealt with both philosophy and sociology during its publication from 1956 through 1959. In that year it split into two journals, one of which, *Sociologija*, is primarily concerned with sociology.
3. The Soviet Union issued one issue of a sociological bulletin in 1959, which has not appeared since (4). Romania issued one edition of the English-language *Romanian Journal of Sociology* in 1962, another journal which failed to achieve second publication (53).
4. A trial issue of a new Soviet sociological periodical, *Social Research,* appeared late in 1965 (65). It is scheduled to begin regular publication soon.

TABLE 10–11. PARTIAL LISTING OF PERIODICALS PUBLISHING SOCIOLOGICAL ARTICLES

I. Poland

A. *Sociological Journals*
 1. *Przeglad Socjologiczne* (1957) (*Review of Sociology*)
 2. *Kultur i Spoleczenstwo* (1958) (*Culture and Society*)
 3. *Studia Socjologia-Politiczne* (1958) (*Studies in Political Sociology*)
 4. *Studia Socjologiczne* (1960) (*Studies of Sociology*)
 5. *Polish Sociological Bulletin* (1961) (English-language)
B. *Others*
 1. *Mysl Filozoficzne* (*Philosophical Thought*)
 2. *Panstwo i Prawo* (*State and Law*)

II. Yugoslavia

A. *Sociological*
 1. *Jugoslovenski Casposis za Filozofiju i Sociologija* (1956–58) (*Yugoslav Journal of Philosophy and Sociology*)
 2. *Sociologija* (1959) (*Sociology*)
B. *Other*
 1. *Socijalna Politika* (*Social Policy*)

III. USSR

A. *Sociological Publications*
 1. One issue of a sociological bulletin published in 1959
 2. *Sotsialnye issledovania* (*Social Research*) (Trial issue, 1965; regular publication scheduled to begin in 1967.)

TABLE 10–11. (Cont'd)

B. *Other*
  1. *Voprosy filosofi* (*Problems of Philosophy*)
  2. *Filosofiskia nauki* (*Philosophical Science*)
  3. *Kommunist* (*The Communist*)
  4. *Partiinaia zhizn* (*Party Life*)
  5. *Vestnik Leningradskogo universiteta* (*Journal of Leningrad University*)
  6. *Vestnik Moskovskogo universiteta* (*Journal of Moscow University*)

IV. Romania

A. *Romanian Journal of Sociology* (One issue, English, in 1962)
B. *Other*
  1. *Revue des Sciences Sociales* (*Review of the Social Sciences*)
  2. *Lupta de Klasa* (*The Class Struggle*)

V. Czechoslovakia

A. *Sociological*
  1. *Sociologicky Casopis* (1965) (*Sociological Review*)
B. *Other*
  1. *Filosoficky Casopis* (*Philosophical Review*)

VI. Hungary

A. *Other*
  1. *Magyar Filozofai Szemle* (*Hungarian Philosophical Review*)
  2. *Magyar Tudomany* (*Hungarian Science*)
  3. *Belpolitikai Szemle* (*Domestic Affairs Review*)
  4. *Valosag* (*Reality*)
  5. *Tarsadalmi Szemle* (*Social Review*)

VII. East Germany

A. *Other*
  1. *Deutsche Zeitschrift für Philosophie* (*German Journal of Philosophy*)
  2. *Einheit* (*Unity*)

VIII. Bulgaria

A. *Other*
  1. *Filosofska Misal* (*Philosophical Thought*)

Principal sources for this material include numbers *22, 44, 53, 65, 71, 3, 8*.

APPENDIX F

TABLE 10–12. THE SCOPE OF EMPIRICAL SOCIOLOGICAL RESEARCH
IN EASTERN EUROPE

SYMBOLS:

1. X indicates that the field in question has undergone empirical sociological investigation.
2. X* indicates that such investigation consisted, in all likelihood, of a single study or has been of a preliminary nature.
3. ___ indicates that on the basis of the available information the field in question has not as yet been subject to empirical investigation.
4. The italicized numbers in parentheses indicate numbers of references in Notes to Tables in which the study or studies denoted by the X directly above are either mentioned or described.
5. Categories denoted by capital letters are the twenty-seven major categories referred to in the text. Subcategories are denoted by numbers.

Area	1 Poland	2 USSR	3 Yugoslavia	4 East Germany	5 Romania
A) INDUSTRY AND LABOR	X (41, 48)	X (64)	X (80, 89)	X (24)	X (60)
1) Management	X (37, 40)	—	X (80, 91)	—	X* (54)
2) Worker attitudes and motivations	X (39, 41)	X (62, 64)	X (77)	—	—
3) Jobs and roles	X (38, 44)	X (62)	X (90)	X (24)	—
B) CHILDREN AND YOUTH	X (48)	X (9, 62)	X (75)	X (23, 24)	X (9)
1) Values	X (36, 52)	X (72, 62)	X (86)	X (23)	—
2) Vocational choice	X (44)	X (64)	X (86)	X (23)	X (59)
3) Ideology and beliefs	X (42, 52)	X* (72, 62)	X (86)	X (23)	—
4) Education	X (50, 48)	X* (64)	X (77, 86)	X (23)	X (9)
5) Juvenile delinquency	X (34)	X (9)	X (86)	X (3)	—
C) RELIGION	X (48)	X (71)	X (86)	—	—
D) CULTURE	X (48)	X (62)	X (86)	X (71)	X (54)
1) Mass culture and leisure-time use	X (33)	X (64)	X (86)	X (23, 24)	X (54)

Area	1 Poland	2 USSR	3 Yugoslavia	4 East Germany	5 Romania
2) Forms of culture	X (44)	X (64)	—	X (23)	X* (20)
E) SMALL GROUPS	X (44, 48)	—	—	—	—
F) SOCIAL STRUCTURE AND MOBILITY	X (44)	X (3)	X (75)	X (24)	X (56)
1) Elites and intelligentsia	X (49)	—	X (91)	X* (24)	X* (56)
2) Changing social rules & conditions	X (44, 48)	X* (64)	—	—	—
G) INTERNAL MIGRATION	X (44, 48)	—	X (88)	—	—
H) COMMUNIST PARTY	X (47)	—	—	—	—
I) LOCAL GOVERNMENT	X (48)	—	X (84, 88)	—	—
J) ELECTORAL	X (32)	—	—	—	—
K) GENERAL TIME USE	X (44, 48)	X (66, 64)	—	X (23, 24)	—
L) MASS COMMUNICATIONS	X (44, 48)	X (62)	X (89)	—	—
M) PROPAGANDA & POLITICAL EDUCATION	X (48)	X (62)	X (88)	X (24)	X (54)
N) URBAN	X (44)	X (71)	X (88)	—	X (57, 58)

Area	1 Poland	2 USSR	3 Yugoslavia	4 East Germany	5 Romania
O) SMALL TOWN	X (44)	—	X (84)	—	—
P) RURAL & AGRICULTURAL	X (31, 46, 48)	X* (9)	X (88)	X (24)	X (57, 58)
Q) HOUSING	X (3)	X (62)	—	—	—
R) MARRIAGE AND FAMILY	X (44, 48)	X (67.70)	X (73)	—	—
S) ROLE OF WOMEN	X (35, 43)	X (3)	X (74)	X* (24)	X (55, 60)
T) CONSUMER PREFERENCES	X (48)	—	X (2)	X* (24)	—
U) SEX	X (44, 48)	—	X (86)	X* (23, 24)	—
V) MILITARY	X (44)	—	—	X (24)	—
W) MEDICINE & HEALTH	X (48)	—	—	—	—
X) ALCOHOLISM, DRUGS, ETC.	—	—	X (88)	X* (71)	—
Y) CRIME AND LAW	X (44, 48)	X* (71)	X (88)	—	X (60)
Z) STANDARD OF LIVING & FAMILY BUDGETS	X (9)	X (79)	X (83)	—	—
AA) SOCIAL PSYCHOLOGY	X (44)	—	X (88)	—	—

Area	6 Hungary	7 Czechoslovakia	8 Bulgaria	Number of Nations Using Empirical Research
A) INDUSTRY AND LABOR	X (26)	X (3)	—	7
1) Management	—	X* (9)	—	2
2) Worker attitudes and motivations	X (26)	X (3)	—	6
3) Jobs and roles	—	—	—	5
B) CHILDREN AND YOUTH	X (9)	—	X (9)	7
1) Values	X (9)	—	X* (21)	6
2) Vocational choice	X (3)	—	—	6
3) Ideology and beliefs	—	—	X (19)	5
4) Education	X (9)	—	X (9)	7
5) Juvenile delinquency	—	X* (9)	—	4
C) RELIGION	—	X* (22)	X (9)	5
D) CULTURE	—	—	X (20)	7
1) Mass culture and leisure-time use	—	—	X (20)	6

Area	6 Hungary	7 Czechoslovakia	8 Bulgaria	Number of Nations Using Empirical Research
2) Forms of culture	—	—	—	4
E) SMALL GROUPS	—	—	—	1
F) SOCIAL STRUCTURE AND MOBILITY	—	—	—	5
1) Elites and intelligentsia	—	—	—	5
2) Changing social rules & conditions	—	—	—	2
G) INTERNAL MIGRATION	—	—	—	2
H) COMMUNIST PARTY	—	—	—	1
I) LOCAL GOVERNMENT	—	—	—	2
J) ELECTORAL	—	—	—	1
K) GENERAL TIME USE	—	—	—	3
L) MASS COMMUNICATIONS	—	—	X (20)	4
M) PROPAGANDA & POLITICAL EDUCATION	—	—	X (20)	6
N) URBAN	—	—	—	4
O) SMALL TOWN	—	—	—	2
P) RURAL & AGRICULTURAL	X (3)	X* (22)	—	7
Q) HOUSING		X* (22)	—	3
R) MARRIAGE AND FAMILY	X* (3)	X (22)	—	5
S) ROLE OF WOMEN	—	X* (22)	—	5

Area	6 Hungary	7 Czechoslovakia	8 Bulgaria	Number of Nations Using Empirical Research
T) CONSUMER PREFERENCES	X (2)	X (9)	—	6
U) SEX	—	—	—	3
V) MILITARY	—	—	—	1
W) MEDICINE & HEALTH	—	—	—	2
X) ALCOHOLISM, DRUGS, ETC.	—	—	—	0
Y) CRIME AND LAW	—	—	—	4
Z) STANDARD OF LIVING & FAMILY BUDGETS	X (2)	X (9)	—	6
AA) SOCIAL PSYCHOLOGY	—	—	—	2

NOTES TO TEXT

1. The most important recent articles dealing with the revival of empirical sociology in Eastern Europe include:
   L. Labedz, "Sociologists in Conference," *Survey*, No. 31 (1960), pp. 20–29; E. Wilder, "Opinion Polls," *Survey*, No. 48 (1963), pp. 118–29; E. Wilder, "Social Research in Soviet Bloc Countries," *American Behavioral Scientist*, VI, No. 5 (1963), pp. 3–4; Ithiel de Sola Pool, *The Fourth World Congress of Sociology*, External Research Paper 136, External Research Division. Department of State, Washington, D.C. (1960); L. Labedz, "Sociology as a Vocation," *Survey*, No. 48 (1963), pp. 57-64; Rene Ahlberg, "Die Sowjetische Gesellschaft und die Empirische Sozial Forschung," *Ost-Europa*, XIII, No. 10 (1963), pp. 679–94; *Current Sociology*, XIII, No. 2 (1964), pp. 69–93; G. Kiss, "Soziologie," *Ost-Europa*, XV, No. 11–12 (1965), pp. 841–45.
   Soviet sociology is treated extensively in G. Fischer, "Science and Politics: The New Sociology in the Soviet Union" (*Cornell Research Papers in International Studies*—I, Ithaca: Center for International Studies, Cornell University, 1964).
   The most thorough study of East German sociology is P. C. Ludz, "Soziologie und Empirische Sozial Forschung in der DDR," in P. C. Ludz (ed.), *Studien und Materiellen zur Soziologie der DDR* (Westdeutscher Verlag, Sonderheft 8; *Kölner Zeitschrift für Soziologie und Sozialpsychologie*, 1964), pp. 327–418.
2. I include the Soviet Union and Yugoslavia in this group. The Soviet Union has traditionally assumed the leadership role among Eastern European communist nations. Yugoslavia is a variant case, not having acknowledged membership in the Soviet "bloc" since 1948.
3. Sources on this subject include Z. Bezeredz, "Die Lage der Soziologie in Ungarn," *Kölner Zeitschrift Für Soziologie und Sozialpsychologie*, XIII, No. 4 (1961), pp. 773–76; J. Chalasinski, "Sociology and Social Mythology in Postwar Poland," *Transactions of the 4th World Congress of Sociology* (London: International Sociological Association, 1959), pp. 139–46; Rene Ahlberg, "Sowjetische Gesellschaft," pp. 679–83.
4. That is, communism in the economic sense, in which all means of production are owned by society as a whole and the fruits of production are shared according to need rather than work.
5. See Table 10–1, Appendix A.
6. See Tables 10–10 and 10–11, Appendix E. Historical materialism is considered a branch of philosophy.
7. G. Osipov and M. Yovchuk, "Some Principles of Theory, Problems and Methods of Research in Sociology in the U.S.S.R.," *American Sociological Review*, No. 4 (1963), p. 620.
8. Ahlberg, "Sowjetische Gesellschaft," pp. 679–81.
9. See Tables 10–9, Appendix D. 10–10, Appendix E, and section III for a detailed analysis.
10. This is plain from sources cited under Footnote 1.
11. Sociology was limited, but never completely suppressed in Yugoslavia. J. S. Roucek, "Soviet Russia's Satellite Europe," in J. S. Roucek (ed.), *Contemporary Sociology* (New York: Philosophical Library, 1958), pp. 957–59.

12. *Ibid.,* p. 939.
13. Chalasinski, "Sociology and Social Mythology," p. 139; S. Nowak, "In Memory of Stanislaw Ossowski," *Polish Sociological Bulletin,* No. 2 (1963), pp. 6–10.
14. "Division of Sociological Research at the Polish Academy of Sciences— Warsaw and Lodz," *International Social Sciences Journal* (ISSJ), IX, No. 2 (1957), p. 229.
15. Bezeredz, "Lage der Soziologie," p. 770.
16. Roucek, "Soviet Russia's Satellite Europe," p. 957.
17. *Ibid.,* p. 959.
18. M. V. Manescu, "Theory of Mechanical Sampling and its Application in Sociological Research of the Population's Living Standards," *Romanian Journal of Sociology (RJS),* I, No. 1 (1962), pp. 81–91; V. Trebici and L. Tövissi, "Aspects of Sociological Research," *RJS,* I, No. 1 (1962), pp. 232–39.
19. Ludz, "Soziologie und Empirische Sozial Forschung," pp. 379–80, lists a study of youth attitudes toward sex carried out in 1950.
20. See Table 10–14 in Section VI, below.
21. "Social Change in Poland" (issue title), *ISSJ,* IX, No. 2 (1957).
22. "Sociology and Communism" (unsigned editorial), *Survey,* No. 25 (1958), pp. 2–8.
23. Roucek, "Soviet Russia's Satellite Europe," p. 959.
24. The Polish rural study was made by the Institute of Agricultural Economics, not primarily a sociological research institute, and its results were not published until 1955. As late as 1962, the leisure-time survey made in Romania was only mentioned in the literature; neither its methods nor its results were described.
25. P. Konstantinov and V. Kelle, "Historical Materialism-Marxist Sociology," *Kommunist,* No. 1 (Jan. 1965), pp. 92–93 as translated in the *Current Digest of the Soviet Press (CDSP),* XVII, No. 8 (1965), pp. 3–8.
26. I. Desmereanu and P. Weiner, "Change Which Took Place in the Working and Living Conditions of the Working People in the Years of People's Democracy," *RJS,* I, No. 1 (1962), pp. 141–64.
27. See "Current Developments," *East Europe,* X, No. 9 (1961), p. 45 (Hungary); "Bulgarian Youth, A Self-Portrait," *East Europe,* XII, No. 10 (1963), pp. 29–30 (Bulgaria); and "*Komsomolskaia pravda*'s Public Opinion Institute," *Komsomolskaia pravda,* May 19, 1960, p. 1 as translated in *CDSP,* XII, No. 20 (1960), pp. 2–4 (USSR).
28. See *CDSP,* XIII, No. 15 (1961), pp. 19–21.
29. *ISSJ,* XV, No. 3 (1963), pp. 436–37; E. Taborsky, "Sociology in East Europe—Czechoslovakia," *Problems of Communism,* XIV, No. 1 (1965), pp. 62–63; M Jollivet, "The Franco-Polish Seminar on Public Opinion Surveys," *ISSJ,* XI, No. 1 (1959), p. 91; Desmereanu and Weiner, "Change Which Took Place," p. 154.
30. Jollivet, "Franco-Polish Seminar." A. Sicinski, "Public Opinion Surveys in Poland," *ISSJ,* XV, No. 1 (1963), pp. 91–110.
31. None of the material consulted in connection with this study indicates that any of these countries has yet established an autonomous faculty or chair in sociology.

32. Ludz, "Soziologie und Empirische Sozial Forschung," pp. 397–409, gives a detailed listing of all the academic institutions engaged in sociological teaching and research. None is a formal teaching institution and only eight or less than twenty-five percent are devoted exclusively to sociological research.

33. See indicators (2), (3), and (7) of Table 10–8, appearing in Appendix D.

34. C. Murgescu, "Field Research as Conducted by the Economic Research Institute of the Academy of the Rumanian People's Republic," *RJS*, I, No. 1 (1962), p. 240.

35. Ludz, "Soziologie und Empirische Sozial Forschung," pp. 378–79, Study No. E 34.

36. *Bulgarian Press Survey*, No. 611, Radio Free Europe Target Area Research Analysis, May 11, 1966, pp. 1–5.

37. This contention could be tested by subjecting articles reporting the results of empirical sociological studies in similar areas published formally and informally to comparative content analysis.

38. G. Fischer, "Current Soviet Work in Sociology," *The American Sociologist*, I, No. 3 (1966), p. 128, and a letter from Professor Fischer dated Sept. 22, 1966.

39. The results of Polish sociological thought and investigation are regularly published in English in the *Polish Sociological Bulletin*. Additional sources include: A. Kloskowska, "General Attitude Towards the Respective Equality of the Two Sexes and Their Children," *ISSJ*, XIV, No. 1 (1962), pp. 66–80; J. Kolaja, "Review of Books by Zygulski, Przeclawski, and Michol," *Social Forces*, XLIV, No. 1 (1965), pp. 133–34; and S. Nowak, "Egalitarian Attitudes of Warsaw Students," *American Sociological Review*, XXV, No. 2 (1960), pp. 219–31.

Examples of Yugoslav sociological research and thought include: K. Kilibaros, "Desire for Specialized Education by Young Workers and Peasants Working on the Autoput," *Socijalna Politika*, X, No. 7/8 (1960), pp. 60–64 (tr. in Joint Publications Research Service [*JPRS*], 1961, No. 13090, pp. 101–16); R. Rajovic, "Studying the Commune System in Yugoslavia," *ISSJ*, XIII, No. 3 (1961), pp. 451–57; and S. Skrzypek, "The Political, Cultural and Social Views of Yugoslav Youth," *Public Opinion Quarterly*, XXIX, No. 1 (1965), pp. 87–106.

For comparison with Soviet sociological research, see the articles published in *Soviet Sociology*, I–V (1962–67): "How Has Your Living Standard Changed?" *Komsomolskaia pravda*, Oct.7, 1960, p. 1 (tr. in *CDSP*, XII, No. 41, pp. 9–18); "Confession of a Generation—17,466 Replies to Youth Poll," *Komsomolskaia pravda*, July 21, 1961, pp. 1–4 (tr. in *CDSP*, XIII, No. 34 [1961], pp. 3–8); and Fischer, "Current Soviet Work," pp. 127–32.

40. Konstantinov and Kelle, "Historical Materialism," pp. 3–5, 7.

41. For references to these studies and those indicated by asterisks below, see bibliographical index numbers included in Table 10–12, Appendix F.

42. A. Kharchev, "Problems of the Family and Their Study in the U.S.S.R.," *ISSJ*, XIV, No. 1 (1962), pp. 539–49; and "Motives of Marriage in the U.S.S.R.," *Acta Sociologica*, VIII, No 1/2 (1965), pp. 142–54.

43. The use of leisure time for self-education, attendance at cultural or political events, and for party-sponsored activities is considered "socially

useful" in most communist nations. On the other hand, attendance at church, visiting friends, "hanging out" on street corners have the opposite connotation for communist elites. They have found no method of exercising direct and efficient political control over the use of leisure time, however, and indirect methods such as exhortation and the arousal of public opinion must be employed.

44. Lewis S. Feuer, "Problems and Unproblems in Soviet Social Theory," *Slavic Review*, XXIII, March 1964, pp. 117–24; and Paul Hollander, "The Dilemmas of Soviet Sociology," *Problems of Communism*, XIV, No. 6 (1965), p. 46.

45. V. Shubkin, "Concrete Research into Social Processes," *Kommunist*, Feb. 1965, pp. 48–57 (tr. in *CDSP*, XVII, No. 17 [1965], pp. 15–19); Konstantinov and Kelle, "Historical Materialism," pp. 157–60.

46. The only exception is Bulgaria, unrepresented at the Fifth Congress held in 1962 in Washington, D.C.

47. Labedz, "Sociologists in Conference," pp. 20–29; Pool, "Fourth World Congress," pp. 4–5, 7; "Activities of the National Sociological Committee," *RJS*, I, No. 1 (1962), pp. 226–29.

48. Chalasinski, "Sociology and Social Mythology," pp. 139–45 (Poland; Radomir Lukic, "Les Conditions Sociales du Development de la Sociologie en Yugoslavie," *Transactions of the 4th World Congress of Sociology*, I, pp. 187–204.

49. *Index Translationum*, VIII-XVI (1956–1963) (Paris: UNESCO).

50. Ludz, "Soziologie and Empirische Sozial Forschung," pp. 366–72.

51. Ahlberg, "Sowjetische Gesellschaft," pp. 679–82.

52. See Footnote 23. Polish articles which have appeared in Western journals include: A Gostkowski, "Popular Interest in the Municipal Elections of Lodz, Poland," *Public Opinion Quarterly*, XXIII, No. 3 (1959), pp. 371–80; A. Kloskowska, "The Negroes as Seen by Polish Children," *International Journal of Comparative Sociology*, III, No. 2 (1962), pp. 189–99; Nowak, "Egalitarian Attitudes," pp. 219–31; and Sicinski, "Public Opinion Surveys," pp. 91–110.

53. These have included O. Buric, "Attitudes Toward Work by Women," *ISSJ*, XVI, No. 9 (1962), pp. 47–58; Rajovic, "Studying the Commune System," pp. 451–57; and Skryzpek, "The Political," pp. 87–106.

54. These have been as follows: Kharchev, "Problems of the Family," pp. 539–49; Kharchev, "Motives of Marriage," pp. 142–54; and A. Zvorikin, "The Social Sciences in the U.S.S.R.—Methods and Trends," *ISSJ*, XVI, No. 4 (1964), pp. 588–99.

55. *Romanian Journal of Sociology*, I, No. 1 (1962).

56. M. Stoian, "Rumanian Teenagers Look at Their Future," *UNESCO Features*, No. 479, April (I), 1966, pp. 13–15.

NOTES TO TABLES

I. General

1. *Index Translationum*, IX–XVI (Paris: UNESCO, 1953–63).

2. *International Social Science Journal* (Formerly *International Social Science Bulletin*) (*ISSJ*), I-XVII (1950–1965).

3. KISS, G. "Soziologie in Ost-Europa," *Ost Europa*, XV, No. 11/12 (1965), 841–45.

4. LABEDZ, L. "Sociologists in Conference," *Survey*, No. 31 (1960), pp. 20–29.

5. POOL, I. DE SOLA. *The Fourth World Congress of Sociology*, External Research Paper No. 136, External Research Division, Department of State, Washington, D. C., 1960.

6. ROUCEK, J. S. "Russian Sociology and Sociology under Communism," in J. S. Roucek (ed.), *Contemporary Sociology*. New York: Philosophical Library, Inc., 1958, pp. 892–921.

7. ————. "Soviet Russia's Satellite Europe," in Roucek, *ibid., pp.* 932–978.

8. WIATR, J. "Political Sociology in Eastern Europe," *Current Sociology*, XIII, No 2 (1964), 1–93. (Pp. 69–93 of this monograph comprise a bibliography of 374 books and articles published on political sociology in Eastern Europe, 1957–1963.)

9. WILDER, E. "Opinion Polls," *Survey*, No. 48 (1963), pp. 118–29.

10. ————. "Social Research in Soviet Bloc Countries," *American Behavioral Scientist*, VI, No. 5 (1963), 3–4.

II. Pre-Communist Sociology

11. MANOIL, A. "Rumanian Sociology," in *Twentieth Century Sociology*, Gurvitch, G., and Moore, W. (eds.). New York: Philosophical Library, 1945, pp. 732–40.

12. OBROLIK, A. "Sociological Activities in Czechoslovakia," *American Sociological Review*, I, No. 4 (1936), 653–56.

13. ROUCEK, J. S. "Czechoslovak Sociology," in Gurvitch and Moore, *Twentieth Century Sociology*, pp. 717–31.

14. ————. "Sociological Periodicals of Czechoslovakia," *American Sociological Review*, I, No. 1 (1936), 168–70.

15. ————. "Sociology in Romania," *ibid.*, III, No. 1 (1938), 54–62.

16. ————. "Sociology in Yugoslavia," Gurvitch and Moore, *Twentieth Century Sociology*, pp. 740–54.

17. ZNANIECKA, E. M. "Polish Sociology," in Gurvitch and Moore, *Twentieth Century Sociology*, pp. 703–17.

18. ————. "Sociology in Poland," *American Sociological Review*, I, No. 1 (1936), 296–98.

III. Bulgaria

19. "Bulgarian Youth, A Self-Portrait," *East Europe*, XII, No. 10 (1963), 29–30.

20. *Bulgarian Press Survey*, No. 565 (*RFE* Target Area Research and Analysis), Mar. 11, 1965.

21. ————, No. 611, May 11, 1966.

IV. Czechoslovakia

22. TABORSKY, E. "Sociology in Eastern Europe—Czechoslovakia," *Problems of Communism*, XIV, No. 1 (1965), 62–66.

V. East Germany

23. LUDZ, P. C. "Soziologie und Empirische Sozialforschung in der DDR," in Ludz, P. C. (ed.), *Studien und Materiellen zur Soziologie der DDR*. Cologne: Westdeutscher Verlag (Sonderheft VIII of the *Kölner Zeitschrift für Soziologie und Sozialpsychologie*), 1964, pp. 327–418.
24. ———. "Ausgewählte Literatur zur Soziologie der DDR: Soziologie und Empirische Sozialforschung," in Ludz (ed.), *ibid.,* pp. 521–31.

VI. Hungary

25. BEZEREDZ, Z. "Die Lage der Soziologie in Ungarn," *Kölner Zeitschrift für Soziologie und Sozialpsychologie,* XIII, heft 4 (1961), 770–76.
26. "Current Developments," *East Europe,* X, No. 9 (1961), 45.
27. ———. *East Europe,* X, No. 6 (1961), 46–47.

VII. Poland

28. CHALASINSKI, J. "Sociology and Social Mythology in Postwar Poland," *Transactions* [15], Vol. 1, pp. 139–146.
29. "The Destiny of Sociology in Postwar Poland," *Survey,* No. 28 (1959), pp. 46–55.
30. "Division of Sociology of the Polish Academy of Sciences—Warsaw and Lodz," *ISSJ,* IX, No. 2 (1957), 229.
31. GALEWSKI, B. "Social Stratification of Rural Areas," *ISSJ,* IX, No. 2 (1957), 193–211.
32. GOSTKOWSKI, Z. "Popular Interest in the Municipal Elections of Lodz, Poland," *Public Opinion Quarterly,* XXIII, No. 3 (1959), 371–80.
33. JOLLIVET, M. "The Franco-Polish Seminar on Public Opinion Surveys," *ISSJ,* XI, No. 1 (1959), 75–92.
34. JORDAN, Z. A. "The Meaning of Juvenile Delinquency," *East Europe,* XII, No. 5 (1963), 5–15.
35. KLOSKOWSKA, A. "General Attitude Towards the Respective Equality of the Two Sexes and Their Children," *ISSJ,* XIV, No. 1 (1962), 66–80.
36. ———. "The Negroes as seen by Polish Children," *International Journal of Comparative Sociology,* III, No. 2 (1962), 188–99.
37. KOLAJA, J. Review of *Sovremana Sociologija* (M. Popovic, author), and *Zagadnien Wspolesnej Socjologii Amerikanskiy* (Z. Bauman, author), *American Sociological Review,* XXVII, No. 3 (1962), 441–42.
38. ———. Review of *The Situation of Polish Journalists, Public Opinion Quarterly,* XXVI, No. 4 (1962), 686–88.
39. ———. "Sociology in Poland," *American Sociological Review,* XXIII, No. 2 (1958), 201–02.
40. KONIG, R. Review of *A Polish Factory* (J. Kolaja, author). *Kölner Zeitschrift für Soziologie und Sozialpsychologie,* XIII, heft 3 (1963), 537–39.
41. MALANOWSKI, J., *et al.* "The Individual Inquiry Card as an Instrument in the Sociology of Work," *ISSJ,* IX, No. 2 (1957), 212–28.

42. NOWAK, S. "Egalitarian Attitudes of Warsaw Students," *American Sociological Review*, XXV, No. 2 (1960), 219–31.

43. PIOTROWSKI, J. "Attitudes Towards Work by Women," *ISSJ*, XIV, No. 1 (1962), 80–91.

44. *Polish Sociological Bulletin*. Warsaw: Polish Academy of Sciences, No. 1–11 (1961–65).

45. SICINSKI, A. "Public Opinion Surveys in Poland," *ISSJ*, XV, No. 1 (1963), 91–110.

46. "Social Change in Poland," *ISSJ*, IX, No. 2 (1957) (theme of issue).

47. "Sociological Studies at the Social Science College of Warsaw," *ISSJ*, XIII, No. 1 (1961), 121.

48. *Studia Socjologiczne*, 1961–1963, 1965.

49; SZCZEPANSKI, J. "Changes in the Structure and Function of the Intelligentsia," *ISSJ*, IX, No. 2 (1957), 180–92.

50. TYMOWSKI, J. "The Efficiency of Studies," *Zycia Szkoly Wyz szoj*, VIII, No. 2 (1960), 20–21. (tr. in *JPRS*, 1960, No. 10104, p. 39.)

51. "University Sociological Center in Cracow," *ISSJ*, XIII, No. 1 (1961), 120–24.

52. ———. "Impact of Poland's Stabilization on Her Youth," *Public Opinion Quarterly*, XXVIII, No. 3 (1964), 447.

VIII. Romania

53. *Romanian Journal of Sociology*, I, No. 1 (1962), Bucharest, Publishing House of the Academy of the Romanian People's Republic (*RJS*). (Only issue published thus far.)

54. CAZACU, *et al.* "Method of Sociological Investigation of Social Consciousness Phenomena in Plants," *RJS*, pp. 165–78.

55. DESMEREANU, I., and WEINER, P. "Changes Which Took Place in the Working and Living Conditions of the Working People of the Industrial Region of Resita in the Years of People's Democracy," *RJS*, pp. 141–64.

56. IONESCU, D. "Achievements and Aptitudes of Rumanian Students," *Contemporanul*, No. 7 (1960). (tr. in *JPRS*, 1960, No. 14246, p. 57.)

57. MANESCU, M. "Theory of Mechanical Sampling and its Application in Sociological Research of the Populations' Living Standards," *RJS*, pp. 81–91.

58. MURGESCU, C. "Field Research as Conducted by the Economic Research Institute of the Academy of the Rumanian People's Republic," *RJS*, pp. 239–47.

59. STOIAN, MIHAI. "Rumanian Teenagers Look at their Future," *UNESCO Features*, No. 479, April (I), 1966, pp. 13–15.

60. TREBICI, V., and TOVISSI, L. "Aspects of Sociological Research," *RJS*, pp. 232–39.

IX. USSR

61. AHLBERG, R. "Die Sowjetische Gesellschaft und die Empirische Sozialforschung," *Ost Europa*, XIII, No. 10 (1963), 679–94.

62. *Current Digest of the Soviet Press*, XII–XVII (1960–1965).

63. FEUER, L. S. "Problems and Unproblems in Soviet Social Theory," *Slavic Review,* XXIII (1964), 117–24.
64. FISCHER, G. "Science and Politics: The New Sociology in the Soviet Union," *Cornell Research Papers in International Studies*—I. Ithaca, N. Y.: Center for International Studies, Cornell University, 1964.
65. ———. "Current Soviet Work in Sociology," *The American Sociologist,* I, No. 3 (1966), 127–32.
66. HOLLANDER, P. "The Dilemma of Soviet Sociology," *Problems of Communism,* XIV, No. 6 (1965), 34–46.
67. KHARCHEV, A. G. "Problems of the Family and Their Study in the U.S.S.R.," *ISSJ,* XIV, No. 1 (1962), 539–49.
68. LABEDZ, L. "Sociology as a Vocation," *Survey,* No. 48 (1963), pp. 57–64.
69. OSIPOV, G., and YOVCHUK, M. "Some Principles of Theory, Problems, and Methods of Research in Sociology in the U.S.S.R.," *American Sociological Review,* XXVIII, No. 4 (1963), 620–23.
70. "Sociology and Communism," *Survey,* No. 25 (1958), pp. 2–8.
71. *Soviet Sociology,* I–IV (1962–1966).
72. YU, K. "How the Soviet Institute of Public Opinion Conducted Three Polls," *Vestnik Statisticki,* June 1961, No. 6, pp. 82–84. (tr. by *JPRS,* 1962, No. 3099, 1–6.)

X. Yugoslavia

73. ANDERSON, N. "Soziologie der Familie," *Kölner Zeitschrift für Soziology und Sozialpsychologie,* XIII, heft 4 (1961), 777–81.
74. BURIC, O. "Attitudes Regarding the Status of Women in Yugoslavia," *ISSJ,* XIV, No. 1 (1962), 166–76.
75. ILIC, M. "Results of the Questionnaire Used in the Study, 'Social Structures and Mobility of the Working Class,'" *Sociologija,* II, No. 2 (1960), 137–47. (tr. in *JPRS,* 1961, No. 7792, pp. 14–29.)
76. ILIC, O. "Results of Questionnaire on the Situation of Children of Employed Mothers in Serbia," *Socijalna Politika,* X, No. 7/8 (1960), 97–99. (tr. by *JPRS,* 1961, No. 4566, pp. 45–46.)
77. KILABAROS, K. "Desire for Specialized Education by Young Workers and Peasants Working on the Autoput," *Socijalna Politika,* X, No. 7/8 (1960), 60–64. (tr. in *JPRS,* 1961, No. 1091, pp. 1–5.)
78. LAKICEVIC, D. "Social Care of Children of Employed Parents in Serbia," *Socijalna Politika,* X, No. 11 (1960), 25–37. (tr. in *JPRS,* 1961, No. 13090, pp. 101–16.)
79. LUKIC, R. "Les Conditions Sociales du Development de la Sociologie en Yugoslavie," *Transactions* [15], I, pp. 187–204.
80. MATIC, S. "Three Studies of the Functioning of Yugoslav Workers Self-Management," *Sociologija,* II, No. 1 (1960), 124–31. (tr. in *JPRS,* 1960, No. 17272, pp. 18–24.)
81. MICUNOVIC, E. "Yugoslav Association for Philosophy and Sociology Divided into Two Associations," *Borba,* No. 271 (1960), p. 9. (tr. in *JPRS,* 1961, No. 12995, pp. 343–44.)
82. "The Network of Yugoslav Advanced Schools," *Jugoslovenskii Pregled,* No. 12 (1960), pp. 535–37. (tr. in *JPRS,* 1961, No. 13146, pp. 77–87.)

83. POPOVIC, M. "Family Budgets of Blue and White Collar Workers' Families in 1959," *Socijalna Politika*, X, No. 10 (1960), 76–83. (tr. in *JPRS*, 1960, No. 13090, pp. 80–86.)

84. RAJOVIC, R. "Studying the Commune System in Yugoslavia," *ISSJ*, XIII, No. 3 (1961), 451–57.

85. "Schools for Ideological and Political Education," *Jugoslovenskii Pregled*, IV, No. 10 (1960), 427–28. (tr. in *JPRS*, 1961, No. 9323, pp. 57–63.)

86. SKRZYPEK, S. "The Political, Cultural and Social Views of Yugoslav Youth," *Public Opinion Quarterly*, XXIX, No. 1 (1965), 87–106.

87. "Social Science Research Institutes in the People's Federative Republic of Yugoslavia," *ISSJ*, XIII, No. 3 (1961), 457–74.

88. *Sociologija*, V–VII (1963–1965).

89. STEPANOVIC, E. "The Surplus Labor Force in Economic Organizations," *Socijalna i Zdrevstvena Politika*, XIII, No. 11 (1960), 39–42. (tr. in *JPRS*, 1961, No. 13258, pp. 46–49.)

90. STIJNER, R. "Problems of Technical Qualification and Industrial Labor Productivity," *Socijalna Politika*, X, No. 10 (1960), 3–22. (tr. in *JPRS*, 1961, No. 13090, pp. 38–60.)

91. SUPEK, R. "The Director in a System of Worker Self-Administration," *Sociologija*, II, No. 1 (1960), 132–37. (tr. in *JPRS*, 1960, No. 17272, pp. 9–17.)

92. VASIC, B. "Higher School for Personnel and Social Services Founded in Kranj," *Socijalna i Zdrevstvena Politika*, XIII, No. 11/12 (1960), 65–68. (tr. in *JPRS*, 1961, No. 13258, pp. 50–53.)

93. VRATUSA, A. "The Sociologists and the Policymakers in Yugoslavia," *Transactions* [16], I, pp. 44–49.

ELEVEN

EXTERNAL CONFLICT AND
INTERNAL COHESION:
THE SINO-SOVIET CASE*

OLE R. HOLSTI

To the student of international relations, one of the most fascinating developments since World War II has been the changing relations among
states within the communist subsystem, and particularly those between
China and the Soviet Union. Apart from their historical and contemporary
significance, these events can provide an example of more general theoretical considerations in the study of international politics. For example,
to what factors should one attribute the dispute? Did the discord between
the USSR and China originate in the clashing personalities of Khrushchev
and Mao? Is this an illustration of the hypothesis that authoritarian states
are invariably expansionist and that, owing to geographical location, these
two nations were bound to clash? Or is the conflict related to a basic
structural change within the international system—a transformation from
a tight bipolar configuration to one with less rigid alliances? Each of these
explanations of Chinese and Soviet policy has its advocates who cite supporting historical examples. The difficulty, as Rosenau[1] has pointed out,
is not the existence of multiple explanations of state behavior, but, rather,
the absence of a theory of international relations to postulate under what
conditions each of these interpretations may be relevant.

* Earlier versions of this chapter were published in *The Journal of Applied
Behavioral Science,* and as a chapter in Philip J. Stone *et al., The General
Inquirer: A Computer Approach to Content Analysis in the Behavioral
Sciences* (Cambridge: Massachusetts Institute of Technology Press, 1966).
1 am indebted to P. Terry Hopmann for making available documents
relating to the crisis in Korea and Vietnam, and the Geneva Conference.

The study of Sino-Soviet relations also brings into focus certain problems of research strategy. Social scientists who seek to analyze political behavior at the international level labor under a number of handicaps, not the least of which concerns the availability of data. Recently, political scientists have become increasingly concerned with the perspective of the actor, and *his* definition of the situation, as opposed to the perspectives and situational definitions of the investigator. Without neglecting the analysis of organizations and institutions, the basic premise underlying this approach is that the behavior of nations "is determined by the way in which the situation is defined subjectively by those charged with the responsibility for making choices."[2] Although we habitually personify nation-states, by referring to "Soviet actions" or "American policies," this is, in fact, while convenient, a sometimes misleading way of identifying decisions made by individuals in Moscow or Washington who are empowered to commit the resources of their respective states in the pursuit of international goals. However, direct access to foreign policy leaders is always severely restricted in time and space. Even the scholar fortunate enough to gain access to decision-makers of his own nation cannot always do so at those times when much of the most theoretically relevant research might be undertaken—for example, during a crisis situation. Moreover, many of the leaders who are deemed important, such as those of communist China, are never available. Usually, the best one can produce under these circumstances is an *ex post facto* study of one party in the crisis situation, such as the analysis of the American decision to resist aggression in Korea.[3]

The research problems inherent in the study of international relations are magnified for the student of Sino-Soviet relations; here the normal difficulties are compounded by cold war politics. Even the post-Stalin thaw in the Soviet Union, which has facilitated some types of research by western scholars, has not materially eased the problems in the study of foreign policy. Clearly, many standard methods of social science research—the personal interview, the questionnaire, or participant observation of decision-makers in action—can rarely be used. What is needed is an instrument for measuring attitudes "at a distance." This is, perhaps, the primary rationale for using content analysis—a technique for making inferences by systematically and objectively identifying specified characteristics within text—of decision-makers' documents. Thus, it is not surprising that many studies of Soviet bloc politics have relied to some extent on one or more of the many available techniques of content analysis.[4]

A major drawback to the use of content analysis is found in the very nature of the technique itself; even elementary forms of the method, such as simple word counts, require extensive expenditure of scarce research resources. Nor do such relatively simple techniques always insure a high level of reliability. For example, in the pioneering Revolution and Development in International Relations (RADIR) studies undertaken by Lasswell and his colleagues, reliability tests indicated only 66, 68, and 70 per cent agreement between coders.[5] Moreover, many manual techniques of content analysis lack flexibility and suffer from a limited ability to deal with complex units of analysis. Finally, content analysis usually requires skilled and sensitive coders, the very type of persons who soon become bored and frustrated by the tedious and repetitive nature of the task. These difficulties lend considerable validity to Berelson's warning that, "Unless there is a sensible, or clever, or sound, or revealing, or unusual, or important notion underlying the analysis, it is not worth going through the rigor of the procedure, especially when it is so arduous and so costly of effort."[6]

Recent developments in programming high-speed computers for content analysis have helped, in part, to resolve the dilemma of the investigator who is faced, on the one hand, with a need for precise data, and, on the other hand, with the costs of content analysis.[7] The "General Inquirer" system of automated content analysis has been modified for measuring attitudes in political documents.[8] This technique permits a substantial reduction of manual effort in data preparation while materially increasing speed, reliability, and flexibility of analysis.

The adaptation of the General Inquirer used in this study is programmed to measure *frequency* and *intensity* of attitudes by means of a dictionary in which words are defined along three dimensions: positive affect—negative affect; strength—weakness; activity—passivity. These correspond to the *evaluative, potency,* and *activity* dimensions which have been found to be primary in human cognition in a variety of cultures.[9] The dictionary thus reflects the assumption that when decision-makers perceive themselves, other nations, events—or any attitude object—the most relevant discriminations are made in a space defined by these three factors. This does not assume that two persons will agree whether a given attitude object is good or bad, strong or weak, active or passive, but, rather, that these three factors account for an overwhelming proportion of the variance.

HYPOTHESIS AND DATA

The hypothesis to be examined in this paper states that intra-bloc relations vary systematically according to the level of inter-bloc conflict. That is, during periods of heightened tensions between the East and the West, relations between China and the Soviet Union will be characterized by a higher consensus, whereas during periods of decreasing tension, there will be a lower level of consensus. The hypothesis can be considered an application of a more general proposition regarding group cohesion; namely, that out-group pressure—in this case resulting from East-West conflict—tends to reduce in-group (Sino-Soviet) dissonance, whereas the absence of external pressure tends to increase those differences.[10] Variations of this hypothesis may be found in many of the classical theories of the causes of war.

One test of the hypothesis might be to examine Chinese and Soviet perceptions of *each other* during periods of high and low inter-bloc conflict. The tendency of communist leaders to use allegory, indirect attack, obscure jargon, and even omission, renders *direct* analysis of Chinese and Soviet decision-makers' attitudes toward each other extremely difficult.

> . . . because the realities of the dispute were carefully concealed, and because in public utterances neither side attacked the other by name, it was impossible, even as late as the early autumn of 1962, to prove the extent and bitterness of the quarrel without the most elaborate documentation; and, although this had up to a point been done, very few people in the West were any the wiser because, to understand the documentation, the reader first had to master the code-language of Communist polemics.[11]

For example, during the October 1962 missile crisis, Chinese decision-makers ignored the role of the Soviet Union in a seemingly calculated manner, preferring to regard the events in the Caribbean as a Cuban-American affair. In all the Chinese documents of October 26–31, 1962 analyzed in this chapter, there are only five direct references to the Soviet Union.

An alternative approach is to adopt an indirect research strategy. There is more or less general agreement among students of Sino-Soviet relations that a major source of friction between China and the Soviet Union concerns the proper policy to be pursued toward the West in general and the United States in particular. The Soviet Union has intermittently taken a position of partial accommodation toward the West, whereas Chinese leaders have opposed any such relaxation as contradictory to the principles of Marxism-Leninism.[12] Thus, it should be possible, through content analysis, to measure the degree of Sino-Soviet cohesion by measuring similarities and differences in perceptions of American policy. That is, perceptions of the United States should provide a useful and valid index of the level of agreement or disagreement between Chinese and Soviet decision-makers. Numerous references to American policy in most Chinese and Soviet documents is a further advantage of this approach.

The hypothesis can now be restated in more operational terms:

Chinese and Soviet perceptions of the United States will tend to be similar in periods of high inter-bloc conflict, whereas, during periods of decreasing tensions, perceptions of American policy will diverge. The data may yield four configurations of Chinese and Soviet perceptions of the United States.

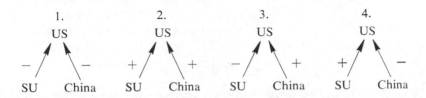

The major theoretical assumption underlying this operational definition of the hypothesis, a premise informed by a considerable literature relating to cognitive balance, is that consensus can be defined as the "existence, on the part of two or more persons, of similar orientations toward something."[13] Or, stated somewhat differently, the four attitude structures above are in "balance" only if the relationship between the Soviet Union and China is associative or cohesive (+) in patterns 1 and 2, and dissociative or conflictual (—) in patterns 3 and 4.[14]

Two further assumptions are incorporated into this research design. If the "strain toward balance" is to be operative: (1) the attitude object must be *salient* for the actors,[15] and (2) the actors must be *aware of each other's attitudes*. Thus, the United States must be an attitude object of central concern to China and the Soviet Union and, further, the latter two nations each must be cognizant of the other's views. Even a casual survey of Sino-Soviet-American relations for the period 1950–1965 indicates that these two conditions are fully satisfied.

The data used in this study consist of 39 Soviet and 45 Chinese documents—totalling nearly 150,000 words—written in eight periods selected from the years 1950–1965. The periods include three during which East-West relations were relatively calm, one in which a major crisis was in the process of resolution without recourse to violence, and four of extremely high tension.

1. June 28–29, 1950   The outbreak of the Korean war.

2. July 17–19, 1955   The Geneva "Summit" Conference.

3. September 15–25, 1959   Premier Khrushchev's visit to the United States.

4. April 12–25, 1961   The American-supported invasion of Cuba.

5. October 22–25, 1962   The most intense period of the
                                    Cuban missile crisis.[16]
6. October 26–31, 1962   The "bargaining period" in
                                    which the missile crisis was
                                    resolved.
7. July 25–August 5, 1963   The signing of the Test Ban
                                    Treaty by the United States,
                                    Soviet Union, and Great Britain.
8. February 8, 1965   The United States decision to
                                    bomb North Vietnam.

After the periods of analysis had been selected, the *entire verbatim text* of publicly available documents authored by designated decision-makers was content analyzed.[17]

Prior to punching the text on IBM cards, three coding operations were performed: (1) complex sentences were separated into one or more themes; (2) the syntactical position of key *words* in the text was identified by a system of numerical subscripts; and (3) each *theme* was characterized as to time and mode of expression. For example:

CV   All freedom-loving/3 peoples/3 of the world/3 must/4
     oppose/4 Washington's/7 policy/7 of nuclear/7 black-
     mail/7.
CD   The Soviet-Union/3 recognizes/4 the industrial/7
     achievements/7 of the United States/7.

These codes identify the subject-verb-object (3-4-7) relationship, links between modifiers and referents, time (C = current), and mode of expression (V = imperative; D = indicative).[18]

The primary analysis was carried out through a *direct table* program written in Balgol. Scores on the evaluative, potency, and activity dimensions were tallied for: (1) actions in themes in which the United States was the agent, and (2) qualitative characteristics attributed to the United States. The General Inquirer dictionary used in this study contains approximately 3600 words—including such terms as "nuclear," "black-mail," "industrial," and "achievement"—which have been tagged and scaled for intensity along the three dimensions.[19] This permits rapid and accurate calculations of perceptions, as revealed in the Soviet and Chinese documents, of the United States. A General Inquirer retrieval program was used on a sample of the data to insure the validity of the scoring in the context of the theme. In addition, the "leftover lists" (words appearing in the text, but not in the dictionary) were checked against the text, and all relevant items were scored by hand.

FINDINGS

The documents analyzed lend strong support to the hypothesis. They also corroborate the assertions by a number of scholars that some aspects of the Sino-Soviet dispute, which was clearly public by 1963, have their roots in the 1950's; Zagoria begins his analysis in 1956, whereas two other recent studies date the conflict from 1958.[20]

During periods of high East-West tension, Soviet and Chinese documents reveal consistently similar perceptions. The American decision to resist the invasion of South Korea brought forth unequivocal denunciation from both the Soviet Union and China. The period of the Bay of Pigs invasion was marked by an absence of censure by Soviet and Chinese leaders regarding the policies of each other, and during the initial days of the missile crisis, in October 1962, both Chinese and Albanian criticism of Soviet policy ceased. Despite two years of increasingly vocal disagreement, the responses from Moscow and Peking to the bombing of North Vietnam revealed few differences.[21] The content analysis data disclose that, during all four crisis periods, Chinese and Soviet attitudes toward American policy were quite similar; both perceived the United States predominantly on the negative, strong, and active ends of the evaluative, potency, and activity dimenisons. The raw scores on the three dimensions for the eight periods are given in Table 11–1, and are converted into percentages for Figure 11–I. These data indicate clearly that Soviet and Chinese perceptions of American policy converged during the periods of intense inter-bloc conflict over Korea, Cuba, and Vietnam.

On the other hand, sharp differences between China and the Soviet Union arose during periods marked by a more relaxed international atmosphere. While Premier Khrushchev was visiting the United States in 1959, the Chinese did not directly denounce the Soviet leader or his policies. Attacks against American conduct were stepped up, however, with a warning that "the imperialists will never give up their policy of war and aggression of their own accord," intimating that accommodation with the West should be avoided.[22] At the same time, compared with Chinese statements, the Soviet documents revealed vastly different perceptions of the United States, particularly along the evaluative dimension.

During October 1962, initial Chinese support for the Soviet Union in regard to the offensive missiles in Cuba did not survive the *détente* which brought the immediate crisis to an end. Direct analysis of the documents (geared to an assessment of each other by Chinese and Soviet leaders) reveals far less of the disagreement than the comparison of their attitudes toward the United States. After the Kennedy-Khrushchev agreement of October 28, for example, *Jen-min Jih-pao* editorialized that "The people of the world cannot under any circumstances lightly put their trust

TABLE 11–1. SOVIET AND CHINESE PERCEPTIONS OF UNITED STATES POLICY—
WEIGHTED (FREQUENCY × INTENSITY) TOTALS

	USSR							
	June 28–29, 1950	July 17–19, 1955	Sept. 15–25, 1959	April 12–25, 1961	Oct. 22–25, 1962	Oct. 26–31, 1962	July 25– Aug. 5 1963	Feb. 8, 1965
Positive	7	18	754	39	23	61	10	6
Negative	49	2	226	211	258	80	10	104
Strong	87	6	746	279	359	126	35	135
Weak	3	2	117	27	16	25	3	3
Active	76	4	530	264	289	159	21	139
Passive	10	7	242	63	53	50	5	2
	CHINA							
Positive	16	16	31	125	3	27	86	1
Negative	157	53	70	1196	269	1040	774	125
Strong	120	93	140	1055	243	816	675	116
Weak	2	7	11	81	17	63	20	2
Active	142	38	114	954	216	818	499	115
Passive	8	0	21	75	18	75	59	2

in the empty promises of United States aggressors," implying that Premier Khrushchev had done so. The same editorial went on to praise Fidel Castro for the "justified and absolutely necessary" opposition to the on-site inspection agreed to by the United States and Soviet Union.

Subsequent developments have confirmed the thesis that the Kennedy-Khrushchev agreement with respect to the missiles in Cuba was a major irritant in the relations between Moscow and Peking. Within weeks after the immediate crisis had passed, differences regarding the settlement in Cuba became more pronounced. The *Jen-min Jih-pao* editorial of November 18 stated that "It is pure nonsense to say that 'peace has been saved by withdrawing Soviet missiles.' " *Pravda*, on the other hand, editorialized that "Neither bourgeois propagandists nor other falsifiers can conceal the main fact that Soviet policy saved world peace and preserved the Cuban revolutionary movement."[23] In a report presented by Mikhail Suslov to the plenary meeting of the Central Committee of the CPSU on February 14, 1964, the following charge was made against China:

> The Chinese leaders tried to paralyze the efforts that the USSR and other socialist countries were making to turn back the menace of world

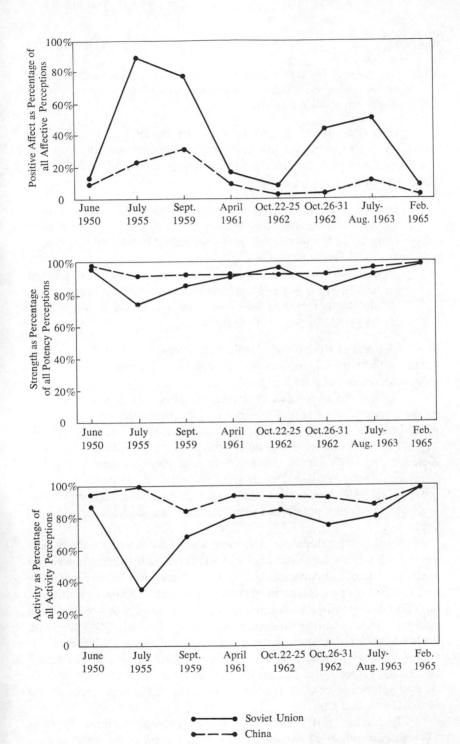

FIGURE 11–I. *Soviet and Chinese Perceptions of the United States*

war. Even at the very moment when the Cuban crisis was at its most intense point, the Chinese Government extended the armed conflict on the Sino-Indian frontier.[24]

Since July 1963, the rift between the Soviet Union and China clearly has been brought out into the open. Documents from the Test Ban Treaty period reveal little of the former reticence against direct attack. For example, the Chinese charged:

> The people of the world can draw only one conclusion. They [Soviet leaders] have betrayed the interests of the Soviet people and of all countries in the world, and have raised their hands and surrendered to United States imperialism.[25]
>
>   Incontrovertible facts show that the Soviet government has sold out the interest of the Soviet people and the interests of the people of the socialist camp, including the Chinese people, and the interests of the people living throughout the world.[26]

The Soviet replies were equally polemical. Premier Khrushchev charged Peking with "political irresponsibility" and lack of respect for the "sovereignty of the Soviet state."

To test the hypothesis regarding the effects of inter-bloc tension on the convergence of Sino-Soviet perceptions, the data have been aggregated into the situations of high and low East-West conflict in Table 11–2. The results indicate that during the peak periods of the crises over Korea, Cuba, and Vietnam, differences in perceptions of American policy were consistently smaller than those of the other three periods. During times of high inter-bloc tension, both Soviet and Chinese decision-makers perceived American policy as overwhelmingly negative, strong, and active.

In the other three periods, there was a considerable divergence. Table 11–2 reveals the existence of wider differences between Chinese and Soviet perceptions of American policy during times of relatively low inter-bloc conflict along all three dimensions. For example, under conditions of high East-West tension, both Chinese and Soviet perceptions of American policy on the evaluative dimension were approximately 90% negative. With more relaxed relations between the East and the West, however, the figures for negative affect were 27.6% and 92.4% for the Soviet Union and China, respectively. The results thus support the hypothesis that decreased inter-bloc conflict tended to increase differences between the Soviet Union and China.

Inspection of the data also reveals another pattern: Whereas Chinese perceptions of American policy are marked by little change, irrespective of the state of the cold war, those of Soviet leaders have

TABLE 11–2.   DIFFERENCES IN SOVIET AND CHINESE PERCEPTIONS OF
THE UNITED STATES DURING PERIODS OF HIGH AND
LOW EAST-WEST TENSION

HIGH INTER-BLOC CONFLICT (June 1950; April 1961; Oct. 22–25, 1962; Feb. 1965)		LOW INTER-BLOC CONFLICT (July 1955; Sept. 1959; Oct. 26–31, 1962; July–Aug. 1963)	
	USSR	CHINA		USSR	CHINA

	USSR	CHINA		USSR	CHINA
Positive	75 (10.8%)	145 (7.7%)	Positive	843 (72.4%)	160 (7.6%)
Negative	622 (89.2%)	1747 (92.3%)	Negative	318 (27.6%)	1937 (92.4%)
Strong	860 (94.6%)	1534 (93.8%)	Strong	913 (86.1%)	1724 (94.5%)
Weak	49 (5.4%)	102 (6.2%)	Weak	147 (13.9%)	101 (5.5%)
Active	768 (85.7%)	1427 (93.3%)	Active	714 (70.1%)	1479 (90.0%)
Passive	128 (14.3%)	103 (6.7%)	Passive	304 (29.9%)	165 (10.0%)

Because the data in Tables 11–2 and 11–3 are based on a weighted (frequency × intensity) score, rather than frequency alone, the chi-square test of statistical significance cannot be used. It is clear from the table, however, that differences between China and the Soviet Union increase during periods of low East-West tension.

tended to be more sensitive to international events. This pattern is not, however, inconsistent with the hypothesis that cohesion (as indexed by similarity of attitudes) varies systematically with the level of inter-bloc conflict. Indeed, it may support the theory that Chinese inflexibility (in the eyes of Soviet elites) and Soviet "softness" (as seen by Chinese leaders) with respect to the United States is one source of the conflict between Moscow and Peking. If so, one would expect such differences to become more salient at both the doctrinal and policy levels when tensions between blocs decline.

Further evidence of the growing differences between China and the Soviet Union is indicated in their attitudes toward the Nuclear Test Ban Treaty. Content analysis of the documents reveals the degree to which the Chinese leaders—who characterized the treaty as a "dirty fraud" and as "a United States-Soviet alliance against China, pure and simple"[27]— differed with the Soviets in regard to the treaty (Table 11–3).

TABLE 11–3. CHINESE AND SOVIET PERCEPTIONS OF THE TEST BAN TREATY,
JULY-AUGUST 1963

	USSR	CHINA
Positive	256	26
	(98.5%)	(31.3%)
Negative	4	57
	(1.5%)	(68.7%)
Strong	209	77
	(80.7%)	(74.8%)
Weak	50	26
	(19.3%)	(25.2%)
Active	161	57
	(49.8%)	(64.8%)
Passive	162	31
	(50.2%)	(35.2%)

Tables 11–2 and 11–3 also indicate that differences between the Soviet Union and China under conditions of high and low tension are registered most clearly along the evaluative dimension. That is, both Chinese and Soviet leaders perceived the United States as strong and active—although in differing proportions—rather than as weak and passive under *both* conditions of intercoalition conflict. Under conditions of low tension, however, Chinese and Soviet perceptions of the United States are on the opposite ends of the evaluative dimension. This result supports other studies that have disclosed the primacy of the evaluative dimension.[28]

SUMMARY AND CONCLUSION

The purpose of this chapter has been to demonstrate the use of automated content analysis in the study of international relations "at a distance." The hypothesis that a high level of intercoalition conflict tends to increase intracoalition unity, whereas more relaxed relations between blocs tend to magnify differences within the alliance, was examined in the context of Sino-Soviet relations. Eighty-four documents written by leading Chinese and Soviet decision-makers in eight periods during the years 1950–1965 were content analyzed through the Stanford version of the "General Inquirer" on the IBM 7090.

The results indicated that during the peak period of the crises over Korea, Cuba, and Vietnam, both Chinese and Soviet perceptions of American policy were overwhelmingly on the negative, strong, and active ends of the evaluative, potency, and activity dimensions. During the four periods of lower East-West tension, differences between Chinese and Soviet perceptions were greater than in the high tension periods on all three dimensions.

Although the data lend strong support to the hypothesis examined here, it seems advisable to interpret the results with great caution. It would be particularly hazardous to conclude that other factors—such as those of personality, ideology, or domestic politics—play no significant role in the relations between China and the Soviet Union. Specifically, the high degree of consensus between Moscow and Peking regarding American policy in Vietnam does not preclude the existence of other factors which might prevent a Sino-Soviet reconciliation. Indeed, neither the mutual escalation of the Vietnam war between February 1965 and March 1968, nor the Soviet-led invasion of Czechoslovakia, events which have clearly raised tensions between the Eastern and Western blocs, appears to have changed the basically antagonistic relations between Peking and Moscow. A more tenable conclusion might be that East-West tension may be a necessary, but is not a sufficient, condition for Sino-Soviet cohesion.

Whether even this limited interpretation of the findings is applicable to other contexts is, of course, a question for further research. A parallel study of the effects of East-West tensions on cohesion within NATO, for example, would shed further light on the generalizability of the findings presented in this paper.[29]

NOTES

1. James N. Rosenau, "Pre-Theories and Theories of Foreign Policy," in R. Barry Farrell (ed.), *Approaches to Comparative and International Politics* (Evanston: Northwestern University Press, 1966), pp. 27–92.
2. Richard C. Snyder, H. W. Bruck, and Burton Sapin, *Foreign Policy Decision Making* (New York: The Free Press, 1962), p. 212.
3. Richard C. Snyder and Glenn Paige, "The United States Decision to Resist Aggression in Korea," *Administrative Science Quarterly*, III (1958), 341–78.
4. Alan Whiting, *China Crosses the Yalu* (New York: Macmillan, 1960); also see Sergius Yakobson and Harold D. Lasswell, "Trend: May Day Slogans in Soviet Russia," in Harold D. Lasswell *et al.* (eds.), *Language of Politics* (New York: George E. Stewart, 1949); Nathan C. Leites and Ithiel de Sola Pool, "Interaction: The Response of Communist Propaganda to Frustration," in Lasswell *et al.*, *Language of Politics;*

and Nathan C. Leites, Elsa Bernaut, and Raymond Garthoff, "Politburo Images of Stalin," *World Politics,* III (1951), 317–39.

5. Harold D. Lasswell, Daniel Lerner, and Ithiel de Sola Pool, *The Comparative Study of Symbols* (Stanford: Stanford University Press, 1952), p. 62.

6. Bernard Berelson, *Content Analysis in Communication Research* (Glencoe: The Free Press, 1952), p. 198. For further discussion of these problems, see Lasswell *et al., Language of Politics;* Ithiel de Sola Pool (ed.), *Trends in Content Analysis* (Urbana: University of Illinois Press, 1959); and Ole R. Holsti, with Joanne K. Loomba and Robert C. North, "Content Analysis," in Gardner Lindzey and Elliot Aronson (eds.), *The Handbook of Social Psychology* (2nd ed.; Reading, Mass.: Addison-Wesley, 1968).

7. Philip J. Stone, Robert F. Bales, J. Zvi Namenwirth, and Daniel M. Ogilvie, "The General Inquirer: A Computer System for Content Analysis and Retrieval Based on the Sentence as a Unit of Information," *Behavioral Science,* VII (1962), 484–98; see also Stone *et al., "The General Inquirer."*

8. Ole R. Holsti, "An Adaptation of the 'General Inquirer' for the Systematic Analysis of Political Documents," *Behavioral Science,* IX (1964), 382–88; Anne Armour, "A Balgol Program for Quantitative Format in Automated Content Analysis" (Stanford University: Studies in International Conflict and Integration, 1964); and, Ole R. Holsti, *Content Analysis for the Social Sciences and the Humanities* (Reading. Mass.: Addison-Wesley, 1969), pp. 164–90.

9. Charles E. Osgood, George Suci, and Percy H. Tannenbaum, *The Measurement of Meaning* (Urbana: University of Illinois Press, 1957); see also Charles E. Osgood, "Studies on the Generality of Affective Meaning Systems," *American Psychologist,* XVII (1962), 10–28.

10. Leighton found a similar phenomenon among groups in Japanese relocation camps during World War II, as did Grinker and Spiegel in their study of cohesion among bomber crews. Alexander Leighton, *The Governing of Men* (Princeton: Princeton University Press, 1945); and Roy R. Grinker and J. P. Spiegel, *Men Under Stress* (Philadelphia: Blakiston, 1945). See also Dorwin Cartwright and Alvin Zander, *Group Dynamics* (Evanston: Row Peterson and Co., 1956), 73–134; Robert R. Blake and Jane S. Mouton, "The Intergroup Dynamics of Win-Lose Conflict and Problem-Solving Collaboration in Union-Management Relations," in Muzafer Sherif (ed.), *Intergroup Relations and Leadership* (New York: John Wiley and Sons, Inc., 1962); Raymond W. Mack and Richard C. Snyder, "The Analysis of Social Conflict—Toward an Overview and Synthesis," *Journal of Conflict Resolution,* I (1957), 212–48; and Lewis A. Coser, *The Functions of Social Conflict* (Glencoe: The Free Press, 1956).

11. Edward Crankshaw, *The New Cold War: Moscow v. Peking* (Baltimore: Penguin, 1963), p. 7. For a further discussion of this point, see the introduction to Zagoria's analysis of recent Sino-Soviet relations. Donald S. Zagoria, *The Sino-Soviet Conflict, 1956–1961* (Princeton: Princeton University Press, 1962).

12. "This Chinese Communist assessment of the likelihood, desirability, and criteria of peaceful coexistence was clearly at variance with the Soviet

view that there was no alternative to coexistence but war and that 'realistic' and 'sober' American circles were beginning to understand that." Zagoria, *Sino-Soviet Conflict,* p. 242.

"The Chinese rejected all three explanations of Soviet coexistence tactics: that nuclear weapons left no other choice but a more moderate approach to the West, that the Bloc could ultimately triumph with a minimum of revolutionary violence, and that it was necessary to pursue Bloc aims with a maximum of flexibility." *Ibid.,* p. 304.

13. Theodore M. Newcomb, "The Study of Consensus," in Robert K. Merton *et al.* (eds.), *Sociology Today* (New York: Basic Books, Inc., 1959), p. 279.

14. Fritz Heider, "Attitudes and Cognitive Organization," *Journal of Psychology,* XXI (1946), 107–12. Also, see Theodore M. Newcomb, "An Approach to the Study of Communicative Acts," *Psychological Review,* LX (1953), 393–404; Charles E. Osgood and Percy H. Tannenbaum, "The Principle of Congruity in the Prediction of Attitude Change," *Psychological Review,* LXII (1955), 42–55; Leon Festinger, *A Theory of Cognitive Dissonance* (Evanston: Row Peterson and Co., 1957); and Milton J. Rosenberg, Carl I. Hovland, William J. McGuire, Robert P. Abelson, and Jack W. Brehm, *Attitude Organization and Change* (New Haven: Yale University Press, 1960).

15. Robert P. Abelson, "Modes of Resolution of Belief Dilemmas," *Journal of Conflict Resolution,* III (1959), 343–52.

16. The division of the missile crisis into two periods at October 25–26 is based on an earlier study: Ole R. Holsti, Richard A. Brody, and Robert C. North, "Measuring Affect and Action in International Reaction Models: Empirical Materials from the 1962 Cuban Crisis," *Peace Research Society, Papers II* (1965), 170–90. This division of the crisis period corresponds to the turning back of the Soviet ships which had been headed for Cuba, the first indication that violence on the high seas might be avoided. For the purposes of this chapter, the first (June 1950), fourth (April 1961), fifth (October 22–25, 1962), and eighth (February 1965) periods are considered to be those of high inter-bloc conflict. The other four periods—highlighted by Soviet-American negotiations at Camp David, the Geneva Conference, the settlement of the missile crisis, and the Test Ban Treaty—are those of lower international tension.

17. For example, during the Cuban missile crisis, every available document written by Premier Khrushchev, Foreign Minister Gromyko, Defense Minister Malinovsky, and Ambassador Zorin was coded and analyzed. In addition, certain unsigned editorials appearing in authoritative organs of government policy, such as the Chinese newspapers *Jen-min Jih-pao* and *Red Flag,* have been included. For the 1950, 1955, and 1965 cases the initial radio commentaries were used.

18. A small second dictionary serves to cross-reference all proper names, permitting references to "Washington" and "United States" to be retrieved together, if desired.

19. The dictionary actually consists of about 3600 word stems—words with regular endings such as *e, s, es, ed,* and *ing* removed. Thus the working capacity of the dictionary is probably closer to 10,000 words.

20. Zagoria, *Sino-Soviet Conflict;* Crankshaw, *New Cold War,* p. 8; and

David Floyd, *Mao Against Khrushchev* (New York: Praeger, 1963), p. 67.

21. A study of the Korean and Vietnam crises has shown a high degree of consensus among nine members of the Communist system (the Soviet Union, China, Albania, East Germany, Poland, Hungary, Romania, Bulgaria, and Czechoslovakia) to both events; on the other hand, during the more relaxed periods of the Geneva Conference of 1955 and the signing of the Test Ban Treaty, the level of consensus dropped sharply. P. Terry Hopmann, "International Conflict and Cohesion in the Communist System," *International Studies Quarterly,* XI (1967), 212–36.

22. Zagoria, *Sino-Soviet Conflict,* p. 242.

23. Quoted in Floyd, *Mao,* p. 325.

24. Quoted in Alain Joxe, "La crise cubaine de 1962—Entraînement contrôlé vers la dissuasion réciproque," *Strategie,* I (1964), 85.

25. Kuo Mo-jo, New China News Agency Broadcast, August 1, 1963.

26. *Jen-min Jih-pao,* July 27, 1963.

27. Unsigned editorials, *Peking Review,* July 30, 1963, and *Jen-min Jih-pao,* July 27, 1963.

28. Osgood, "Studies on the Generality of Affective Meaning Systems." Also, see Sheldon G. Levy and Robert Hefner, "Multi-dimensional Scaling of International Attitudes," *Peace Research Society, Papers I* (1964), 129–65.

29. Such a study is being undertaken by P. Terry Hopmann at the University of Minnesota.

TWELVE

SOVIET OPENNESS TO CHANGING SITUATIONS: A CRITICAL EVALUATION OF CERTAIN HYPOTHESES ABOUT SOVIET FOREIGN POLICY BEHAVIOR

RICHARD A. BRODY
JOHN F. VESECKY

Almost as old as the October Revolution itself are attempts to account for the behavior of the nation born in that upheaval;[1] but this long line of shared interest has not produced a shared conceptual framework within which Soviet behavior can be viewed.[2] Outside of some agreement on the proposition that the Soviet Union is a unique phenomenon—in a class by itself—there is little common ground among schools of Soviet studies. These "schools" differ particularly as to their choice of factors explaining Soviet behavior.

One might expect to find more agreement on the factors accounting for Soviet foreign policy—in contradistinction to domestic policy—because of reduced independence of nations acting in the international realm. But systems of explaining Soviet international behavior are more polymorphous than those applied to domestic policy. Consider, for example, the variety of factors listed by Triska:

> . . . Some authors have considered Marxist philosophy the key; others have stressed the over-all significance of Soviet ideology; still others claim that Soviet foreign policy represents simply a continuation of Russian nationalism, traditionalism, and imperialism; the theory of bureaucratic tyranny has been advanced in several variants; the Byzantium theory of Russian-Western conflict explains Soviet foreign policy in terms of its inherent antagonism towards the West; the need for security or the necessity for expansion is another rationale; and geo-

graphical location, Asiatic influence and heritage, urge to the sea, Gorer's swaddling hypothesis, social psychological explanations of "national character," and many other theories have been developed to clarify, explain, and interpret Soviet foreign policy, either by themselves or in combination with others.[3]

When one adds to this list factors hypothesized—by theorists of international politics who do not single out the Soviet Union as a special case—as affecting any nation's foreign policy,[4] the task of sorting among alternative plausible explanations of Soviet behavior becomes extremely complex. The complexity emerges from the fact that the "factors" involved in the single-factor explanations are palpably true of the Soviet Union—there *is* an ideology (or ideologies), a Russian past, a geographical position, a nation with a leadership position in the cold war, and so forth. Nevertheless, the obvious presence of these factors does not guarantee their influence on Soviet policy; to argue that it does is to commit the logical fallacy *"post hoc, ergo propter hoc."*

The problem comes down to this: Although many social scientists are loath to acknowledge it, as scientists we are engaged in discovering causes of—in this case, Soviet—foreign policy behavior. We are offered numerous competing models which purport to explain the phenomenon, but crucial experiments (which would provide a means of choosing between models) are by and large missing. This is a very familiar problem in the history of science; the attempt to solve it supplies the dynamic underlying the growth in scientific knowledge.

Professor Platt's idealization of scientific method, which he calls "strong inference,"[5] depends upon the very presence of competing plausible explanations and the creation of empirical tests for choosing among them; the approximation of this ideal can serve the social scientist no less than the physical scientist.

This paper proceeds with Platt's model as an outline. We will, at the outset, offer competing hypotheses about the roots of Soviet behavior, which have been drawn from the literature on Soviet international politics and international politics in general. We will then confront these formulations with three empirical studies of Soviet openness to change in an attempt to choose among alternative explanations.

A SURVEY OF HYPOTHESES ABOUT SOVIET FOREIGN POLICY BEHAVIOR

Social scientists' assertions are not always easy to reconstruct in terms of standard logical formats, and the assertions of Soviet specialists do not violate this norm. For certain purposes, such reconstruction would be indispensable, for example, to ascertain the consistency among the elements of a theory,[6] but our aim here can be served as well by allowing these specialists to speak for themselves.

We have gathered these hypotheses and counterhypotheses into four substantive domains (ideology, nationhood, history, and geography) and ordered them within domains from least to most specific. While many Soviet specialists are represented here, many are not; we feel, however, that, in sum, the statements presented here give a fair picture of the state of theorizing about Soviet foreign policy behavior.

1. Hypotheses about the impact of ideology on Soviet policy.[7]

1.1: [Although] it is sometimes argued that Communist ideology has now ceased to possess any importance . . . such unqualified assertions are erroneous.[8]

1.2: . . . At the least there are presuppositions and influences of . . . ideology which distinguish Soviet foreign policy from that of a state merely seeking power.[9]

1.3: . . . In Moscow . . . policies are shaped by basic Marxist assumptions.[10]

1.4: Marxist-Leninist-Stalinist ideology plays an extremely important role in determining the direction and motivation of Soviet foreign policy. . . .[11]

1.5: Certainly, the leaders shape and phrase their domestic and foreign policies to fit the general framework established by [theoretical principles that distinguish communist regimes from other forms of dictatorship], and the latter often do not allow much room for maneuver.[12]

1.6: . . . Soviet Communists are impelled by—and limited by —ideological considerations. . . .[13]

1.7: Ideology . . . plays a more important role in influencing the foreign policies of closed societies [for example, the Soviet Union] than it does in open societies.[14]

1.8: The closed system decision-maker is . . . to some extent a prisoner of dogma—dogma which has precepts about foreign policy or of relevance to foreign policy; dogma which is only to a very limited degree susceptible to questioning about its utility and factual relationship to changing world conditions.[15]

We also found the following counterhypotheses about the role of ideology:

1.9: . . . In the cold war between the Soviet and the United States . . . it is easy to exaggerate the role of the ideo-

logical conflict. Russia and America are two very great
powers; and great powers have always been a threat to
each other's security and vital interest, even where no
ideological hatred was involved.[16]

1.10: . . . The transcendental goal of world revolution was
subordinated to the security and power interests of the
Soviet state during Stalin's lifetime [and thereafter].[17]

2. Hypotheses about the impact of Soviet nationhood on its policy.

In one sense, the propositions emphasizing the importance of
Soviet nationhood all stand as counterhypotheses to those emphasizing
ideology; hypothesis 1.9, above, is typical of these. This is the case because the theorists emphasizing nationhood root Soviet policy in her power
and the "realities" of the international situation. The ideology of nations
so conceived is "power enhancement," which is shared by all states (according to the theory), irrespective of the rhetoric (for instance, Marxism-
Leninism) in which it is couched. According to Arnold Wolfers, "[for
theorists of this persuasion] States are conceived of as the sole actors in
the international arena. . . . They constitute a multistate system. . . . All
the units of the system behave essentially in the same manner; their goal
is to enhance if not maximize their power."[18]

But to justify assigning the "nationhood" hypotheses to the "coun-
terideology" category we would have had to assume that their authors
subscribed to the "realists" position; it seemed less risky to establish a
separate category.

2.1: Soviet policy, whether in spite of or because of its ideological overtones, is predominantly based upon a calculation of power.[19]

2.2: The Soviets observed those agreements when and while
it served their interests to do so, and violated them
when their interests seemed to require it. Such international amorality is by no means uniquely Soviet.[20]

2.3: . . . Communists claim a theoretical justification for the
basic principles in which they believe. But these principles must be translated into appropriate action; and
action, if directed by the rulers of a powerful country
like the Soviet Union, will take the form of *Real-
politik*.[21]

2.4: . . . The policy-makers of the Soviet Union act in what
they believe to be the best interests of the state over
whose destinies they are presiding. . . . The Soviet Union

is an actor, a protagonist, on the stage of international politics. . . . Its actions can be interpreted most fruitfully in terms of behavior *germane* to the practice of international politics.[22]

2.5: . . . The pursuit of ultimate [Soviet] goals has been circumscribed in time and scope by considerations of the *feasible*.[23]

2.6: The foreign policy of any country, the Soviet Union included, is not . . . simply the sum total of its avowed intentions. . . . In order to draw a proper appraisal of Soviet diplomacy at any given time, the voluntaristic aspects of Soviet foreign policy must always be measured against the power to overcome the deterministic impediments of international reality.[24]

2.7: . . . Soviet expectations of political gains depend in part on Soviet military posture. . . . Only minimal gains can be expected from minimal posture. . . . Soviet attention is not simply a function of the intensity of their attachment to their ultimate political objectives. Technological opportunities and constraints, U. S. military policy, and competing demands for economic resources enter into the equation.[25]

2.8: The fundamental Soviet objective which determines political and military strategies may be concisely summarized in one: Advance the power of the Soviet Union in whatever ways are most expedient so long as the survival of Soviet power itself is not endangered.[26]

We also found the following counterhypotheses about the impact of Soviet nationhood:

2.9: . . . Actions [of Soviet leaders] proved that they were quite ready to sacrifice Russian strengths and interests to promote Bolshevik [that is, ideological] successes elsewhere.[27]

2.10: The Communist movement cannot and must not be identified with Russia, even though it uses Russia as its chief instrument of power. What confronts us in the present conflict is not the nation Russia with its power interests, but rather a militant enterprise with a revolutionary design of destruction. This design creates a political interest of its own, an interest not merely in the reduction of power of other nations, in the change of boundaries and spheres of influence, but beyond this in the disintegration and destruction of Western society

as an order of life. This is not merely the ultimate objective, but also an operational objective of Communist
conflict management.[28]

3. History as a determinant of Soviet foreign policy.

3.1:   Most Russian statesmen and diplomats are deeply affected by the antique Russian tradition, a product of
history and environment, of, when in doubt, pushing
outwards along the line of least resistance to infinity—
until continued progress becomes manifestly dangerous.[29]

3.2:   . . . Russia was . . . put, by an autocratic ruler, through
a forced march to catch up with Western technology that
had [for the third time] shot ahead of hers. . . . This renewal of the technological race is another of the very
serious difficulties now besetting the relations between
these two ex-Christian societies.[30]

As counterhypotheses we were able to find the following:

3.3:   . . . Pre-revolutionary Russian imperialism was essentially no different from the imperialism of other great
powers. . . . [The] identity between pre-revolutionary
and Soviet foreign policy [is illusory].[31]

3.4:   . . . Pre-Communist Russian policy, in contrast to Soviet
diplomacy, had no global *aims.* It did not have these
because it possessed no *all-embracing political plan,* with
an *over-all* idea underlying it. The idea of world revolution underlies an all-embracing Soviet plan, contained in
the body of literature the Communists call Marxism-
Leninism-Stalinism. The Tsars had no such aims or
plan.[32]

4. Hypotheses emphasizing geographical determinants.

4.1:   . . . The Heartland position has granted to the Soviet
Union [extremely important political assets]—the ability which the Soviet Union possesses to influence and
manipulate its neighbors for political ends short of war.[33]

4.2:   Russia's geographical propinquity to . . . areas of [polit-
ical] instability and [power] vacuum has been of im-
mense service to her political goals.[34]

4.3:   . . . There exists a political aspect to the Heartland concept . . . [which] derives from the fact that Russia possesses a common frontier with a score of nations situated

in the turbulent and explosive rimland. The precise political advantage . . . varies from region to region, but it nevertheless constitutes a major weapon in Russia's outward expansion.[35]

4.4: . . . Geography is . . . the most permanent conditioning factor in a country's foreign policy; for location, topography, and natural resources are significant—and often decisive—determinants of a country's economic and military power.[36]

As a counterhypothesis we found the following:

4.5: [With respect to the Soviet Union] the formation of geopolitical laws is not possible.[37]

Before turning to our attempt to shed critical light on some of these hypotheses, it is necessary to draw out of these four postures[38] the implications for the dependent variable under consideration—Soviet openness to changing situations. Of each of the postures, we will query assertions about the nature and extent of rigidity or openness to change.

With varying degrees of emphasis, those who single out ideology agree that Soviet decision-makers respond in terms of a relatively rigid set of predispositions or assumptions.[39] Soviet responses are said to be "shaped" (H1.3, H1.5),[40] "influenced" (H1.2, H1.7), "impelled" (H1.6), "determined" (H1.4) by principles which leave "little room for maneuver" (H1.5). If these hypotheses are true, then it cannot be true that Soviet leaders respond differentially to different American administrations (which publicly are assigned to the same category, Imperialist) nor could it be true that Soviet leaders exhibit rapid attitude change in situations where American policy behavior is changing.

Those who emphasize the impact of nationhood would not deny a general rigidity to Soviet (or any nation's) motivation but the rigidity would derive from concern over "power" (H2.1), "security" (H2.8), and "interest" (H2.2, H2.4). However, this rigidity does not extend uniformly to behavior and attitudes. It would not be incompatible with the realist posture to predict Soviet behavioral changes in response to changes in the United States' administration, but the tenor of these assertions would not lead one to predict rapid changes in attitude in response to changes in behavior. The realist asserts that national leaders hold uniformly negative or unaffective views of other nations—attitude is simply not a variable. Thus, while it would be true that nations would change their behavior, it would not be true (in accordance with the theory) that attitude changes would take place.

The differences in time-scales between the hypotheses based on historical factors and the studies we carried out preclude any confrontation between them. Whether the fluctuations we unearthed are or are not contained within a more general historical trend is a question upon which our data will shed no light.

The hypotheses emphasizing geographical factors, presented above, are not representative of what the Sprouts call "environmental determinism" which "hypothesizes an invariable correlation between some set of environmental 'causes' and environing 'effects' ";[41] rather, they belong to the orientation the Sprouts identify as "environmental possibilism," which holds that "the milieu . . . is . . . a sort of matrix which limits the operational results of whatever is attempted."[42] Geographical factors, so conceived, become part of the power equation (H4.4) and are logically antecedent to the nationhood hypotheses; they would have to be combined with these hypotheses before they would yield falsifiable propositions about openness to change.

One other theory of openness to changing situations can be considered in view of one of the studies to follow, L. F. Richardson's model of "arms and insecurity."[43] Richardson's basic premise in the description of an arms race (one type of response situation) was originally given in a pamphlet written by Bertrand Russell in 1914.[44] Russell's contention was that in the period prior to World War I, the motives of the two sides were essentially the same, that is, each side was afraid of the other; and it was fear (perceived provocative threat) that prompted each side to increase its warlike preparations as a defense against the other. A second premise accepted by Richardson states that a high level of warlike preparation in a nation tended to restrain further increases in such preparations, for instance, as a greater and greater amount of national resources is devoted to war goods it becomes more and more difficult to gain the assent of the population to further increases. Finally, a third group of factors was considered by Richardson. He noted that there were certain factors of good will and grievance or ambition which would influence warlike preparations in addition to the other two factors.

These premises were collected (or restated) by Richardson in compact mathematical form:

$$\frac{dx}{dt} = ky - \alpha x + g \dots \dots \dots \dots [1]$$

$$\frac{dy}{dt} = lx - \beta y + h \dots \dots \dots \dots [2]$$

These two coupled first-order differential equations state in mathematical form that the time-rate of change of one nation's warlike preparation is equal to the sum of three factors: a term directly proportional to the warlike preparation of the opposing nation representing the perceived threat, a negative term proportional to the nation's own level of warlike preparations representing fatigue under high levels of warlike preparations, and a constant term representing grievances or ambitions (g or h greater than 0) or good will (g or h less than 0). The constants k and l are termed defense coefficients and are always positive. The constants a and β are called fatigue coefficients and are also always positive. The constants g and h are termed grievance coefficients.

For the above model, changes in behavior are responses to either changes in behavior (the warlike preparation of the other nation) or fatigue (domestic reaction to extended effort); changes in attitude (grievance) and changes in the constants a, β, k, l are not consistent with the model. In essence, Richardson's model yields the same predictions about openness to change that we are attributing to the scholars emphasizing Soviet nationhood.

We will now turn to three studies of Soviet policy in order to gauge the validity of the propositions derived from our explorations of the literature.

SOVIET MILITARY DOCTRINE: OPENNESS TO CHANGES IN TECHNOLOGY

Those who conceive of the Soviet Union as an ideological monolith have a great deal of diversity to explain away when they address themselves to Soviet military doctrine. Hanson Baldwin's contention that "Russian military thought is plainly in the process of transition, of major change"[45] is not only difficult to dispute but is a point of view which has been popular for quite a while.[46]

The debate over the correct military posture, which became public shortly after Stalin's death[47] and waxed throughout Khrushchev's regime, has yet to be settled.[48] The existence of this debate has afforded observers in the West an unusual opportunity to observe the dialectic in operation and an opportunity to discover to which aspects of reality the formation of thesis and antithesis are responsive. Our plan in this section is to recount the principal features of this debate in order to extract the sources of change.

Soviet military doctrine cannot be said to have its roots deep in the classics of Marxism-Leninism. Lenin's pronouncements on the subject cite Engels as a guide and are pragmatic in tone. Thus, in July 1905, Lenin wrote:

> No Social-Democrat at all familiar with history, who has studied Engels, the great expert on this matter, ever doubted the tremendous importance of military knowledge, the tremendous importance of military technique and military organisation as an instrument in the hands of the masses

of the people and classes of the people for deciding the issue of great historical conflicts. Social-Democracy never stooped to the game of military conspiracies, it never advanced military questions to the fore-front until the conditions of incipient civil war had arisen. But *now* all Social-Democrats have advanced military questions, if not to the very first, at least to one of the first places, and are now making it their business to study these questions. . . . The revolutionary army must employ military knowledge and military weapons in deciding the fate of the Russian people. . . .[49]

In September of the same year, he asserted a determinative role for tech-nology: "Military tactics are determined by the level of military technique [that is, technology]. . . . We can and must take advantage of improve-ments in technique. . . ."[50]

On the nature of war, Lenin was offhandedly derivative of von Clausewitz: ". . . All war is the continuation by violent means of the politics which the belligerent states and the classes that rule in them have been conducting for many years, sometimes for decades before the out-break of war. . . ."[51]

Lenin's relative silence on questions of military doctrine left the field open to Stalin, whose contribution is typified by his speech following the successful defense of Moscow (February 23, 1942). Stalin made the following points:

(a) That there are five constant factors which win wars: (i) the stabil-ity of the home front; (ii) the morale of the armed forces; (iii) the quantity and quality of divisions; (iv) the armament of the armed forces; (v) the ability of the commanders.

(b) That there are a number of non-constant temporary factors which influence the course of the war and may prolong it, but which do not affect the outcome. The most important temporary factor is strategic and tactical surprise.

(c) That Western military thought, being unable to progress because capitalism cannot develop the five constant factors to a sufficient de-gree to win a war, relies on adventuristic strategy and on temporary factors such as surprise. Therefore capitalist countries are doomed in advance to defeat in any war with the Soviet Union.

(d) That the defence policy of the Soviet leaders in peacetime should be to prepare the country for active defence, using its vast land space, that is, a planned retreat into the interior of the country which would wear down the advancing enemy. Once full mobilization had been achieved, all five constant factors would come into play and the enemy would be destroyed after a massive counter-offensive.[52]

While this speech neatly summarized the factors operating in the defense of Moscow, their elevation to the level of indisputable dogma probably handicapped the development of strategic thinking in the Soviet Union.[53]

Two comments about Stalinist doctrine seem warranted: Whatever its justification during World War II, it was substantially out of date in the nuclear era, into which it persisted, nonetheless, for almost a decade. Stalin, speaking in 1946, reaffirmed his faith in the five constants and said of nuclear weapons, "I do not believe that the atomic bomb is as serious a force as certain politicians are inclined to regard it. Atomic bombs are intended to intimidate the weak-nerved. But they cannot decide the outcome of war, since atomic bombs are by no means sufficient for this purpose."[54] It must also be noted that, its force as dogma notwithstanding, Stalin's doctrine did not preclude substantial changes in Soviet military organization and technology before 1953.[55]

The five constants outlived Stalin, the first major change in their substance coming with the substitution of Lenin as their author. But in the mid-1950's the debate over military doctrine broke open.

In 1955, Marshal Rotmistrov for the first time gave emphasis to one of the "temporary factors" (strategic surprise) and in so doing posed a challenge to Stalinist doctrine. He claimed that "it is necessary to state clearly that in certain cases of surprise aggression the use of atomic and hydrogen weapons may appear to be one of the decisive conditions for the achievement of success not only in the initial period of a war, but in the war as a whole."[56] One year after this pronouncement, Marshal Zhukov entered a note of caution into the enthusiasm over nuclear weapons, but in so doing he refined Stalinist doctrine along lines more appropriate to 1956. During his speech to the Twentieth Party Congress he asserted: "The need to have [nuclear] weapons is demanded by the interests of the Fatherland. . . . However, the importance of land forces, the navy and the tactical air force is not lessened by this. Without their joint action with the new weapons, a modern war cannot be waged successfully."[57] Zhukov included in this speech two major departures from Stalinist theory: (1) Land mass was no longer sufficient for defense; atomic weapons were needed. (2) He remarked upon the possibility of losing a war if the stated conditions were not met.

From the time of the Twentieth Party Congress, Soviet armed forces developed along the lines stressed by Marshall Zhukov, that is, the preparation for all-out nuclear war and convential war. Zhukov and other military figures continued to reformulate doctrine through a series of statements covering three points: (1) the impossibility of future large-scale war not being atomic; (2) the inherent failure in policies based on the assumption that nuclear weapons could decide the outcome of wars; and (3) the need to develop weapons for both types of war.[58]

Even with the reformulation of military doctrine along these lines, the discussion of the impact of nuclear weapons on the nature of war was not ended in the Soviet Union. On the contrary, it became a part of the internal political struggle which followed Stalin's death. Such debate over military doctrine played a part in the deposition of Malenkov, for example.[59]

Malenkov, in 1954, took what was considered, at the time, a very radical position on the mutual deterrent effect of nuclear weapons. He maintained:

> The Soviet government stands for a further reduction of international tension for a stable and lasting peace. It takes a strong stand against the policy of cold war because this policy is one of the preparations of a new world slaughter, which with the existence of modern means of destruction would mean the destruction of world civilization.[60]

Khrushchev took issue with this position. He asserted in 1954:

> We can state with full justification that the mighty camp of democracy and socialism, which unites the Soviet Union, the Chinese People's Republic, the Czechoslovak Republic, and all countries of the people's democracies, united by strong friendship, is capable of giving a worthy rebuff to the lovers of military adventures. Should the imperialists unleash a new, third world war, they will choke on it, and it will end in catastrophe for the imperialist world.[61]

Where Malenkov predicted the destruction of world civilization, Khrushchev asserted that a third world war would result in the destruction of the imperialist camp. Whether Khrushchev believed this, or whether his statement was for local consumption (as part of his struggle with Malenkov) we cannot know. In either case, he still adhered to this line as late as 1958, when he stated in *Pravda*,[62] "if the imperialists unleash another war, it will inevitably lead to the destruction of those who started it. . . ."

Since Khrushchev emerged from his struggle with Malenkov clearly in command of the political forces of the Soviet Union, one might assume that his views on military doctrine unchangingly characterized that of the Soviet government during his regime. However, this was not the case. Khrushchev, unlike Stalin, was willing to change his mind, or line, when faced with altering realities in the international environment and a changing military technology. Thus, while he stated in 1956 that "as long as capitalism survives in the world, the reactionary forces representing the interests of the capitalist monopolists will continue their drive toward military gambles in aggression and may try to unleash war,"[63] this sentiment did not continue to designate his position. In later pronouncements, Khrushchev came to accept the idea of a deterrent effect deriving from Soviet military capability. But, as of 1956, he was apparently still unconvinced of this factor. However, by 1959, Khrushchev accepted Soviet deterrence of the West; in May, he declared:

> What the imperialists fear at this time are the successes of the Soviet Union. . . . They realize that it would be folly to fight us. . . . [If] the imperialists start a war, they are threatened with inevitable disaster.[64]

It will be noted that even at this late date, Khrushchev was still restricting destruction to the Western nations. However, in 1960, when addressing himself to the hypothetical situation of the strategic position of the Soviet Union relative to the West should a capitalist country achieve parity with them in strategic missiles, he stated:

> Since the possibility is not excluded that some capitalist states may equal us in the field of modern weapons, could they not act perfidiously and strike us first to exploit the factor of surprise attack by means of such a ferocious weapon as the nuclear missile and thereby have advantages for gaining victory? No. Modern means of war give no such advantage to either side.[65]

Taken together, Khrushchev's statements of 1959 and 1960 amount to an acceptance on his part of the essence of the position held by many deterrence theorists in the United States, that the possession of a relatively invulnerable retaliatory capability will preclude the calculated selection of first strike by any potential aggressor.[66]

So far had Soviet military doctrine evolved by 1961 that General Talensky was able to voice an implicit rejection of the Leninist concept of war: "The development of the technique of exterminating people," wrote Talensky in *International Affairs* (Moscow), "has resulted in a situation which makes it impossible to resort to war as a means of solving political disputes as was done throughout the age-long history of mankind."[67] But the evolution of Soviet strategic thought did not end with this rejection of Leninist thought. Colonel Korotkov, writing in 1964, succinctly summarized the continued ferment of the early 1960's:

> Important means of activating military thought were theoretical conferences at armed forces academies and discussions on the pages of military journals. . . . Two viewpoints were brought out [in 1960–1961] on the subject and content of military science. Unfortunately, this discussion did not reach a conclusion. There is still no unified view on the subject. . . .[68]

The publication of *Military Strategy* in 1962[69] did little to stem the decade-long debate; it seems rather to have fueled it.[70]

In the course of recounting the postwar development of Soviet military doctrine, several factors have emerged as stimuli for this debate. It appears to us that technological change has been a constant challenge to Soviet doctrine and doctrinal changes have thus been the response to a changing reality—Colonel Korotkov refers to the "decisive influence" of technology.[71] However, domestic politics also appears as a factor, as do Soviet interservice rivalries. To this list must also be added responses to the development of strategic thinking in the United States.

To the extent that Soviet military doctrine relates to Soviet foreign policy, the contentions of those who emphasize the influence of Marxist-Leninist-Stalinist ideology seem to fall far short of explaining Soviet behavior. The development of military doctrine seems more responsive to factors dominant in the hypotheses of those emphasizing Soviet nationhood, but this qualitative content analysis still leaves much ambiguity; we will now turn to our second study in hopes of reducing this uncertainty.

ARMS AND INSECURITY IN THE SOVIET-AMERICAN DYAD

The great utility of a mathematical model is that it is precise to begin with, and, further, that by the application of reliable techniques precise implications can be obtained. The Richardson model, insofar as it holds true, is a valuable tool in examining hypotheses concerning Soviet foreign policy behavior. In the following sections, the Richardson model will be applied to warlike preparations in the period 1955–1964.

First, certain implications concerning stability will be drawn from the model. A discussion of the measures of warlike preparations utilized in the study is presented with the data in tabular as well as graphical form. Next, the validity of the Richardson model is discussed in light of the data and certain implications are drawn concerning stability and coefficient trends during the Eisenhower and Kennedy-Johnson administrations. Finally, the validity of the ideological and nationhood hypotheses is discussed in view of the data and conclusions are drawn.

Several rather simple, but instructive, implications follow immediately from equations (1) and (2). Consider the situations in which two rather bellicose powers face each other such that the perceived provocative threat from the opposite power is much greater than the fatigue of high armaments spending (kl is much greater than $a\beta$). Equations (1) and (2) reduce to $dx/dt = ky + g$ and $dy/dt = lx + h$. They describe a mutually stimulated runaway arms race which has often ended in war.

The most important implications of the Richardson theory for the present study concern equilibrium and stability. Equilibrium is reached when both dx/dt and dy/dt reach zero, and thus the warlike preparations of each side remain constant in time. A situation of equilibrium can be of either a stable or an unstable character. A stable equilibrium exists when a small change in x or y results only in a subsequent reestablishment of the previous equilibrium. An unstable equilibrium, on the other hand, is an equilibrium situation in which a small change in x or y tends to upset the equilibrium completely, and the warlike preparations x and y move away from the previous equilibrium point. The stable situation could be represented by a child balancing on a small rock—if the child slips off his perch, he can easily regain it—whereas the unstable situation would correspond to a tightrope walker high above the earth.

The following equations show the conditions for stable and unstable equilibrium in the Richardson model as represented by equations (1) and (2).

Stable Equilibrium: $a\beta > kl$, $g > 0$, $h > 0$ (3)
Unstable Equilibrium: $a\beta < kl$, $g > 0$, $h > 0$ (leads to a runaway
arms race)   (4)

Conditions for stability also exist when g and h are less than or equal to 0, but these cases will not be of interest in the present application of the model. These conditions, as well as a wealth of other information, are discussed by Richardson.[72]

Richardson sought to apply his model to the arms race which preceded World War I. In order to do this, he examined the warlike preparation of Germany and Austria-Hungary on one side and France and Russia on the other. These data were entered into a new equation (5), derived from equations (1) and (2), which described the relationship of the combined warlike preparations of the two alliances to the time-rate of change in that preparation. For his measure of warlike preparation, the arms expenditures of the blocs (U and V) less a constant symbolizing cooperation between the two alliances (U_0 and V_0) was used; that is, in terms of equations (1) and (2), $x = U - U_0$ and $y = V - V_0$. For convenience he let $k = 1$ and $a = \beta$. This allowed him to rewrite equations (1) and (2) with the following equation resulting:

$$\frac{d(U+V)}{dt} = (k-a)\left\{(U+V) - \left[U_0 + V_0 - \frac{g+h}{k-a}\right]\right\}$$

This expression implies that the rate of change of the combined armaments expenditures of the two sides is proportional to the level of combined armaments expenditure. Data for the years 1909–1913 was collected by Richardson and the plot shown in Figure 12–I was made.[73]

The agreement of the actual case with Richardson's theory is remarkable, indeed, and the close fit of the straight line is doubly impressive, since the vertical axis represents a difference quantity. It should be noted that the trend along the line with time is important.

A statistical measure for warlike preparations is essential for appli-

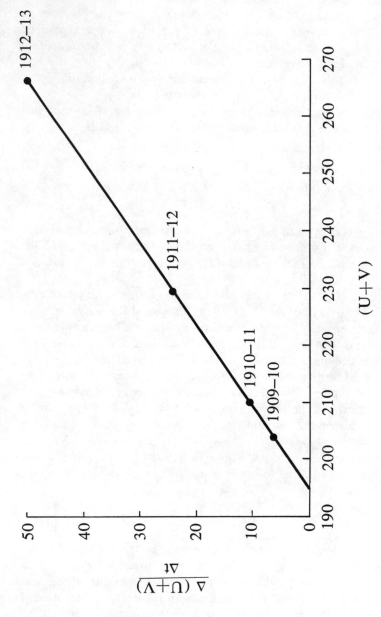

FIGURE 12–I. *The European Arms Race of 1908–1914 (after L. F. Richardson)*

cation of Richardson's theory and the credibility of the analysis rests to a considerable degree on the accuracy of the measure of warlike preparations. The measures to be considered here are defense expenditure regarded in several ways, that is, as an absolute amount, as a percentage of the total government budget, and as a percentage of the Gross National Product.

The use of defense expenditure as a measure of warlike preparations is not without its difficulties. The defense budget of the United States is well known and quite detailed. Hence, figures for the defense spending of the United States are easily obtained both in dollars as well as percentages of the total budget and the Gross National Product. On the other hand, Soviet defense spending is difficult to estimate. In fact, "one gets the strong impression from the 1964 state budget that the Soviet authorities try to render figures concerning the Soviet economy as confusing as possible."[74] One purpose of the obscure budget is to support Soviet claims as to the "peaceable character of the Soviet Government."[75] The method

TABLE 12–1. GENERAL METHOD FOR COMPUTING SOVIET
DEFENSE EXPENDITURE

Direct Defense Spending (the "defense" item in the Soviet budget)	(1)
Indirect Defense Spending (concealed in the Soviet budget)	+ (2)
Soviet Defense Expenditure	= (3)

used in this paper to estimate Soviet defense spending is a composite of the procedures used by Timothy Sosnovy[76] of the Library of Congress and Abraham Becker of RAND.[77] This method is based on the assumption that all defense expenditure is contained within the Soviet state budget either in the category for "defense" or secreted in other portions of the budget. Item (1) is the portion of the Soviet budget publicly reported to be for defense and is easily obtained over the years under consideration from Soviet public sources. Item (2), the concealed portion of defense expenditure, will be estimated by taking the sum of the military portions of various other items in the state budget.

Becker contends[78] that the indirect military outlays in the Soviet budget can be approximated by the sum of the following items: a portion of the funds devoted to "science"; a portion (from a low of 25 per cent to a high of 75 per cent) of the budgetary expenditure residual, BE (the residual obtained by subtracting all known outlays from the total budget); a portion (25 per cent to 75 per cent) of the national economy residual,

NE (unidentified outlays in the budgetary category "national economy"); and a portion (25 per cent to 75 per cent) of the industry and construction residual, IE (obtained by deducting all known outlays from the budgetary category "industry and construction"). Item (1) plus Becker's estimate of indirect defense spending above is intended to cover the following defense expenditures: military pay and subsistence, operations and maintenance, military construction, military research and development, stockpiling, nuclear energy, and a part of procurement.[79] This excludes the bulk of investment in the armaments industry which is "presumably financed by investment grants in the budget allocation to 'industry and construction' under the heading 'national economy.' "[80] Sosnovy contends that the portion of "industry and construction" utilized for defense purposes has remained approximately constant since the years 1930–1940 at 29 per cent.[81] The total estimate for item (2) will be Becker's estimate indirect defense spending plus the 29 per cent of "industry and construction" funds for defense industry. Table 12–2 illustrates the details of the Soviet defense spending calculation. The results are given in Table 12–3.

TABLE 12–2. DETAILS OF SOVIET DEFENSE SPENDING CALCULATION

Direct Defense Spending		(1)
Indirect Defense Spending		+ (2)
Science	(A)	
NE, IE, and BE Residuals	+ (B)	
Defense Industry	+ (C)	
	= (2)	
Total Soviet Defense Expenditure		= (3)

The total Soviet governmental budget figures are made public and are easily available so that Soviet defense spending as a percentage of the total state budget can be easily calculated using the estimates described above. The results and sources are given in Table 12–3.

Figures on the Soviet Gross National Product are not made public by the Soviet government and no estimates are published by Soviet economists. However, estimates are made by Western economists. These estimates vary considerably and thus the average of several compatible estimates is used to obtain a figure with which to calculate Soviet defense spending as a percent of the Gross National Product.

In none of the above calculations was any attempt made to take inflation into account. With regard to United States defense spending, compensations for inflation are available and, in fact, figures for defense spending in constant dollars are readily available.[82] However, for the Soviet Union "no adequate basis exists for an attempt to deflate the military expenditure series for price changes."[83]

TABLE 12–3. MEASURES OF WARLIKE PREPARATIONS FOR THE UNITED STATES AND THE SOVIET UNION[a]

	Defense Spending					
	Soviet Union			United States		
Year	Billions of Rubles	% of GNP	% of Budget	Billions of Dollars	% of GNP	% of Budget
1964	24.7	15.3	30.0	57.7	9.0	59.1
1963	28.4	16.7	33.0	56.9	9.7	59.8
1962	27.2	16.8	33.1	53.2	9.6	59.0
1961	30.8	19.4	40.4	49.3 (46.5)	9.5 (9.0)	58.2 (57.8)
1960	21.6	14.7	29.6	46.6	9.1	59.0
1959	21.3	15.5	30.3	46.1	9.5	58.8
1958	18.6	14.2	29.0	45.4	10.1	60.0
1957	18.2	14.8	30.0	43.8	10.0	62.4
1956	18.5	16.2	32.8	42.1	9.6	62.3
1955	18.2	17.2	33.6	40.7	9.8	62.3
1954	17.0	17.2	30.8	43.9	11.3	66.7

a. The figures in the second column for Soviet defense spending were calculated according to the method described in the text.

The Soviet Union GNP estimates were made by taking an average of several sources as follows: M. Bornstein, *Comparison of the U. S. and Soviet Economies* (Washington: Government Printing Office, 1959), p. 391; T. Sosnovy, "The Soviet Military Budget," *Foreign Affairs*, XLII, No. 3, 1964, 493; *United Nations Statistical Yearbook, 1963*, New York: Statistical Office of the United Nations Department of Economic and Social Affairs, p. 516; Joint Economics Committee, 1964, *Annual Economic Indicators for the USSR*, Washington: Government Printing Office, p. 93.

The figures for the Soviet governmental budget were ascertained as follows: 1963–64, A. S. Becker, *Soviet Military Outlays Since 1955* (Santa Monica: RAND, 1964), p. 53; 1955-62, Joint Economic Committee, *Annual Economic Indicators for the USSR* (Washington: Government Printing Office, 1964), p. 101; 1954, Joint Economic Committee, *Comparisons of the United States and Soviet Economies* (Washington: Government Printing Office, 1959), p. 398.

The figures for United States defense spending, total budget, and GNP were taken from L. B. Johnson, *The Economic Report of the President* (Washington: Government Printing Office, 1965), pp. 258, 259, and 189, respectively.

The figures in parentheses for the year 1961 are for the proposed budget of the Eisenhower administration, that is, Bureau of the Budget, *The Federal Budget in Brief for the Fiscal Year 1961* (Washington: Government Printing Office, 1962), p. 16. In cases where high and low estimates were given, an average was taken.

From the data of Table 12–3, a plot of the same type as shown in connection with the 1909–1913 arms race can be easily constructed. Such plots were made for the three measures of warlike preparations mentioned earlier and the one for absolute defense spending is shown in Figure 12–II. The other plots coincide with Figure 12–II in essential features. During the period 1955–1964, there can be no doubt that the points are far too scattered to be approximated by a single straight line. Thus, it must be concluded that *with a single set of coefficients* the Richardson model does not apply to the United States-Soviet dyad over this period. In fairness to Richardson, it must be mentioned that he made efforts to go beyond the simple theory described here and these efforts are recorded in his book *Arms and Insecurity*.

If one were to accept the notion that the Soviet-American international system is mechanistic and independent of the effects of changes in national decision-makers and the policies they pursue, then the inadequacy of the Richardson model to fit the total period 1954–1964 would preclude further consideration of it. If the opposite view is taken, that is, that national decision-makers and their defense policies influence to a great extent the American-Soviet international system, it would seem likely that the coefficients for defense, fatigue, and grievance in Richardson's model would undergo considerable change following changes in national decision-makers and possibly change slowly with time during periods in which the set of these remained constant. We might hypothesize that k, 1, a, β, g and h are factors which change slowly, if at all, when the set of national decision-makers remains constant, but undergo drastic changes following changes in national leadership. Thus, for the case at hand, this hypothesis states that changes in United States national leadership do indeed affect the mutual responsiveness in the United States-Soviet dyad.

On the Soviet side, Khrushchev came to power in 1955, displacing Malenkov, and remained in power until the latter half of 1964. In the United States, two administrations were in office; we might expect a change in coefficients with this change in administration. Since there were no major changes in national leadership (Johnson continued the Kennedy policies through 1964) during either of the periods (1955–1960) or (1961–1964) and no major wars occurred during this time, it is reasonable to assume that the long-term average values of the defense, fatigue, and grievance coefficients remained relatively constant over both periods in question. During the pre-World-War-I arms race described by the Richardson model, there was little change in national leadership. The two periods have been analyzed separately in Figure 12–II using the same method that was used by Richardson in connection with the 1909–1913 period. In addition, a straight line approximation to the points for each

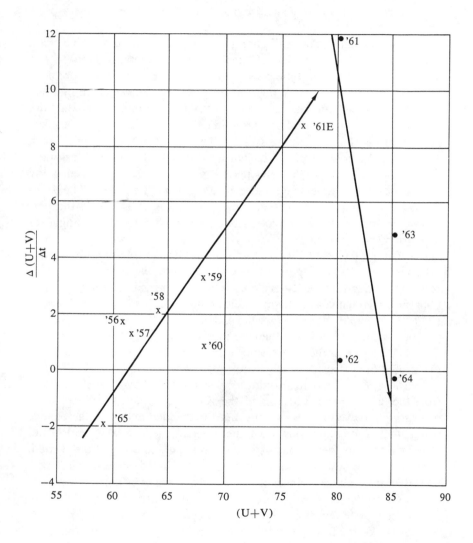

FIGURE 12–II.   *Magnitude of the Combined United States and Soviet Union Warlike Preparations vs. the Annual Change of This Magnitude (U + V vs.* $\frac{\Delta (U + V)}{\Delta t}$ *Where the Measure of Warlike Preparations is the Defense Spend-ing of the Two Powers in Rubles or Dollars*

period was made and the direction of the trend in time noted by the arrow-head on each line.

The straight line approximations drawn in the figures cannot be said to confirm the Richardson model in detail. However, there does seem to be a trend which is in general agreement with the qualitative aspects of the model.

Upon examination of Figure 12–II, one notices an unstable trend during the 1955–1961 period of the Eisenhower administration (x's in Figure 12–II); that is, as time passed, annual changes in warlike prepara-tions tended to become more positive. In terms of the Richardson model, this pattern appears to be headed for a "runaway arms race" situation. Indeed, the 1961 point is a large jump in exactly that direction. Consider-ing Figure 12–II and equations (4) and (5) the equilibrium point is seen to be unstable, in terms of the Richardson model $a\beta<kl$. (It is assumed that during the entire 1955–1964 period grievances greatly exceeded any good will in Soviet-American relations; hence, g and h are >0). The Rich-ardson model implies, then, that during the years 1955–1961, the per-ceived provocative threat on both sides was higher than the fatigue of high armaments spending.

During the years 1961–1964 of the Kennedy-Johnson administra-tion, the trend (0's in Figure 12–II) had an entirely different character. It was toward lower (more negative) annual changes in warlike prepara-tions and, eventually, a relatively stable equilibrium point. From equations (3) and (5) and Figure 12–II we have, then, $a\beta>kl$; that is, that perceived provocative threat was lower than the fatigue of high armaments spending.

It is evident, then, that some very gross changes in the nature of the United States-Soviet conflict took place with the change of adminis-tration in 1961. The detailed nature of change, however, is not evident from the data at hand. In terms of the Richardson model, the fact of kl decreasing relative to $a\beta$ is evident, but the detailed nature of the change is not, that is, it is not known whether $a\beta$ remained constant and kl de-clined, or kl remained constant and $a\beta$ rose, or both quantities varied. More detailed knowledge of behavior in the United States-Soviet dyad than that given above is necessary to answer these questions.

Given the data and the resultant coefficient trends implied by the Richardson model, what can now be said concerning openness to change on the part of the Soviet Union? In particular, what relevant comments can be made concerning the hypotheses derived from the literature? It should be noted that these comments are relevant to openness to change only insofar as it is involved with warlike preparation. While this behavior is quite important in international relations, it may follow principles dif-ferent from those accounting for other behavior, such as, trade, voting, in the UN, etc.

It is clear from the data that mutual responsiveness exists in Soviet-American relations. It is quite unlikely that Russian and American defense spending just happened by chance to fall into the form described even approximately by the Richardson model. Hence, the data imply that factors which preclude responding to change are not of first importance in the decision processes of the Soviet and American governments. Soviet leaders tend to regard United States actions as germane and they appear to act in part on the basis of those actions. The findings imply that Soviet leaders respond differently to changes in American behavior. Thus, if ideology requires the "imperialist" administrations be indistinguishable to Soviet decision-makers, then ideology has not been a dominant factor in Soviet warlike preparations.

Contrary to their inconsistency with the role of Soviet ideology, the observed differences in the coefficients of the Richardson model for the periods of the Eisenhower and Kennedy-Johnson administrations are not inconsistent with the nationhood hypotheses. The findings indicate that changes in United States leadership have an effect on the behavior exhibited jointly by the two nations. During both administrations, the pattern of warlike preparation is indicative of mutual responsiveness. Taken together, these statements argue that Soviet warlike preparation changed with the change in American leadership.

If we consider this evidence of Soviet openness to change, we must acknowledge that our evidence is found in Soviet behavior, in this case, warlike preparation. This accords with the nationhood hypotheses. What do we know about changes in Soviet attitudes which would not accord with the nationhood hypotheses? Our analysis of warlike preparation (since it assumed constant "grievances") tells us nothing about attitude change. It is to this question that we now turn.

SOVIET ATTITUDINAL RESPONSES IN THE CUBAN CRISIS[84]

The data presented in this section are designed to answer a single question: Is there evidence of changes in the attitudes of Soviet leaders toward American policy correlated with changes in American behavior?

Consider the situation where actions taken by the United States, which counter Soviet interests, decrease the positive evaluation of the United States expressed by Soviet leaders and where actions which do not counter Soviet interests increase the positive evaluation.[85] If, and only if, both these conditions are present, Soviet attitudes will be said to be "open" to American actions.

A test situation, which would permit evaluation of Soviet openness, would contain a sequence of American actions classified according to

whether or not they counter Soviet interests and expressions by Soviet
leaders from which assessments of attitudes could be derived. A segment
of the October 1962 Cuban missile crisis provides such a test situation.

The segment chosen is the seven-day period following President
Kennedy's announcement of the "quarantine" on October 22. We will be
reviewing American actions from October 22 through October 27 and
analyzing Soviet perceptions from October 23 through October 28.[86]

The following are highlights of United States actions during the
period:[87]

10/22:   United States missions abroad were notified to inform
         foreign offices of the quarantine decision.
         At 6:00 P.M., Ambassador Dobrynin was given a copy
         of the President's speech and a letter to Khrushchev.
         At 7:00 P.M., the President made public the decision.
         An airborne alert for an increased portion of Strategic
         Air Command was instituted.

10/23:   Secretary Rusk presented a resolution to the Organiza-
         tion of American States seeking authorization for the
         use of force. Secretary McNamara ordered the tours of
         duty of all Navy and Marine Corps personnel extended.
         He also revealed, later in the day, that the interception
         of twenty-five Soviet ships had been ordered.

10/24:   At 10:00 A.M., the U. S. quarantine went into effect.
         President Kennedy ordered low-level reconnaissance
         flights over Cuba.

10/25:   The U. S. Navy intercepted the Soviet tanker, *Bucharest*.
         Officials in Washington announced a rejection of U
         Thant's pleas for negotiation.
         Ambassador Stevenson issued a challenge to Soviet Am-
         bassador Zorin in the Security Council.

10/26:   Two United States destroyers halted a Soviet-chartered,
         Lebanese freighter but allowed it to proceed after search.
         Secretary Rusk convened a meeting to consider at note
         from Khrushchev.
         The President was briefed on the contents of Khrush-
         chev's note.
         14,000 air reservists were called to active duty.

10/27:   The Kennedy "no invasion in return for the removal of
         missiles" letter was delivered to the Soviet Union.

10/28:   At noon, a statement was released in which the President
         referred to Khrushchev's "statesmanlike decision."

The actions described in this summary and the other American
actions gathered in the Kunz-Osteen Chronology[88] were given to three

independent judges who were instructed to rank each of the days of the crisis on the basis of the relative level of violence of that day's total activity.[89] The rankings of the six days in question appear in Table 12–4.

TABLE 12–4. RANKINGS OF SELECTED DAYS DURING OCTOBER 1962
ON THE BASIS OF RELATIVE LEVEL OF VIOLENCE
OF TOTAL AMERICAN DAILY ACTIVITY

Day	Rank
10/22	5
10/23	4
10/24	6
10/25	3
10/26	2
10/27	1

We assume that "level of violence" is a measure of effort to counter Soviet interest. This assumption, given the nature of United States actions and the Soviet activities they were designed to thwart, seems plausible. We will now turn to an analysis of Soviet expressions in order to prepare for an answer to the question with which we began this section.

The source materials for determining Soviet evaluation of American actions are a series of ten documents produced by official Soviet spokesmen between October 23 and October 28, 1962.[90] The *verbatim* text of these documents was submitted to the General Inquirer/Stanford Political Dictionary computer content analysis program.[91] The daily profiles of Soviet perceptions of United States action generated by this content analysis appear as Figure 12–III.

The correlation of the attitude components of these daily profiles, that is, the positive and negative evaluations, with our measure of American efforts to counter Soviet interests supplies our test of Soviet responsiveness. These correlations appear in Table 12–5.

Using two different bases for computing the correlation of increases in Soviet positive evaluation with decreases in American actions countering Soviet interests, we find evidence of Soviet responsiveness. On the other hand, however, the expression of negative attitudes by Soviet leaders is less sensitive to changes in American behavior.

CONCLUSIONS

From an examination of matters related to Soviet foreign policy, in three instances, it appears that knowledge of ideology (in any of its

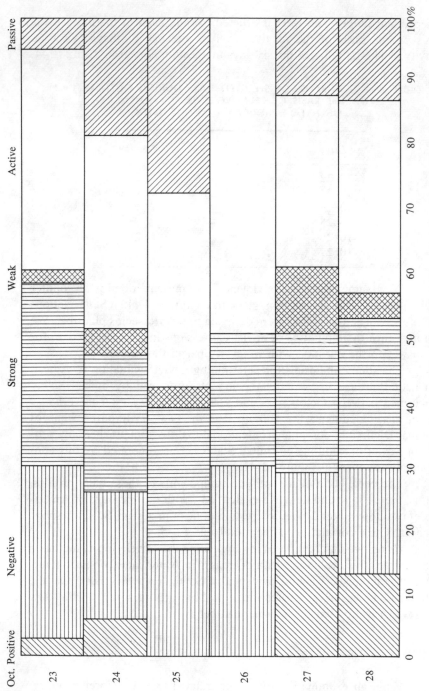

FIGURE 12–III. *Soviet Perceptions of United States Actions During the Missile Crisis*

TABLE 12–5. RANK-ORDER CORRELATIONS (r_s) OF SOVIET POSITIVE AND NEGATIVE EVALUATIVE EXPRESSIONS WITH EACH OTHER AND WITH UNITED STATES ACTIONS[a]

Relationship	r_s	N	P[b]
U. S. Actions with Soviet Positive Evaluative Expressions as a percentage of total expressions	−.73	6	.046
U. S. Actions with Soviet Positive Evaluative Expressions as a percentage of total evaluative expression	−.67	6	.064
U. S. Actions with Soviet Negative Evaluative Expressions as a percentage of total expression	+.57	6	.210
Soviet Positive Evaluative Expressions with Soviet Negative Evaluative Expressions	−.67	6	.064

a. Where correlations with U. S. actions were computed, a one-day lag was introduced; thus, for example, the rank of U. S. actions on October 22 was correlated with the rank of Soviet expression on October 23.

b. These are exact probabilities drawn from: D. B. Owen, *Handbook of Statistical Tables* (Reading, Mass.: Addison-Wesley, 1962), pp. 400ff.

doctrinaire guises) is not sufficient to account for the actions or expressions of Soviet leaders. Substantial shifts in military doctrine (in response to technology and other factors), changes in rate of warlike preparations (in response to different American administrations), and changes in attitude during the Cuban crisis amply indicate that it is not always necessary to take into account Soviet ideology.[92] Whether it is ever necessary to include ideological factors cannot be established with so limited a sample of Soviet foreign policy.

The nationhood hypotheses were found to be consistent with the results of the examination of changes in military doctrine and warlike preparation. However, the openness of Soviet positive attitudes to changes in American behavior and even the less sensitive responsiveness of their negative attitudes during the Cuban missile crisis raise questions about the adequacy of a model, such as the realists', which predicts tactical shifts in behavior but denies changes in underlying attitude. It is probable that concerns over power, security, and interest are necessary ingredients in the analysis of foreign policy; their sufficiency is subject to doubt.

NOTES

    * A preliminary version of this paper was read at the convention of the American Association for the Advancement of Science, Berkeley, California, December 27, 1965. A number of scholars took time to make critical comments on the earlier draft. We especially wish to thank Davis Bobrow, Ernst Haas, Carey Joynt, Thomas Milburn, Jan Triska, and Albert Wohlstetter for their suggestions for improving the paper. We have tried to take account of this criticism, but since none of these individuals has seen the current version, we will follow convention and absolve them of any responsibility for it.

1. For example, two articles on the Soviet Union appeared in Volume XIII (1919) of the *American Political Science Review:* R. G. Gettell, "The Russian Soviet Constitution," 293–97, and R. M. Story, "Observations on Soviet Government," 460–67.

2. See the reviews of the many conceptual frameworks contained in: D. Bell, "Ten Theories in Search of Reality," *World Politics,* X (1958), 327–65; J. Triska, "A Model for the Study of Soviet Foreign Policy," *American Political Science Review,* LII (1958), 64–83; W. Glaser, "Theories of Soviet Foreign Policy: A Classification of the Literature," *World Affairs Quarterly,* XXVII (1956), 128–52; and J. S. Reshetar, Jr., *Problems of Analyzing and Predicting Soviet Behavior* (Garden City: Doubleday, 1955).

3. Triska, "A Model," p. 64.

4. See S. Hoffmann, *Contemporary Theory in International Politics* (Englewood Cliffs: Prentice-Hall, 1959), for a representative sample of theories of international politics which are postulated as applying to any and all nations.

5. J. R. Platt, "Strong Inference," *Science,* CXLVI (1964), 347–53. We refer to Platt's characterization of inductive method as an "idealization" because of the questions raised by E. M. Hafner and S. Presswood about its soundness as a description of what goes on in science; "Strong Inference and Weak Interactions," *Science,* CXLIX (1965), 503–10. See also T. Kuhn, *The Structure of Scientific Revolutions* (Chicago: University of Chicago Press, 1962).

6. D. G. Sullivan, "Towards an Inventory of Major Propositions Contained in Contemporary Textbooks in International Relations" (Ph. D. Thesis, Department of Political Science, Northwestern University, 1963).

7. All these statements will be direct quotations and the customary uses of brackets and ellipses apply. We have taken the liberty of adding identification numbers to ease future reference. These quotations are quite obviously "out of context" and the works they are drawn from are more sophisticated than an isolated sentence can possibly indicate;

nevertheless, these are the assertions of scholars expert in the field of Soviet studies and, as such, tests of them need to be devised if science is to progress. It is not our intention to pass judgment on any of the *works* from which these propositions are drawn; we will be satisfied if we can say something about the assertions.

8. R. N. Carew Hunt, "The Importance of Doctrine," in A. Brumberg (ed.), *Russia Under Khrushchev* (New York: Praeger, 1962), p. 7.
9. R. Garthoff, *Soviet Strategy in the Nuclear Age* (New York: Praeger, 1958), p. 4.
10. P. E. Mosely, *The Kremlin in World Politics* (New York: Vintage, 1960), p. 501.
11. R. S. Tarn, "Continuity in Russian Foreign Policy," in R. Goldwin and M. Zetterbaum (eds.), *Readings in Russian Foreign Policy* (Chicago: American Foundation for Political Education, 1953), p. 273.
12. Hunt, "Importance of Doctrine," p. 11.
13. F. W. Neal, "The Sources of Soviet Conduct," in D. Pentony (ed.), *Soviet Behavior in World Affairs* (San Francisco: Chandler, 1962), p. 145.
14. R. B. Farrell, "Foreign Policies of Open and Closed Political Societies," in R. B. Farrell (ed.), *Approaches to Comparative and International Politics* (Evanston: Northwestern University Press, 1966), p. 173.
15. *Ibid.,* p. 176.
16. P. H. Partridge, "The Conflict of Ideologies," in D. McClellan, W. Olson, and F. Sondermann (eds.), *The Theory and Practice of International Relations* (Englewood Cliffs: Prentice-Hall, 1960), p. 77.
17. V. Aspaturian, "Soviet Foreign Policy," in R. Macridis (ed.), *Foreign Policy in World Politics* (2nd edition; Englewood Cliffs: Prentice-Hall, 1962), p. 197.
18. A. Wolfers, "The Pole of Power and the Pole of Indifference," *World Politics,* IV (1951), 40.
19. Garthoff, *Soviet Strategy,* p. 5.
20. W. B. Walsh, "Soviet Foreign Policy from Petrograd to Yalta," in S. Brown (ed.), *Great Issues* (New York: Harpers, 1951), p. 263.
21. Hunt, "Importance of Doctrine," p. 14.
22. S. L. Sharp, "National Interest: Key to Soviet Politics," in Brumberg, *Russia under Khrushchev,* p. 16.
23. *Ibid.,* p. 20.
24. Aspaturian, "Soviet Foreign Policy," p. 133.
25. H. Dinerstein, "Future Soviet Foreign Policy," in D. Abshire and R. Allen (eds.), *National Security* (Stanford and New York: Hoover and Praeger, 1963), p. 34.
26. Garthoff, *Soviet Strategy,* p. 5.
27. Walsh, "Soviet Foreign Policy," p. 254.
28. G. Niemeyer, "Political Requirements," in D. Abshire and R. Allen (eds.), *National Security,* p. 258.
29. E. Crankshaw, *Khrushchev's Russia* (Baltimore: Penguin, 1959), pp. 145–46.
30. A. Toynbee, "Russia and the West," in Goldwin and Zetterbaum, *Readings,* p. 269.
31. M. Karpovich, "Russian Imperialism or Communist Aggression," in Goldwin and Zetterbaum, *Readings,* p. 235.

32. *Ibid.*, p. 237.

33. D. McClellan, "Mackinder's Heartland Concept: A Note," in Pentony, *Soviet Behavior,* p. 47.

34. *Ibid.*, p. 48.

35. *Ibid.*, p. 50.

36. Aspaturian, "Soviet Foreign Policy," p. 134.

37. D. Mills, "The USSR: A Reappraisal of Mackinder's Heartland Concept," in Pentony, *Soviet Behavior,* p. 46.

38. It is not our contention that these four postures exhaust all the "theories" of Soviet foreign policy; on the contrary, as we indicated earlier, a great many factors have been advanced to account for Soviet behavior. These four (especially, ideology and nationhood) have been the most frequently cited factors. More recently, factors relevant to the characteristics and motives of the Soviet elite have been put forth as explanatory of Soviet actions. For example, V. Aspaturian states in a recent paper, "The foreign policy of the Soviet Union, like that of other states, is shaped by the interests of the dominant social groups in society, ideologically rationalized as the will of all social classes . . . and legalized as the official interests of the state" ("Internal Politics and Foreign Policy in the Soviet System," in Farrell, *Approaches,* p. 214).

39. Soviet specialists disagree about how rigid is the doctrine informing Soviet ideology. At one extreme we find statements like Farrell's about the role of dogma in closed systems (H1.8, above); at the other, statements claiming that Soviet ideology is ever flexible, ever accommodating to changes in political reality. This position is attributed to Brzezinski, but it is incompatible with his assertions on the subject (for example, "Communist Ideology and International Affairs," *Journal of Conflict Resolution,* IV [1960], 266–91). Brzezinski labels "ignorant" assertions that the Soviet leaders are abandoning their Marxism or communism" (*ibid.*, p. 266). He defines ideology "as an action program derived from certain doctrinal assumptions about the nature of reality and expressed through assertions [which] include an explicit guide to action" (*ibid.*, p. 266). What kind of guide to action could a flexible ideology provide? If ideology is ever responsive to changes in reality, it could provide no guide. Since changes in reality occasion decisions, if ideology is responding to these changes, it can hardly function as a standard for evaluating alternatives. A "flexible ideology" is a mixture in terms. The notion is a semantic cover for those who treat ideology as a way of rationalizing decisions constrained by other factors but who also wish, for some reason, to continue using the term. Thus, we accept Brzezinski's *definition* of ideology; this of course does not preclude the possibility that he and others who argue as he does are mistaken about the role of ideology as a factor in decision-making.

40. The numbers in parentheses refer back to propositions listed above.

41. H. and M. Sprout, "Environmental Factors in the Study of International Politics," *Journal of Conflict Resolution,* I (1957), 312.

42. *Ibid.*, p. 313.

43. L. F. Richardson, *Arms and Insecurity* (Chicago: Quadrangle, 1960).

44. B. Russell, *War the Offspring of Fear* (London: Union of Democratic Control, 1914).

45. H. Baldwin in R. D. Crane, ed., *Soviet Nuclear Strategy*, Washington: Center for Strategic Studies, Georgetown University, 1963, p. 1.
46. See, for example, "Changing Military Thought in the Soviet Union," *World Today*, XIII (1957), 517–28; and N. Galay "Guided Missiles and Soviet Military Doctrine," *Bulletin: Institute for the Study of the USSR*, IV (1957), 14–21.
47. Compare Marshal Rotmistrov's statements quoted in "Changing Military Thought," p. 520, with Marshal Zhukov's statements quoted by Galay, "Guided Missiles," p. 16.
48. T. W. Wolfe, *Problems of Soviet Defense Under the New Regime*, (P-3098) Santa Monica: RAND Corp., March 1965. See also V. Sokolovskii and M. Cherednichenko, "Several Aspects of Soviet Military Development in the Post War Period," *Voyenno-Istoricheskii zhurnal* (Journal of Military History), Moscow, No. 3, March 1965, pp. 3–16 [Soviet Military Translations, No. 193, *Joint Publications Research Bureau:* 31351, 02 Aug. 65].
49. "Revolutionary Army & Revolutionary Government" (July 1905) in V. I. Lenin, *Selected Works* (New York: International Publishers, 1943), III, 315.
50. "Lessons of the Moscow Uprising" (Sept. 1905), in *ibid.*, III, 351–52.
51. "Proposals Submitted by the Central Committee of the Russian Social-Democratic Labour Party to the Second Socialist Conference" (April 1916), in *ibid.*, V, 232.
52. J. Stalin, as paraphrased in "Changing Military Thought," p. 518.
53. The handicap of the "five constants" is discussed quite openly in the Soviet military literature. See, for example, Sokolovskii and Cherednichenko, "Several Aspects," p. 7. Also, I. Korotkov, "The Development of Soviet Military Theory in the Post War Years," *Voyenno-Istoricheskii zhurnal*, No. 4 (April 1964), pp. 39–50 [Soviet Military Translations, No. 144, *JPRS:* 24667, 19 May 1964, pp. 14–38].
54. *Pravda*, September 25, 1946 [page no. unavailable—issue missing at Stanford].
55. Sokolovskii and Cherednichenko, "Several Aspects," pp. 1–7. See also Garthoff, *Soviet Strategy*, pp. 149–240.
56. Rotmistrov, "Changing Military Thought."
57. Zhukov, quoted by Galay, "Guided Missiles," p. 16.
58. Garthoff, *Soviet Strategy*, Chapter IV.
59. *Ibid.*, p. 23.
60. *Pravda*, March 13, 1954, p. 2.
61. *Pravda*, June 13, 1954, p. 3.
62. *Pravda*, January 26, 1958, p. 2.
63. *Pravda*, February 15, 1956, p. 2.
64. *Pravda*, May 12, 1959, p. 4.
65. *Pravda*, January 15, 1960.
66. R. Brody, "Deterrence," in *International Encyclopedia of the Social Sciences*, Vol. IV, 1968.
67. N. Talensky, "On the Character of Modern Warfare," *International Affairs* (Moscow), No. 10 (October 1960), p. 23.
68. Korotkov, "Development," p. 29.
69. Published in the United States as *Soviet Military Doctrine* by both Prentice-Hall and Praeger.

70. See T. Wolfe, *Soviet Strategy at the Crossroads* (Cambridge, Mass.: Harvard University Press, 1964) and T. Wolfe, *Problems of Soviet Defense Policy.*

71. Korotkov, "Development," p. 14.

72. Richardson, *Arms and Insecurity,* Chapters III and VII.

73. L. F. Richardson, "The Mathematical Psychology of War," *Nature,* CXLII (1919), 792.

74. T. Sosnovy, "The Soviet Military Budget," *Foreign Affairs,* XLII (1964), 489.

75. *Finance of the Soviet Union,* quoted in Sosnovy, "The Soviet Military Budget."

76. Sosnovy, "Soviet Military Budget," p. 489.

77. A. S. Becker, *Soviet Military Outlays Since 1955,* Santa Monica: RAND, 1964.

78. *Ibid.*

79. *Ibid.,* pp. 12 and 34.

80. *Ibid.,* p. 12.

81. Sosnovy, "Soviet Military Budget," p. 489.

82. S. P. Huntington, *The Common Defense* (New York: Columbia University Press, 1961), p. 281.

83. Becker, *Soviet Military Outlays,* p. 39.

84. Material for this section was drawn primarily from O. R. Holsti, R. A. Brody, and R. C. North, "Measuring Affect and Action in International Reaction Models: Empirical Materials from the 1962 Cuban Crisis," *Papers, Peace Research Society (International),* 2 (1965), pp. 170–90.

85. C. E. Osgood and P. H. Tannenbaum, "The Principle of Congruity in the Prediction of Attitude Change," *Psychological Review,* XLIX (1952), 251–62. The concept of "attitude" employed in our study is drawn from Osgood and Tannenbaum who single out "evaluation" as the attitude dimension in a multidimensional perceptual space. The Stanford Political Dictionary (O. Holsti, "An Adaptation of the 'General Inquirer' for the Systematic Analysis of Political Documents," *Behavioral Science,* IX [1964], 382–87) is designed to extract Osgood's three principal perceptual dimensions—evaluation, potency, activity—from diplomatic communication.

86. We have introduced a systematic one-day lag in our comparison of United States behavior and Soviet attitudes to avoid assumptions of instantaneous communication and also to take account of differential time zones.

87. Drawn from T. Kunz and A. Osteen, Jr., "Appendix C: Chronology—October 1962," in R. C. North *et al., The Analysis of International Tension,* Report to Behavioral Sciences Group, USNOTS, China Lake, California, June 15, 1964.

88. *Ibid.*

89. The interjudge agreement on this task was quite high: the *lowest* level of agreement was reflected in a correlation coefficient of $r_s = .84$ which with $N = 10$ is significant beyond $p = .01$.

90. "Zorin's address to the U.N.," *New York Times,* October 24, 1962; p. 25. "Text of Soviet Statement Challenging the U. S. Naval Quarantine," *ibid.,* p. 20. "Resolution to the Security Council on Cuban Question," *ibid.,* p. 25.

"Khrushchev's Letter to Bertrand Russell," *ibid.,* October 25, 1962; p. 22.
"Zorin's Address in Debate in U. N. Security Council," *ibid.,* October 26, 1962; p. 16.
"Khrushchev's Reply to Thant," *ibid.,* p. 16.
"Khrushchev's Reply to Thant's Appeal," *ibid.,* October 27, 1962; p. 8.
"Khrushchev's Message to Kennedy," *ibid.,* October 27, 1962; p. 30.
"Khrushchev's Message to Thant," *ibid.,* October 29, 1962; p. 16.
"Khrushchev's Message to Kennedy via Broadcast," *ibid.,* p. 16.

91. Holsti, "An Adaptation," p. 382.

92. Perhaps with respect to the Cuban crisis this goes too far; the relatively weaker sensitivity of Soviet negative ("bad") expressions to changes in U. S. behavior recalls Pruitt's contention that, ". . . ideologies sometimes give guidance concerning how to evaluate another nation. For example, *communism teaches its adherents that capitalist nations are bad. . . ."* D. Pruitt, "The Definition of the Situation as a Determinant of International Action," in H. Kelman (ed.), *International Behavior* (New York: Holt, Rinehart, Winston, 1965), p. 410, emphasis added.

INDEX